Nordic Approaches to Peace Operations

THE CASS SERIES ON PEACEKEEPING
ISSN 1367-9880
General Editor: Michael Pugh

This series examines all aspects of peace-keeping, from the political, operational and legal dimensions to the developmental and humanitarian issues that must be dealt with by all those involved with peacekeeping in the world today.

Nordic Approaches to Peace Operations

A New Model in the Making?

Peter Viggo Jakobsen

Routledge
Taylor & Francis Group

LONDON AND NEW YORK

First published 2006
by Routledge
2 Park Square, Milton Park, Abingdon, Oxon, OX14 4RN

Simultaneously published in the USA and Canada by Routledge
270 Madison Ave, New York NY 10016

Routledge is an imprint of the Taylor & Francis Group

Transferred to Digital Printing 2009

© 2006 Peter Viggo Jakobsen

Typeset in Times by Keyword Group

British Library Cataloguing in Publication Data
A catalogue record for this book is available from the British Library

Library of Congress Cataloging in Publication Data
A catalog record has been requested

ISBN10: 0-415-38360-9 (hbk)
ISBN10: 0-415-54491-2 (pbk)

ISBN13: 978-0-415-38360-8 (hbk)
ISBN13: 978-0-415-54491-7 (pbk)

To Charlotte and Pia

Contents

Tables

Preface

Contrary to popular opinion, the Nordic model for peace operations is not a relic of the Cold War. The Nordic countries remain relevant for the study and practice of peace operations. A survey of the literature conveys a different impression as most non-Nordic analysts continue to view Denmark, Finland, Norway and Sweden as a bastion of traditional peacekeeping. The Nordic approach is consequently dismissed as irrelevant at best. At worst it is viewed as positively dangerous and 'morally bankrupt'.[1] This book proves the critics wrong. It demonstrates that the Nordics have moved with the times and changed their approaches to peace operations radically. Denmark became the first nation to employ tanks in a United Nations (UN) peace operation in Bosnia in 1993; Norway took the lead in developing civilian rapid reaction capacities for peace operations; Finland has developed a model for civil–military cooperation (CIMIC) which is generally regarded as second to none; the Nordics have taken intelligence sharing in peace operations to a new level through the establishment of joint intelligence cells; the first multinational rapid reaction brigade made available for UN peacekeeping (SHIRBRIG) was the result of a Danish initiative; and the Nordics made a multinational brigade-size force (NORDCAPS) available for peace operations led by the European Union (EU), the North Atlantic Treaty Organization (NATO) and the UN in 2003. The Nordics, in short, continue to have plenty to offer to other nations in this field.

Proving the critics wrong is not the principal ambition of this book, however. The main objective is to evaluate the new Nordic model that has developed since the end of the Cold War. This is done by means of an analytical framework consisting of eleven success conditions that personnel contributors must meet to be successful in the post-Cold War era. These conditions are derived from an analysis of the lessons learned since the early 1990s and the framework established for evaluating the efforts of the Nordic countries is of general value since it can be used for all personnel contributors. The creation of this framework is thus a theoretical contribution to the field of peace operations in its own right.

The actual analysis of the four Nordic countries is structured and focused around the eleven success conditions to ensure that the results of the individual case studies are directly comparable. By implication these results will also be directly comparable to analyses of other nations that rely on the theoretical framework developed in this book.

The study of the national efforts is supplemented by an analysis of their collective efforts to replace their old Cold War peacekeeping model with a new one that meets the requirements of the new era. The components of the new model (personnel pool, institutional framework and the Nordic strategic culture) are assessed in a separate chapter. The overall conclusion is that the Nordics have succeeded in meeting the post-Cold War requirements for success, individually and collectively, and that a new effective model is in the making. However, it is also pointed out that the Nordic brand name in peace operations is likely to disappear due to the growing Nordic involvement in peace operations as part of the EU, NATO and coalitions of the willing. The preservation of a high Nordic profile will require additional Nordic initiatives and an increased willingness to provide joint Nordic contributions to peace operations. The establishment of a Nordic civilian rapid reaction capacity is identified as a must if a clear and distinct Nordic profile is to be maintained.

The book fills two gaps in the academic literature on Nordic peace operations. It is the first to provide a comprehensive analysis of the old Nordic Cold War model, explaining how and why it developed and how it functioned. It also provides the first systematic overview of the reforms undertaken by the four Nordic countries since the end of the Cold War. It explains the pace and shape of the reform processes in the four countries and assesses the strengths and weaknesses of the new Nordic model. At the practical level, it highlights the areas in which the Nordics continue to make contributions and initiatives that could be of value to other countries, and it also offers a number of policy recommendations that would strengthen the Nordic profile in the field.

The ambition has been to write a book that bridges the gap between theory and practice, having something to offer to academics and practitioners alike. I will leave it to others to decide whether I have succeeded in doing so, but I hope that at the very least I have succeeded in demonstrating that the Nordic experiences remain relevant to the world of peace operations and that it is a mistake to ignore them.

This eternally forthcoming book has been a standard joke among my friends and colleagues for a longer time than I care to remember. The idea first came to me in 1996 and I have been working on it on and off since then. Unsurprisingly, my editor Michael Pugh had all but forgotten the project's existence when I finally sent him the manuscript. The number of people who helped me on this project along the way is far too numerous to be mentioned here. I would, however, like to thank the many officers and officials from the four Nordic countries who kindly let me interview them or who helped me with information. Without their help this book could not have been written. At the Danish Institute for International Studies (DIIS) Stine Lehmann-Larsen and Martin Fernando Jakobsen provided valuable research assistance and Ib M.C. Nielsen read the entire manuscript and prepared it for publication.

I am also grateful for the financial support received from the Danish Research Council (grant no. 9800332); the working group on Peace Support Operations in the Nordic Research Program on Security (1998–2004), which was funded by the Nordic ministries of defence and the Nordic Council of Ministers; and the Defence and Security Studies Programme at DIIS, which is funded by the Danish Ministry of Defence.

Copenhagen, September 2005

Notes

1. Stedman, Stephen John (1996) 'Consent, Neutrality, and Impartiality in the Tower of Babel and on the Frontlines: United Nations Peacekeeping in the 1990s', in *Managing Arms in Peace Processes: The Issues* (New York, Geneva: United Nations), p. 56.

Abbreviations

APC	Armoured personnel carrier
ASEAN	Association of Southeast Asian Nations
AU	African Union
BALTBAT	Baltic Battalion
BALTRON	Baltic Naval Squadron
CIMIC	Civil–military cooperation
CIS	Commonwealth of Independent States
CNN	Cable News Network
CSCE	Conference for Security and Cooperation in Europe
D	Germany
DANCON	Danish Contingent
DIIS	Danish Institute for International Studies
DANOR	Danish–Norwegian Battalion
DK	Denmark
DKK	Danish krone
DPKO	Department of Peacekeeping Operations
DRB	Danish Reaction Brigade
ECOWAS	Economic Community of West African States
EU	European Union
EUR	Euro
FIM	Finnish marks
FINCENT	Finnish Defence Forces International Centre
FRDF	Finnish Rapid Deployment Force
Gen.	General
GB	Great Britain
ICRU	Iceland Crisis Response Unit
IHS	International Humanitarian Service
Innst.S.nr.	*Innstilling til Stortinget*. Assessments and recommendations for decisions from a Committee in Stortinget, the Norwegian parliament, to Stortinget
Lt Gen.	Lieutenant General
MFA	Ministry of Foreign Affairs
MoD	Ministry of Defence

N	Norway
NATO	North Atlantic Treaty Organization
NATO HR	NATO High Readiness Forces
NATO NRF	NATO Response Force
NGO	Non-governmental organization
NMCG	NORDCAPS Military Coordination Group
NOA HRF	Norwegian Army High Readiness Force
NOK	Norwegian krone
NORDBAT	Nordic Battalion
NORDCAPS	Nordic Coordinated Arrangement for Military Peace Support
NORDEM	Norwegian Resource Bank for Democracy and Human Rights
NORDPOLBDE	Nordic–Polish Brigade
NORDSAMFN	Nordic cooperation group for military UN matters
NORSTAFF	Norwegian Standby Arrangements of Professionals
NOU	*Norges Offentlige Utredninger.* Norwegian governmental reports from various specialist committees
NPBG	Nordic–Polish Battle Group
NSG	NORDCAPS Steering Group
NST	Norwegian Support Teams
OAS	Organization of American States
OAU	Organization of African Unity
OSCE	Organization for Security and Cooperation in Europe
Ot.prp. nr.	*Odelstingsproposisjon.* Norwegian government bill
PARP	Planning and Review Process
PfP	Partnership for Peace
PRT	Provincial Reconstruction Team
REACT	OSCE Rapid Expert Assistance and Cooperation Teams
RDT	Rapid Deployment Team
ROE	Rules of Engagement
S	Sweden
SADC	Southern African Development Community
SEK	Swedish krona
SF	Finland
SHIRBRIG	Multinational UN Standby High Readiness Brigade
SHO	Sector Humanitarian Officer
SOU	*Statens Offentliga Utredningar.* Swedish governmental reports from various specialist committees or appointed investigators
SRSG	Special Representative of the United Nations Secretary-General

St.meld. nr.	*Stortingsmelding*. Reports from the government to Stortinget on the state budgets, current and planned activities, etc.
St.prp. nr.	*Stortingsproposisjon*. Proposals for decisions from the government to Stortinget
SWEDINT	Swedish Armed Forces International Centre
TR	Turkey
UN	United Nations
UNDAC	United Nations Disaster Assessment and Coordination Team
UNHCR	United Nations High Commissioner for Refugees
UNICEF	United Nations Children's Fund
UNSAS	United Nations Standby Arrangements System
UNSMAS	United Nations Senior Management Seminar
USA	United States of America
WEU	Western European Union
WFP	World Food Programme

1 Introduction

A Nordic instructor training US troops in border patrol techniques told his class, 'You've got to be shot [as opposed to shot at] first before you can return fire.' To which one American soldier laconically replied, 'Ain't gonna be that way'.[1]

During the Cold War the four Nordic countries, Denmark, Finland, Norway and Sweden, made a name for themselves in United Nations (UN) peacekeeping operations. The Nordics were seen as one actor due to their close cooperation with respect to standby forces earmarked for UN peacekeeping, training, doctrine and personnel contributions. Their cooperation became known as the 'Nordic Model',[2] and it was generally regarded as the quintessence of traditional peacekeeping.[3] Its influence was evident from the popularity of the 'Blue Book', the Nordic Standby Forces manual, which became widely used as a basis for establishing and training UN peacekeeping contingents,[4] and it was also to the Nordic Model that the British Army, the United States (US) Army and the Western European Union (WEU) turned when they began to take an interest in peace operations in the early 1990s.[5]

Unfortunately for the Nordics, their model did not survive the fall of the Berlin Wall. Peace operations moved from the margins to the centre of Western security policy and many new states, including the great powers, entered the scene. As a consequence, it became impossible for the Nordics to maintain their status as major troop contributors. During the 1990s 67 new nations joined the contributors club, which during the Cold War had been limited to 56.[6] This put pressure on the Nordics to field larger forces than before. Their traditional battalion-sized contributions were no longer enough to obtain operational influence and autonomy in operations led by the great powers. On NATO-led operations, brigade-sized contributions became the admission card for influence, and the *Brahimi Report* also called upon member states to make brigades available to the UN.[7] On EU-led operations, 1,500-strong battle groups seem destined to become the minimum required following the adoption of the battle group concept in 2004.[8]

Also, and more important, the erosion of consent rendered the traditional (Nordic) approach to peacekeeping ineffective and some observers even condemned it as morally bankrupt.[9] The experiences from Bosnia, Cambodia, Rwanda and Somalia where lightly armed peacekeepers were deployed in environments characterized by limited consent showed that a peace force to be effective under these circumstances had to be able to fight and stop attempts by the parties to prevent it from achieving its mission. This realization led to the development of new doctrines and the increased use of Chapter VII mandates authorizing peace forces to use force beyond self-defence.[10]

Aims and arguments

The big question asked by this book is therefore whether the Nordics have been able to meet these challenges and bring their approach(es) up to speed with the post-Cold War era. Many non-Nordic analysts believe this not to be the case. The Nordics are commonly still seen as a bastion of traditional peacekeeping with little relevance for contemporary operations. This perception is not surprising. The principal Nordic contribution to the field in the 1990s, the UN Standby Forces High Readiness Brigade (SHIRBRIG), a Danish initiative that gave the UN an effective rapid reaction capability, was based on traditional peacekeeping principles.[11] Similarly, the main work produced by Nordic scholars on peace operations in the 1990s made the case that the lessons learned from the UN operation in Bosnia (UNPROFOR) had vindicated the traditional Nordic peace-keeping principles.[12] Apart from this work very little has been written on the Nordic approaches to post-Cold War peace operations, and even less has been published in English. It has, in short, not been easy for analysts, who do not master one of the Nordic languages, to keep track of what the Nordics have been up to since the end of the Cold War.

One of the aims of this book is to fill this gap and set the record straight. It does so by proving wrong the conventional wisdom regarding the Nordic approaches to peace operations after the Cold War. The Nordic countries are no bastion of traditional peacekeeping and they have, as this book shows, led the charge to reform the traditional approach in several areas. To give a few examples, the Danish tank squadron serving in UNPROFOR was the first ever to be deployed in a UN-commanded peace operation, and the Danish tanks inflicted the largest military defeat upon Bosnian Serb forces prior to the Croat offensives and NATO's Operation Deliberate Force in 1995. In Operation Hooligan Buster conducted on 29 April 1994, the Danish tanks fired seventy-two shells taking out all the Bosnian Serb units that opened fire upon them.[13] According to the American NATO ambassador Robert Hunter and UNPROFOR commander Michael Rose, the Danish use of tanks in UNPROFOR later served as a model for the operation that NATO launched in Bosnia in 1995.[14]

General Rose's characterization of the Swedish battalion serving in UNPROFOR is also difficult to square with the traditionalist view:

> Although Sweden has not been at war for 300 years, it was plain that they had lost nothing of the martial quality that allowed them to dominate northern Europe in the seventeenth century. They could be extremely bloody-minded and always returned fire immediately with their heavy weapons if they were fired upon ... Henricsson [the Swedish battalion commander] had personally led their first convoy across the conflict line. At a Bosnian Serb roadblock, he was confronted by an aggressive soldier who told him he had orders not to allow him to pass. Henricsson immediately put a loaded pistol to the soldier's head and informed him that he had just received a new set of orders ... Because of their tough-minded approach, the Swedes were respected by all of the warring parties.[15]

The Nordics have not just contributed to the 'militarization' of traditional peacekeeping, however. They have also contributed to the development of the civilian components in the new breed of multifunctional or complex peace operations that have become the dominant mission type of the post-Cold War era. Norway was the first country in the world to set up a civilian rapid reaction capacity for peace operations, and the Norwegian standby arrangements were an important source of inspiration for the arrangements subsequently set up by the other Nordic countries, Canada, the UN and the Organization for Security and Cooperation in Europe (OSCE).[16]

Finland has created an effective CIMIC model, and Finnish CIMIC contingents have gained a reputation for being among the best in the field. A Swedish study published in 1998 comparing the Danish, British, Finnish and Swedish CIMIC contingents in Bosnia concluded that the Finnish rotation system was superior to the one used by the other nations which rotated all personnel every six months. In contrast, the Finnish CIMIC personnel serve for 12 months, only a third of a unit is rotated at a time, and a rotation is carried out with an overlap period of two weeks. As a result, the Finnish model ensures greater continuity and less loss of local knowledge than the models employed by most other nations.[17] Another strongpoint of the Finnish model is the ready availability of considerable funds for CIMIC projects and procedures allowing for their quick dispersal. For instance, the Finnish CIMIC contingent in Bosnia had been provided with an annual budget of more than FIM 1 million (EUR 168,000).[18]

Finally, the Nordics have also taken the lead with respect to intelligence sharing in the field. The establishment of joint Nordic Intelligence Cells in Bosnia and Kosovo took intelligence sharing in peace operations to a new level, and the creation of these cells was hailed by an impressed KFOR commander, General Juan Ortuño Such, as an example for others to follow.[19]

Proving conventional wisdom wrong is merely a sideshow to the war, however. The principal aim of this book is to determine whether a new Nordic Model is in the making. That is to say, whether the Nordics have established a new model for post-Cold War peace operations that may become as influential as their Cold War one; and whether the Nordics continue to have something of value to offer to other small- and medium-sized personnel contributors with limited budgets and capabilities.

The answer to both questions is yes. This book shows that all four Nordic countries have succeeded in meeting the requirements for success in the post-Cold War era, and that they have established a new effective model of cooperation. The Nordic Co-ordinated Arrangement for Military Peace Support (NORDCAPS), which replaced the old institutional framework the Nordic cooperation group for military UN matters (NORDSAMFN) in 1997, represents a deepening and widening of the old model. The joint training programme has been expanded and widened, the old Blue Books have been replaced by new manuals covering the full spectrum of peace operations, and the force pool is considerably larger and includes all three services. NORDCAPS thus enables the Nordics to provide sizable military contingents to peacekeeping and enforcement operations, not involving offensive operations, as well as critical enablers in high demand such as logistics, headquarters staff, combat support services and communications. It has also ensured that the Nordic expertise in peace operations remains a commodity in high demand. The training assistance provided to other countries has grown, the Nordics are deeply involved in the development of training programmes within the EU, NATO and the UN, and they have also been involved in the establishment of multinational forces ear-marked for peace operations such as the Baltic Battalion (BALTBAT) and SHIRBRIG. The new Nordic Model, in short, continues to have something of value to offer to other countries.

Somewhat paradoxically this book also finds that these achievements may not be enough to ensure the survival of the Nordic 'brand name' in the field of peace operations. As demonstrated in the final chapter, Nordic cooperation does not enjoy the same level of support in all the Nordic governments as it used to. Denmark has all but abandoned Nordic cooperation in favour of bilateral cooperation with the great powers and informal alliances within the EU and NATO. The importance of these channels, which did not exist during the Cold War, has also increased significantly in the other three Nordic capitals. The problem for NORDCAPS is, in other words, that Nordic cooperation no longer is the 'only game in town' with respect to generating influence and prestige within the field of peace operations. The new reality is illustrated by the fact that the most notable 'Nordic' successes in the post-Cold War era, SHIRBRIG which the *Brahimi Report* held up as a model for others to follow,[20] BALTBAT and the multinational Baltic Defence College which served as the model for the defence college established in Bosnia-Herzegovina, all included several non-Nordic countries. These successes and the growing Nordic involvement in other multinational arrangements dilute the Nordic profile and threaten to dissolve it completely in the longer term. The preservation of a clear and distinct Nordic profile in the field of peace operations will consequently require new initiatives, which set Nordic cooperation apart from the growing number of cooperative arrangements that characterize post-Cold War peace operations.

The most effective way to give the Nordic brand name a longer shelf life would be to give the military NORDCAPS framework a fully fledged civilian rapid reaction component. The building blocks for a Nordic civilian rapid reaction arrangement already exist as the Nordics have established civilian standby arrangements at the national level and made civilian personnel available to the EU, the OSCE and the UN. By pooling their resources the Nordics could develop indispensable niche capabilities in short supply that would enhance their political profile and give them a lead-nation capacity. Civilian rule-of-law teams (judges, jailers, prosecutors and correctional staff), civilian administration teams and police mission leadership teams are examples of such capabilities. These capabilities can also be established in other multinational settings, most notably the EU, but Nordic teams would hold two key operational advantages over multinational teams composed by personnel from a much larger group of states: they would be easier to deploy and more effective as a result of similar decision-making procedures and a high degree of convergence in national interests and strategic cultures. As pointed out in Chapter 8, ambitious EU plans for establishing an effective civilian rapid reaction capacity have thus far been frustrated by the absence of these factors.

The establishment of a joint Nordic civilian rapid reaction capacity would not only enable the Nordic countries to offer much sought-after civilian capacities at short notice. It would also enable them to establish unique joint civil–military force packages with a higher degree of integration than is the case in the existing rapid reaction arrangements. Effective civil–military coordination and cooperation have been a problem on all the major peace operations conducted since the end of the Cold War, so the Nordics could really add value in this area.

Approach

The peace operations literature is preoccupied with an interest in practical problems. It has a reputation for being atheoretical and has been criticized repeatedly for its failure to draw on relevant insights from other parts of political science.[21] In addition, post-Cold War scholarship has been characterized by an almost complete lack of knowledge about UN peacekeeping experiences prior to 1989. Most of the analysts rushing in when the study of peace operations became sexy in the early 1990s have never bothered going back to take a look at the operations conducted prior to 1989, and much contemporary work consequently suffers from a complete lack of historical perspective.

Two factors help to explain this sorry state of affairs. The first is the popularity of the 'generation' concept, i.e. the notion that the first generation of operations conducted during the Cold War has been superseded by a second and a third generation of operations in the course of the 1990s.[22] The second factor is the strong criticism levelled against the established peacekeeping experts for their failure to acknowledge the need for a new approach to peace operations in the early 1990s.[23] These two factors probably convinced a lot of the newcomers that it would be pointless to mine the Cold War operations for nuggets of insight. This was a fatal mistake as many of the problems encountered in the first part of the 1990s could have been foreseen if greater attention had been paid to the experiences of the UN in the Congo, in Cyprus during the early years, and in Lebanon.[24] The ONUC operation in the Congo was effectively a second-generation operation that came too early, and many of the operational mistakes committed during UNPROFOR in Bosnia could have been avoided by heeding the lessons learned during ONUC.[25]

This book is firmly rooted in the policy-relevant tradition but designed to overcome the two shortcomings described above. The principal motivation behind it is the desire to determine how the Nordic approaches to post-Cold War peace operations can be improved and to demonstrate that they still have something of value to offer to other nations. This ambition is not pursued in an atheoretical or ahistorical way, however. A historical perspective is required to permit a comparison between the old and the new Nordic models. A comprehensive analysis of the origins, the creation and the running of the old Nordic model is therefore undertaken. This analysis not only provides the baseline against which the post-Cold War reforms can be compared, but its explanation of how and why the old model was developed also fills a gap in the literature on Nordic peacekeeping. Surprising as it may sound, such an analysis has not been undertaken before.

The analysis of the new Nordic approaches to peace operations is guided by the structured, focused comparison method developed by Alexander L. George to ensure that case studies are conducted in a theoretically informed manner.[26] The case studies undertaken here of the four Nordic countries are structured by eleven conditions for success which personnel contributors must meet to be successful in the post-Cold War era. These success conditions are derived from a detailed analysis of the lessons learned since the end of the Cold War and then used to evaluate the reforms undertaken in each of the four Nordic states. The study of each country is structured and focused around the eleven research questions that the success conditions provide. This approach not only ensures that the results obtained in the case studies are directly comparable, but it also fills yet another gap in the literature, as systematic comparative studies of the Nordic countries relying on the same theoretical framework are rare. This study is the first of its kind in the field of peace operations and the number of such studies carried out in other issue areas is very limited indeed. The vast majority of comparative books on the Nordic countries are thus collaborative efforts by scholars from the four Nordic countries, using a variety of different approaches.[27]

Finally, it should be noted that the framework made up by the eleven success conditions constitutes a theoretical contribution in its own right. It is a general tool derived inductively from the existing body of knowledge in the field, which can be used to evaluate the approaches to peace operations employed by all countries in the world.

Structure of the book

In Chapter 2 I start out by explaining where the old Nordic model came from and how it developed and functioned. Chapter 3 explains what changed and why in the field of peace operations after the Cold War. The new operational challenges to peace operations are identified and eleven conditions for success are derived from the lessons learned. These conditions then structure the case studies of Denmark, Finland, Norway and Sweden that follow in Chapters 4–7. The dual objective pursued in these chapters is to determine whether the Nordics meet the eleven conditions for success and to explain the nature of their reform processes. Chapter 8 focuses on their collective efforts to establish a new Nordic model. The personnel pool, the institutional framework for planning and decision making and the willingness to use the NORDCAPS framework as a basis for joint deployments are analysed in order to determine whether the new model is likely to become as effective and influential as the old one. The strengths and weaknesses of the new model are identified and a number of policy recommendations for the Nordic governments to consider are outlined at the end.

Notes

1. Scalard, Douglas (1997) 'People of Whom We Know Nothing: When Doctrine Isn't Enough', *Military Review*, Vol. 77, No. 4 (July–August), p. 6 (4–11).
2. Eknes, Åge (1995) 'The Nordic Countries and UN Peacekeeping Operations', in Åge Eknes (ed.) *The Nordic Countries in the United Nations: Status and Future Perspectives* (Copenhagen: Nordic Council), p. 65 (65–83).
3. Smith, Richard (1994) 'A Study into the Requirement for the United Nations to Develop an Internationally Recognized Doctrine for the Use of Force in Intra-State Conflict', *Strategic and Combat Studies Institute Occasional Paper*, No. 10 (Camberley: Strategic and Combat Studies Institute); Stedman, Stephen John (1996) 'Consent, Neutrality, and Impartiality in the Tower of Babel and on the Frontlines: United Nations Peacekeeping in the 1990s', in *Managing Arms in Peace Processes: The Issues* (New York, Geneva: United Nations), pp. 35–56.

4. Egge, Bjørn (1978) 'FN's fredsbevarende operasjon i Libanon. En oversikt ved årsskiftet og noen tanker om Norges rolle', *Internasjonal Politikk*, No. 4 B (Supplement), p. 751 (751–765); Fetherston, A.B. (1994) *Towards a Theory of United Nations Peacekeeping* (New York: St Martin's Press), p. 183.

5. Mackinlay, John and Randolph Kent (1997) 'Complex Emergencies Doctrine, The British are Still the Best', *RUSI Journal*, Vol. 142, No. 2 (April), p. 40 (31–49); WEU (1993) 'United Nations Operations – Interaction with WEU', *WEU Document*, No. 1366 (19 May 1993), pp. 2–3, 23–27; Wilkinson, Philip (1998) 'Sharpening the Weapons of Peace: The Development of a Common Military Doctrine for Peace Support Operations', *British Army Review*, No. 118 (April), p. 3 (3–7).

6. This number continues to grow. As of March 2004 some 130 countries had contributed to UN peace operations. UN Department of Peacekeeping Operations (2004) 'Who contributes Personnel?', *United Nations Peacekeeping – FAQ – Meeting New Challenges.* < http://www.un.org/Depts/dpko/dpko/faq/q8.htm > (20 July 2004).

7. *Brahimi Report* (Official title *Report of the Panel on the United Nations Peace Operations*, UN Doc. A/55/305-S/2000/809), 21 August 2000, p. xi.

8. European Council (2004) *Progress Report on the Battle Group Concept* (Brussels: Council of the European Union), 9 June.

9. Findlay, Trevor (2002) *The Use of Force in UN Peace Operations* (Oxford: Oxford University Press for Stockholm International Peace Research Institute), pp. 122–123; Kane, Angela (1996) 'Other New and Emerging Peacekeepers', in Trevor Findlay (ed.) *Challenges for the New Peacekeepers*, SIPRI Research Report No. 12 (Oxford: Oxford University Press), p. 102 (99–120); Mackinlay, John (1990) 'Powerful Peace-keepers', *Survival*, Vol. 32, No. 3 (May/June), pp. 241–250; Scalard, 'People of Whom We Know Nothing'; Smith, 'A Study into the Requirement for the United Nations to Develop an Internationally Recognized Doctrine for the Use of Force in Intra-State Conflict', p. 16; Stedman, 'Consent, Neutrality, and Impartiality in the Tower of Babel and on the Frontlines', p. 56.

10. Jakobsen, Peter Viggo (2000) 'The Emerging Consensus on Grey Area Peace Operations Doctrine: Will It Last and Enhance Operational Effectiveness?', *International Peacekeeping*, Vol. 7, No. 3 (Autumn), pp. 36–56.

11. In late 2002 the SHIRBRIG members agreed to consider participation in UN-commanded peace operations with enforcement authority on a case-by-case basis, but they had yet to do so with infantry by mid-2004.

12. Biermann, Wofgang and Martin Vadset (eds) (1998) *UN Peacekeeping in Troubles – Lessons Learned from the Former Yugoslavia* (Aldershot: Ashgate Publishing Group).

13. Jakobsen, Peter Viggo (1998) 'The Danish Approach to UN Peace Operations After the Cold War: A New Model in the Making?', *International Peace-keeping*, Vol. 5, No. 3 (Autumn), p. 106 (106–123).

14. Andersen, Simon and Jesper Larsen (1997) 'Høj cigarføring', *Jyllands-Posten,* 2 March.

15. Rose, Michael (1998) *Fighting for Peace* (London: Harvill Press), p. 34.

16. Olesen, Gunnar (Team Leader), Ole Espersen, Birthe L. Nautrup, Lisbeth Pilegaard, Ulrik Sørensen Rohde, Eilís Ward (2002) *Evaluation of the Norwegian Resource Bank for Democracy and Human Rights (NORDEM)* (Copenhagen: T&B Consult).

17. Eriksson, Pär (1998) *Civil-militär samverkan på taktisk nivå i fredsfrämjande operationer. Motiv, metoder och förutsättningar* (Stockholm, FOA, FOA-R–98-00968-170–SE), p. 28.

18. Madsen, Kai (2000) 'Manglende dansk bidrag stopper processen', *FOV Nyhedsbrev*, No. 14, p. 6.
19. Valpolini, Paolo (2000) 'Interview with Lt Gen Juan Ortuño Such, Commander Kosovo Force and Commander Eurocorps', *Jane's Defence Weekly*, Vol. 3, No. 1 (2 August).
20. *Brahimi Report.*
21. Fetherston, A.B. (1994) 'Putting the Peace Back into Peacekeeping: Theory Must Inform Practice', *International Peacekeeping*, Vol. 1, No. 1 (Spring), pp. 3–29; Neack, Laura (1995) 'UN Peace-keeping: In the Interest of Community or Self?', *Journal of Peace Research*, Vol. 32, No. 2 (May), p. 185 (181–196); Paris, Roland (2000) 'Broadening the Study of Peace Operations', *International Studies Review*, Vol. 2, No. 3 (Fall), pp. 27–44; Pugh, Michael (2004) 'Peacekeeping and IR Theory: Phantom of the Opera?' *International Peacekeeping*, Vol. 10, No. 4 (Winter), pp. 104–112.
22. The generational concept was popularized by Ratner, Steven R. (1995) *The New UN Peacekeeping: Building Peace in Lands of Conflict After the Cold War* (New York: St Martin's Press).
23. Mackinlay, John (1994) 'Improving Multifunctional Forces', *Survival*, Vol. 36, No. 3 (Autumn), pp. 149–173.
24. The value of analysing Cold War operations with an eye to learn lessons of contemporary value is perhaps best illustrated by Findlay, *The Use of Force in UN Peace Operations.*
25. For UN mission acronyms see Appendix 1, for non-UN missions see Appendix 2.
26. This method stipulates that the researcher must derive a set of general research questions from the existing body of knowledge in the relevant field of study and use these questions to structure the analysis of each case. Moreover, each case study should focus selectively on those aspects that are relevant for the research question only. See George, Alexander L. (1979) 'Case Studies and Theory Development: The Theory of Structured, Focused Comparison', in Paul Gordon Lauren (ed.) *Diplomacy: New Approaches in History, Theory and Policy* (New York: Free Press), pp. 43–68 and George, Alexander L. and Timothy J. Mckeown (1985) 'Case Studies and Theories of Organizational Decision Making', in Robert F. Coulam and Richard A. Smith (eds) *Advances in Information Processing in Organizations*, Vol. 2 (Greenwich, CT: JAI Press), pp. 21–58. The method is essentially the same as the one advocated for multiple case studies in Robert K. Yin (1989) *Case Study Research. Design and Methods*, revised edn (London: Sage Publications).
27. Østergaard, Uffe (2003) 'Prøv at kalde Norden for Nordeuropa', *Jyllands-Posten*, 6 December.

2 The old Nordic Model: Nordic peacekeeping during the Cold War (1947–87)

> The deep involvement and close cooperation that evolved amongst the Nordic countries gradually led to their being referred to in UN contexts as a single actor rather than as separate countries with regard to participation in peacekeeping. This collaboration ... is often referred to as 'the Nordic Model'.
>
> Åge Eknes[1]

Although other nations, most notably Canada, played a key role in UN peacekeeping operations during the Cold War,[2] the Nordic Model is generally viewed as the quintessence of traditional (Cold War) peace-keeping.[3] Its influence was evident from the popularity of the 'Blue Book', the Nordic Standby Forces manual which became widely used as a basis for establishing and training UN contingents.[4] It was also to the Nordic Model that the British Army, the US Army and the WEU turned when they began to take an interest in peacekeeping in the early 1990s as a result of the operation in the former Yugoslavia.[5]

The Nordic Model was composed of four elements: an institutional framework made up of regular meetings between the Nordic ministers of defence and a number of working groups; a series of joint special UN peacekeeping courses for officers; national standby forces which generally consisted of volunteers recruited at short notice on an individual basis and deployed in the field with only a few weeks of preparation and a minimum of logistical support; and finally a high willingness to provide personnel for UN operations. By the end of the Cold War approximately 125,000 troops, or about 25 per cent of the personnel that had served on UN peacekeeping operations, had come from the four Nordic countries.[6] It was their cooperation that set the Nordics apart from Canada and the other traditional troop contributors. They were the first to set up joint multinational training programmes and manuals, and their close cooperation at the UN Head-quarters in New York and in the field gave them a disproportionate influence on the evolution of UN peacekeeping operations.

In spite of the Nordic Model's influence, no study provides an overview of its origins, evolution and operating procedures. This chapter is therefore written with a dual objective in mind. It fills a gap in the literature on Cold War peacekeeping and provides the historical perspective that is required to understand why the changing nature of peace operations in the 1990s forced the Nordics to engage in a process of radical reform. The traditional Nordic Model is analysed by means of four general questions: (1) Where did it come from? (2) How did it develop? (3) Why did it develop? (4) How was the model's flagship, the standby force, organized and used?

The origins of the Nordic involvement in peacekeeping

Born as an improvised response to crises in the Middle East and Kashmir, peacekeeping evolved to become the hallmark of the UN's efforts to maintain international peace and security during the Cold War. By the end of 1987, when the Cold War deadlock of the Security Council had been broken as a result of a more positive Soviet attitude towards the organization and the use of peacekeeping,[7] a total of 13 UN peacekeeping operations had been conducted.[8]

These operations were generally of a diplomatic rather than military nature, seeking to contribute to the diplomatic resolution of conflicts. Accordingly, they were conducted under Chapter VI of the Charter dealing with peaceful conflict resolution.[9] Cold War peacekeeping fell largely in two categories: observer missions and peacekeeping missions. Observer missions were carried out by small numbers of unarmed officers who were tasked to monitor ceasefire agreements, troop withdrawals and/or borders. Peacekeeping operations were performed by national contingents of lightly armed troops who in addition to monitoring were also tasked to separate the parties to the conflict. These operations took place with the consent of the parties and peacekeeping forces were only allowed to use force in self-defence (the Congo operation (ONUC), the early stage of the Cyprus mission (UNFICYP) and the mission in Lebanon (UNIFIL) were the main exceptions to the rule, being characterized by limited consent and, in the case of ONUC, offensive operations).[10]

Although the UN can rightly claim to have invented peacekeeping as a term, a closer look at the historical record reveals that military operations serving essentially the same functions as UN peacekeeping and observer missions during the Cold War were conducted long before the world organization was founded. Some of these operations had Nordic participation. The earliest instance is found in 1849–50 when a joint 3,800-strong Norwegian–Swedish force carried out what was essentially a peacekeeping operation to prevent further fighting between Denmark and Prussia. The 1,100 Norwegian and 2,700 Swedish troops were deployed in Schleswig as part of the armistice that was agreed upon in July 1849. The force conducted control and police duties until a peace agreement was signed in July the following year.[11]

Nordic troops and military observers also participated in observer and peacekeeping operations under the auspices of the League of Nations during the 1920s and 1930s. Denmark, Norway and Sweden pledged to provide troops to a 1,500-strong international force that the League intended to send to Vilna to supervise a plebiscite in 1920. All three governments had made preparations for the deployment and raised volunteer units when the operation was finally cancelled in March 1921.[12]

The League was more successful in 1935 when it deployed a 3,300 international military force to establish a secure environment for a plebiscite in the Saar. Sweden provided 261 troops to the military contingent as well as personnel to the civilian staff that managed the vote supervision. Norway also made a contribution to the civilian staff.[13]

In addition to these 'peacekeeping' operations, the Nordic states also made military observers available to the League on a number of occasions. Following the League's successful effort to establish a ceasefire in the Greek–Bulgarian crisis in 1925, Sweden provided the two military observers who supervised the reorganization of the frontier guards and served in the conciliation commission that was set up to prevent new incidents and defuse any that might nonetheless occur.[14]

All four Nordic states participated in the 130-strong military observer force that was deployed on the border between France and Spain from 1937 to 1939 by the Non-Intervention Committee to contain the Spanish Civil War.[15] The force was commanded by the Danish colonel C.D.O. Lunn, and the Nordics contributed a total of 50 observers to the force: Denmark provided 30, Finland 14, Norway one and Sweden five.[16] Finally in 1938–39 one Danish, one Finnish, two Swedish and two Norwegian officers were made available to the League's international military commission which in 1939 supervised the withdrawal of the foreign units which fought in the Spanish Civil War.[17]

During the League years the Nordics not only provided military personnel to peace operations conducted by the organization. Denmark, Norway, Sweden and, to a lesser extent, Finland also established a practice of diplomatic cooperation.[18] Within the League, the three Scandinavian countries constituted an inner circle of a group of small member states who sought to act as a counterweight against great power domination and promote the rule of law and the peaceful settlement of disputes. The Scandinavian countries tended to hold common views on the chief issues discussed at Geneva, and when a Scandinavian country had a seat on the Council of the League, it acted as spokesperson for the group as a whole.[19] As a consequence, other states began to take close cooperation on the basis of common interests for granted and referred to the existence of a 'Scandinavian bloc'.[20]

In summary, Scandinavian/Nordic cooperation and involvement in peacekeeping operations did not begin with the founding of the UN. The seeds were sown during the League years. It is equally clear that the UN did not invent peacekeeping; rather the UN perfected what the League had begun. Some might object to this conclusion that the operations described above differ from UN peacekeeping in that they were not guided by the three principles that became the trademark of the UN operations during the Cold War: impartiality, consent from the parties and non-use of force except in self-defence. However, this objection does not even seem to hold true with respect to the Norwegian–Swedish force that was deployed in Schleswig as part of the armistice in 1849. The armistice stipulated that Schleswig would be administered from Flensburg by an impartial administration consisting of a Dane, an Englishman and a Prussian, and that the northern part of the area would be occupied by Norwegian and Swedish troops and the southern part by Prussian troops. The Norwegian–Swedish force was tasked 'to maintain law, order and justice in northern Schleswig under observance of the strictest neutrality between Danes and Germans.'[21] Impartiality, in order words, was a factor and since the force was deployed with the consent of parties, the UN principles were respected at least to some extent. That the League of Nations operations mentioned above did respect the three UN peacekeeping principles to such an extent that they can be regarded as examples of 'proper' peacekeeping is convincingly documented in a 1971 study by Larry Fabian.[22]

How did the Nordic Model develop?

The establishment of the UN did not induce the Nordic states to embark on policies that differed markedly from the ones they had pursued during the League years. Their cooperation continued. From 1946 onwards the Danish, Norwegian and Swedish foreign ministers met each year prior to the opening of UN General Assembly to coordinate their policies, and Finland began to take part in 1956, having been admitted to the UN the previous year. That Denmark and Norway joined NATO in 1949 and Finland and Sweden stayed neutral did not result in major changes in Nordic cooperation either. Nils Ørvik was thus able to conclude in the early 1960s that:

> In most [international] organizations where the Nordic countries are represented their delegations cooperate intimately. The fact that Sweden is pursuing a neutral policy whereas Norway and Denmark are members of NATO has had remarkably little impact on their attitude towards international cooperation. As a rule the Nordic countries take a common position.[23]

They also continued their active participation in peacekeeping. The three Scandinavian countries became involved in UN peacekeeping from day one. Sweden played a key role in the first official UN observer mission which was set up in Palestine in 1948. In addition to military observers, Sweden also provided the first two chiefs of staff and the first UN mediator for this operation. The following year all the Scandinavian countries provided personnel to the second observer mission in Kashmir (UNMOGIP), which was the first operation to which all UN member states were invited to contribute.[24] Finland joined the club of troop contributors when the world organization launched its first peacekeeping operation in Egypt (UNEF I) in 1956.

Since then Nordic troops have served in UN peacekeeping operations on a continuous basis. As can be seen in Table 2.1, Nordic military personnel participated in all but two of the official 13 UN operations that were initiated before 1988, and a large number of Nordic officers served as chiefs of staff, chiefs of military observers and force commanders.

The Nordic involvement went beyond the provision of personnel. All four states were deeply involved in the birth of UN peacekeeping in 1956. Hans Engen, the Norwegian ambassador to the UN, was one of four representatives who helped the Secretary-General to produce the preliminary plan for the establishment of UNEF on 4 November, and Norway co-sponsored the resolution proposing the establishment of UNEF I together with Canada and Columbia later that day; Engen also served on the UNEF advisory committee that was set up after the establishment of the force had been approved by the General Assembly;[25] all four Nordic states made military officers available for the informal UNEF military staff at the UN Headquarters in New York that planned the deployment of UNEF I; and Finnish Major General (retd) A.E. Martola acted as special military advisor to the Swedish Secretary-General Dag Hammarskjöld, who formulated the three peacekeeping principles of consent, impartiality and non-use of force that continue to guide the conduct of peacekeeping operations to this day.[26]

UNEF I also marked the starting point of the Nordic cooperation on peacekeeping that eventually developed into what was to become known as the Nordic Model. Cooperation began almost immediately after the UN requests for troops arrived in the four Nordic capitals between 3 and 5 November 1956. All four states decided within hours to send troops, and on Danish initiative the three Scandinavian defence ministers met in Copenhagen on 12 November to coordinate policy. Finland did not participate in this meeting because of its policy of strict neutrality and because it needed more time to put its UN contingent together.[27] The Finns only began to arrive in the mission area on 11 December, some three weeks after the Scandinavian contingents.[28]

The meeting in Copenhagen between the Scandinavian defence ministers led to the establishment of a joint Danish–Norwegian battalion (DANOR)

Table 2.1 Nordic participation in the 13 UN peacekeeping and observer missions conducted during the Cold War (1948–87)[a]

Mission	Duration	Denmark	Finland	Norway	Sweden
UNTSO – United Nations Truce Supervision Organization in the Middle East	1948–	X	X	X	X
UNMOGIP – United Nations Military Observer Group in India and Pakistan	1949–	X	X	X	X
UNEF I – First United Nations Emergency Force (Gaza)	1956–67	X	X	X	X
UNOGIL – United Nations Observation Group in Lebanon	1958	X	X	X	X
ONUC – United Nations Operation in the Congo	1960–64	X	. .	X	X
UNSF – United Nations Security Force in West New Guinea (West Irian)	1962–63	. .	. .	. .	. .
UNYOM – United Nations Yemen Observation Mission	1963–64	X	. .	X	X
UNFICYP – United Nations Peacekeeping Force in Cyprus	1964–	X	X	. .	X
DOMREP – Mission of the Representative of the Secretary-General in the Dominican Republic	1965–66	. .	. .	. .	. .
UNIPOM – United Nations India–Pakistan Observation Mission	1965–66	X	X	X	X
UNEF II – Second United Nations Emergency Force (Egypt)	1973–79	. .	X	. .	X
UNDOF – United Nations Disengagement Observer Force (Golan Heights)	1974–	X	X	. .	X
UNIFIL – United Nations Interim Force in Lebanon	1978–	. .	X	X	X
Mission total		9	9	8	11

Notes

a The Nordics also participated in some of the UN observer missions that do not appear in the statistics such as UNSCOB – United Nations Special Committee on the Balkans (Norway and Sweden) and UNTEA – United Nations Temporary Executive Authority in West New Guinea (West Irian) (Sweden).

and a joint Scandinavian air transport service (SCANAP).[29] A UN request for the establishment of a joint Finnish–Swedish battalion was not implemented, however. On 22 November Sweden made clear in a letter to the UN that it regarded the establishment of a joint Finnish–Swedish battalion as impractical because separate Finnish and Swedish battalions were already being set up, and because the Swedish contingent would be ready for deployment much quicker than the Finnish.[30]

Whereas Denmark and Norway continued to hold frequent defence minister meetings to coordinate policy, Sweden took part only occasionally, and Finland stayed away. Both countries were concerned that such cooperation with NATO countries might jeopardize their neutrality in the eyes of Moscow. This concern also led the Finnish leadership to withdraw its contingent after a year once it became apparent that UNEF would be required to stay in the mission area longer than initially expected. Officially, the decision to withdraw was motivated by economic and practical considerations, but the Finnish diplomat Max Jakobson makes clear in his memoirs that the principal reason was fear that a prolonged engagement might jeopardize Finnish neutrality.[31]

UNEF I's success led to repeated calls for the establishment of a permanent international UN peace force,[32] and in September of 1958 the Nordic foreign ministers discussed the issue without agreeing on a common position at a meeting in Copenhagen.[33] A request from UN Secretary-General Dag Hammarskjöld and a new chaotic UN deployment was required before concrete action was taken. In a letter dated 12 June 1959 Hammarskjöld asked all the nations that had provided troops for the UN peacekeeping operations in the Middle East whether they would be prepared to incorporate possible future UN requests for peacekeeping contingents in their national military planning.[34] The Danish government declared itself willing to initiate informal discussions with the UN Secretariat on the matter, but since the latter never took up the invitation, no action was taken.[35] Nothing happened in Norway and Sweden either until the chaotic establishment of ONUC in July 1960 once again underlined the need for greater preparedness.

Before the dust whirled up by the difficulties created by the ONUC deployment had time to settle, the Swedish minister of defence, Sven Andersson, asked his chief of defence to draw up plans for a Swedish standby force.[36] The three Scandinavian defence ministers discussed the Swedish initiative at a meeting in September and similar studies were subsequently undertaken in Denmark and Norway.[37] The defence ministers met again in March 1961 to discuss the results of their national studies and they agreed to continue this work at the national level and at the UN. Following requests from the Scandinavian countries, the UN Secretariat on 10 May 1961 provided the three states with detailed lists of the types of personnel that it wanted them to make available to the UN.[38]

At a meeting in Oslo on 27–28 September 1961 the Scandinavian defence ministers decided to set up a joint working group to develop a plan for how the three states could jointly meet the wishes of the UN.[39] Draft proposals were discussed at meetings during 1962 and on 23 April 1963 the establishment of standby forces for UN service was approved by the three defence ministers at a meeting in Stavanger. Finland joined the working group the following month after the Finnish UN ambassador Ralph Enckell and Max Jakobson, then head of the Political Department in the Finnish Ministry of Foreign Affairs, had succeeded in persuading President Kekkonen that it would not compromise Finnish neutrality.[40] A year later in May 1964 all the Nordic parliaments approved the establishment of national standby forces for UN service. Two years later the relevant data concerning the Nordic standby units were forwarded to the UN Security Council.[41] However, the standby forces were still not fully developed, making it more appropriate to regard the publication of the Nordic standby manual, the so-called 'Blue Book', in 1973 as the event that marks the birth of the fully fledged Nordic Model.[42]

Why did the Nordic Model develop?

That the UN's first two Secretary-Generals, Trygve Lie and Dag Hammarskjöld, came from Norway and Sweden, respectively, is often regarded as an important factor in explanations of why the Nordic Model developed.[43] There is no doubt that the early involvement of the Scandinavian countries in the late 1940s, and of Finland from 1956 onwards, to some extent can be explained by this fact. The selection of Lie and Hammarskjöld was (and is) a source of national pride in both countries, and it made the two governments more inclined to support UN policies than they might otherwise have been.[44] At the same time, it also made the Secretary-Generals naturally inclined to seek support from the Nordic countries and to select Nordic mediators. Evidence of this can be found in Norway's participation in the observer mission authorized by the UN General Assembly in Greece (UNSCOB) in 1947;[45] Lie's proposal of the Swedish Count Folke Bernadotte as UN mediator in Palestine in 1948;[46] Hammarskjöld's request for a Finnish military advisor in connection with the establishment of UNEF; the strong Nordic involvement in the planning of this operation; and Hammarskjöld's request for a Swedish officer to head UNTSO in 1958.[47] Moreover, Tage Erlander, former Swedish prime minister, argues in his memoirs that Hammarskjöld succeeded in persuading the Swedish government to involve itself deeper in the Congo operation than it had originally intended.[48]

Although the nationalities of the first two secretary-generals undoubtedly helped to make the relationship between the UN Secretariat and the Nordic governments more intimate than would otherwise have been the case, the policies pursued by the latter would arguably have been much the same in any event. Six additional factors made the Nordic involvement in UN peacekeeping an obvious policy choice. The first factor is the successful experience from the League of Nations which made the three Scandinavian states predisposed towards cooperation and active participation in peace operations in the UN. However, the fact that the Scandinavian countries continued their League policies in the UN does not explain why the decisions to do so were taken. Five factors must be invoked to do so: (1) the suitability of the Nordic states; (2) common interests; (3) national interests; (4) an unusually high overlap between national interests and values and UN goals and ideals; and finally (5) that the Nordic involvement in UN peacekeeping became a success story. Each of these five factors are addressed in turn below.

Suitability: the Nordics were perfect for the job

One obvious, but sometimes overlooked, factor explaining the extensive Nordic involvement in UN peacekeeping is that they were eminently suitable for the job. To qualify for UN peacekeeping, a potential contributor had to fulfil four conditions. First, it could not be a permanent member of the Security Council as they were ruled out to avoid local conflicts becoming part of the global confrontation between the super-powers. Second, it could not come from the region in which the conflict was taking place nor be thought to have a special interest in the conflict at hand. Third, it had to be acceptable to the host government. Fourth, a contributor had to be able to provide without delay units sufficiently large to be relatively self-contained.[49]

The four Nordic states generally met all four conditions. They were too small to pose a threat to anyone and had no special political or economic interests, no recent colonial histories, and no presumed imperial designs that could create problems in the areas of operation. Finland and Sweden were declared neutrals and the Scandinavian countries, as we have seen, had established a record of active involvement in the attempts made by the League of Nations to solve disputes peacefully. All this helped to give the four Nordic states a reputation for impartiality that made them natural candidates for UN peacekeeping service. Although Denmark and Norway joined NATO in 1949, both governments insisted that this did in no way prevent them from pursuing an independent policy at the UN, and they continued to act as mediators, to promote peaceful conflict resolution and do their utmost to stay aloof of great power conflicts in much the same way as they had done during the League years.[50] Their quasi-neutral UN policies and the impartial behaviour displayed by Danish and Norwegian UN personnel on the ground explain why their NATO membership did not prevent the two states from playing key roles in UN peacekeeping operations.[51]

Finally, the Nordic countries were able to provide trained and equipped troops without delay. In some of the early operations, the Scandinavian states made troops available to the UN in a matter of hours rather than days, a feat they would be hard pressed to repeat today. To give one example, Norway was the first state to declare a contingent ready for deployment in the UNEF I operation, needing less than 24 hours to prepare its 190-strong company for departure.[52] Moreover, use of the Scandinavian contingents also had practical advantages as extensive Scandinavian cooperation reduced the problems related to transport and logistics. That the Scandinavian troops understood each other's languages also facilitated cooperation on the ground. Using the Nordic contingents did have one serious drawback from the UN perspective since they were among the most expensive to deploy. This problem was partly addressed in 1967 when the Nordic governments agreed to pay a greater share of the costs themselves.[53]

Summing up, the Nordic involvement in peacekeeping can in part be explained as demand driven. There was a great need for impartial, non-threatening states capable of fielding military forces for UN operations at short notice, and the Nordics fitted this job description perfectly. That the Nordics were suitable and capable does not explain why they were willing to do the job, however. An explanation of their willingness requires an analysis of their interests and values.

Common small state interests

The Nordic willingness to participate in UN peacekeeping was shaped by common interests emanating from the cultural, historical, social and political similarities that characterize the four countries and their common fate as small states whose security in the final instance depended on the great powers. This naturally resulted in foreign policies whose long-term objectives aimed at strengthening the rule of law and promoting the peaceful settlement of all disputes in order to limit the risk of great power abuses. Since these were also the long-term objectives that the League and subsequently the UN were set up to achieve, supporting peacekeeping operations under the auspices of these organizations was evidently in the Nordic interest. The Danish minister for foreign affairs Per Hækkerup explained well the rationale behind the Nordic support for UN peacekeeping in an article in *Foreign Affairs* in 1964 that was written to increase international awareness of the establishment of the Nordic standby forces:

> Small countries have a vital stake in supporting the development of the United Nations so that it becomes an effective instrument of the international rule of law. Obviously, this is not an aim that can be achieved at once. But by helping to preserve and strengthen the United Nations as an effective instrument for peace in the current international

situation, we can help in the longer run to bring about conditions which foster gradual progress toward the distant but all-important goal.[54]

This argument has been repeated time and time again in statements from the leaders of all four Nordic states. The view of the Norwegian minister of defence Johan Jørgen Holst is typical. He explained the long-standing Norwegian support for peacekeeping in an article in 1990 in the following way:

> Norway's engagement in peacekeeping is based on its interest in upholding certain basic principles of international conduct which are of vital importance to small states everywhere, particularly those that find themselves in exposed positions in the geometry of international power relations. One of those basic principles is that territorial conquest by military force is unacceptable. Might does not make right. Borders can only be changed legitimately by agreement. If that principle be violated and weakened anywhere the security of small states will be weakened everywhere.[55]

Peacekeeping was not merely regarded as an instrument for attaining such long-term objectives, however. It was also seen as a way of addressing more pressing security concerns. Concern that local conflicts might escalate into superpower confrontations that would draw the Nordic states into a general war was thus a principal factor motivating the Nordic support for peacekeeping. The Korean War and the Suez crisis had brought this risk home to Nordic decision makers, and the interest in preventing escalation and great power involvement in local conflicts statements is a constant refrain in Nordic statements on UN peacekeeping. One example is the explanation for the Finnish support for UN peacekeeping provided by President Kekkonen in his memoirs:

> This policy has not been unselfish idealism only; it has been based on a realistic assessment of our national security. In the present world situation, the interdependence of all states has attained such a degree that every conflict, even a remote one, which endangers international security in general also threatens our security in the final analysis.[56]

A second factor behind the active support for UN peacekeeping was the interest in avoiding entrapment in great power conflicts. Participation in UN peacekeeping was seen as useful in this respect in two ways. First, it enabled the Nordics to signal independence of the two emerging power blocs since personnel from the great powers were barred from participation. Second, it carried little risk of entrapment in great power conflicts because the great powers usually consented to them.

The Nordic fear of entrapment in the East–West confrontation was particularly strong in the early stages of the Cold War. It plays an important part in the explanation as to why none of the Nordic states sent combat troops to Korea,[57] and the Finnish unwillingness to send troops to Congo in 1960 must also be seen in this light. This fear is also evident in the Nordic voting pattern in the General Assembly where the Nordic states usually abstained in votes where the superpowers clashed. Initially, the Nordic states were also very reluctant to accept seats on the Security Council out of fear that it might force them to choose sides. Thus, Denmark declined the offer to serve on the Security Council in 1950 giving its seat to Holland, and it kept a very low profile when it served for the first time in 1953–54. In the words of Preben Askgaard: 'Denmark's membership of the Security Council in 1953 and 1954 passed off very quietly. It is literally not mentioned with a single word in either books or journals.'[58]

Sweden was also very concerned when it served for the first time in 1957–58,[59] and Finland did not seek election to the Security Council until 1968.[60] That Norway was the exception to this rule serving its first period on the Council in 1949–50 can probably be explained by the fact that the Secretary-General at the time, Trygve Lie, was a Norwegian. The outbreak of the Korean War made it very difficult for Norway to steer a middle course between the superpowers while it served on the Security Council, and these difficulties cannot but have discouraged Denmark and Sweden from following in Norway's footsteps.[61]

Although Norway and Sweden played a more active role than Denmark and Finland in the 1950s, it is nevertheless fair to say that all the Nordic states kept a low profile at the UN during this period. Their principal objective was to stay out of trouble and keep a good relationship with the great powers on which their security depended. Denmark and Norway regarded a good relationship with London and Washington as a priority whereas Finland gave first priority to its relations with Moscow. For Sweden the name of the game was to keep a middle course between the two blocs.[62] It was not until the late 1950s and early 1960s that the Nordics began to play the more active role that resulted in the establishment of the Nordic Model.

The existence of common interests does not always lead to cooperation, but in this case Nordic cooperation on peacekeeping was facilitated by the shared belief that the Nordics had to cooperate in order to maximize their influence at the UN. As Edvard Hambro, the Norwegian ambassador to the UN, explained in 1966:

> We attempt as far as possible to maintain the same policies in the United Nations since we think that the Nordic voice receives increased authority and weight if the Nordic countries stand together. Therefore we always attempt to consult with each other, but we are not legally bound, on any occasion, to take exactly the same stand.[63]

National interests

For all their similarities and common bonds, their different geographical locations and different experiences from the Second World War still gave rise to different dilemmas inducing the Nordic states to choose different solutions to their security problems. Finland never had much of a choice as it received an offer it could not refuse to sign a 'Treaty of Friendship, Cooperation and Mutual Assistance' with the Soviet Union in 1948, but it retained sufficient autonomy to pursue a policy of neutrality. Negotiations between the three Scandinavian states to establish a Scandinavian Defence Union in 1948–49 collapsed and resulted in Denmark and Norway joining NATO, whereas Sweden adopted a policy of alliance-free neutrality which was underpinned by secret cooperation with NATO. These differences meant that each of the four Nordic states, in addition to the shared interests outlined above, also had specific interests which shaped their peacekeeping policies.

The Danish and Norwegian security and defence policies during the Cold War are best characterized as delicate balancing acts between deterrence and reassurance.[64] The NATO membership served to deter a possible Soviet attack, while a low profile in NATO and active support for impartial UN mediation and peacekeeping served to demonstrate to the world (and especially the Soviet Union) that in spite of their NATO membership they were peace-loving, 'neutral' states which did not pose a threat to anyone (particularly the Soviet Union). Domestically, support for the UN served the additional purpose of muting criticism of the NATO membership that both states only opted for *faute de mieux*.

For Finland the situation was quite different. While Denmark and Norway had to convince the Soviet Union that they did not pose a threat and at the same time demonstrate solidarity with their alliance partners in NATO, Finland faced the challenge of convincing the Western states that it was capable of maintaining a genuinely neutral position between East and West without at the same time arousing suspicion in Moscow.[65] President Kekkonen formulated the challenge for Finland in the following way in March 1959:

> Finland's relations to the West depend on the way we handle our relations to the East. When we make decisions (in the West), we naturally have to take into account the fact that Finland's vital interests require that the neighbourly relations to the Soviet Union and the trust of the Union remain intact.[66]

After initial concern that the UN membership and participation in peacekeeping operations might drag Finland into great power conflicts and compromise its neutrality,[67] Kekkonen in 1963 finally became convinced that active support for UN mediation and peacekeeping missions had the opposite effect.[68] His decision to support the establishment of the Finnish standby force signalled this change of heart, and active support for peacekeeping from 1963 onwards became an important instrument in the Finnish efforts to safeguard its neutrality and enhance its international room of manoeuvre.

In addition, as pointed out by Jakobson, Finland and the other neutral states were also 'anxious to persuade the world that their policy was not merely a way of saving their own skin, but actually served the higher interests of the international community.'[69] Support for peacekeeping, mediation and conciliation was therefore repeatedly presented as a moral obligation that Finland had to make in support of international peace and security.[70]

Like its neighbour, Sweden also came to see peacekeeping as a valuable way of enhancing international respect for its neutrality and demonstrating international solidarity. However, in Sweden an activist UN policy also served the domestic purpose of silencing critics of the neutrality policy. Sweden's active involvement in the UN was thus based on the belief that the 'credibility of neutral policies would be judged primarily according to how it contributed to the construction of a new system of peaceful international relations.'[71]

Its UN and peacekeeping policy developed in much the same way as that of the Finnish. Initially, Sweden shared the Finnish concern that an active role at the UN might compromise its neutrality. As mentioned already, Sweden refrained from sending troops to Korea and worried that it might get caught in a superpower conflict when it served on the UN Security Council in 1957–58. In the 1960s this concern gradually gave way to greater involvement as the Swedish leadership became convinced that support for peacekeeping operations actually enhanced Sweden's international reputation. Sweden also went to great lengths to convince the world and domestic critics of the neutrality policy that neutrality did not equal egoistic free-riding. In March 1964 the Swedish minister for foreign affairs Torsten Nilsson thus argued that:

> the very existence of large alliances creates a need for the taking of a neutral stand by countries that can be of use by undertaking assignments in certain situations in which the aligned Powers are not readily acceptable. This is particularly true of UN missions and the examples are manifold: Korea, Gaza, the Congo.[72]

Sweden went much further than Finland in its efforts to signal its independence from the two superpowers both at the UN and in general. This was particularly true in the mid-1960s and early 1970s where the Swedish prime minister Olof Palme made criticism of the superpowers a main feature of Swedish foreign policy.[73] This policy differed markedly from the low-key policy pursued by Finland prompting the Finnish president Mauno

Koivisto to make the following quip about the difference between Finnish and Swedish foreign policy: 'Finland strives for equally friendly relations with all countries, Sweden for equally bad relations.'[74]

Overlap between national interests and UN ideals

Although the high degree of overlap between national interests and UN ideals is evident from the two previous sections, it should still be emphasized as an independent factor in the explanation of the Nordic involvement in peacekeeping operations. In their support for peacekeeping the Nordics were doing exactly the same as all the other members: trying to promote their national interests – and one must not forget that national defence always was accorded a much higher priority than peacekeeping.

As is clear from the legislation on the UN standby forces, decisions to commit troops would only be made if they did not have a negative impact on national defence, and alliance/neutrality considerations were an important determinant. Effective national defence was seen as a prerequisite for peacekeeping participation, and the latter invariably lost out if it was perceived to have a detrimental effect on the former. Peacekeeping in this sense remained a sideshow to the Cold War, and it is quite telling that it was not considered part of Nordic defence and security policy. It is thus conspicuously absent from Cold War analyses of Nordic security, and peacekeeping forces were not even considered part of the defence forces in Finland and Sweden.

This said, one should be careful not to exaggerate the distinctions between defence and peacekeeping and between interest and idealism in the Nordic case.[75] The key to understanding the strong Nordic support for peace-keeping is that it allowed the Nordic governments to promote their interests (prevent great power conflicts, reduce the scope for great power abuse, keep the great powers at an arms length, avoid accusations of free-riding and enhance international prestige) and ideals (support the peaceful resolution of conflicts, the rule of law and decolonization) at the same time. It was the ability of peacekeeping to unite realists and idealists that made it so popular in the Nordic countries and its proponents used it as a selling point time and time again.[76]

While this strong overlap between interest and idealism goes some way towards explaining the Nordic engagement, it would probably have been short-lived if the experience with UN peacekeeping had not proved so successful.

Nordic peacekeeping: a success story

It did not look that way in the beginning and early setbacks would almost certainly have induced the Nordic leaders to stop their involvement. The Nordics were reluctant peacekeepers at first. Finland withdrew its contingent from UNEF after a year and rejected a request for troops to the Congo in 1960 out of fear that it might compromise its neutrality. Sweden rejected the first UN request for troops to Cyprus in 1964 and it took a lot of UN/great power pressure to induce the Swedish government to change its mind. However, the political concerns gradually disappeared as the benefits became visible. Once the Nordic politicians realized that their involvement in peacekeeping operations enhanced their international status and prestige markedly, they quickly began to make the most of it. In a speech in 1965 the Swedish minister for foreign affairs, Torsten Nilsson, made no bones about the fact that the Swedish support for peacekeeping was 'calculated to give a small country status in the minds of other countries.'[77] The Finnish leadership also wanted to make the most of its involvement in peacekeeping and did not allow General Ensio Siilasvuo to decline an offer for the position as deputy chief of staff of UNTSO in 1967. A chance to get a top post in a UN peacekeeping operation was an opportunity to enhance Finland's international profile that the Finnish government did not want to miss.[78]

The military leaderships were harder to convince. In their view peacekeeping was a sideshow to the (Cold) war, and only acceptable to the extent it did not have a negative impact on their core mission: deterring a Soviet attack on their homelands. The heads of the Finnish armed forces were initially concerned that this was the case and continued to regard peacekeeping as an unwelcome burden until the 1980s.[79] The military opposition was also strong in Sweden, where the commander-in-chief, General Nils Swedlund, complained that the Swedish participation in UNEF resulted in 'an indefensible bloodletting of our officers' corps.'[80] The Swedish military tried in vain to prevent the subsequent involvement in the Congo in 1960, the reinforcements of the Congo operation in 1961 and 1962 and the deployment in Cyprus in 1964.[81] Moreover, several Swedish regimental commanders actively discouraged their younger officers from volunteering for UN service in the early 1960s.[82]

The only partial exception I have been able to find to the 'defence first' rule is the statement by the Norwegian chief of the army and the chief of defence in the bill proposing the establishment of the Norwegian standby force to the Norwegian parliament in 1964, that the establishment of the Nordic standby forces was 'of such importance that it should be carried out even if it involves certain adverse effects on the defence activity.'[83]

Generally speaking, the Nordic military leaderships eventually came to accept UN peacekeeping as a task they had to do. In Sweden where the resistance had been most visible, the army leadership began to take a more positive view towards peacekeeping in the course of the 1960s. According to Nils Sköld, this was primarily due to the fact that the Swedish personnel gained valuable training and experience that proved useful with respect to improving the defence forces. He adds that it probably was also a factor that the Swedish contingents did well compared to other contingents in UNEF and ONUC, thus enhancing the reputation of the Swedish Army abroad.[84]

The Nordic military leaderships never learned to love peacekeeping, however. Their continued disdain for peacekeeping was reflected in the fact that peacekeeping experience never became a trump in the promotion game. UN service continued to be seen as 'pure holidaying' as one Danish officer put it in 1969.[85]

The benefits accruing from the participation in peacekeeping were not limited to the international scene. Domestically, it became a source of national prestige. The policy enjoyed strong support across the political spectrum and bills authorizing the deployment of troops abroad passed through the parliaments unanimously in most cases. This was also the case when the legislation to establish the standby forces was passed in the four countries in 1964. There was consequently remarkably little domestic debate about the growing Nordic involvement in peacekeeping operations in the 1950s and 1960s.[86] Public support remained strong throughout the Cold War, although participation in difficult operations characterized by high tension and the loss of lives generated debate and criticism from time to time. Examples include the Swedish participation in the Congo mission and the Finnish and Norwegian participation in UNIFIL.[87] However, these episodes underline the strength of popular and political support for peacekeeping in that criticism never resulted in a revision of policy or a withdrawal of Nordic UN contingents. In today's political climate, characterized by a strong Western aversion towards casualties in peace operations that do not pose a threat to national security, it is noteworthy that the loss of 18 Swedish soldiers during the Congo operation did not cause domestic support for peacekeeping to collapse.[88]

In sum, the Nordic enthusiasm for UN peacekeeping is not difficult to understand in retrospect. As we have seen, participation in peacekeeping allowed the Nordic governments to kill several birds with one stone. It enabled them to further their long-term objectives of a more idealistic nature concerning the establishment of an international system characterized by respect for international law, peaceful conflict resolution and the absence of great power abuse; it enabled them to address pressing short-term security considerations related to the perceived need to deter and reassure the Soviet Union; it enabled them to signal independence from the two power blocs and show 'international solidarity'; it enabled them to silence domestic critics who opposed the membership of NATO in Denmark and Norway and the policy of neutrality in Sweden; it resulted in international praise and an enhanced international reputation; it became a source of national pride; and last but not least, the costs were negligible. The military drawbacks were limited as the UN contingents were equipped with basic military equipment and made up by volunteers who could be raised outside of the defence forces. The economic burden was to some extent alleviated by reimbursements from the UN and the human costs were low.

The development of the Nordic Model can, in short, be explained by the fact that it generated power, pride and prestige on the cheap.

How was the Nordic Model (standby force) organized and used?

Things did not go as planned after the Nordic parliaments had approved the establishment of the standby forces in 1964. According to the original plan Denmark, Norway and Sweden would only set up their standby forces once their existing UN commitments in the Congo and in Gaza had ended. However, Denmark, Finland and Sweden never got the breathing space required to establish the standby forces because they got involved in the peacekeeping operation in Cyprus in 1964, and recruitment difficulties prevented Norway from establishing its standby force in accordance with the original plan after UNEF I was terminated in 1967. The discrepancy between theory and practice remained throughout the Cold War and the actual use of the standby forces never corresponded entirely with the descriptions provided in the original plans and the three editions of the Nordic standby manual that were published between 1973 and 1986. This section therefore analyses how the standby forces were organized and employed by looking at the (1) conditions for their use; (2) finance; (3) organization and readiness; (4) recruitment and training of personnel; (5) doctrine, armaments and rules of engagement; and (6) logistics.

Readers familiar with the peace operations of the 1990s may wonder why crucial mission components such as intelligence, humanitarian assistance, public information and CIMIC are not analysed. The reason is simply that they generally played a marginal role in Cold War operations. The UN forces did not have intelligence officers because it was considered incompatible with the notions of impartiality and neutrality. UN forces were generally limited to using ears and eyes only, and due to its sensitive nature such intelligence was simply referred to as 'military information'.[89] Exceptions were made as commanders sometimes found this untenable and set up their own intelligence system.[90] Some humanitarian assistance was provided during most peacekeeping operations, and from the 1960s onwards Danish UN contingents had a sector humanitarian officer (SHO), who dealt with such activities as part of normal duties.[91] The same system was used to deal with the press. UN contingents were only responsible for dealing with their national press at home and public information was handled by the battalion commander or a designated officer as part of their normal duties. Finally, there was little need for CIMIC because UN peace operations were primarily of a one-dimensional, military nature. Civilian components were the exception, not the rule.[92]

Conditions for use

Although the legislation varied, the general guidelines for deployment were the same in all four Nordic states. Activation of the standby forces required an official request from the UN, consent from the parties to the conflict, a peacekeeping mandate as use of the standby forces for enforcement operations under Chapter VII of the Charter was explicitly ruled out, and, finally, approval from the national parliaments with respect to deployment of larger contingents. Decisions to commit troops and observers were made on a case-by-case basis. Each government reserved the right to say no to a UN request if it was considered incompatible with the national defence requirements, alliance commitments, domestic support, etc.[93] The right to say no or make participation conditional was exercised on a few occasions. Finland rejected a request for troops for the Congo in 1960 and again in 1987 when the UN wanted Finland to fill the gap created by the withdrawal of the Swedish battalion from Cyprus.[94] Sweden initially rejected requests for troops to Cyprus in 1964 and for a logistics battalion to Lebanon in 1986.[95] Yet on both occasions the Swedish government was persuaded to change its mind. However, the Swedish participation in UNFICYP was made contingent upon the participation of other neutral states. Likewise, Finland would only participate if Sweden took part.[96]

The guidelines for deployment were not always followed to the letter. The Swedish government thus accepted the transition of ONUC in Congo from peacekeeping to enforcement and responded positively to a UN request for fighter planes. The Swedish forces played a central role in the defeat of Katanga's defence forces.[97]

Finance

In theory the UN was to have reimbursed the Nordic governments for the costs associated with the deployment of their standby contingents. According to an agreement reached between the Scandinavian governments and the UN in July 1962, the UN would pay a fixed sum per person per day to cover the cost of clothes, weapons and other personal equipment. The equipment for the unit would be paid in accordance with a fixed devaluation percentage. In addition, if special equipment were put at the disposal of the UN, it would be paid for all at once.[98]

In reality the UN was never able to honour these obligations and following criticism that their contingents were too expensive, the Nordic governments in 1967 agreed to pay a greater share of the costs themselves.[99] However, since the UN was not able to pay its reduced share of the costs either and continued to suffer from chronic financial difficulties, the Nordics ended up footing most of the bill themselves.[100]

Organization and readiness

The strength and organization of the standby forces evolved slightly between 1964 and 1987 as new lessons were learned, the compositions of units were altered and new equipment went into service. In addition,

Table 2.2 The Nordic standby force (1978–86)

Units	Denmark	Finland	Norway	Sweden
Max strength (1986)	950	2,000	1,330	2,000
Army units				
UN battalion	1	1	1	2
Zone HQ company	1			
Workshop unit			1	
Medical company			1	
Movement control unit	1	1	1	
Military police unit	1	1	1	1
Naval units				
Naval vessel			1	
Harbour command			1	
Air force units				
Air transport unit			1	
Helicopter wing			1	
Other units				
Survival unit				1
Health care unit				1
Technical assistance unit				1
Transportation and stores unit				1
Individuals				
HQ staff personnel	15	20	25	15
Observers	15	25	25	26
Movement control personnel			10	20

Based on *Nordic Standby Forces* 1978 and 1986 (Stockholm: NORDSAMFN).

Sweden boosted its initial contribution with 700 during this period. An overview of the units in the national standby forces as they appeared in 1986 can be found in Table 2.2.[101] There was a clear separation between the armed forces organized for national defence and the UN standby forces, and the Finnish standby force was not even considered part of the Finnish armed forces.[102] The standby units were organized, equipped, trained and mobilized on a national basis and they could be deployed separately, jointly or in part depending on specific UN requests. The standby forces were never deployed as a joint Nordic force, and joint battalions consisting of personnel from more than one Nordic state were never deployed either after the standby forces came into existence. The only joint battalion deployed during the Cold War was the Danish–Norwegian DANOR in UNEF I.[103] A UN attempt to establish a joint Scandinavian battalion in UNEF I in 1966 failed due to Swedish fears that the establishment of a joint battalion together with two NATO members would compromise its neutrality.[104]

While some units, such as the Norwegian naval units, were never used at all, the Nordic states occasionally responded positively to requests for units that were not listed in their standby forces. Denmark and Sweden thus provided civilian police officers for the operation in Cyprus for many years.[105] Moreover, the Nordic states also exceeded the force level indicated in the standby force on a few occasions. On 30 April 1964, the same day that the Danish parliament approved the establishment of the 950-strong standby force, it also decided to provide 980 troops and 40 civilian police officers for UNFICYP. This commitment, which in itself exceeded the 950 personnel ceiling in the standby force bill just passed, was made at a time when Denmark was also participating in UNEF I, ONUC and a number of observer missions.

The official response times provided in the standby manuals gradually became longer between 1973 and 1986, and the following figures from the 1986 manual are the most conservative. Individuals such as staff personnel and observers, who were on immediate standby, could be posted within 24 hours after their government had approved a UN request for personnel. A battalion or a larger formation would be ready for departure 19 days after approval had been granted. The preparation would take place in three stages. A small 20-strong advance party would be ready to depart for the mission area four days after approval had been granted. A second advance party (44 personnel) would be ready in eight or nine days and the main party would then be ready after 19 days.[106] Since none of the Nordic countries had the capacity to airlift the main party themselves, the speed of the actual deployment depended on whether airlift was made available by the UN or other member states, but this was never a problem during the Cold War.

In most cases the Nordic states needed less time to prepare their contingents than the 1986 manual suggests. As mentioned already, the Norwegian contingent for UNEF I was ready for departure less than 24 hours after the government had approved the UN request for troops, and all the Scandinavian contingents had arrived in the mission area less than two weeks after the decisions to participate had been taken.[107] Only the Finns needed more time than the 19 days indicated in the manual to prepare their contingent for deployment.[108]

When ONUC was established in 1960, the Swedish battalion arrived in the Congo three days after the decision to participate had been taken. Sweden accomplished this feat by simply transferring its UN battalion serving in Gaza as part of UNEF I to the Congo.[109] With respect to the UNFICYP operation, the Danish troop contingent departed for Cyprus 20 days after the decision to participate was taken,[110] the Finnish main force was deployed six weeks after the Finnish Ministry of Defence had been ordered to establish it, and the Swedish contingent was in place approximately one month after the operation had been approved by the government.[111] The longer reaction times for this operation can in part be explained by the fact that it stretched the capacity of the Scandinavian countries that were also contributing to UNEF I and ONUC at the time. The establishment of the contingents was further complicated by a UN request for larger contributions which was made in the middle of the force generation process.[112]

In connection with UNEF II in 1973 Sweden deployed its contingent in Egypt in only 27 hours. This was possible because most of the personnel were taken from the Swedish battalion already serving in UNFICYP.[113] UNFICYP companies from Austria, Ireland and Norway were transferred to UNEF II in the same manner.[114]

Sweden used the same procedure when UNIFIL was established in 1978. Then a 250-strong advance guard was raised from the Swedish UNEF II battalion and transferred to Lebanon in a matter of hours.[115] The advance guard of the Norwegian contingent arrived in Tel Aviv on 25 March, six days after the UN Security Council had established the force.[116] The Finns were also quick to arrive as they had formed a 'fire brigade' within their UNFICYP contingent which was ready to move at short notice.[117]

Recruitment and training of personnel

Although recruitment and training of UN personnel was a national responsibility and the procedures varied among the Nordic countries, the model was basically the same in all four countries. The Nordic UN contingents were almost exclusively made up of volunteers and most of the personnel volunteered on an individual basis in response to recruitment campaigns. To qualify for service, the volunteers had to have completed (or be near the completion of) their basic military training with a satisfactory result. Relevant civilian skills were also a factor in the recruitment because of a desire to ensure that each contingent had a number of electricians, plumbers, carpenters and so on. Approximately 90 per cent of the volunteers were civilians who had completed their military training as conscripts while the remaining 8–10 per cent were regulars serving in the defence forces.[118]

Once selected, the volunteers signed a standby contract requiring them to standby for deployment at short notice on a UN mission. The terms and lengths of the standby period and the operational deployment varied between the countries. The Scandinavian states occasionally ordered regular personnel to serve on UN operations to make up for shortfalls, and Denmark even ordered conscripts abroad in a few instances. Although this practice apparently ended after a conscript had filed a complaint to the ombudsman in 1966, the Danish legislation continued to allow the ordering of conscripts abroad throughout the Cold War.[119] Finland appears to have based its contingents entirely on volunteers, although, as we have seen, saying no was not an option for Ensio Siilasvuo when he was offered the post of deputy chief of staff of UNTSO in 1967.

A combination of unexpected recruitment difficulties and the continuous nature of the Nordic peacekeeping commitments meant that the Nordic standby forces ended up functioning more as a system for raising rotation units for ongoing peacekeeping missions than as a 'proper' standby force made up of volunteers who had signed contracts with an obligation to stand by for deployment at short notice on a UN mission at an unknown time and location anywhere in the world.[120] Whereas it generally proved relatively easy to get volunteers in sufficient numbers to fill the rotation units in ongoing peacekeeping missions, getting people to sign up for unknown peacekeeping missions proved much more difficult. Because the large majority of the Nordic UN contingents were rotation units serving on ongoing missions, these difficulties did not prevent the standby forces from functioning. Most Nordic volunteers knew the exact location, nature and duration of the mission for which they signed up, and when the Nordics helped to set up new peacekeeping missions, the shortfall of volunteers on 'blind' standby contracts was overcome by recruiting volunteers from UN contingents already serving on (or training for) existing missions. Sweden used this method when UNEF II, UNDOF and UNIFIL were set up, and Finland did it in a similar way with respect to UNEF II. The first Norwegian contingent that was sent to Lebanon in March 1978 to participate in UNIFIL appears to have been the only Nordic peacekeeping contingent to be made up of volunteers who had signed standby contracts without knowing where and when they might be going during their standby period.[121]

The national training programmes lasted three to four weeks and consisted of three main components: a general introduction to the UN and peacekeeping, mission-oriented training and training in specific peacekeeping skills such as controlling check-points, handling of weapons, and so on. The Nordic training programmes were based on the philosophy that peacekeeping was fundamentally different from conventional military operations. The traditional 'warfighting skills' that the troops had been taught during their basic military training as conscripts were considered necessary, but not sufficient, for peacekeeping because peacekeepers had to rely on negotiation skills and diplomacy rather than their weapons in order to accomplish their mission.[122]

In addition to the general training programme, the Nordics set up a joint UN training programme for officers and non-commissioned officers in the 1965–73 period. The 1973 programme consisted of UN observer courses hosted by Sweden and Finland, a UN staff course hosted by Sweden, a course for movement control personnel hosted by Norway, a military police course hosted by Denmark and a logistics officers course hosted by Norway.[123] Later a Nordic UN seminar dealing with questions related to UN peacekeeping operations for persons at command level within the ministries of foreign affairs and defence and the defence staffs was added to the training programme. The training programme in 1985 is summarized in Table 2.3.

Far from all the Nordic UN personnel went through the training programmes just described. Sometimes the establishment of new operations

Table 2.3 The joint Nordic UN training programme 1985

Course	Host country	Frequency
UN military police course	Denmark	Once a year
UN military observer course	Finland	Twice a year
UN logistics officers course	Norway	Every second year
UN movement control course	Norway	Once a year
UN staff officers course	Sweden	Once a year
Nordic UN seminar	Rotating	Every third year

Source: *Nordic UN Standby Forces*, 3rd edn, 1986 (Stockholm: NORDSAMFN).

did not leave sufficient time to go through the programme. Training schedules sometimes had to be shortened and shortages of officers and specialized personnel such as doctors also created difficulties. Moreover, the training of rotation contingents for known missions allowed for much more mission-related training. For instance, the pre-deployment training of all the Swedish UNEF II and UNFICYP rotation units became entirely mission-oriented once these missions had become routine.[124]

Doctrine, armaments and rules of engagement

The standby forces were based on the peacekeeping principles set out by Hammarskjöld in 1958 and configured for peacekeeping operations enjoying the consent of the parties to the conflict. The Nordic contingents were trained to rely on negotiations in crisis situations. Use of force was only permissible as a last resort in self-defence. The rules of engagement (ROE) employed by the Swedish contingents during UNEF II were typical of the ones employed during the Cold War. The Swedish UNEF II contingents were only allowed to use force:

1 when UN personnel were deliberately fired at
2 when UN personnel (or materiel) were attacked or threatened with attack by armed personnel
3 to support a UN unit under armed attack.[125]

The use of force was further limited by the fact that the UN contingents were usually thinly deployed, carried light weapons and travelled in soft-skinned vehicles. If subject to a determined attack with heavy weapons they had no means to defend themselves. Tanks, armoured personnel carriers and heavy mortars were usually not employed in peacekeeping operations because they were viewed as too aggressive and as increasing the risk of escalation.[126]

The use of force by the Nordic contingents was in general very restrained, usually casualties had to occur for less restrictive ROE to be introduced. Exceptions to the rule do exist, however. The principal exception is the

ONUC operation where Swedish forces as already mentioned engaged in offensive combat operations. The ROE were also wider than usual in the beginning of UNFICYP where the UN contingents were given permission to use force to protect civilians under attack.[127]

Logistics

Logistical support was a UN responsibility and the UN agreed in advance with contributors what their contingents should bring with them to the mission area. UN contingents were usually asked to bring rations for a short period of time, personal equipment including weapons, tents and essential light equipment. The UN logistics system seldom worked satisfactorily, however. As the Nordic 1978 manual pointed out, it generally took between one and three months for the central UN logistic organization to become operational when a new mission was established, and it added that 'shortage of funds, bureaucratic procedure, choice of supplies, abnormal delays in delivery of equipment and spare parts, etc., may obstruct the smooth running of the logistic organization and render it cumbersome and unwieldy.'[128] That this was indeed the case is clear from the complaints about logistical and administrative shortcomings and lack of equipment that can be found in virtually all accounts of the peacekeeping operations conducted by the UN during the Cold War.[129] The exception is UNFICYP where the British forces stationed in Cyprus handled the logistics.[130]

The Nordic countries therefore set up air or sea services to the mission areas to keep their peacekeeping contingents supplied with medicine, spare parts and other essentials that the UN system either could not or took too long to provide.[131] Following the chaotic start-up of UNEF I and ONUC, the Nordics also began to provide their contingents with supplies for longer periods of time, and the first Finnish and Swedish UNEF II contingents thus arrived with supplies for a month.[132]

Summing up, the Nordic standby forces enabled the Nordic governments to field troops at short notice when they decided to participate in a UN operation. The training programmes proved adequate as the Nordic troops generally acquitted themselves well in the field,[133] and the logistical backup system made it possible to overcome some of the problems generated by inadequate UN support. At the same time, the actual use of the Nordic standby forces reveals their name to be something of a misnomer. In practice they did not function as 'proper' standby forces, but as systems for raising rotation units for ongoing operations. As a consequence, most volunteers knew where and when they were going before signing up. The only exception to this rule appears to be the first Norwegian UNIFIL contingent.

Conclusion

This chapter has sought to describe and explain the evolution and functioning of the traditional Nordic peacekeeping model. The Nordics were, surprising as it may sound, reluctant UN peacekeepers at first, although they had experience from similar operations under the auspices of the League of Nations.[134] The initial reluctance at the political level was replaced by enthusiasm once it became clear that their participation in peacekeeping was welcomed by the superpowers and served to enhance their prestige on the world scene. The Nordics were among the first to establish standby forces for UN service, and their development of joint training programmes and manuals were unique during the Cold War. The standby forces and the continuous deployment of UN forces in the field enabled the Nordics to respond to UN requests for troops at very short notice – sometimes within hours.

The Nordic enthusiasm for UN peacekeeping is not difficult to understand. Conceived as a small-/medium-power instrument of peaceful conflict resolution, it enabled the Nordics to make a much respected, if limited, contribution to world peace with a minimum of risk and resources. It enhanced their national security and international prestige while promoting their vision of an international system characterized by respect for international law, peaceful conflict resolution and a strong UN at one and the same time. It was popular at home (except in the military) and became part of their national identities.

The Nordic peacekeeping model sounds almost too good to be true. While it was an unqualified success seen from the perspective of Nordic foreign policy, the overall impact of UN peacekeeping was limited during the Cold War. It was a useful instrument in the relatively limited number of conflicts where peacekeepers were invited in by the parties and continued to enjoy their consent and cooperation. Alan James said it best when he characterized Cold War peacekeeping as a 'secondary activity' that was nonetheless 'one of the more fruitful developments of the twentieth century.'[135] The limitations of the traditional peacekeeping concept were highlighted during the Congo operation, which foreshadowed many of the challenges that were to confront UN peace operations in the 1990s. A Norwegian evaluation of this operation conducted in 1964 warned that:

If haphazardly composed UN forces are assigned more complicated tasks than they are able to solve and the opponent finds ways to exploit the weak points of such an instrument, the UN would suffer a serious defeat. Under unfavourable circumstances this might have an impact on world opinion seriously complicating future use of a UN instrument of force to maintain world peace.[136]

Unfortunately, this was precisely what happened in the 1990s in Bosnia, Somalia, Rwanda and elsewhere. The nature of peace operations changed and pulled the rug from under the Nordic Model. The factors behind these changes and the resulting need for a new model are addressed in the next chapter.

Notes

1. Eknes, Åge (1995) 'The Nordic Countries and UN Peacekeeping Operations', in Åge Eknes (ed.) *The Nordic Countries in the United Nations: Status and Future Perspectives* (Copenhagen: Nordic Council), p. 65 (65–83).
2. Canada was the only state to contribute to all of the 13 UN operations launched between 1948 and 1987, and the Canadian foreign minister Lester Pearson is usually credited for the invention of peacekeeping because of the key role he played in connection with the deployment of UNEF I. In addition to the Nordic countries, the other top contributors were Australia, Austria, Fiji, Ghana, India, Ireland, Nepal, New Zealand, Pakistan and Senegal.
3. Smith, Richard (1994) 'A Study into the Requirement for the United Nations to Develop an Internationally Recognized Doctrine for the Use of Force in Intra-State Conflict', *Strategic and Combat Studies Institute Occasional Paper*, No. 10 (Camberley: Strategic and Combat Studies Institute); Stedman, Stephen John (1996) 'Consent, Neutrality, and Impartiality in the Tower of Babel and on the Frontlines: United Nations Peacekeeping in the 1990s', in *Managing Arms in Peace Processes: The Issues* (New York, Geneva: United Nations), pp. 35–56.
4. Egge, Bjørn (1978) 'FN's fredsbevarende operasjon i Libanon. En oversikt ved årsskiftet og noen tanker om Norges rolle', *Internasjonal Politikk*, No. 4 B (Supplement), p. 751 (751–765); Fetherston, A.B. (1994) *Towards a Theory of United Nations Peacekeeping* (New York: St Martin's Press), p. 183.
5. Mackinlay, John and Randolph Kent (1997) 'Complex Emergencies Doctrine, the British are Still the Best', *RUSI Journal*, Vol. 142, No. 2 (April), p. 40 (31–49); WEU (1993) 'United Nations Operations – Interaction with WEU', *WEU Document*, No. 1366 (19 May 1993), pp. 2–3, 23–27; Wilkinson, Philip (1998) 'Sharpening the Weapons of Peace: The Development of a Common Military Doctrine for Peace Support Operations', *British Army Review*, No. 118 (April), p. 3 (3–7).
6. Eknes, Åge (1993) 'Prepared for Peacekeeping: The Nordic Countries and Participation in UN Military Operations', in Winrich Kühne (ed.) *Blauhelme in einer Turbulenten Welt. Beiträge internationaler Experten zur Fortenwicklung des Völkerrechts und der Vereinten Nationen* (Baden-Baden: Nomos Verlag), p. 509 (509–523).
7. Weiss, Thomas G. and Meryl A. Kessler (1990) 'Moscow's UN Policy', *Foreign Policy*, No. 79 (Summer), p. 98 (94–112).
8. See Appendix 3 for a complete list of UN peace operations 1948–2005 (March).
9. The traditional peacekeeping operations were sometimes referred to as Chapter VI½ operations, an expression first used by Dag Hammarskjöld, UN secretary-general 1953–61. The reason was that peacekeeping operations are not mentioned in the Charter and that they are situated in a grey area between Chapter VI, dealing with the pacific settlement of disputes, and Chapter VII, referring to enforcement actions and measures. The term 'Chapter VI½ operations' thus had a different meaning during the Cold War

than is the case today where the term is usually employed to describe 'robust peacekeeping operations', i.e. operations that fall somewhere between traditional peacekeeping operations and full-scale enforcement operations.

10. For UN mission acronyms see Appendix 1, for non-UN mission acronyms see Appendix 2.

11. Bjørgo, Narve, Øystein Rian and Alf Kaartvedt (1995) *Norsk utenrikspolitikks historie Bind 1: Selvstendighet og union. Fra middelalderen til 1905* (Oslo: Universitetsforlaget), p. 279; Gäfvert, Björn (1995) 'Swedish Troops in International Cooperation – North Africa, 1802 and Fyn-Schleswig, 1848–1850', in Lars Ericson (ed.) *Solidarity and Defence: Sweden's Armed Forces in International Peace-keeping Operations during the 19th and 20th Centuries* (Stockholm: Swedish Military History Commission), pp. 30–32 (22–33).

12. Ericson, Lars (1995) 'The Swedish Military in League-of-Nations-Operations-Vilna, the Saar and Spain, 1921–1939', in Lars Ericson (ed.) *Solidarity and Defence: Sweden's Armed Forces in International Peace-keeping Operations during the 19th and 20th Centuries* (Stockholm: Swedish Military History Commission) p. 37 (35–52); Fabian, Larry L. (1971) *Soldiers Without Enemies: Preparing The United Nations For Peacekeeping* (Washington, DC: Brookings Institution), pp. 45, 47.

13. Ericson, 'The Swedish Military in League-of-Nations-Operations', p. 40; Wambaugh, Sarah (1933) *Plebiscites since the World War: With a Collection of Official Documents* (Washington, DC: Carnegie Endowment for International Peace), p. 328.

14. Wainhouse, David W. (1966) *International Peace Observation: A History and Forecast* (Baltimore, MD: Johns Hopkins University Press), p. 52.

15. This study uses the term Scandinavian to refer to Denmark, Norway and Sweden, and the term Nordic when referring to Denmark, Finland, Norway and Sweden. The fifth Nordic nation, Iceland, has played a marginal role in peace operations and is not included in the term Nordic unless it is explicitly mentioned.

16. Lunn, C.D.O. (1993) *I fredens tjeneste. Udgivet og kommenteret af Gerda Gram* (Odense: Odense Universitetsforlag), p. 24.

17. Ericson, 'The Swedish Military in League-of-Nations-Operations', p. 49.

18. The Finnish foreign minister did not begin to take part in the regular meetings between the three Scandinavian foreign ministers until 1934. See Gripenberg, G.A. (1960) 'Finnish Neutrality', in Urhu Toivola (ed.) *Introduction to Finland 1960* (Porvoo: Werner Söderström), p. 57 (55–69).

19. Lönnroth, Erik (1953) 'Sweden: The Diplomacy of Östen Undén', in Gordon A. Craig and Felix Gilbert (eds) *The Diplomats 1919–1939* (Princeton, NJ: Princeton University Press), p. 90 (86–99); Pedersen, Ole Karup (1970) *Udenrigsminister P. Munchs opfattelse af Danmarks stilling i international politik* (København: Københavns Universitets Fond til Tilvejebringelse af Læremidler), p. 178; Åhman, Brita Skottsberg [1950] (1979) 'Scandinavian Foreign Policy: Past and Present', in Henning Friis (ed.) *Scandinavia – Between East and West* (Westport, CT: Greenwood Press), pp. 266–267 (255–306).

20. Jones, S. Shepard [1939] (1969) *The Scandinavian States and the League of Nations* (New York: Greenwood Press), p. 3.

21. Gäfvert, 'Swedish Troops in International Cooperation', p. 31; Kristiansen, Rolf (1970) *Norsk militær innsats for de Forente Nasjoner 1949–1970* (Oslo: Forsvarets Krigshistoriske Avdeling), p. 13; Norberg, Erik (1995) 'Solidarity or National Defence', in Lars Ericson (ed.) *Solidarity and Defence: Sweden's*

Armed Forces in International Peace-keeping Operations during the 19th and 20th Centuries (Stockholm: Swedish Military History Commission), p. 10 (9–22).

22. Fabian, *Soldiers Without Enemies*, pp. 44–56. See also James, Alan (1999) 'The Peacekeeping Role of the League of Nations', *International Peacekeeping*, Vol. 6, No. 1 (Spring), pp. 154–160.

23. Ørvik, Nils (1961–62) 'Hovedlinjer i norsk utenrikspolitikk', *Tidens ekko*, No. 5 (Oslo: Chr. Michelsens Institutt og Norsk Udenrigspolitisk Institut), p. 27.

24. Fabian, *Soldiers Without Enemies*, p. 68.

25. Frye, William R. (1957) *A United Nations Peace Force* (New York: Oceana Publications), pp. 7–8, 12, 25.

26. Kalela, Jaakko (1975) 'The UN Peace-keeping Operations', *Yearbook of Finnish Foreign Policy 1974* (Helsinki: Finnish Institute of International Affairs), pp. 50–54; Kristiansen, *Norsk militær innsats for de Forente Nasjoner 1949–1970*, pp. 66–68; Rosner, Gabriella E. (1963) *The United Nations Emergency Force* (New York: Columbia University Press), pp. 135–136; Urquhart, Brian (1987) *A Life in Peace and War: Memoirs* (New York: Harper & Row), pp. 133–134; Wainhouse, David W. (1973) *International Peacekeeping at the Crossroads: National Support, Experience and Prospects* (Baltimore, MD: Johns Hopkins University Press), pp. 248–250.

27. Jakobson, Max (1982) *Den finländska paradoxen: Linjer i Finlands utrikespolitik 1953–1965* (Stockholm: P.A. Norstedt), p. 94.

28. Kettinen, U. (1967) 'Observations and Experience Derived from the Activities of the UN Finnish Company in the Middle East', *IPKO Documentation*, No. 9 (June), p. 4 (3–7).

29. Kristiansen, *Norsk militær innsats for de Forente Nasjoner 1949–1970*, pp. 70, 80; Sköld, Nils (1990) *United Nations Peacekeeping after the Suez War. UNEF I: The Swedish Involvement* (London: Hurst), p. 31. Joint Scandinavian air services were also employed during the ONUC, UNFICYP and UNIFIL operations. See Rigsrevisionen, *Beretning om Det Danske FN-kontingent (DANCON) på Cypern* (København: Statsrevisoratet, 1992), p. 18; and Wainhouse, *International Peacekeeping at the Crossroads*, p. 357.

30. Sköld, Nils (1990) *I fredens tjänst – Sveriges medverkan i Förenta Nationernas fredsbevarande styrka i Mellanöstern 1956–67* (Stockholm: Almqvist & Wiksell International), p. 46.

31. Jakobson, *Den finländska paradoxen*, p. 95.

32. See for instance the statements before the UN General Assembly by Ernst Christiansen, head of the Danish UN delegation on 22 November 1957 cited in *Udenrigsministeriets Gråbog:Dansk sikkerhedspolitik gennem tyve år* (1969) (København: J. Vintens Forlags boghandel), p. 215; and the foreign minister of Pakistan, Firaz Khan Noon, on 29 November 1957, *Official Records of the General Assembly, Eleventh Session, Plenary Meetings (1957)*, p. 417. See also the introduction to the Annual Report of the Secretary-General on the Work of the Organization, 1956–57, *Official Records of the General Assembly, Twelfth Session, Supplement No. 1A* (UN Doc. A/3594/Add. 1), pp. 1–2; Frye, *A United Nations Peace Force*; Munroe, Leslie (1958) 'The Case for a Standing UN Army', *The New York Times Magazine*, 27 July; and Pearson, Lester B. (1957) 'Force for UN', *Foreign Affairs*, Vol. 35, No. 3 (April), pp. 395–404.

33. *Udenrigsministeriets Gråbog:Dansk sikkerhedspolitik gennem tyve år*, p. 215.

34. Haekkerup, Per (1964) 'Scandinavia's Peacekeeping Force For UN', *Foreign Affairs*, Vol. 42, No. 4 (July), p. 676 (675–681).

35. *Udenrigsministeriets Gråbog: Dansk sikkerhedspolitik gennem tyve år*, p. 216.

36. Sköld, *United Nations Peacekeeping after the Suez War*, pp. 210–211.
37. Kristiansen, *Norsk militær innsats for de Forente Nasjoner 1949–1970*, p. 214.
38. For these lists see Engnér, Eskil (1992) 'Norden och FN's fredsbevarande operationer: Nordiska insatser igår, idag och imorgon', *FOA Rapport*, A 10037-1.4 (October), p. 30.
39. Kristiansen, *Norsk militær innsats for de Forente Nasjoner 1949–1970*, p. 216; Sköld, *United Nations Peacekeeping after the Suez War*, p. 212.
40. Jakobson, *Den finländska paradoxen*, p. 297. Kekkonen did not allow the Finnish minister of defence to take part in the biannual Nordic defence minister meetings until October 1966. See Kristiansen, *Norsk militær innsats for de Forente Nasjoner 1949–1970*, p. 221.
41. See UN Doc. A/AC 121/11, 20 March 1968 (Sweden), A/AC 121/12, 29 March 1968 (Denmark), A/AC 121/13, 29 March 1968 (Finland) and A/AC 121/14, 29 March 1968 (Norway).
42. On the incomplete nature of the standby forces in the late 1960s see Fabian, *Soldiers Without Weapons*, pp. 98–129. It is also clear from the differences between the data submitted to the UN in 1968 and the data provided in the first standby force manual: *Nordic Standby Forces in United Nations Service* (Stockholm: UN-department, Army Staff in conjunction with NORSAMFN, 1973).
43. See for instance Eknes, 'The Nordic Countries and UN Peacekeeping Operations', p. 69; Pellnäs, Bo (1998) 'Internationella operationer i ett säkerhetspolitiskt perspektiv', *Royal Swedish Academy of War Sciences Proceedings and Journal*, Vol. 202, No. 1, p. 7 (6–14).
44. Thus Tage Erlander, former Swedish prime minister, argues in his memoirs that a desire to support Hammarskjöld influenced the Swedish UN policy in general and the decision to take a seat in the Security Council in 1957–58 in particular. Erlander, Tage (1976) *1955–1960* (Stockholm: Tidens Förlag), p. 285; Möller, Yngve (1986) *Östen Undén. En biografi* (Stockholm: Norstedts), pp. 420, 424.
45. The observer force was established in October 1947 as part of the United Nations Commission for the Balkans (UNSCOB). It does not appear on the list of official UN operations, because the observers were not officially under the authority of the UN secretary-general acting instead as members of the national delegations in the area. Norway provided an observer and two civilians to this force although it did not have a seat on the commission. Sweden also contributed with observers to a follow on force between 1952 and 1954 when the operation was terminated. For a detailed analysis of UNSCOB see Nachmani, Amikam (1990) *International Intervention in the Greek Civil War: The United Nations Special Committee on the Balkans, 1947–1952* (New York: Praeger).
46. Lie, Trygve (1954) *In the Cause of Peace: Seven Years with the UN* (New York: Macmillan), p. 185.
47. Jarring, Gunnar (1984) 'Swedish Participation in UN Peacekeeping Operations', *Revue internationale d'historie militaire*, No. 57 (Stockholm), p. 64 (59–67).
48. Erlander, *1955–1960*, p. 285.
49. For the most detailed elaboration of the principles guiding the selection of UN contingents during the Cold War see UN Doc. A/3943, 9 October 1958.
50. Haagerup, Niels Jørgen (1956) *De Forenede Nationer og Danmarks sikkerhed: Træk af den danske udenrigs- og forsvarsdebat siden 1945* (Århus: Institut for Presseforskning og Samtidshistorie, Universitetsforlaget i Aarhus), p. 88; Ørvik, 'Hovedlinjer i norsk utenrikspolitikk', pp. 15–16.

51. The NATO membership did create difficulties during the establishment of UNEF I as the Egyptian government initially expressed concern about the inclusion of Danish and Norwegian contingents in the force because they were allies of France and Great Britain in NATO. UN Secretary-General Hammarskjöld then made clear that an Egyptian rejection of the Danish and Norwegian offers of troops would probably induce Finland and Sweden to withdraw their offers, and that this would endanger the entire operation. This caused the Egyptian government to back down. See Kristiansen, *Norsk militær innsats for de Forente Nasjoner 1949–1970*, p. 68. In 1986 the Soviet Union also blocked the appointment of a Norwegian force commander for UNIFIL because a NATO commander member was unacceptable. See Skogmo, Bjørn (1989) *International Peacekeeping in Lebanon, 1978–1988* (Boulder, CO: Lynne Rienner), note 4, p. 161.

52. Kristiansen, *Norsk militær innsats for de Forente Nasjoner 1949–1970*, p. 67.

53. Kristiansen, *Norsk militær innsats for de Forente Nasjoner 1949–1970*, p. 226.

54. Haekkerup, 'Scandinavia's Peacekeeping Force For UN', p. 675. This article was regarded as a semi-official position paper on the Scandinavian force at the time. See Fabian, *Soldiers Without Enemies*, note 33, p. 288.

55. Holst, Johan Jørgen (1990) 'Support and Limitations: Peacekeeping from the Point of View of Troop Contributors', in Indar J. Rikhye and Kjell Skjelsbaek (eds) *The United Nations and Peacekeeping. Result, Limitations and Prospects* (London: Macmillan Press), p. 113 (111–124). See also Hartling, Poul (former Danish prime and foreign minister) (1976) 'Dansk deltagelse i FN's Fredsbevarende Operations som Led i Danmarks Udenrigs- og Sikkerhedspolitik', in L.M.K. Skern (ed.) *Danmark i FNs fredsstyrke*, Vol. I (København: Edvard Henriksen), pp. 43–52.

56. Kekkonen, Urho (1982) *A President's View* (London: Heinemann), p. 190.

57. UN/US pressure eventually resulted in Danish and Norwegian offers to send troops to Korea. Norway formally offered 50–60 specialists in winter warfare whereas the Danish foreign minister Ole Bjørn Kraft publicly expressed his willingness to consider a contribution involving a 1000-strong battalion. No troops were ever dispatched to Korea, however. Skogrand, Kjetil (1994) 'Norge og Koreaspørsmålet. 1945–1953' (unpublished MA thesis, Universitetet i Oslo), pp. 206–207, 213, 218.

58. Askgaard, Preben V. (1967) *Sikkerhedsrådet gennem tyve år: I anledning af Danmarks medlemsskab 1967–68* (København, Det udenrigspolitiske Selskabs skrifter), p. 95.

59. Mörth, Ulrika (1991) 'Sverige i FN:s säkerhetsråd. En neutral stat på estraden', *FOA Rapport* C 10334-1.2 (Stockholm: Försvarets forskningsanstalt), pp. 39–40.

60. Jakobson, Max (1983) *Trettioåttonde våningen: Hågkomster och anteckningar 1965–1971* (Stockholm: P.A. Norstedt), p. 111.

61. Skogrand, 'Norge og Koreaspørsmålet 1945–1953', p. 68.

62. Eriksen, Knut Einar and Helge Øystein Pharo (1997) *Norsk utenrikspolitikks historie. Bind 5: Kald krig og internasjonalisering* (Oslo: Universitetsforlaget), pp. 381–403; Jespersen, Morten (1997) 'FN og Danmarks sikkerhed 1949–1965. En undersøgelse af dansk FN-politik set i relation til Danmarks NATO-medlemskab' (unpublished MA thesis, Historisk Institut, Aarhus Universitet), pp. 31–70, 88–91; Mörth, 'Sverige i FN:s säkerhetsråd', pp. 33–40; Pajunen, Aimo (1972) 'Finland's Security Policy in the 1970s: Background and Perspectives', in Johan Jørgen Holst (ed.) *Five Roads to Nordic Security* (Oslo: Universitetsforlaget), p. 44 (39–60).

63. Interview on Norwegian radio on 30 June 1966, cited by Jacobsen, Kurt (1967) 'Voting Behaviour of the Nordic Countries in the General Assembly', *Cooperation and Conflict*, Vol. 2, No. 3–4, p. 139 (139–157). For the same view see the memoirs by the former Danish ambassador to the UN and foreign minister: Tabor, Hans (1995) *Diplomat blandt politikere* (København: Gyldendal), p. 126.

64. This is the generally accepted way to conceptualize the Danish and Norwegian NATO policies. See for instance Faurby, Ib (1995) 'Danish Alliance Policy 1967–1993: From Quiet Adaptation via Loud Disagreement to Cautious Involvement', in Carsten Due-Nielsen and Nikolaj Petersen (eds) *Adaptation and Activism: The Foreign Policy of Denmark 1967–1993* (Copenhagen: DJØF Publishing), pp. 55–91; Holst, Johan Jørgen (1966) 'Norwegian Security Policy: The Strategic Context', *Cooperation and Conflict*, Vol. 2, No. 2, p. 65 (64–79); Holst, Johan Jørgen (1985) 'Norway's Role in the Search for International Peace and Security', in Johan Jørgen Holst (ed.) *Norwegian Foreign Policy in the 1980s* (Oslo: Norwegian University Press), pp. 144–165; Villaume, Poul (1999) 'Denmark and NATO through 50 Years', in Bertel Heurlin and Hans Mouritzen, (eds) *Danish Foreign Policy Yearbook 1999* (Copenhagen: Danish Institute of International Affairs), p. 32 (29–61). The role played by the UN policies in this balancing act has generally been ignored, however. The only exceptions to this rule are: Jespersen, 'FN og Danmarks sikkerhed', pp. 92–94; and Midtgaard, Kristine K.N. (1998) 'Denmark and the United Nations, 1949–63. The Role of the Danish UN Membership and Danish UN Policy in the General Danish Security Policy', paper presented at the third joint ISA-ECPR conference, Vienna, 16–19 September.

65. Jakobson, Max (1998) 'Finland in the New Europe', *The Washington Papers*, No. 175 (Westport, CT: Praeger Publishers for Center for Strategic and International Studies, Washington, DC), p. 74.

66. Cited by Giverholt, Helge (1961–62) 'Finland og Sovjetsamveldet', *Tidens ekko*, No. 7 (Oslo: Chr. Michelsens Institutt og Norsk Udenrigspolitisk Institut), p. 8. My translation.

67. Jakobson, *Den finländska paradoxen*, pp. 83, 88, 95.

68. Jakobson, *Den finländska paradoxen*, p. 297.

69. Jakobson, 'Finland in the New Europe', p. 74.

70. For examples of official statements making this point see Brodin, Katarina, Kjell Goldmann and Christian Lange (1968) 'The Policy of Neutrality: Official Doctrines of Finland and Sweden', *Cooperation and Conflict*, Vol. 3, No. 1, pp. 18–51; and Vesa, Unto (1980) 'Determining Finland's Position in International Crises', in *Yearbook of Finnish Foreign Policy 1979* (Helsinki: Finnish Institute of International Affairs), pp. 2–19.

71. Dohlman, Ebba (1989) *National Welfare and Economic Interdependence: The Case of Sweden's Foreign Trade Policy* (Oxford: Clarendon), p. 55.

72. Cited in Brodin *et al.*, 'The Policy of Neutrality', p. 37.

73. The anti-American rhetoric coincided with secret diplomacy and intelligence cooperation that opened up the possibility of American/NATO military assistance in the event of a war between the superpowers in Europe. *Had there been a war: Preparations for the reception of military assistance 1949–1969: Report of the Commission on Neutrality Policy* (Stockholm: Fritze, Statens Offentlige Utredningar, SOU 1994: 11E); and Tunander, Ola (1999) 'The Uneasy Imbrication of Nation-State and NATO: The Case of Sweden', *Cooperation and Conflict*, Vol. 34, No. 2 (June), pp. 169–203.

74. Mauno Koivisto was president of Finland 1982–94. Cited by Andrén, Nils (1991) 'Mellan fredsegoism och världssamvete', *Svensk tidskrift*, Vol. 78,

No. 8–9, p. 581 (575–583). For the Finnish view of the Swedish policy see also: Jakobson, *Trettioåttonde våningen*, pp. 68–69.

75. There is a tendency in the academic literature to treat interest and ideals as opposites, even mutually excluding. However, as experienced policy makers know, effective policy has to incorporate elements of both. To both the Danish foreign minister Per Hækkerup and his Swedish colleague Östen Undén this was what foreign policy making was all about: Hækkerup, Per (1965) *Danmarks udenrigspolitik* (København: AOF Fremad); Undén, Östen (1962) 'Realism och idealitet i utrikespolitiken', *Nordisk tidsskrift for International Ret*, Vol. 32, No. 3, pp. 139–146. On this point see also the thoughtful analysis of the Danish UN policy by Midtgaard, 'Denmark and the United Nations, 1949–63.'

76. See for instance Enckell, Ralph (1968) 'Finland och omvärlden', in Ilkka Hakalehto (ed.) *Finlands utrikespolitik 1809–1966* (Halmstad: Prisma), p. 149 (145–152); Hækkerup, *Danmarks udenrigspolitik*, pp. 15–16; Kekkonen, *A President's View*, p. 190.

77. Cited by Pedersen, Ole Karup (1967) 'Scandinavia and the UN "Standby Forces"', *Cooperation and Conflict*, Vol. 2, No. 1, p. 39 (37–46).

78. Siilasvuo, Ensio (1992) *In the Service of Peace in the Middle East* (London: C. Hurst/New York: St Martin's Press), pp. 2–3.

79. Kronlund, Jarl and Juha Valla (1996) *Suomi rauhanturvaajana, 1956–1990* (Porvoo: WSOY), p. 452.

80. Jarring, 'Swedish Participation in UN Peacekeeping Operations', p. 63; Sköld, *United Nations Peacekeeping after the Suez War*, pp. 76, 78.

81. Persson Sune O. (1991) 'Svensk militär på Cypern: SWEDBAT och UNFICYP 1964, 1974 och 1987' (Stockholm, FOA C 10335-1.2), pp. 29–30; Sköld, Nils (1994) *Med FN i Kongo. Sveriges medverkan i den fredsbevarande operationen 1960–1964* (Stockholm: Probus förlag), pp. 67, 110, 115.

82. Fabian, *Soldiers Without Enemies*, p. 120.

83. Cited in Frydenberg, Per (ed.) (1964) *Peace-Keeping: Experience and Evaluation. The Oslo Papers* (Oslo: Norwegian Institute of International Affairs), p. 321.

84. Sköld, *United Nations Peacekeeping after the Suez War*, pp. 218–220.

85. Gustafsson, Poul E. (1988) *Afrika-missionen. FN-soldater i stammekrig* (København: Forlaget Europa), p. 194. For the other Nordic countries see Eknes, Åge and Tom Henry Knutsen (1994) 'Flernasjonale operasjoner og norsk deltagelse', *Norsk Militært Tidsskrift*, Vol. 164, No. 5/6, p. 11 (9–12); Sköld, *Med FN i Kongo*, pp. 205, 208–209.

86. Cited by Pedersen, 'Scandinavia and the UN "Standby Forces"', pp. 38–39.

87. Siilasvuo, *In the Service of Peace*, p. 357; Skjelsbæk, Kjell (1985) 'UNIFIL: Forutsetninger, vanskeligheter og resultater', *Internasjonal Politikk*, Vol. 43, No. 2–3, pp. 253–276; Stanghelle, Harald (1985) 'UNIFIL og Norge – holdninger og myter', *Internasjonal Politikk*, Vol. 43, No. 2–3, pp. 225–240.

88. Huldt, Bo (1995) 'Working Multilaterally: The Old Peacekeepers' Viewpoint', in Donald C.F. Daniel and Bradd C. Hayes (eds), *Beyond Traditional Peacekeeping* (New York: St Martin's Press), p. 114 (101–119).

89. Harbottle, Michael (1970) *The Impartial Soldier* (London: Oxford University Press), pp. 28–29. One exception exists. The UN did establish a small intelligence service in the Congo after the operation was given an enforcement mandate in 1961. At its height in 1962, the Military Information Branch employed 27 intelligence officers. See Dorn, A. Walter and David J. H. Bell (1995) 'Intelligence and Peacekeeping: The UN Operation in the Congo, 1960–64', *International Peacekeeping*, Vol. 2, No. 1 (Spring), pp. 11–33.

90. Horn, Carl von (1966) *Soldiering For Peace* (London: Cassell), p. 98; Wærn, Jonas (1980) *Katanga: Svensk FN-Trupp i Kongo 1961–1962* (Stockholm: Atlantis), pp. 54, 61–68.

91. For descriptions of humanitarian activities carried out by Nordic forces see Hansen, Rolf (1978) 'Norske styrker i Libanon', *Internasjonal Politikk*, No. 4 B (Supplement), p. 771 (767–772); Sköld, *I fredens tjänst*, pp. 142–143; and Stjernfelt, Bertil (1992) *The Sinai Peace Front: UN Peace-keeping Operations in the Middle East, 1973–1980* (London: Hurst), p. 34.

92. Exceptions include the ONUC mission in Congo (1960–64) which had a 2,000-strong civilian component tasked to provide technical assistance to the government; the UNSF/UNTEA mission in West New Guinea (1962–63) in which civilian personnel ran the civilian government and set up a new police force; and the UNFICYP mission in Cyprus (1964–) which had a civilian police contingent of 174 personnel.

93. Hartling, 'Dansk deltagelse i FN's Fredsbevarende Operationer'; Haekkerup, 'Scandinavia's Peacekeeping Force for UN'.

94. Welin, Gustaf and Christer Ekelund (1999) *FN på Cypern. Den svenska fredsbevarande insatsen 1964–1993* (Stockholm: Probus Förlag), p. 265.

95. Persson, Sune (1995) 'The Swedish Army on Cyprus. SWEDBAT and UNFICYP 1964, 1974, and 1987', in *Peacekeeping 1815 to Today: Proceedings of the XXIst Colloquium of the International Commission of Military History* (Ottawa: National Defence Headquarters), p. 353 (347–355).

96. James, Alan (1998) 'Reluctant Heroes. Assembling the United Nations Cyprus Force, 1964', *International Journal*, Vol. 53, No. 4 (Autumn), pp. 733–754; Persson, 'Svensk militär på Cypern'.

97. Sköld, *Med FN i Kongo*, pp. 97–169.

98. Sköld, *United Nations Peacekeeping after the Suez War*, pp. 205–206.

99. Kristiansen, *Norsk militær innsats for de Forente Nasjoner 1949–1970*, p. 226.

100. In 1999 the UN still owed the Danish government US$106 million for its participation in UNEF I, ONUC and UNFICYP. See Rødsgaard, Solveig (1999) 'Ingen regning', *Weekendavisen*, 15 January, p. 2.

101. For a detailed description of the units see *Nordic UN Standby Forces*, 3rd edn, 1986 (Stockholm: NORDSAMFN).

102. Skern, L.M.K. (1966) 'United Nations Peacekeeping Operations From a Danish Viewpoint', *Revue Militaire Generale*, October, p. 365 (353–367); Stenqvist, Nils (1967) 'The Swedish UN Standby Force and Experience', *Monograph*, No. 4 (Paris: International Information Center on Peace-keeping Operations), p. 16.

103. According to the Danish commander of the first DANOR contingent Carl Engholm, all the commanding officers agreed that the joint arrangement was impractical and uneconomical. Given the lack of preparation and joint training this is hardly surprising, and this probably explains why joint battalions never were employed again. Engholm, Carl (1996) *Fremmedlegionær og dansk oberst: Carl Engholms erindringer i krig og fred 1913–1979* (Lyngby: Dansk Historisk Håndbogsforlag), p. 242.

104. Pedersen, 'Scandinavia and the UN "Standby Forces"', p. 41; Sköld, *United Nations Peacekeeping after the Suez War*, p. 93.

105. Denmark provided civilian police for UNFICYP in 1964–75; Sweden in 1964–93.

106. *Nordic UN Standby Forces* (1986), pp. 11, 39–40.

107. Engholm, Carl (1976) 'UNEF United Nations Emergency Force', in L.M.K. Skern (ed.), *Danmark i FNs fredsstyrke*, Vol I, p. 121 (119–162); Kristiansen, *Norsk militær innsats for de Forente Nasjoner 1949–1970*, p. 67.

108. Once the process began, the Finnish contingent did not take longer to prepare than the 19 days indicated in the 1986 manual. A fortnight passed from the time the Finnish government had approved the UN request for troops until the officers in charge of the contingent were appointed. These officers were then given 19 days to prepare the contingent, a deadline they met successfully. See Kettinen, 'Observations and Experience', pp. 3–4.

109. Ericson, Lars (1999) 'Solidaritet eller försvar? Den svenska militären och de fredsbevarande operationerna 1956–96', *Militärhistorisk Tidskrift*, p. 189 (181–199).

110. Forsvarets Oplysnings- og Velfærdstjeneste (1967) *Dansk soldat på Cypern* (København: Forsvarets Oplysnings- og Velfærdstjeneste og Hærkommandoen, med enkelte rettelser), p. 24.

111. Wainhouse, *International Peacekeeping at the Crossroads*, pp. 375, 380–381.

112. Persson, 'Svensk militär på Cypern', pp. 33–34.

113. Stjernfelt, *The Sinai Peace Front*, p. 32.

114. Erskine, Emmanuel A. (1989) *Mission with UNIFIL: An African Soldier's Reflections* (London: C. Hurst), p. 23.

115. Stjernfelt, *The Sinai Peace Front*, p. 125.

116. Erskine, *Mission with UNIFIL*, p. 23; Jevne, Per ø. (1978) *Farlig fred* (Oslo: Cappelen), p. 16.

117. Kronlund and Valla, *Suomi rauhanturvaajana*, p. 450.

118. Stjernfelt, *The Sinai Peace Front*, p. 43.

119. Fabian, *Soldiers Without Enemies*, p. 115.

120. For a general discussion of this problem in each of the four countries see Fabian, *Soldiers Without Enemies*, pp. 98–129.

121. Gisvold, Marius (1979) *Møte med Libanon: En norsk FN-soldats beretning* (Oslo: Gyldendal Norsk Forlag), pp. 12–13.

122. Fetherston, A.B. (1994) *Towards a Theory of United Nations Peacekeeping* (New York: St Martin's Press), p. 192; Skern, L.M.K. (1976) 'Konklusion og vurdering af dansk deltagelse i FN-operationer', in Skern (ed.), *Danmark i FNs fredsstyrke*, Vol. II, pp. 174–176.

123. Kristiansen, *Norsk militær innsats for de Forente Nasjoner 1949–1970*, p. 225; Skerning, Aage (1976) 'Nordiske FN-kurser: Logistikkursus', in Skern (ed.), *Danmark i FNs fredsstyrke*, Vol. II, p. 198 (198–209).

124. Stjernfelt, *The Sinai Peace Front*, p. 204.

125. Stjernfelt, *The Sinai Peace Front*, p. 151.

126. Mackenzie, Lewis (1993) *Peacekeeper: The Road to Sarajevo* (Vancouver/ Toronto: Douglas & McIntyre), pp. 201, 205; Wærn, Jonas (1995) *Cypern. Svenskarnas inledande FN-aktion 1964* (Stockholm: Atlantis), pp. 25, 52.

127. Stegenga, James A. (1968) *The United Nations Force in Cyprus* (Columbus, OH: Ohio State University Press), pp. 133, 135–136.

128. *Nordic Standby Forces in United Nations Service*, 2nd revised edn, 1978 (Stockholm), pp. 73, 115–116. For analyses of the problems see Bowman, Edward H. and James E. Fanning (1963) 'The Logistics Problems of a UN Military Force', *International Organization*, Vol. 17, No. 2 (Spring), pp. 355–376; Johnsen, Arne Holm and Odd Øyen (1964) 'Experiences Relating to Logistics in Gaza and the Congo', in Frydenberg, *Peace-Keeping: Experience and Evaluation*, pp. 163–171.

129. See Horn, *Soldiering For Peace*, pp. 62, 90, 359–60; Kristiansen, *Norsk militær innsats for de Forente Nasjoner 1949–1970*, pp. 88–91; Siilasvuo, *In the Service of Peace*, pp. 11–12, 158, 175, 181–182; Sköld, *United Nations Peacekeeping after the Suez War*, pp. 16–118, 185, 215; Stjernfelt, *The Sinai Peace Front*, pp. 68, 168, 171–176.

130. Harbottle, *The Impartial Soldier*, pp. 132–144; Stegenga, *The United Nations Force in Cyprus*, pp. 159–165.
131. *Nordic Standby Forces in United Nations Service* (1978), p. 113.
132. Siilasvuo, *In the Service of Peace*, p. 175.
133. Although it is difficult to generalize, Nordic peacekeepers were generally praised for their effectiveness, and Michael Harbottle, the British chief of staff of UNFICYP (June 1966–August 1968) regarded the Danish and Finnish UNFICYP contingents as better suited for peacekeeping than the British. Harbottle, *The Impartial Soldier*, pp. 69–78.
134. The same was true for Canada, see Granatstein, J.L. (1992) 'Did Canada Make a Difference? And What Difference Did Peacekeeping Make to Canada?', in John English and Norman Hillmer (eds) *Making a Difference: Canada's Foreign Policy in a Changing World Order* (Toronto: Lester Publishing), pp. 225–227 (222–236).
135. James, Alan (1990) *Peacekeeping in International Politics* (London: Macmillan), pp. 1, 369–370.
136. Frydenberg, *Peace-Keeping: Experience and Evaluation*, p. 14.

3 Peace operations after the Cold War: the need for a new model

[N]o amount of good intentions can substitute for the fundamental ability to project credible force if complex peacekeeping, in particular, is to succeed. But force alone cannot create peace; it can only create the space in which peace may be built.

Brahimi Report[1]

It is often said that change was the only constant characterizing peace operations during the 1990s. While it is a great way to start a chapter or a lecture, it is still an exaggeration and quite illustrative of the lack of historical perspective which characterizes most of the post-Cold War literature on peace operations. Many of the 'new' problems confronting the peace operations of the 1990s were actually old; the UN had already struggled with them in the Congo and in Lebanon. This said, the geo-political and normative context and the operations themselves changed fundamentally. The traditional peacekeeping and observer missions did not disappear, but they were overshadowed by a new breed of multifunctional or complex peace operations, mandated by the UN, or regional organizations such as the EU or the OSCE, to achieve humanitarian goals, create the basis for lasting peace settlements, or at their most ambitious, as in Kosovo and East Timor, to build democratic states virtually from scratch. Most operations enjoyed limited consent from the parties, the threat and use of force beyond self-defence was required more often than not and the traditional concept of impartiality became morally untenable in the face of gross violations of human rights.

These changes pulled the rug from under the Cold War peacekeeping model, and the purpose of this chapter is to analyse what changed and why, identify the challenges post-Cold War peace operations are up against and finally use the lessons learned in the 1990s to outline the new requirements for success that the Nordic countries and other personnel contributors must honour to be effective in the new era. The chapter falls in three parts. The first part presents the changes and explains why they took place. The second part identifies the operational challenges posed by the new operations as well as the lessons learned in the course of the 1990s. The final part derives the requirements for success that personnel contributors must meet to be effective in post-Cold War peace operations.

The changing nature of peace operations

To better understand what changed and why, it is useful to make a distinction between changes in the operations themselves and changes in the international context in which they are conducted. With respect to the operations themselves, three changes stand out: a dramatic increase in the number of operations; a corresponding leap in ambitions and objectives; and finally a vast proliferation of mission types and tasks. The single most important contextual change was the end of the Cold War and the geopolitical and normative changes resulting from it, but it is best thought of as the permissive factor that made change possible in the first place. The contents and direction of the changes that did occur were primarily shaped by four other contextual factors: the rise of democracy and human rights, a change in the nature of the armed conflicts, the advent of real-time television and finally recent operational outcomes. Each of the three operational changes are presented in turn below and explained with reference to the five contextual changes.

The explosion in numbers

The numbers speak for themselves. If we focus on the peace operations with UN involvement,[2] which constitute the vast majority, and classify them according to their command and control arrangements and the legal basis of their mandates (Chapter VI or VII of the UN Charter), we find an increase in all of the three main types of operations that were undertaken during the Cold War (Table 3.1): UN-commanded peacekeeping and observer missions conducted under Chapter VI adhering to the principles of impartiality, consent and non-use of force except self-defence; UN-commanded operations that *de facto* went beyond these principles; and delegated enforcement

Table 3.1 Overview of UN peace operations during and after the Cold War

Operation type	Cold War (1947–87)	Post-Cold War (1988–2004)
UN-commanded Chapter VI operations	12	35
UN-commanded beyond Chapter VI – *de facto/de jure*	1	12
UN-delegated Chapter VII enforcement operations	1	20

operations with Chapter VII authorization to take offensive action to compel compliance with UN resolutions. The number of UN-commanded peacekeeping and observer missions has tripled from 12 to 35.[3] The number of UN-commanded operations that went beyond peacekeeping principles, either *de facto* because force was used beyond self-defence or *de jure* because of Chapter VII authorization, has risen from 1 (ONUC) to 12.[4] Finally, the number of delegated Chapter VII operations has gone up from 1 (Korea) to 20.

The dramatic rise in the number of operations has not surprisingly translated itself into a major increase in the number of troop contributors. Whereas 56 nations had contributed personnel to UN peace operations by the end of 1988, the number had risen to 123 by 31 October 2000, meaning that 67 nations got their debut in UN peace operations during the 1990s.[5] This was also the case for many regional organizations. The Commonwealth of Independent States (CIS), the EU, the Economic Community of West African States (ECOWAS), NATO, the Organization of African Unity/African Union (OAU/AU), the Organization of American States (OAS), the OSCE and the WEU have all taken part in peace operations in one way or another since 1988, most of them for the first time, and several other organizations such as the Southern African Development Community (SADC) and the Association of Southeast Asian Nations (ASEAN) are gearing up for such tasks.[6] Although the UN remains the key player, a division of labour between it and regional organizations is emerging in several parts of the world, particularly with respect to Chapter VII operations, which the UN lacks the capacity to conduct.[7]

As was the case during the Cold War, the post-Cold War operations have been launched in waves. In the first six years characterized largely by success (1988–93) 23 operations were authorized. Overstretch problems and the traumatic failure in Somalia then brought the expansion to an abrupt halt. In the next five years (1994–98) only eight new operations were launched and the majority of them were small with less than 1,000 personnel.[8] Since then (1999–2004) a revival has occurred with the launch of major UN-commanded and UN-delegated operations in Kosovo, East Timor, Sierra Leone, Ethiopia/Eritrea, Afghanistan, Democratic Republic of Congo, Liberia, Côte d'Ivoire, Haiti and Burundi. The 'never again' reaction created by the collapse of the UN operation in Rwanda and the subsequent genocide, which cost 800,000 people their lives in 1994, and the successful conduct of operations in Bosnia and Albania explain the start of the latest wave. The 'never again' effect was visible in the reaction to the near collapse of the peace operation in Sierra Leone in May 2000. Instead of a withdrawal, the response chosen in Somalia and Rwanda, the response came in the form of a unilateral intervention by Great Britain, which played a pivotal role in stabilizing the situation.

The latest wave received a further boost by the attacks on the World Trade Center and the Pentagon on 11 September 2001. The subsequent

US-led attacks on Afghanistan and Iraq not only created the need for peace operations in both countries, but the attacks also made the launch of peace operations aimed at preventing state failure more likely. As the British foreign secretary Jack Straw observed following the 11 September attacks: 'When we allow governments to fail, warlords, drug barons, or terrorists fill the vacuum... Terrorists are strongest when states are weakest.'[9] As a result of the attacks, state failure was singled out as an important threat in the September 2002 *National Security Strategy of the United States of America* and the *Security Strategy* presented by the EU in December 2003.[10] Moreover, the urgency felt about the threat of state failure also paved the way for the launch of new major peace operations in Africa in 2003 and 2004.

While operational outcomes fresh in the minds of decision makers can explain why peace operations come in waves (successes generate optimism and expansion whereas failures generate pessimism and contraction), the successes in the late 1980s and early 1990s cannot explain the scale of the increase. To do this we must turn to the four contextual changes that were set in motion by the end of the Cold War.

The end of the Cold War lit the fuse to the explosion by increasing both the demand for and the supply of peace operations at the same time. Central to this development was the termination of the unconditional economic and military assistance that the two superpowers and their allies had provided to many Third World regimes because of their strategic importance. The loss of this assistance had destabilizing effects which helped spark internal wars in some countries (examples include Liberia, Somalia, Yugoslavia and Zaire),[11] and stabilizing effects in others where it helped to end conflicts that had been fuelled by superpower support (e.g. Angola, Mozambique and Namibia).

Contrary to what is often assumed, the latter effect was stronger than the former. The widely held belief that the explosion in peace operations can be explained by a major increase in the number of ethnic and internal conflicts triggered by the end of the Cold War is mistaken. The number of armed conflicts only rose from 47 to 55 between 1987 and 1992 and it has been declining ever since.[12] There was a sharp rise in the number of internal wars that ended, however.[13] The demand for new operations was thus boosted more by a need to end existing wars than a need to quell new ones; a quarter of the internal conflicts that ended in the 1990s incorporated international peace operations as part of the solution.[14]

A rise in demand does not necessarily trigger an increase in supply. So to understand why the number of operations rose, we need to take a look at the 'supply side.' The end of the Cold War facilitated an increase in the supply in two ways. The first was the removal of the geopolitical and ideological barriers to cooperation in the Security Council. This enabled the great powers to use peace operations pragmatically as a means to (1) disengage themselves from Cold War conflicts that had lost their strategic importance (e.g. UNAVEM I in Angola 1988–91, UNTAC in Namibia 1989–90 and ONUMOZ in Mozambique 1992–94); (2) share the burden of managing new armed conflicts with other states (e.g. UNPROFOR in former Yugoslavia 1992–95 and UNOSOM I in Somalia 1992–93); (3) delegate part of this burden to coalitions of willing states and regional organizations (e.g. NATO's Bosnia operations); and (4) obtain legitimacy for operations led by the permanent members themselves or other regional great powers in their own spheres of influence (e.g. the French-led Chapter VII operation in Rwanda 1994; the US-led Chapter VII operation in Haiti 1994–95; the Italian-led Chapter VII operation in Albania 1997; the Nigerian-led ECOMOG Chapter VII operation in Liberia 1990–99; and the Australian-led Chapter VII operation in East Timor 1999–2000).

'Spheres of influence' operations were a novel development as they discarded two of the principles that had guided the selection of contributors for UN peacekeeping operations during the Cold War: the non-use of troops from the permanent members of the Security Council, and the non-use of troops from countries in the region in which the conflict was taking place, or countries which were thought to have a special interest in the conflict at hand.[15] This new practice undoubtedly helped to boost the number of peace operations in the 1990s as great power operations previously undertaken independently of the UN increasingly were launched with a UN mandate.[16] The American interventions in Panama and Grenada in the 1980s do not count as peace operations because they lack authorization from the Security Council, but if they had taken place in the 1990s, they would probably have been carried out with UN authorization, as was the case with the American intervention in Haiti in 1994. Peace operations in other words no longer contribute to international security by keeping the great powers out of regional conflicts. Instead, peace operations get them in either by legitimizing their involvement in the regional conflicts in which they take an interest, or by generating pressure on them to 'do something' about conflicts that they would have preferred to ignore.

The end of the Cold War also facilitated the rise in the supply in a second way. By removing the Soviet threat to the West, it enabled the Western states and the former members of the Warsaw Pact to devote more resources to peace operations.[17] At the turn of the century peace operations had not only become the most important operational activity conducted by the Western armies except the American; the ongoing restructuring of the European armies and NATO and the establishment of the EU rapid reaction forces are also to a large extent driven by an interest in increasing the capacity for peace operations.

That this change in the balance of power made it possible for the West to increase the supply of peace operations does not in itself explain why the willingness to do so increased, however. This willingness is actually quite difficult to understand from a geopolitical perspective. Whereas the Cold

War balance gave the two superpowers and their respective allies a geopolitical incentive to take an interest in conflicts anywhere on the globe, the new balance of power emerging in the 1990s gave the remaining superpower and the other states little geopolitical incentive to involve themselves in conflicts outside their own spheres of influence. From being a strategic imperative during the Cold War, involvement in 'faraway conflicts' became a matter of choice in the 1990s because such conflicts no longer were perceived as direct threats to national security. This did not change until September 11 induced the Western powers to readopt a global perspective on their security.

As a result, the Western states not only became less inclined to intervene in faraway conflicts outside their own spheres of influence, they also became more vulnerable to casualties because casualties are harder to justify in conflicts not involving national interests. A comparison between the American engagements in Vietnam and Somalia illustrates the point. The involvement in Vietnam in the 1960s was justified with reference to the global struggle with the Soviet Union and the USA proved willing to sustain 50,000 dead and numerous setbacks before it withdrew. The intervention in Somalia in 1992 was justified in humanitarian terms and the USA decided to throw in the towel following the death of 18 soldiers in a single engagement in October 1993.

However, if the Third World 'didn't matter,' as Van Evera provocatively put it in 1990,[18] why did the willingness to provide troops for peace operations increase so drastically in the first part of the 1990s? The answer to this question must be found in the new goals and ambitions that were driving these operations.

New goals and higher ambitions

This second change in the nature of the operations was as drastic as the explosion in numbers. The Security Council adopted a far more ambitious approach to peace operations. It no longer sat back and waited until the parties had tired of fighting, agreed to a stable ceasefire and invited the UN in. Instead, it began to deploy peacekeepers in conflicts where ceasefires and consent from the parties were either extremely fragile or nonexistent. Many peacekeeping operations were effectively peace-creating ones, and it was not peace in the negative Cold War sense (ceasefire preservation and suppression of violence) for which the Security Council was aiming; it was the creation of positive (lasting) peace. Success became defined in terms of peace building involving the (re)building of civil society, state institutions and democracy.[19] Peace forces now sought to create the conditions for sustainable peace so that their withdrawal did not result in renewed violence. The ambitions peaked with the peace operations launched in Kosovo and East Timor in 1999 where the UN assumed all government functions for a transitional period and is trying together with other actors to build democratic states virtually from scratch.[20]

This jump in ambitions and change of objectives was driven by the rise of democracy and human rights, which was facilitated by the end of the Cold War, early successes on the ground, the advent of real-time television and changes in the nature of the armed conflicts. The new (im)balance of power created by the collapse of the Soviet Union made it easier to promote democracy and human rights at the global level. That the opportunity to do so was seized was all but inevitable in the context of the collapse of the communist model and the wave of democracy sweeping through Eastern Europe. Liberal democracy was generally (in the West at least) seen as the only model on offer,[21] and a coalition of Western states and non-governmental organizations (NGOs) used their influence in the various international organizations involved in peace operations to make sure that 'free and fair' elections and human rights became part and parcel of all the peace processes in which the international community became involved.[22] Moreover, there was also an increasing demand for human rights and democracy in many Third World countries where NGOs and opposition groups began to put pressure on Western governments to help them in their struggles for human rights and democracy.[23]

These efforts benefited from operational success in the beginning. The successful outcomes of the first two major attempts to implement peace agreements and hold elections, UNTAG in Namibia (1989–90) and UNTAC in Cambodia (1992–94), set precedents that helped to make electoral support a principal feature of the operations that followed. Similarly, the successful US-led intervention in northern Iraq in April 1991 set a precedent that paved the way for a number of UN-authorized enforcement operations under Chapter VII of the Charter to bring an end to massive human rights violations.[24]

A third factor helping to put humanitarian issues on the agenda was real-time television coverage of unfolding humanitarian crises and atrocities. Intense live media coverage of some of the armed conflicts resulting in large-scale human suffering increased the pressure on Western governments to 'do something'. The so-called CNN effect became a factor in the policy-making process that made it much harder to apply the Cold War rules of peacekeeping and refrain from intervening until the parties tired of fighting and invited outsiders in. It helped to trigger the military intervention in northern Iraq in 1991, the delegated Chapter VII enforcement operations in Somalia in 1992 and in Rwanda in 1994,[25] and concern that inaction would trigger a barrage of criticism appears to have played a role in the British intervention in support of the UN peace operation in Sierra Leone in 2000.[26] Although the large majority of armed conflicts still fail to make the news, 'giving war a chance,' as a much cited critic of the UN's post-Cold War peace operations has demanded, is not as easy as it once was.[27]

The fourth factor that helped to put humanitarian issues on the agenda was a drastic increase in the number of civilian casualties and atrocities, which resulted from a change in the nature of the armed conflicts. This change does not, as many mistakenly believe, simply result from a shift from interstate to intrastate conflicts. Intrastate conflicts have been the predominant type of armed conflict in the international system since 1945,[28] and the conduct of peace operations in intrastate conflicts is not a new phenomenon either; five out of the UN's 13 Cold War operations took place in the context of internal conflicts.[29] Moreover, contemporary conflicts are never wholly internal in nature because of strong outside involvement by state and non-state actors such as diasporas, criminal networks, private military companies and transnational firms. The 'internal conflicts' in Sierra Leone and Democratic Republic of Congo are cases in point.

What changed was the complexity of the conflicts. The complexity increased because many of the conflicts took place within the context of failing or very weak states. They differed from traditional wars, in which at least one of the parties was a conventional army under central control, in the following ways: none of the parties were capable of conducting conventional military campaigns with regular armies; the fighting was conducted by irregular forces, some of whom were driven more by commercial and criminal interests than political agendas; there were no clear front lines; the distinction between civilians and combatants was blurred; there was an absence of law and order and little respect for the laws of war; civilians were deliberately targeted and preyed upon by the warring factions, the result of which was a high number of refugees and internally displaced persons and an unprecedented high proportion of civilian casualties; and the fighting was protracted because none of the parties had the capacity to win a decisive victory and because some of them wanted the conflict to continue in order to benefit from the criminal opportunities that the absence of law and order created. Somalia is the archetypal example of such a complex conflict.[30]

New mission types and tasks

The third major change in the nature of the peace operations themselves was a vast proliferation of mission types and tasks. This development was a logical consequence of the new goals, the rising ambitions and the increased complexity of conflicts in which the operations were conducted. The rebuilding of war-torn societies and collapsed states is a complex undertaking involving many different missions and tasks, and if coercion is required the number involved increase further still. Complex conflicts require complex peace operations and all major peace operations undertaken since the launch of UNTAG in Namibia in 1989, which is generally regarded as the first multifunctional peace operation, have taken this form.

A complex or multifunctional peace operation distinguishes itself from a traditional peacekeeping operation or observer mission by having both civilian and military contingents and a combination of civilian and military tasks.

Peace operations did not just become multifunctional or complex, however. A number of new mission types were also added to the traditional ones. It thus became common practice to distinguish between conflict prevention, peacemaking, peacekeeping, peace enforcement, peace building and humanitarian operations (Table 3.2). All these mission types have become a source of terminological confusion because most operations incorporate several mission types and tasks. A good example is UNPROFOR in former Yugoslavia. It started out as a traditional peacekeeping operation but slid into peace enforcement because consent proved fragile. One

Table 3.2 Overview of mission types

Peacekeeping: operations generally undertaken under Chapter VI of the UN Charter with the consent of all the major parties to a conflict, to monitor and facilitate the implementation of a peace agreement.

Peace enforcement: operations coercive in nature and undertaken under Chapter VII of the UN Charter when the consent of any of the major parties to the conflict is uncertain. They are designed to maintain and re-establish peace or enforce the terms specified in the mandate. Two main types of enforcement operations have evolved: enforcement of existing peace agreements, which do not typically involve large-scale offensive operations, and enforcement aimed at stopping/undoing acts of aggression that do.

Conflict prevention: activities normally conducted under Chapter VI of the UN Charter. They range from diplomatic initiatives to preventative deployments of forces intended to prevent disputes from escalating into armed conflicts or from spreading. Conflict prevention can also include fact-finding missions, consultation, warnings, inspections and monitoring. Preventative deployment within the framework of conflict prevention is the deployment of operational forces possessing sufficient deterrence capabilities to avoid a conflict.

Peacemaking: covers the diplomatic activities conducted after the commencement of a conflict aimed at establishing a ceasefire or a rapid peaceful settlement. They can include the provision of good offices, mediation, conciliation, diplomatic pressure, isolation and sanctions.

Peace building: actions that support political, economic, social, and military measures and structures, aiming to strengthen and solidify political settlements in order to redress the causes of conflict. This includes mechanisms to identify and support structures that tend to consolidate peace, advance a sense of confidence and well being, and support economic reconstruction.

Humanitarian operations: operations conducted to relieve human suffering. Military humanitarian activities may accompany, or be in support of, humanitarian operations conducted by specialized civilian organizations.

Adapted from *JWP 3–50: Peace Support Operations* (Northwood, UK: Ministry of Defence, 1998), para. 101. NATO uses these terms also. UN terminology is very similar, see *An Agenda for Peace*, paras 20–59; and the relevant entries in: < http://www.un.org/Depts/dpko/glossary > (16 November 2001).

of UNPROFOR's central missions was humanitarian operations and its military personnel also became involved in peace-building activities. Finally, mediators representing different international organizations and states engaged in peacemaking during the course of the operation. It is for this reason that peace operations increasingly have been referred to as complex, multidimensional or multifunctional.[31]

Matters have been complicated further still by the blurring of the distinction between consent-based peacekeeping operations and peace enforcement operations conducted without consent. Most post-Cold War peace operations are conducted in the grey area or middle ground between peacekeeping and peace enforcement, which is characterized by limited and uncertain consent from the parties. Attempts to come up with a new term to describe such operations have clouded rather than clarified the matter. The British Army, NATO and the USA use the term peace enforcement for such operations. The French military prefers the term peace restoration (*restauration de la paix*) whereas the EU has opted for the term peacemaking.[32] UN Secretary-General Kofi Annan initially tried to promote the term 'inducement operations' but since it did not catch on, he has now begun to push the term 'robust peacekeeping'.[33] This study employs the term peace enforcement and distinguishes between enforcement operations mandated to enforce existing peace agreements relying primarily on deterrence through strength (essentially Annan's definition of robust peacekeeping) and offensive enforcement operations mandated to conduct offensive operations to enforce compliance with UN resolutions. NATO's SFOR and KFOR operations and the UN-commanded operations in Sierra Leone and Liberia belong in the first category, whereas Operation Desert Storm in 1991 belongs in the latter.

Terminology aside, the practical solution to the problem presented by the erosion of consent has been to equip peacekeeping forces with better protection and more firepower to deter potential spoilers. Moreover, peacekeeping forces are increasingly provided with a Chapter VII mandate and the authority to use force beyond self-defence to protect themselves and civilians from attack. The traditional peacekeeper equipped with light weapons and soft-skinned vehicles has thus become an endangered species in the course of the 1990s – military observers remain unarmed though.

As illustrated in Box 3.1 the many missions have been accompanied by a never ending list of tasks. This proliferation of tasks has had two implications: the military personnel have been given many new tasks in addition to their traditional monitoring duties, and there has been a drastic increase in the number and size of the civilian mission components.

The military tasks associated with deterrence, show of force and combat operations have grown in importance due to the increased deployment of peace forces in ongoing conflicts. In addition to keeping and sometimes creating the peace, the military personnel have also become heavily involved in peace-building activities. Not just tasks requiring military expertise such

---

Box 3.1 Tasks undertaken as part of peace operations in the 1990s

1   Political negotiations and diplomatic collaborative projects.
2   Security tasks to contain and control the conflict.
3   Weapons control, disarmament, demobilization and rehabilitation (DDR).
4   De-mining.
5   Emergency relief.
6   Repatriation of refugees and displaced persons.
7   Elections and other democratization activities.
8   Reintroduction of police and legal, justice and penal systems.
9   Re-establishment of basic utilities (water, sanitation, etc.) and facilities (communications, education, etc.).
10 Public information and establishment of a free press.
11 Development activities, economic restoration and investment.
12 Reconciliation activities.

Source: JWP 3-50: Peace Support Operations, para. 206.

---

as de-mining, disarmament, destruction of collected weapons and the creation of new armed forces, but also civilian ones such as civilian administration, rebuilding of infrastructure, the running of radio stations, schools and hospitals, delivery of humanitarian assistance, construction of refugee camps, law and order activities including riot control, electoral support, etc.

The civilian mission components grew in number and importance throughout the 1990s as the peace operations took on more civilian tasks. Civilian police, electoral assistance, human rights, rule of law and civil administration can all be described as 'growth industries' within peace operations, and the number of civilian organizations involved has grown tremendously. A major multifunctional operation will typically involve the four big UN agencies: UN Development Programme (UNDP), the UN High Commissioner for Refugees (UNHCR), the UN Children's Fund (UNICEF) and the World Food Programme (WFP); the Bretton Woods institutions: the World Bank and the International Monetary Fund (IMF); regional organizations; private military companies; and hundreds of national and international NGOs. The high number of actors in the field is yet another factor which adds to the complexity of these operations.

Section summary

Five changes in the international context interacted to change the nature of peace operations fundamentally: the end of the Cold War; an increased emphasis on human rights and democracy; increasingly complex armed conflicts; the advent of real-time television; and recent operational outcomes. The number of operations skyrocketed and the goals and objectives changed from ceasefire monitoring and the preservation of negative peace to creation of the conditions for sustainable peace through the holding of elections, implementation of comprehensive peace agreements and the rebuilding of societies and states. As a result, new mission types, tasks and actors entered the scene and the Cold War one-dimensional military peace operation was marginalized by highly complex multifunctional ones.

All these changes produced a host of challenges with which the international community struggled to come to terms throughout the 1990s. Many lessons were learned the hard way by peace forces that were literally learning by doing in the mission areas. It is to these challenges and the resulting learning process that we now turn.

Challenges and lessons learned

In retrospect it took surprisingly long for the international community to get to the heart of the problems presented by the changing nature of peace operations. Agreement on a workable doctrine for peace operations characterized by limited consent was not achieved until the end of the 1990s,[34] and the political and organizational barriers that hampered operations throughout were not addressed head on until the publication of the *Brahimi Report* in 2000. Although it did not solve these problems plaguing post-Cold War peace operations, this report, which was prepared by a high-level panel appointed by the UN Secretary-General, certainly succeeded in putting them on the agenda.

The following analysis of the challenges and the lessons learned will address both the practical and political problems and their possible solutions. It identifies eleven challenges culled from the vast lessons-learned literature produced since the birth of UN peacekeeping. They have been separated into three different levels: the political, the managerial and the operational (Table 3.3), and are analysed briefly by means of three questions: (1) What is the problem? (2) How has it been addressed? (3) To what extent has it been overcome?

Table 3.3 Challenges to post-Cold War peace operations

Levels	Challenges
Political	Unrealistic mandates
	Failure to match ends with means
Managerial	Inadequate planning, management and support
Operational	Short-circuited command and control
	Inappropriate armaments, doctrines and rules of engagement
	Long response times
	Poor training standards
	Public security gap
	Ineffective public information capacity
	Inadequate intelligence capacity
	More clash than coordination and cooperation

Unrealistic mandates

> [The] UN Secretariat should always request resources for individual peacekeeping operations that reflect a realistic estimate – a conservative estimate, not an exaggerated one, but a realistic mandate – of what is needed to do the job properly, rather than a perception of 'what the traffic will bear'.
>
> Margaret J. Anstee,
> UN Special Representative of the Secretary-General for Angola[35]

The tendency of the Security Council to ignore the realities on the ground and disregard recommendations from fact-finding missions when setting up new peace operations posed a key challenge to commanders and heads of mission throughout the 1990s. A combination of a desire to save money, a reluctance to provide troops and use of best-case planning scenarios often resulted in the launch of operations that were understaffed, under-financed and entirely dependent upon the willingness of the parties to cooperate with the UN force. The use of best-case planning scenarios and rejection of force estimates from fact-finding missions and the UN Secretariat could almost be likened to a standard operating procedure. It was employed prior to the launch of UNTAG in Namibia, UNAVEM II and III in Angola and UNAMIR I in Rwanda, and when UNPROFOR in Bosnia was tasked to set up the 'safe areas' in 1993.[36]

All of these operations except UNTAG failed, and the political unwillingness of the permanent members to face up to the fact that peace operations conducted in an environment characterized by limited consent require bigger, better equipped and hence more expensive forces capable of overcoming setbacks was heavily criticized in the *Brahimi Report*.[37]

These problems are not peculiar to the UN. NATO's operations in the Balkans have suffered from similar problems.[38] The problem took on a mission-threatening character following the US invasion of Iraq in 2003. The USA was totally unprepared for the post-war phase because it had entered the war on the best-case assumption that it somehow would not require detailed planning and preparation.[39]

The failure to match ends with means

> I don't read the SC resolutions anymore because they don't help me. There is a fantastic gap between the resolutions of the Security Council, the will to execute those resolutions and the means available to commanders in the field.
>
> General Francis Briquemont,
> commander of UN forces in Bosnia[40]

Related to the first problem was the tendency of the Security Council to expand mandates and place additional tasks on existing peace operations without providing them with additional resources. UNPROFOR in the Balkans suffered from this problem throughout its existence, which culminated with the creation of the safe areas. Although the commander of UN forces in Bosnia estimated that the establishment and protection of the safe areas would require 34,000 additional troops, the Security Council was unwilling to authorize more than 7,600.[41] The Srebrenica massacre of some 6,500 Muslims in July 1995 was the predictable consequence of this policy.[42]

Another more recent example can be found in Sierra Leone where the members of the Security Council once again proved unwilling to provide anything but token support for the Chapter VII operation that they had authorized. The result was a UN force composed mainly of ill-equipped Third World contingents that were neither willing nor capable of carrying out the tasks demanded of them. The result was another disaster, namely the near collapse of UNAMSIL in May 2000 where more than 500 UN soldiers were taken hostage.[43]

The problem of unrealistic mandates and the failure to match ends and means are as old as the UN itself and remedies exist. In spite of this, they are likely to continue to plague peace operations in the foreseeable future as they can be boiled down to a lack of political will on the part of the Western UN member states with the capacity to do something about them. The attempt in the *Brahimi Report* to shame these states into acting in a more responsible manner is unlikely to work.

Inadequate planning, management and support

> Do not get into trouble as commander in the field after five p.m. New York time, or Saturday and Sunday. There is no one to answer the phone.
>
> Major General Lewis MacKenzie,
> commander of UN peacekeeping forces, Sarajevo, 1992[44]

The managerial capacity of the UN Secretariat remained minimal throughout the Cold War, and it was no surprise that it was completely overwhelmed by the explosion in the number of peace operations in the early 1990s. In 1989, when the expansion began, a staff of nine was involved in the management of peace operations. Since then institutional reform in the Secretariat has been continuous,[45] and the recommendations in the *Brahimi Report* led to a significant strengthening of the UN Department of Peacekeeping Operations (DPKO).[46] However, the creation of 191 new posts by 2003 does not alter the fact that the UN Secretariat's managerial capacity remains limited. By mid-2004 the DPKO only had one person managing operations for every 100 personnel in the field,[47] and it remained short-staffed in the police/rule of law area and in planning for the civilian elements of peace operations. In addition, the DPKO continued to suffer from a shortage of funds and pre-stocked materiel, a highly uneven quality of personnel and cumbersome standard operating procedures.[48]

These problems are not new. They also existed during the Cold War and reform proposals have been made regularly since the organization became involved in peacekeeping.[49] If we go further back, the commander of the League of Nations' monitoring force in the Saar made a reform proposal in 1935 that is all but identical to the ones that have been tabled since 1988.[50] The fate of all these proposals serve to underline a basic truth: The UN will never be more effective than its member states want it to, and many of them do not want the organization to be too effective.[51]

The preferred solution to these problems has been to delegate operations to regional organizations and ad hoc coalitions of the willing. On top of the eleven operations delegated by the Security Council to other actors since 1988 come the many observer missions, mandated and conducted by the O/AU, EU, OSCE and other organizations.

The delegation practice is but a partial solution to the managerial problems, however. Only the Western countries have the capacity to plan and conduct larger operations effectively, and the operations delegated to non-Western states, especially the ones in Africa, have suffered from the same managerial problems as the UN-commanded ones. This will not change in the foreseeable future as Western efforts to improve the management capacity of the regional organizations in Africa have made little headway.

Short-circuited command and control

> Instead of OPCON [operational control], it was OPNO in the British sector, OPNON in the French sector and UP YOURS in the American sector.
>
> Lt General Michael Walker,
> commander of IFOR's land component[52]

The increased risks caused by the erosion of consent made effective command and control more important and at the same time harder to achieve, because governments responded by placing restrictions on the use of their military contingents in order to minimize the risk of casualties. Although interference and micro-management from national capitals also occurred in peace operations during the Cold War, it reached unprecedented levels in the 1990s. As a consequence, force commanders who in theory had operational control over their contingents, in practice had to learn to live with the fact that they often refused to carry out orders that their governments deemed too risky or inappropriate.

That governments place restrictions on the use of their military contingents in high-risk operations is understandable because they risk getting voted out of office if their soldiers are killed in conflicts that pose no direct threats to national security. Demanding that governments stop their interference as many have done is therefore unrealistic. In recognition of this, the doctrinal solution has been to regard national interference as a fact of life and use a lead or framework state to ensure some unity of command in peace operations not commanded by the UN, i.e. let the state supplying the largest military contingent assume command of the peace force.[53]

This model was employed in the 1991 Gulf War, where the USA acted as lead nation, and in most of the subsequent enforcement operations that followed in the 1990s. The interventions led by Nigeria in Liberia and Sierra Leone, the US-led intervention in Somalia, the Italian-led operation in Albania and the Australian-led intervention in East Timor all belong in this category, and experience shows that the lead nation model provides a satisfactory solution to the problem. In the Balkans NATO has been forced to employ a model with several 'lead nations' because of the simultaneous involvement of several major member states with sizable contingents. As indicated in the quote above, NATO's IFOR/SFOR force in Bosnia effectively had three lead nations as the force commander had little influence over the three multinational divisions nominally under his command led by Britain, France and the USA. The situation was the same in Kosovo where the KFOR commander had little influence over the five multi-national brigades led by Britain, France, Germany, Italy and the USA.[54] The effectiveness of the lead nation model is, in short, negatively correlated with the number of lead nations in the operation. The unity of command that the NATO model achieves within the lead nation sectors is offset by weakened operational control.

The lead nation model is usually not on option on UN-commanded operations because it runs counter to the principle of equitable geographical representation, which is defended vigorously by the Non-Aligned Movement (114 mainly Third World countries), and the reluctance of the great powers to act as lead nations on operations under UN command. Instead, the UN has tried to reduce the problem caused by national interference on operations under its command by improving consultation with troop contributors who do not have a seat in the Security Council. An increase in the number of meetings and briefings held by the UN Security Council and the UN Secretariat with troop-contributing nations have improved the situation in recent years,[55] but they are unlikely to be sufficient to reduce significantly the problem posed by national interference in high-risk situations. This can only be done by the adoption of the lead nation principle on UN operations as well.

Inappropriate armaments, doctrines and rules of engagement

> Go in too light and, in the end, instead of keeping the peace, the Blue Helmets become vulnerable targets.
>
> DPKO's Lessons Learned Unit[56]

Lightly armed peacekeepers operating according to traditional rules of engagement (ROE) ran into serious trouble in Angola, the Balkans and Rwanda where consent was limited or withdrawn upon the arrival of the peacekeepers. The lightly armed peacekeepers could neither defend themselves nor the civilians at risk and were subjected to harassment, attacks or hostage-taking from the parties. Such problems proved to be the norm in all major peace operations launched in the 1990s, and they triggered a heated doctrinal debate that raged during most of the decade.

Two fundamentally different doctrinal solutions were offered to address the problem.[57] The traditionalist solution was to stick with the traditional peacekeeping principles of impartiality and non-use of force except in self-defence, take additional protective measures and emphasize the need to promote consent and avoid inadvertent escalation to peace enforcement. The British *Wider Peacekeeping* doctrine exemplifies this solution.[58]

The reformist solution was initially formulated in doctrinal form by the French.[59] It advocates the deployment of a well-armed force which is militarily superior vis-à-vis all the parties and capable of using both carrots and sticks to promote consent, deter non-compliance and, if necessary, enforce compliance. Negotiation and a wide array of consent-promoting techniques, including rewards for cooperation, must be employed to win the 'hearts and minds' of the local population. To enhance deterrence the force must be provided with ROE based on 'active impartiality' permitting the use of force as a last resort in a discriminate and proportionate manner against parties threatening the civilian population or preventing the peace force from achieving its mandate.

NATO successfully employed the reformist solution in the Balkans, and it has been embraced and elaborated upon in the latest batch of American, British and NATO doctrines.[60] It is spreading to non-NATO countries,[61] UN Secretary-General Kofi Annan has advocated it using the terms inducement operations and robust peacekeeping,[62] and it is also supported by the key recommendation in the *Brahimi Report* on peacekeeping doctrine and strategy which states that:

> United Nations peacekeepers must be able to carry out their mandates professionally and successfully and be capable of defending themselves, other mission components and the mission's mandate, with robust rules of engagement, against those who renege on their commitments to a peace accord or otherwise seek to undermine it by violence.[63]

While the new doctrine is sound and has proved its worth in the field, it is also creating problems because most non-Western states and regional organizations are incapable of meeting its requirements for success. The new doctrine requires contingents with better training, better logistical backup, heavier equipment and higher interoperability than was the case during the Cold War, and most non-Western states simply lack the resources to train, equip and sustain such forces. The new doctrine will therefore only be employed in operations that are led by Western states using NATO standards. Moreover, the inability of the UN and non-Western actors to honour the doctrinal requirements for success is also likely to make Western leaders even more reluctant to provide troops for UN-commanded operations and delegated operations led by non-Western states.

Long response times

> The first six to 12 weeks following a ceasefire or peace accord is often the most critical period for establishing both a stable peace and the credibility of the peacekeepers. Credibility and political momentum lost during this period can often be difficult to regain.
>
> *Brahimi Report*[64]

Long response times and deployment delays of both military and civilian mission components characterized all major peace operations during the 1990s, and although the problem was recognized early on, an effective solution has thus far proved elusive. If we look at the military personnel first, then the UN Standby Arrangements System (UNSAS) that was set up in 1994 to speed up UN deployments has not made a significant difference.[65] The *Brahimi Report* improved the situation resulting in the establishment of a 147-strong list of on-call military officers available within seven days' notice to establish a rapidly deployable mission headquarters, but the support from UN members states remain half-hearted. Shortfalls in critical areas such as engineering, communications, logistics, transport, intelligence and strategic lift continue to make it difficult for the UN to establish a new peace operation within the rather conservative 90-day deadline that the organization has set itself.[66]

The UN does have a limited rapid reaction capability in the 4,500-strong UN Standby Forces High Readiness Brigade (SHIRBRIG), which is available for deployment at short notice (15–30 days) for peace operations for a maximum period of six months. SHIRBRIG was used for the first time in UNMEE in Ethiopia and Eritrea in 2000 and praised by the UN Secretary-General for its contribution allowing 'a quick and efficient deployment.'[67] SHIRBRIG also provided rapid stop-gap deployments of staff to facilitate the deployments of MINUCI in Côte d'Ivoire and UNMIL in Liberia in 2003,[68] and in the autumn of 2004 SHIRBRIG provided seven personnel to the 14-strong advance team authorized by the Security Council to prepare the UNMIS operation in Sudan. In mid-2005 SHIRBRIG deployed the nucleus of the force headquarters support elements (some two hundred personnel) for this operation.[69]

The establishment of up to nine 1,500-strong EU battle groups may provide the UN with the robust rapid reaction capability it needs by 2007.[70] The EU demonstrated its willingness to deploy robust forces at short notice at the request of the UN with its 90-day deployment of 1,800 personnel in and around Democratic Republic of Congo in 2003 (Operation Artemis), but it remains unclear to what extent the UN will be able to rely on the EU for such assistance. The willingness of the Western powers to provide the UN with the military rapid reaction capacity they possess has often been lacking in the past and there is nothing to suggest that this is about to change. It therefore seems safe to conclude that military rapid reaction will remain problematic in peace operations that are not led or supported by the Western powers, the EU or NATO.

This also holds true with respect to civilian rapid reaction, but here the problem is compounded by a serious lack of capacity. The UN has established three 120-personnel civilian rapid deployment teams (RDTs) drawn from its own personnel that are supposed to be available at short notice for a period of up to 90 days to start up new missions. That this is not necessarily the case became clear when the RDT roster was used for the first time for the start up of UNMIL in Liberia in 2003. Although 32 RDT personnel were deployed, it proved impossible to deploy an adequate number of qualified personnel through the RDT roster, in part because managers refused to release their personnel. Moreover, the UN was unable to recruit replacements in time for all the RDT personnel when their 90-day tour of duty was up.[71] In the area of civilian police and rule of law the UN has made very little progress in terms of establishing a reliable rapid reaction capacity.[72]

The EU has established a considerable rapid reaction capacity involving some 5,000 police, 282 rule of law, 2,083 civil protection and 248 civil administration experts,[73] and the OSCE, individual states and many NGOs have also established and continue to enhance civilian rapid reaction capabilities. Although clearly more than a drop in the ocean, the international community still has a long way to go before the demand for civilian rapid reaction personnel is met. For the foreseeable future it will remain a challenge for the international community to deploy civilian personnel with the right qualifications, in the right number, in the right place and at the right time.

Finally, it is important to bear in mind that the proliferation of civil and military rapid reaction forces and standby arrangements is no guarantee of rapid deployment. States retain the right to say no to specific deployments in all of them, and they exercised this right rather frequently during the 1990s. Standby forces, as John Mackinlay has pointed out, 'tend to be exactly what the name implies: forces standing by.'[74]

Poor training standards

> Equipment and adequate training is another area of growing concern...Increasingly...Member States offer troops without the necessary equipment and training.
>
> Boutros Boutros-Ghali, UN Secretary-General, 1992–96[75]

The increased complexity and the erosion of consent have placed greater demands on the personnel involved in peace operations than ever before.[76] Soldiers must be able to function effectively in a multinational setting, to engage in high-intensity combat, riot control, delivery of humanitarian relief, mediation and conflict resolution, and to cooperate with civilian actors. In addition to mastering their specific area of expertise the civilian personnel must be able to function in a conflict zone and cooperate with military personnel. The need to function effectively in a multinational setting has put a premium on multinational pre-deployment training and the formation of multinational civilian and military units. A civilian police force can only function properly from day one if it deploys as a formed, pre-trained unit and the same is true for the military contingents that usually have to rely on each other for support in crisis situations. The need for increased force integration and interoperability is one reason why the *Brahimi Report* recommended the establishment of more SHIRBRIG-type multinational brigades within the UNSAS system.[77]

No such brigades have yet been established, and many military contingents from former Warsaw Pact and developing countries are incapable of meeting these requirements. The problem is equally bad if not worse on the civilian side due to critical shortages of personnel in many areas, and the internal problems within the UN system which made it difficult to attract and retain highly qualified staff.[78] Many steps to increase the pool of qualified civilian and military personnel have been taken during the 1990s. Since its establishment in 1993, the Training and Evaluation Unit at the UN Department of Peacekeeping (DPKO) has sought to coordinate and standardize training among member states that contribute to peace operations. The Training and Evaluation Unit has established a UN staff college in Turin, made considerable headway with respect to developing common standards for peace operations training, created training assistance teams that provide specialized training to member states upon request at short notice, and it conducts a wide range of different training programmes and courses for both civilian and military personnel.[79] NATO has also set up a comprehensive training programme to prepare its members and partner countries for participation in peace operations led by the alliance, the EU is in the process of establishing comprehensive training programmes for its civilian rapid reaction personnel, the Nordic countries have beefed up their joint training programme, new regional training centres dedicated to peace operations have been established in Argentina, Canada, Ghana, Malaysia and Zimbabwe, and several Western countries have begun to provide training assistance to African countries.

In spite of these improvements UN-commanded operations continue to suffer from the deployment of both civilian and military personnel lacking even the most basic qualifications. The near-collapse of UNAMSIL in Sierra Leone in the Spring of 2000 could to a large extent be attributed to the deployment of badly trained and ill-equipped personnel, and in the first year of UNMIK in Kosovo the police commissioner had to send as many as 383 police officers home shortly after their arrival because they were incapable of performing basic police skills.[80] This was also the case with the majority of those interviewed for CIVPOL positions for the UNMIL operation in the autumn of 2003.[81] These examples speak volumes about the problems that remain unsolved in this area.

The public security gap

> For those who say this [public security] is not for the military, my next question to them would be, for whom is it when there is nobody else there?... Or do you just let it go? Do you allow anarchy?... You don't have a secure environment with murderers running around.
>
> Lt General Michael Jackson,
> KFOR commander[82]

Post-Cold War peace operations are often conducted in an environment characterized by a general breakdown of law and order. The local public security triad consisting of law enforcement agencies, courts and the penal system has often ceased to function effectively, and this creates a public security gap in the early stages of a peace operation which the peace force has to fill. The military has been dragged into gap-filling against its will on all major peace operations in the 1990s because international civilian police, judges and jailers are unavailable for rapid deployment in the numbers required. This is not about to change in the foreseeable future, although the EU, the UN and individual countries are building up their civilian rapid reaction rule-of-law capacities. Moreover, the increased use of gendarmerie forces to close the enforcement gap between the military and the police will not let the military off the hook either, because these gendarmerie forces, like police officers, are limited in supply and on occasion will need military assistance. NATO has thus been incapable of providing gendarmes and multinational specialized units (police with military status) in adequate numbers in the Balkans.[83]

The solution proposed by the *Brahimi Report* and other experts is to establish rapid reaction law and order teams consisting of judges and jailers and other legal experts and to develop an interim criminal code for use in the emergency phase until the local security triad is re-established.[84] Unfortunately, this ideal solution will not be implemented in the near future. The political will to order the military to set up such teams is lacking, and it will take a considerable time to build the capacity required for civilian ones. As a result, the challenge will be to construct the optimal force mix from the personnel available when the need arises, and the military will have to play a major part whether it likes it or not.[85]

Ineffective public information capacity

> When mission planners or, especially mission financiers must choose between public information and other capabilities, public information is usually what gets left behind on the dock.
>
> William Durch et al.[86]

The increased deployment of peace forces in semi-hostile environments and intense media coverage made an effective public information and communications capacity and strategy imperative for mission success. In the mission area the peace forces had to counter propaganda and misinformation campaigns launched by the parties to mobilize local and international support for their cause and/or to incite violence. At the international level, an ability to react quickly and provide the ever-present international press with precise information proved crucial to mobilize and sustain international support for an operation because the parties were quick to put their spin on events, or because journalists would make up their own stories if the peace force proved incapable of providing them with information. Finally, a public information capacity proved important with respect to mobilizing and sustaining domestic support for the personnel contributors. This task became much harder than before because higher risks equal higher costs in terms of both blood and treasure. It is more expensive to equip contingents for high-risk operations and harder to convince the public of the need to accept casualties in faraway places to stop conflicts that pose no clear and present danger to national security.

While the personnel in the field quickly realized all this, the UN system was slow in reacting. The General Assembly turned down an application for a radio station for UNTAC, forcing the force commander to find the necessary funds for it himself.[87] UNPROFOR also lacked funds to establish an effective public information campaign,[88] and the story repeated itself in Somalia where it took 10 months before UNOSOM II got an official spokesperson, and a request for funds to establish a radio station was turned down.[89] UNOSOM II was therefore unable to counter the propaganda campaign that the radio stations controlled by clan leader Aideed directed against the UN force. The problem was the same when the genocide began in Rwanda.[90]

Since then some improvement has taken place. The use of radio stations has become standard in UN peace operations launched since 1995,[91] and the UN has also prepared guidelines and a manual for the use of information components in the field.[92] This did not prevent the launch of UNAMSIL in Sierra Leone in 1999 without a strong public information component and this 'proved near fatal to the credibility' of operation during the crisis of May 2000.[93] More improvements will therefore be needed, including the establishment of a rapidly deployable capacity for public information recommended by the *Brahimi Report*.[94] Although the UN succeeded in providing UNMIL in Liberia in 2003 with the equipment to allow early start-up of radio broadcasting, a lack of trained personnel kept the radio off the air for the first month.[95] Moreover, this operation all but exhausted the UN's rapid reaction public information capacity.[96] The situation does not look any better with respect to UN-delegated peace operations led by non-Western states. Only Western-led and NATO peace operations have the necessary capacity for public information. NATO has regarded it as a priority since it became involved in peace operations. IFOR, NATO's first ever peace operation, deployed with a public information organization of around 90 people in Bosnia in 1995.[97]

Inadequate intelligence capacity

> The United Nations...must develop better capacities to prevent and manage threats by improving the mechanisms for gathering information from the field, as well as the ability to use that information effectively by developing it into useful intelligence.
>
> Kofi Annan, UN Secretary-General[98]

During the Cold War intelligence gathering was viewed as too aggressive and incompatible with the principles of impartiality and neutrality that guided the traditional UN peacekeeping operations.[99] The UN Secretariat therefore continued to discourage such activities on UN-commanded Chapter VI operations in the early 1990s.[100] However, recognition that intelligence was crucial for both force protection and mission success in an operational environment characterized by limited consent gradually led to a change of heart in the Secretariat. The importance of an effective intelligence capacity was officially acknowledged in the wake of the failure of UN operation in Rwanda in 1994.[101] This change of mentality has not solved the problem, however. Although the UN by early 2004 had established 'joint mission analysis cells' on four of its missions, its capacity for gathering and analysing intelligence information from the field remained extremely limited. The *Brahimi Report*'s proposals for a strengthening of this capacity were met by stiff resistance from Third World governments, and they successfully defeated the various attempts made by the UN secretary-general to enhance the intelligence capacity in the Secretariat.[102] The UN therefore continues to rely on its members for intelligence information.

The capacity available on NATO or Western-led operations is much greater, but not without weaknesses. In KFOR in 2001 as many as 34 per cent of the staff in the Intelligence Unit had no previous experience with intelligence work when deployed, forcing KFOR to provide on-the-job training for the personnel.[103] Moreover, intelligence sharing within NATO is limited and uneven, and it has also proved difficult for non-NATO members participating in NATO-led operations to get access to NATO intelligence. Similarly, NATO was initially also unwilling to share intelligence and cooperate with the UN civilian police in Kosovo. It took over a year before a limited intelligence cooperation was established.[104]

National interests and concern about the level of security in international organizations and multinational mission headquarters will continue to limit the flow of intelligence information and prevent the establishment of effective intelligence capabilities in multinational settings. It will therefore be up to the contributors themselves to ensure that their personnel can obtain the intelligence they require for their own protection and mission success.

More clash than coordination and cooperation

Experience in Kosovo and Sierra Leone, as in other cases, reveals very serious limits to the extent to which the various regional organizations or NGOs recognize the coordinating authority of the UN or of any other actor.

Bruce D. Jones,
UN Office for the Coordination of Humanitarian Affairs[105]

The vast increase in the number of actors involved in peace operations in the course of the 1990s made coordination and cooperation imperative for mission success. At the same time, barriers and differences of interests at all levels from the strategic to the tactical and the vast increase in the number of actors in the mission areas made such coordination and cooperation very hard to achieve. Civil–military friction resulted from differences in ideology, organizational culture, resources and purpose;[106] coordination efforts within the UN system were frustrated by turf battles and rivalries among the 'big four' (UNDP, UNHCR, UNICEF and WFP) and their unwilling-ness to subordinate themselves to coordination by other UN bodies;[107] the NGOs tended to view coordination efforts in the field as an infringement upon their independence and impartiality;[108] lack of coordination between the UN and the Bretton Woods institutions had counterproductive effects because the structural adjustment programmes forced upon governments by the latter undermined the UN's peace-building efforts;[109] and the cooperation between the UN and regional organizations suffered from rivalries and jealousy.

After a decade of continuous reform, overall coordination at the strategic level remains weak, as does the level of internal coordination within the UN system.[110] At the operational level, cooperation between the various international organizations has improved, and joint civil–military coopera-tion has become institutionalized in the command structure in UN-commanded operations as the civilian and military components have been subordinated the head of mission, usually a Special Representative of the Secretary-General (SRSG). In operations with NATO involvement the command arrangements have moved from *de facto* separation between the civilian and military components during IFOR towards joint command arrangements during KFOR.

At the tactical level, CIMIC benefits from the use of CIMIC centres and specially trained CIMIC personnel, which have become standard in peace operations undertaken by the Western armies and NATO. Joint training and field exercises with the participation of the principal civilian and military actors are also beginning to bear fruit. Another potentially promising development at this level concerns the increased tendency of Western governments to channel their humanitarian assistance directly through their own military forces and NGOs in the field. This practice has obvious advantages for national governments as it reduces the risk of waste, speeds up the delivery of assistance and makes it easier to use humanitarian assistance in pursuit of national interests. However, it also has its drawbacks as it tends to undermine coordination efforts at the operational and strategic levels and defeat efforts aimed at ensuring that the humanitarian assistance is provided according to the same standards throughout the mission area.[111]

The balance sheet is, in sum, mixed. While progress is clear at all levels, it is equally clear that bureaucratic barriers, diverging organizational and state interests and the sheer number of actors ensure that coordination and cooperation will remain a challenge.

Section summary

This overview of challenges and lessons learned (Table 3.4) indicates that many problems remain unsolved, and that UN-commanded peace operations will continue to suffer from many of the same problems that have plagued them in the past. The reform efforts have not yet been able to match the challenges posed by the complex peace operations, and lack of political will has prevented many lessons learned from being acted upon. The UN and non-Western coalitions and organizations do not have the managerial capacity to plan and support effectively anything but small-scale operations, and non-Western actors lack the economic and military resources required to field personnel with the right equipment and training. This makes Western support the principal factor determining whether operations led by the UN and non-Western actors will be able to overcome the challenges discussed above.

The situation looks brighter for operations delegated to Western coalitions and organizations. The Western states have the management and operational capacity required for success, and they are making steady progress in their efforts to tackle the remaining challenges posed by the lack of civilian rapid reaction, the public security gap and coordination. For Western-led operations the key challenge lies at the political level. Western willingness to support peace operations outside their own spheres

Table 3.4 Overview of challenges and lessons learned

Challenges	Lessons learned		
	UN-commanded Chapter VI	UN-commanded beyond Chapter VI – de facto/de jure	UN-delegated Chapter VII operations
Unrealistic mandates	Lack of funds and staff and use of best-case scenarios continue to cause problems	Lack of funds and staff and use of best-case scenarios continue to cause problems	Less of a problem in Western-led operations
Failure to match ends with means	Still a problem	Still a problem	Less of a problem in Western-led operations
Inadequate planning, management and support	Still a problem; capacity far too small	Still a problem; capacity far too small	No problem in Western-led operations
Short-circuited command and control	Still a problem; consultation with contributors not enough	Still a problem; consultation with contributors not enough	Use of lead nation partial solution
Inappropriate armaments, doctrines and ROE	No problem as long as consent is high	Still a problem because new doctrine cannot be implemented	Capacity to implement doctrine only exists in Western-led operations; they are hampered by limited political will
Long response times	Still a problem with respect to both civilian and military personnel. Response time depends on great power support	Still a problem with respect to both civilian and military personnel. Response time depends on great power support	Rapid military reaction possible in Western-led operations, but civilian deployments remain a problem
Poor training standards	Still a problem; many non-Western contingents lack adequate training	Still a problem; many non-Western contingents lack adequate training	Standards not a problem in Western-led operations; new members struggle to meet NATO standards
Public security gap	Still a problem; lack of military will and civilian capability	Still a problem; lack of military will and civilian capability	Still a problem; lack of military will and civilian capability
Ineffective public information capacity	Still a problem due to limited capacity	Still a problem due to limited capacity	No problem in Western-led operations
Inadequate intelligence capacity	Still a problem; dependence on great powers and contributors	Still a problem; dependence on great powers and contributors	Capacity exists in Western-led operations but intelligence sharing is limited
More clash than coordination and cooperation	Challenges at all levels despite improvements	Challenges at all levels despite improvements	Challenges at all levels despite improvements

of influence that are not related to the 'war on terror' remains limited. The number of Western personnel serving in UN-commanded peace operations remains low and Western states have not sent major military units to serve under UN command in Sub-Saharan Africa since 1994. This so-called 'commitment gap' has become a source of friction within the UN.[112]

These challenges, the lessons learned and the differences between UN- and non-Western-led peace operations and Western-led ones must be taken into account by states wanting to make effective contributions to contemporary peace operations. How they can do that is the topic of the final section of this chapter.

Implications for the construction of a new (Nordic) model

Since small- and medium-sized contributors like the Nordics usually have limited influence on political and managerial decisions, the only thing they can do to address the challenges at these levels is to specify the conditions under which they are willing to participate in peace operations, and say no to requests for personnel for operations that do not have realistic mandates, adequate resources, appropriate rules of engagement and so on.

The principal challenges facing small- and medium-sized contributors are operational. To be effective contributors to contemporary peace operations they must tackle all the operational challenges outlined above as well as the legal and political ones to which the changing nature of peace operations gives rise. The *ideal* personnel contributor must be able to meet the eleven requirements for success listed in Box 3.2, which is why they constitute the blueprint for a new Nordic model. The Nordics will only be able to preserve their high profile and influence in peace operations if they are capable of honouring these requirements.

Political will, an appropriate legal framework and economic resources are preconditions for participation. Political will is ultimately a function of domestic support, and the task of mobilizing and sustaining domestic support has been complicated by the increasing risks, higher costs and, in the Western countries at least, a weaker link between the peace operations and national security. The ultimate challenge for governments wanting to participate in contemporary peace operations is to convince domestic audiences that body bags are acceptable even though the link to national security is weak. While September 11 increased the American willingness to accept casualties in operations related to the 'war on terror', the American willingness to accept losses remains low in other operations. September 11 did not make a major difference in other Western countries since they do not perceive terrorism as an existential threat to the same extent as is the case in the USA. This is perhaps best illustrated by a comparison of the differences in tone and approach in US *National Security Strategy* from September 2002 and the EU *Security Strategy* presented in December the following year.[113]

Box 3.2 Blueprint for a new Nordic model

 1 Political will, legal framework and money for all types of operations.
 2 Civilian and military personnel deployable at short notice.
 3 Training and preparing the civilian and military personnel for their many different tasks.
 4 Interoperability with most likely partners.
 5 Armaments and rules of engagement permitting use of force beyond self-defence if necessary.
 6 Logistics support.
 7 Medical, psychological and family support.
 8 Intelligence capacity.
 9 Public information capacity.
10 Coordination and cooperation capacity.
11 Public security capacity.

Although legal obstacles are usually overcome if the political will to participate is present, a legal framework facilitating participation is still important, not least with respect to mobilizing domestic support. A personnel contributor must therefore ideally have national laws permitting the deployment of civilian and military personnel abroad on both Chapter VI and VII operations that are mandated and conducted by a variety of international organizations. If national laws, as was the case in the Nordic countries during the Cold War, restrict participation to Chapter VI operations mandated by the UN only, then the ability to participate in post-Cold War operations is significantly reduced as a result of the increased resort to Chapter VII and the increase in the number of organizations authorizing and undertaking peace operations.

Participation in peace operations has become far more expensive due to the need for heavier and more advanced equipment, better protection, improved back-up systems, modern communications and the delegation practice. Operations delegated to coalitions of the willing and regional organizations are more expensive for participants than UN-commanded ones because personnel contributors do not receive UN reimbursements for delegated operations. The chronic inability of the UN to honour its reimbursement obligations may make the latter factor more theoretical than real, though.

As for personnel contributions, the challenges and lessons learned point to the need for larger contingents, ideally brigade-sized contributions to enhance force protection and operational autonomy and influence on peace operations with great power involvement. They also create a need for more advanced training programmes reflecting the multifunctional nature of contemporary peace operations and the greater need for multinational integration and cooperation. Both civilian and military personnel must be able to deploy at short notice as slow deployments increase the risk that fragile peace processes or ceasefires break down. The military contingents must be able to operate effectively in a multinational setting as soon as they arrive in the mission area to deter spoilers and win the respect of the local population. This requires a high degree of interoperability that can only be attained if the various national contingents use common standards or have conducted joint training in advance. To enhance effectiveness, small- and medium-sized contributors incapable of fielding brigades on their own should therefore establish multinational brigades together with like-minded partners or allies, or at a minimum establish common standards and engage in joint training with them.

The armaments and the rules of engagement must reflect the higher risks in the mission areas. If the level of consent is limited or uncertain, military contingents must be provided with heavy equipment to enhance force protection and deterrence and robust rules of engagement based on 'active impartiality' permitting the use of force beyond self-defence if necessary. Their logistics, medical, psychological and family systems must be designed accordingly, and a high degree of self-sufficiency is clearly needed given the inability of the UN to provide the logistics support it is supposed to, and given that logistics support is a national responsibility on peace operations commanded by other actors.

The increased risks also increase the importance of intelligence activities and public information campaigns. The lessons learned in the 1990s show that intelligence activities are essential for force protection and mission success in conflicts where consent is limited, and none of the parties have full control over their forces. A clear media and information strategy is required from the outset to generate support for a peace operation at home, at the international level and locally in the mission area.

The large number of actors in the mission areas has created a need for increased cooperation and coordination among mission components. A CIMIC capacity is therefore a must for the military contingents, as is joint training and preparation for the civilian and military personnel.

Finally, the lessons learned demonstrated the need to close the public security gap quickly. This challenge calls for the rapid deployment of specially trained soldiers, gendarmes, police, judges, jailers and legal experts. A model hence needs such a capacity to be complete.

Now that the blueprint for a new model has been developed, it is time to determine to what extent the Nordic countries can honour its eleven conditions for success. This is the purpose of the next four chapters.

Notes

1. *Brahimi Report* (official title *Report of the Panel on the United Nations Peace Operations*, UN Doc. A/55/305-S/2000/809), 21 August 2000, p. viii.
2. To qualify as a peace operation in this study, an operation has to be legal under international law. A peace operation authorized to use force beyond

self-defence must consequently have a UN mandate, whereas a peace operation authorized to use force in self-defence only also can be mandated by regional organizations such as the AU, ECOWAS, NATO, OSCE, etc. NATO's air campaign over Kosovo in 1999 (Operation Allied Force) does therefore not qualify as a peace operation. The KFOR operation that followed does qualify, however, since it, unlike Operation Allied Force, was authorized by the UN Security Council.

3. This number includes operations launched with a UN mandate as well as operations that were authorized or welcomed *post hoc* by the Security Council. For an overview of these operations see Appendix 3.

4. ONUC in Congo (1960–64) was a de facto but not de jure enforcement operation since no explicit reference to Chapter VII was ever made. See Huldt, Bo (1995) 'Working Multilaterally: The Old Peacekeepers' Viewpoint', in Donald C.F. Daniel and Bradd C. Hayes (eds) *Beyond Traditional Peacekeeping* (New York: St Martin's Press), pp. 103–104 (101–119).

5. *The Blue Helmets: A Review of United Nations Peace-keeping* (New York: United Nations Publications, 1990); and UN Department of Peacekeeping Operations (2004) 'Who Contributes Personnel?', *United Nations Peacekeeping – FAQ – Meeting New Challenges*. <http://www.un.org/Depts/dpko/dpko/faq/q8.htm> (21 February 2002).

6. Dobson, Hugo J. (1999) 'Regional Approaches to Peacekeeping Activities: The Case of the ASEAN Regional Forum', *International Peacekeeping*, Vol. 6, No. 2 (summer), pp. 152–171; Morris, Justin and Hilaire McCoubrey (1999) 'Regional Peacekeeping in the Post-Cold War Era', *International Peacekeeping*, Vol. 6, No. 2 (summer), pp. 129–151.

7. For an elaboration of the division of labour argument see Jakobsen, Peter Viggo (2000) 'Overload, Not Marginalization, Threatens UN Peacekeeping', *Security Dialogue*, Vol. 30, No. 2 (June), pp. 167–178.

8. In this number I exclude the 'new' UN and NATO missions in former Yugoslavia that resulted from the reorganization and termination of UNPROFOR; the 'new' UN mission that was set up as UNMIH in Haiti was scaled down; and the observer mission that stayed on in Angola after the withdrawal of UNAVEM III. Although my decision to regard UNPROFOR and NATO's IFOR/SFOR as one continuing operation is debatable, I think it is reasonable in this context given that many UNPROFOR contingents stayed on in Bosnia and simply repainted their equipment. See Eide, Espen Barth and Per Erik Solli (1995) 'From Blue to Green: The Transition from UNPROFOR to IFOR in Bosnia and Herzegovina', *NUPI Working Paper*, No. 539 (Oslo: Norwegian Institute of International Affairs).

9. Quoted in Paris, Roland (2004) *At War's End: Building Peace after Civil Conflict* (Cambridge: Cambridge University Press), p. 2.

10. *A Secure Europe in a Better World: A European Security Strategy* (Brussels: European Council, 12 December 2003); and *The National Security Strategy of the United States of America* (Washington, DC: White House, 17 September 2002).

11. It was not just their loss of strategic importance that cost these and other countries their economic support. It also resulted from their unwillingness to accept the new conditions for market reforms, democratization, respect for human rights and good governance that Western donors, the International Monetary Fund and the World Bank began to attach to their offers of economic support. This introduction of economic and political conditions in Western assistance and development programmes was also facilitated by the end of the Cold War. See Jakobsen, Peter Viggo (2002) 'The Transformation

of United Nations Peace Operations in the 1990s: Adding Globalization to the Conventional "End of the Cold War" Explanation', *Cooperation and Conflict*, Vol. 73, No. 3 (September), pp. 267–282.

12. The number of armed conflicts fluctuated in the period between 1985 and 1993 as follows: 1985: 40; 1986: 45; 1987: 49; 1988: 42; 1989: 47; 1990: 49; 1991: 51; 1992: 55; and 1993: 46. E-mail communication from Margareta Sollenberg, 5 March 2002. For the numbers covering the 1989–2002 period, see Eriksson, Mikael, Peter Wallensteen and Margareta Sollenberg (2003) 'Armed Conflict, 1989–2002', *Journal of Peace Research*, Vol. 40, No. 5 (September), pp. 593–607.

13. Marshall, Monty G. and Ted R. Gurr (2003) *Peace and Conflict 2003: A Global Survey of Armed Conflicts, Self-Determination Movements, and Democracy* (College Park, MD: University of Maryland, Center for International Development and Conflict Management).

14. Durch, William J., Victoria K. Holt, Caroline R. Earle, and Moira K. Shanahan (2003) *The Brahimi Report and the Future of UN Peace Operations* (Washington, DC: Henry L. Stimson Center), p. 13.

15. Needless to say, great power interventions without UN authorization continue to occur, as Russia's interventions in Chechnya (1994 and 1999), South Africa's intervention in Lesotho (1998), NATO's air campaign against Serbia (1999) and the US-led invasion of Iraq (2003) illustrate.

16. For these principles see UN Doc. A/3943, 9 October 1958.

17. In addition, the absence of the Soviet threat also made it imperative for the armed forces to find alternative employment in order to protect their budgets and raison d'être, and peace operations proved crucial in this respect.

18. Van Evera, Stephen (1990) 'Why Europe Matters, Why the Third World Doesn't: US Grand Strategy After the Cold War', *Journal of Strategic Studies*, Vol. 13, No. 2 (June), pp. 1–51.

19. UN Secretary-General Boutros Boutros-Ghali's *Agenda for Peace* (UN Doc. A/47/277–S/24111, 17 June 1992) played an important agenda-setting role in this respect.

20. For these two operations see Griffin, Michèle and Bruce Jones (2000) 'Building Peace Through Transitional Authority: New Directions, Major Challenges', *International Peacekeeping*, Vol. 7, No. 4 (winter), pp. 75–90. The American nation-building operation, which started in Iraq in 2003, was obviously even more ambitious, but its initial phase does not qualify as a peace operation since it lacked a UN mandate.

21. The mood at the time is perhaps best captured by the popularity of Fukuyama's 'end of history' thesis, i.e. the idea that history had ended and that liberal democracy was the only model left standing. See Fukuyama, Francis (1992) *The End of History and the Last Man* (New York: Avon Books).

22. Paris, *At War's End*; Ratner, Steven R. (1995) *The New UN Peacekeeping: Building Peace in Lands of Conflict After the Cold War* (New York: St Martin's Press), p. 15.

23. Clapham, Christopher (1996) *Africa and the International System: The Politics of State Survival* (Cambridge: Cambridge University Press), pp. 195–196, 201.

24. For an in-depth analysis of this process see Knudsen, Tonny B. (forthcoming 2006) *Humanitarian Intervention: Contemporary Manifestations of an Explosive Doctrine* (London: Routledge).

25. Jakobsen, Peter Viggo (1996) 'National Interest, Humanitarianism or CNN: What Triggers UN Peace Enforcement After the Cold War?', *Journal of Peace Research*, Vol. 33, No. 2 (May), pp. 205–215; and Jakobsen, Peter Viggo

(2000) 'Focus on the CNN Effect Misses the Point: The Real Media Impact on Conflict Management is Invisible and Indirect', *Journal of Peace Research*, Vol. 37, No. 2 (March), pp. 131–143.

26. Jakobsen, Peter Viggo (2002) 'UN Peace Operations in Africa Today and Tomorrow', in Michael Bothe and Boris Kondoch (eds) *The Yearbook of International Peace Operations, Volume 7, 2001* (The Hague: Klüwer Press International), p. 175 (153–180).

27. Luttwak, Edward. N. (1999) 'Give War a Chance', *Foreign Affairs*, Vol. 78, No. 4 (July/August), pp. 36–44. For an argument that this is impossible in many conflicts see Jakobsen, 'UN Peace Operations in Africa Today and Tomorrow'.

28. Holsti, Kalevi J. (1996) *The State, War, and the State of War* (Cambridge: Cambridge University Press), pp. 21–26.

29. The five UN operations conducted in internal conflicts were UNOGIL in Lebanon, ONUC in the Congo, UNYOM in Yemen, UNFICYP in Cyprus and DOMREP in the Dominican Republic. See James, Alan (1995) 'Peacekeeping in the Post-Cold War Era', *International Journal*, Vol. 50, No. 2 (spring), pp. 243–245 (241–265).

30. While there is no consensus whether these complex conflicts should be called complex emergencies, postmodern wars, privatised wars, new wars, or wars of the third kind, there is general agreement that they share most of the features mentioned here. See Holsti, *The State, War, and the State of War*; Kaldor, Mary (1999) *New and Old Wars: Organized Violence in a Global Era* (Stanford, CA: Stanford University Press); Keen, David (1998) 'The Economic Functions of Violence in Civil Wars', *Adelphi Paper*, No. 320 (Oxford: Oxford University Press for the International Institute for Strategic Studies).

31. See UN Department of Peacekeeping Operations (2001) 'The Logic of Peacekeeping', in *An Introduction to United Nations Peacekeeping* (New York: United Nations Department of Public Information) <http:// www.un.org/Depts/dpko/dpko/intro/2.htm> (16 November 2001); *JWP 3–50: Peace Support Operations* (Northwood, UK: Ministry of Defence, 1998), para. 101.

32. Tardy, Thierry (2003) *Limits and Opportunities of UN–EU Relations in Peace Operations: Implications for DPKO* (New York: UN DPKO Peacekeeping Best Practices Unit), p. 4.

33. Other candidates in the literature include wider peacekeeping, aggravated peacekeeping, middle ground operations, muscular peacekeeping, grey area operations, and strategic peacekeeping. For an analysis of the evolution of British, French, NATO, UN and US doctrinal thinking in the 1990s with respect to this type of operation see Jakobsen, Peter Viggo (2000) 'The Emerging Consensus on Grey Area Peace Operations Doctrine: Will It Last and Enhance Operational Effectiveness?', *International Peacekeeping*, Vol. 7, No. 3 (autumn), pp. 36–56.

34. For an overview of this debate and the emerging consensus see Jakobsen, 'The Emerging Consensus'.

35. Anstee, Margaret J. (1993) 'Angola: The Forgotten Tragedy. A Test Case for UN Peacekeeping', *International Relations*, Vol. 11, No. 6 (December), p. 498 (495–511).

36. Fortna, Virgina Page (1993) 'United Nations Transition Assistance Group', in William J. Durch (ed.) *The Evolution of UN Peacekeeping: Case Studies and Comparative Analysis* (New York: St Martin's Press), p. 362 (353–375); Jakobsen, 'UN Peace Operations in Africa'.

37. *Brahimi Report*, paras 48–64.

38. Jakobsen, Peter Viggo (2003) 'Military Forces and Public Security Challenges', in Michael Pugh and Waheguru Pal Singh Sidhu (eds) *The UN and Regional Security: Europe and Beyond* (Boulder, CO: Lynne Rienner), p. 145 (137–153).
39. Fallows, James (2004) 'Blind into Baghdad', *The Atlantic Monthly*, Vol. 293, No. 1 (January/February), pp. 52–77.
40. Reuters (1993) 'UN Bosnia Commander Wants More Troops Fewer Resolutions', *The New York Times*, 31 December, p. A3.
41. See UN Doc. S/1995/444, 30 May 1995.
42. This estimate is provided by Honig, Jan Willem and Norbert Both (1996) *Srebrenica. Record of a War Crime* (London: Penguin Books), p. 65. For another in-dept analysis of the Srebrenica massacre see *The Fall of Srebrenica*, UN Doc A/54/549, 15 November 1999.
43. For analyses of UNAMSIL see Deen, Talif and Ian Kemp (2000) 'Shoestring Peacekeeping', *Jane's Defence Weekly*, Vol. 33, No. 20 (17 May); Farah, Douglas (2000) 'Old Problems Hamper UN in Sierra Leone', *The Washington Post*, 11 June, p. A25; Gordon, Stuart and James Higgs (2000) 'Briefing UN Mission in Sierra Leone: Peace At What Price?', *Jane's Defence Weekly*, Vol. 34, No. 13 (27 September); MacAskill, Ewen (2000) 'UN Gets Warning Shot on Peacekeeping', *The Guardian*, 9 September; Peacekeeping Best Practices Unit (2003) *Lessons Learned From United Nations Peacekeeping Experiences in Sierra Leone* (New York: UN Department of Peacekeeping Operations); Wilkinson, Philip R. (2000) 'Peace Support Under Fire: Lessons From Sierra Leone', *ISIS Briefing on Humanitarian Intervention*, No. 2/June (London: International Security Information Service).
44. Jones, Simon (1993) 'General MacKenzie Slams UN's Nine-to-Fivers', *The Independent*, 31 January.
45. The reform process can be followed in the updates provided each year since 1993 in the *SIPRI Yearbook* (Oxford: Oxford University Press, 1993ff.).
46. Durch, William J. et al., *The Brahimi Report and the Future of UN Peace Operations*, p. xix.
47. Guéhenno, Jean-Marie (2004) 'A Plan to Strengthen UN Peacekeeping', *International Herald Tribune*, 19 April.
48. Durch, William J. et al., *The Brahimi Report and the Future of UN Peace Operations*; interviews in the UN Department of Peacekeeping Operations, 12 May 2004.
49. See for instance Frydenberg, Per (1964) (ed.) *Peace-Keeping: Experience and Evaluation. The Oslo Papers* (Oslo: Norwegian Institute of International Affairs).
50. Brind, J. [1935] (1968) 'League of Nations: Report by the Commander in Chief, International Force in the Saar, 26 October 1935', *IPKO Documentation*, No. 29 (February) (Paris: International Information Center on Peace-Keeping Operations).
51. The cool reception that the *Brahimi Report* received in the Third World is a case in point. See Brahimi, Lakhdar (2001) *Peacekeeping and Conflict Resolution*, 2001 Alastair Buchan Memorial Lecture delivered on 22 March at Arundel House (London: International Institute for Strategic Studies).
52. The remark is attributed to Walker by Børresen, Jacob (1997) 'Nato som krise-handteringsverktøy', *Norsk Militært Tidsskrift*, Vol. 166, No. 10, p. 12 (4–15).
53. FM 3–07 (100–20) *Stability Operations and Support Operations* (Washington, DC: Headquarters Department of the Army, 2003), paras 4–72; *JWP 3–50: Peace Support Operations*, paras 167, 311.

54. Blome, Nikolaus (2000) 'Als Kfor-Kommandeur hat man wenig zu kommandieren', *Die Welt*, 19 June; Børresen, 'Nato som krisehandteringsverktøy'; Fischer, Paul-Georg (2000) 'Personal Experience from Kosovo September 1999–March 00', talk given at the Danish Institute of International Affairs, 23 August.
55. UN Doc. A/58/694, 26 January 2004, para. 8. See also UN Doc. S/res/1353, 13 June 2001.
56. Quoted from Lessons Learned Unit (1996) *Comprehensive Report on Lessons Learned From United Nations Assistance Mission For Rwanda* (UNAMIR) October 1993–April 1996 (New York: UN Department of Peacekeeping Operations), Part II, para. 8.
57. For a detailed analysis of the doctrinal debate see Jakobsen, 'The Emerging Consensus'.
58. *Wider Peacekeeping* (London: HMSO, 1995).
59. *Principles for the Employment of the Armed Forces Under UN Auspices* (Paris: Ministère de la Défense, 10 March 1995), p. 8.
60. AJP-3.4.1 *Peace Support Operations*, Ratification Draft, NATO, 1 December 2000; FM 3-07 (100-20) *Stability Operations and Support Operations; JWP 3-50: Peace Support Operations*.
61. See Joint Military Doctrine *Peace Support Operations* (Swedish Armed Forces, October 1997); *Peace Support Operations: A Working Draft Manual for African Military Practitioners, DWM 1-2000* (Harare: SADC Regional Peace-keeping Training Centre; Pretoria: Institute for Security Studies, February 2000).
62. Annan, Kofi A. (1998) 'Challenges of the New Peacekeeping', in Michael Doyle and Olara A. Otunnu (eds) *Peacemaking and Peacekeeping for the New Century* (Lanham, MD: Rowman and Littlefield), p. 173 (169–188); Annan, Kofi A. (1999) 'The Future of United Nations Peacekeeping', *UN Press Release*, SG/SM/6901/PKO/80, 23 February.
63. *Brahimi Report*, para. 55.
64. *Brahimi Report*, para. 87.
65. For the various rapid reaction initiatives and reforms made during the 1990s see Langille, Peter H. (2000) 'Conflict Prevention: Options for Rapid Deployment and UN Standing Forces', *International Peacekeeping*, Vol. 7, No. 1 (spring), pp. 219–253.
66. UN Doc. A/58/694, 26 January 2004, paras 20, 24–25; Peacekeeping Best Practices Unit (2004) *Lessons Learned Study on the Start-up Phase of the United Nations Mission in Liberia* (New York: UN Department of Peace-keeping Operations), p. 1.
67. UN Doc. S/2001/202, 7 March 2001, para. 25. As of March 2005, 16 nations had signed one or more SHIRBRIG documents, with five more nations participating as observers. See the SHIRBRIG website <http://www.shirbrig.dk> (5 March 2005).
68. UN Doc. A/58/694, 26 January 2004, para. 22.
69. UN News Service (2004) 'Press Briefing by UN Readiness Brigade', 23 June <http://www.un.org/News/briefings/docs/2004/SHIRBIRG.brf.doc.htm> (15 September 2004).
70. AFP (2004) 'EU Approves Rapid-Reaction Battlegroups', *The Australian*, 18 May.
71. Peacekeeping Best Practices Units, *Lessons Learned Study on the Start-up Phase of the United Nations Mission in Liberia*, pp. 9–10.
72. Durch, William J. et al., *The Brahimi Report and the Future of UN Peace Operations*, pp. 80–83.
73. Interview in the EU Council Secretariat, Brussels, 6 May 2004.

74. Quoted from Jakobsen, Peter Viggo (ed.) (2000) 'CIMIC – Civil–military Cooperation. Lessons Learned and Models for the Future', *DUPI Report*, No. 9/2000 (Copenhagen: Danish Institute of International Affairs), p. 47.
75. *Supplement to An Agenda for Peace* (UN Doc. A/50/60-S/1995/1, 3 January 1995), para. 45.
76. For a direct comparison of the different (training) requirements for both civilian and military personnel for Cold War and post-Cold War peace operations see Tiihonen, Ilkka (1998) 'Upgrading Pre-Deployment Training for UN Peace Operations', in *Managing Arms in Peace Processes: Training* (Geneva: UNIDIR), pp. 52–53 (35–73).
77. *Brahimi Report*, p. xi.
78. *Brahimi Report*, paras 133–145; Jett, Dennis C. (2000) *Why Peacekeeping Fails* (Houndmills: Palgrave Macmillan), p. 48.
79. See the UN website for peacekeeping training: <http://www.un.org/Depts/dpko/training/>.
80. Jakobsen, 'CIMIC – Civil–military Cooperation', p. 37.
81. Durch, William J. *et al.*, *The Brahimi Report and the Future of UN Peace Operations*, p. 80.
82. Quoted from Wilkie, Edith B. and Beth C. DeGrasse (2002) *A Force for Peace and Security: US and Allied Commanders' Views of the Military's Role in Peace Operations and the Impact on Terrorism of States in Conflict* (Washington, DC: Peace Through Law Education Fund), p. 38.
83. 'No Early Exit: NATO's Continuing Challenge in Bosnia', *ICG Balkans Report*, No. 110 (Sarajevo/Brussels: International Crisis Group, 22 May 2001), p. 5; Chauveau, Guy-Michel and Gian Giacomo Migone (2000) 'CIMIC and Police: Forging the "Missing Links" in Crisis Management', Draft Report, Sub-committee on Civilian Security and Cooperation, North Atlantic Assembly, 3 October, para 15; Piatt, Gregory (2001) 'Long-term Policing Options for Bosnia are High on NATO, UN Agendas', *Stars and Stripes European edition*, 21 November.
84. *Brahimi Report*, paras 76–83; Kelly, Michael J. (1999) 'Responsibility for Public Security in Peace Operations', in Helen Durham and Timothy L. H. McCormack (eds) *The Changing Face of Conflict and the Efficacy of International Humanitarian Law* (The Hague: Martinus Nijhoff), pp. 141–172; Strohmeyer, Hansjorg (2001) 'Collapse and Reconstruction of a Judicial System: The United Nations Missions in Kosovo and East Timor', *American Journal of International Law*, Vol. 95, No. 1 (January), pp. 46–63.
85. Jakobsen, 'Military Forces and Public Security Challenges'.
86. Durch, William J. et al., *The Brahimi Report and the Future of UN Peace Operations*, p. 107.
87. See Skov-Christensen, Per (1998) *FN på vrangen – en militær vurdering* (København: Borgen), p. 344.
88. Eknes, Åge (1993) 'Blue Helmets in a Blown Mission: UNPROFOR in Former Yugoslavia', *NUPI Research Report*, No. 174 (Oslo: Norwegian Institute of International Affairs), p. 49.
89. Lessons Learned Unit (1995) *The Comprehensive Report on Lessons Learned from United Nations Operation in Somalia (UNOSOM) April 1992–March 1995* (New York: UN Department of Peacekeeping Operations), para. 65.
90. Kühne, Winrich (1995) 'Lessons From Peacekeeping Operations in Angola, Mozambique, Somalia, Rwanda and Liberia', *Chaillot Papers*, No. 22 (December), p. 36.
91. *Supplement to An Agenda for Peace*, para. 46.
92. UN Doc. A/52/1, 3 September 1997, para 38.

93. Peacekeeping Best Practices Unit, *Lessons Learned From United Nations Peacekeeping Experiences in Sierra Leone*, p. 65.

94. *Brahimi Report*, p. 56. See also UN Doc. A/55/977, 1 June 2001, pp. 4, 90–92.

95. Peacekeeping Best Practices Unit, *Lessons Learned Study on the Start-up Phase of the United Nations Mission in Liberia*, p. 14.

96. UN Doc. A/58/694, 26 January 2004, paras 54–55.

97. Siegel, Pascale Combelles (1997) *Target Bosnia: Integrating Information Activities In Peace Operations* (Washington, DC: NDU Press).

98. UN Doc. A/58/694, 26 January 2004, para. 8.

99. For a treatment of intelligence that is illustrative in this respect, see International Peace Academy (1986) *The Peacekeeper's Handbook* (New York: Pergamon), p. 39.

100. Eriksson, Pär, Nils M. Rekkedal and Wegger Strømmen (1995) 'Militær informasjon ved internasjonale operasjoner', *FFI Rapport*, No. 95/02445 (Kjeller: Forsvarets Forskningsinstitutt), pp. 27–28; Raevsky, Andrei (1996) *Managing Arms in Peace Processes: Aspects of Psychological Operations and Intelligence* (Geneva: United Nations), p. 1.

101. Lessons Learned Unit, *Comprehensive Report on Lessons Learned From United Nations Assistance Mission For Rwanda (UNAMIR) October 1993–April 1996*.

102. Durch, William, J. *et al.*, *The Brahimi Report and the Future of UN Peace Operations*, pp. 38–39.

103. Aaser, Josefine Ingela (2003) 'Tackling Terrorism Together. Potential Benefits of Civil–Military Cooperation in Post-Conflict Territories – The Kosovo Case', *FFI Report*, 2003/00329 (Kjeller: Norwegian Defence Research Establishment), p. 32.

104. Hancock and Lord Ponsonby, 'International Policing in South-Eastern Europe', *WEU Document*, C/1721, 15 November 2000, para. 40; Piatt, Gregory (2000) 'Law-and-Order Duties Shifting Away From US Troops in Kosovo', *Stars and Stripes European edition*, 27 November.

105. Jones, Bruce D. (2001) *The Challenges of Strategic Coordination: Containing Opposition and Sustaining Implementation of Peace Agreements in Civil Wars*, IPA Policy Paper Series on Peace Implementation, CISAC-IPA Project on Peace Implementation (New York: International Peace Academy), p. 22.

106. Jakobsen Peter Viggo (2002) 'Samarbejdet mellem militære enheder og humanitære organisationer under fredsstøttende operationer: Et tvangsægteskab med lykkelig udgang?', *Militært Tidsskrift*, Vol. 131, No. 1 (marts), pp. 133–146; Williams, Michael C. (1998) 'Civil–Military Relations and Peacekeeping', *Adelphi Paper*, No. 321 (Oxford: Oxford University Press for IISS).

107. Weiss, Thomas G. (1998) 'Civilian–Military Interactions and Ongoing UN Reforms: DHA's Past and OCHA's Remaining Challenges', *International Peacekeeping*, Vol. 5, No. 4 (winter), pp. 49–70.

108. Aall, Pamela (2000) 'NGOs, Conflict Management, and Peacekeeping', *International Peacekeeping*, Vol. 7, No. 1 (spring), pp. 121–141.

109. Paris, Roland (1997) 'Peacebuilding and the Limits of Liberal Internationalism', *International Security*, Vol. 22, No 2. (fall), pp. 54–89; de Soto, Alvaro and Graciana del Castillo (1994) 'Obstacles to Peacebuilding', *Foreign Policy*, No. 94 (spring), pp. 69–83.

110. Jones, *The Challenges of Strategic Coordination: Containing Opposition and Sustaining Implementation of Peace Agreements in Civil Wars*; Suhrke,

Astri (2001) 'Peacekeepers as Nation-builders: Dilemmas of the UN in East Timor', *International Peacekeeping*, Vol. 8, No. 4 (winter), pp. 75–90.

111. For a more detailed analysis see Jakobsen, 'CIMIC – Civil–Military Cooperation'.

112. UN Department of Peacekeeping Operations (2004) *United Nations Peacekeeping Year in Review 2003. Para. X. Issues related to deployment of Peace Operations*, <http://www.un.org/Depts/dpko/dpko/pub/year_review03/Issues_related.htm> (11 November 2004).

113. *A Secure Europe in a Better World;* and *The National Security Strategy of the United States of America.*

4 The Danish approach to peace operations after the Cold War

> The Danish tanks changed the way to solve wider peacekeeping tasks forever. The tanks became a model for the existing NATO force in Bosnia.
> Lt General Michael Rose,
> commander of UNPROFOR, 1994–95[1]

Denmark reacted quicker than the other Nordic countries to the new situation created by the end of the Cold War. It was the first of the Nordics to initiate a fundamental restructuring of its armed forces, and the first to begin revising the traditional Nordic approach to peace operations. This makes Denmark the logical country to start with as Danish actions have influenced the other Nordic countries. As will become clear in the course of the next chapters, Denmark set examples that the other Nordic countries follow(ed). This chapter serves two objectives. The first and primary objective is to determine to what extent the new Danish approach meets the eleven requirements for success established in the previous chapter, but an effort is also made to explain why the Danish approach changed the way it did. The main points are summed up in a conclusion at the end.

Political will, legal framework and funds for all types of operations

The most straightforward way to determine the political willingness of a state to participate in peace operations is to look at the rhetoric employed by decision makers, the number and nature of its contributions, the level of domestic support, and finally the role played by the government in mobilizing and sustaining domestic support. Taken together these indicators will make it possible to estimate the strength, depth and evolution of the political willingness to participate in peace operations. In the Danish case they all point in the same direction, indicating a significant increase in political will.

Rhetoric

Although the participation in UN peacekeeping played an important role in Danish foreign policy at the rhetorical level during the Cold War, it was generally conspicuous by its absence in official statements and documents about Danish defence and security policy. This is no longer the case. In the course of the 1990s peace operations took centre stage in documents and statements related to defence and security policy as well. Firstly, these operations were constantly singled out for praise by the Danish defence, foreign and prime ministers. To give but one example, Foreign Minister Niels Helveg Petersen declared peacekeeping 'a matter of the highest priority' for Denmark in his address to the UN General Assembly in 1994.[2] Secondly, peace operations were defined as a main task of the armed forces when the law on the objectives, tasks and organization of the armed forces was revised in 1993, and their importance was further underlined in another revision in 2001.[3] Finally, their importance is visible in the strong concern voiced by former and current defence and foreign ministers that the defence opt-out preventing Danish participation in EU-led peace operations will destroy the prestige and influence generated by Denmark's active involvement in peace operations in the 1990s.[4] The defence opt-out is also perceived as a direct threat to the new post-Cold War foreign policy doctrine known as 'active internationalism'.[5] Niels Helveg Petersen even claimed that it played a role in his decision to resign as foreign minister in December 2000.[6]

Participation on the ground

By the end of 2002 the total number of Danish military personnel who had served on peace operations was close to 62,000.[7] This means that Denmark's annual average contribution of military personnel to peace operations has more than doubled since the end of the Cold War, jumping from 831 during the Cold War to 2,129 in the 1990–2002 period. Since Danish military personnel generally serve six-month tours, it follows that Denmark has sustained an average of approximately 1,000 personnel abroad on peace operations on a continuous basis in the post-Cold War era. Although this level has been established as the maximum that the armed forces should be able to sustain abroad, this ceiling has been exceeded each year since 1997. A record total deployment of 2,323 troops at the same time was set when the Danish Kosovo battalion was deployed in August 1999.[8] The need to sustain more than 1,000 personnel abroad on a continuous basis put considerable strain on the armed forces, and the sustainable international capacity of the armed forces was therefore doubled to 2,000 in the 2005–09 Defence Agreement passed by the Danish parliament (Folketinget) in 2004.[9]

Qualitatively the changes are equally dramatic. As is clear from Table 4.1 the navy and the air force became involved in the 1990s and the tasks have

Table 4.1 Danish military personnel in peace operations 1948–99

	1948–89	*1990s*	*Total*
Army	34,100	17,700	51,800
Navy	0	1,200	1,200
Air force	0	500	500
Total	34,100	19,400	53,500

Source: Lyng, Jørgen (ed.) (2000) Ved forenede kræfter: forsvarets øverste militære ledelse: forsvarschefsembedet og forsvarets udvikling 1950–2000 (Vedbæk: Forsvarskommandoen).

also changed. During the Cold War Denmark said no to requests for combat troops to Korea and restricted its involvement to traditional peacekeeping operations where the troops were allowed to use force in self-defence only. The Congo operation, which started out as peacekeeping and ended up as peace enforcement, is the only exception to this rule, but the Danish troops serving in the Congo, mainly military police, did not become involved in combat operations. This restriction was lifted in the 1990s where Danish forces took part in several peace enforcement (Chapter VII) operations. Denmark was thus one of the few nations that volunteered to deploy troops to defend the 'safe areas' in Bosnia in 1993, and the tank squadron deployed in Tuzla in 1994 became involved in direct combat with the Bosnian Serbs on a number of occasions. In one of them, which made international headlines, the Danish tanks fired 72 shells successfully taking out all the Serb positions that had opened fire on them.[10] The Danish Army subsequently participated in NATO's IFOR, SFOR and KFOR operations in Bosnia and Kosovo and ISAF in Afghanistan. Danish F-16s took part in bombing missions during Operation Allied Force in 1999, and Danish special forces were involved in combat operations during Operation Enduring Freedom in Afghanistan in the spring of 2002. Denmark also contributed a submarine and a corvette to the US-led war against Iraq in 2003 and sent a 500-strong army contingent to take part in the occupation after Baghdad had fallen.

Danish contributions are, in other words, no longer limited to the UN as was the case during the Cold War. Danish forces have participated in UN-commanded operations, operations delegated by the UN to other organizations and coalitions of the willing. The ban on the participation in peace enforcement has been lifted, and Denmark has even gone so far as to participate in offensive enforcement/warfighting operations without UN mandates.

Denmark's civilian personnel contributions have also grown considerably. The Danish Ministry of Foreign Affairs (MFA) established a civilian rapid reaction mechanism, the International Humanitarian Service (IHS), in 1995 and more than 1,100 civilian experts, mainly election monitors, were deployed abroad through the IHS between 1995 and 2001.[11] The Danish police have sent an ever growing number of police officers abroad since 1992, and the rescue personnel and experts from the Danish Emergency Management Agency (DEMA) spent 5,664 man-days abroad on international missions in the 1991–2001 period.[12]

Domestic support

After a shaky start the increased international involvement has been characterized by strong political and public support. In 1990–92 the growing international involvement was characterized by some hesitancy and controversy. It was only with difficulty that Uffe Ellemann-Jensen, the Danish foreign minister, managed to obtain the necessary support in parliament for his proposal to send a corvette to the Gulf in August 1990 to take part in the naval blockade against Iraq. The Social Liberal Party (Det Radikale Venstre), which was part of the coalition government, and the largest opposition party, the Social Democratic Party (socialdemokratiet), only accepted the deployment on condition that the corvette did not take part in combat operations, and these parties also blocked subsequent attempts by Ellemann-Jensen and the Progress Party (Fremskridtspartiet) to allow it to do so after the Gulf War had begun in 1991.[13] In addition, the Social Democrats prevented Danish participation in the humanitarian intervention to save the Kurds in April of 1991.[14] This disagreement was also reflected among the public at large. As Table 4.2 demonstrates, opinion polls from January and February 1991 showed slight majorities either in favour or against military participation.[15]

Controversy reappeared the following year when parliament debated whether Denmark should contribute to the UN force being established in Bosnia with an expanded mandate to use force beyond self-defence. Participation in the mission was not controversial; the problem was whether international service should be voluntary or mandatory for regular personnel in the armed forces. Intense negotiations resulted in a compromise allowing regulars to say no to international service. Again the political disagreement was reflected in public opinion with 53 per cent believing that international service should be voluntary and 46 per cent believing that it should be mandatory.[16] The issue was finally laid to rest when a new law made international service mandatory for all regulars joining the armed forces after 1 January 1994. The personnel already serving before this date were given the option to declare once and for all whether they were willing to serve on international missions or not. Only 5 per cent said no to international service.[17]

Since then the international engagement has enjoyed strong political and public support. The political parties situated in the centre on the traditional left–right continuum, which make up the large majority in the Danish parliament (the Centre Democrat Party (Centrumdemokraterne), the Christian People's Party (Kristeligt Folkeparti), the Conservative People's Party (Det Konservative Folkeparti), the Liberal Party (Venstre), the Social

Table 4.2 Public support for Danish participation in specific military operations since 1990

Operation	Polling dates	For (%)	Against (%)
Naval embargo against Iraq	August 1990	73	11
Operation Desert Storm in Kuwait	January–February 1991	44–47	44–47[a]
Possible operation to end the civil war in Bosnia expected to involve a risk of high Danish losses	July–August 1992	54	37
Operation Alba in Albania	April 1997	45	39
Possible attack on Iraq	February 1998	61	31
Possible attack on Serbia	June 1998	66	15
Operation Allied Force in Serbia	March–May 1999	63–74	20–25[b]
Operation Enduring Freedom in Afghanistan	December 2001	63	24
Operation Iraqi Freedom	March–April 2003	35–46	42–56[c]
Peace operation in Iraq	October 2003	77	21

The polls were conducted for various Danish newspapers and *Eurobarometer* by professional polling institutes using representative samples of 500–1343 persons (Arnum, Sten, 'Dansk støtte til landkrig er faldende,' *Jyllands-Posten* <http://www.jp.dk>, 5 May 1999; Cordsen, Christine, Kristian Klarskov and Jakob Nielsen, 'Danskerne imod krig i Irak,' *Politiken*, 19 March 2003, p. 1; Due-Nielsen, Carsten and Nikolaj Petersen (eds) *Dansk Udenrigspolitisk Årbog 1992* (København: Jurist- og Økonomforbundets Forlag, 1993), p. 510; Eurobarometer, 'Iraq and Peace in the World,' *Flash Europarometer*, No. 151, 8–16 October 2003; Gallup, 'NATOs bombning af Serbien,' *Berlingske Tidende*, 28 March 1999, p. 6; Hansen, Eva Rymann, 'MEGAFON: Danskerne mere positive over for krigen,' <http://nyhederne.tv2.dk> 5 May 2003; Heurlin, Bertel and Hans Mouritzen (1998) (eds) *Danish Foreign Policy Yearbook 1998* (Copenhagen: Danish Institute of International Affairs), p. 155; Heurlin, Bertel and Hans Mouritzen (1999) (eds) *Danish Foreign Policy Yearbook 1999* (Copenhagen: Danish Institute of International Affairs), pp. 220–221, 223; Møller, Peter and Eva Rymann Hansen, 'MEGAFON: Folkelig krigsmodstand, men støtte til Fogh,' <http://nyhederne.tv2.dk> 27 March 2003; Sonar (1999) 'Danskernes holdning til NATO's aktion,' *Jyllands-Posten*, 9 April 1999, Section 2, p. 4; Vilstrup-instituttet, 'Danskernes reaktion på NATO-aktionen,' *Politiken*, 31 March 1999, p. 8; Weiss, Jakob, 'Gallup: Dansk ja til krig,' *Berlingske Tidende*, 26 March 2003, p. 1.)

Notes
a   Based on two polls.
b   Based on four polls.
c   Based on four polls.

Democratic Party and the Social Liberal Party), have voted yes to the bills involving deployment of Danish forces abroad on international missions passed between 1993 and January 2004, except one: the decision to partici-pate in the US-led war against Iraq in 2003. The failure of the USA to obtain a UN mandate for the war split the Danish parliament down the middle, and the decision to go to war was based on a slim 11-vote majority (61 in favour versus 50 against). The political consensus was quickly re-established, however. Only two months later a large majority supported the deployment of a contingent to take part in the post-war stabilization of Iraq.

The parties on the Left, the Red-Green Alliance (Enhedslisten) and the Socialist People's Party (Socialistisk Folkeparti), have voted no on most occasions whereas the parties on the Right, the Progress Party and Danish People's Party (Dansk Folkeparti, founded in 1995 by breakaway members of the Progress Party), have voted yes to all deployments except one (UNMEE in Ethiopia/Eritrea) since 1999.

The broad political consensus has not surprisingly translated itself into strong support in the Danish media and in the public for the new international role played by the Danish military. As Table 4.2 makes clear, public support for military participation in UN operations has grown steadily during the 1990s, and the same pattern is visible if we look at the figures with respect to Danish military participation in specific operations in Table 4.3. It is worth noting that the breakdown and quick re-establishment of the political consensus over Iraq in 2003 is mirrored in public opinion as well.

Government role in mobilizing and sustaining domestic support

An important part of the explanation of the domestic consensus on peace operations is revealed in Table 4.2: the public has been convinced that there is a link between the supposedly 'idealistic' (UN) peace operations and national security. This link is generally regarded as difficult to establish, but as mentioned in Chapter 2, all the Nordic governments have successfully made this case consistently since their involvement in UN peacekeeping began during the Cold War. The Danish politicians supporting the international engagement continued to rely on a combination of national

Table 4.3 Public support for participation in UN operations in general

	Do you support Danish military participation in UN operations in the Balkans?		Do you support Danish military participation in UN operations outside of Europe?		Will Danish participation in UN operations help secure the peace in Denmark and in Europe in the longer term?	
	Yes (%)	No (%)	Yes (%)	No (%)	Yes (%)	No (%)
April 1994	69.5	30.5	55.1	44.9	72.3	27.8
October 1996	74.8	25.3	52.5	47.4	76.7	23.2
October 1998	85.7	14.3	61.2	38.9	82.8	17.2
October 2000	85.1	14.8	59.4	40.6	79.5	20.5
October 2002	82.2	7.8	73.6	26.4	81.4	18.6

Source: Danish Armed Forces Faculty of Leadership and Psychology. The polls were conducted by Statistics Denmark and based on representative samples of 939–1472 persons (Kousgaard, Erik (1998) *Befolkningens forsvarsvilje maj 1975–oktober 1998*, FCLPUB, No. 147 (København: Forsvarets Center for Lederskab), p. 7; Kousgaard, Erik (2000) *Befolkningens forsvarsvilje maj 1975–oktober 2000*, FCLPUB, No. 151 (København: Forsvarets Center for Lederskab), p. 8; Kousgaard, Erik (2003) *Befolkningens forsvarsvilje maj 1975–oktober 2002*, FCLPUB, No. 153 (København: Forsvarsakademiet), p. 7).

interest and idealism to justify the growing involvement in peace operations in the 1990s. They displayed strong and sustained leadership on the issue, missing no opportunity to spell out the linkage between national and international security to the Danish public. An early example of these efforts can be found in a newspaper article by the Danish foreign minister Uffe Ellemann-Jensen from October 1992:

> Events in former Yugoslavia also bear the seed to another – and far more direct – threat to us. If the rest of Europe watch passively while human rights and minority rights are trampled in former Yugoslavia, it sends the signal to future combatants that violence pays. This example can quickly become a threat to all of us if it is allowed to spread ... we in Europe have reached a level of civilization that does not allow us to ignore war in our own part of the world. The war in the Balkans is not a distant war. It is our values, our way of life and, in the final instance, our freedom that are being challenged in former Yugoslavia. If we are not ready to actively defend these values, we undermine our own security in the long run. War and peace is no longer a question of defending Denmark's borders. If the stability in Europe is to be made secure – and that goes without saying – we have to do our part. We have to contribute to prevent and solve conflicts and keep the peace – also in areas which are not close to our own borders. If we remain passive, we risk undermining our own security.[18]

Preparing the public for casualties was also seen as important for sustaining public support from the beginning. As Helge Adam Møller, member of parliament for the Conservative People's Party, pointed out in October 1993:

> Unless we succeed in explaining the background and the idea behind the establishment of the Danish Reaction Brigade to the entire popula- tion ... including that it will involve greater risks than before ... and we must not hide this, we risk getting into serious difficulties the day some of these units become involved in combat and take casualties.[19]

The emphasis placed on preparing the public for possible casualties helps to explain why the eleven deaths suffered by the Danish armed forces in international missions between 1990 and 2003 have had no impact on the strong political and public backing that the Danish participation in peace operations enjoys.[20] Whether it will be sufficient to sustain the high level of support in the face of significant casualties remains to be seen, but odds are that it will. Recent research has thus found that Western publics are prepared to accept high casualties provided that the military operation in question is backed by a united political elite, has a clear humanitarian and/or national security objective, a reasonable chance of success and the government has explained to the public why it is necessary to put the armed forces in harm's way. Danish policy makers have followed this recipe with great success since the end of the Cold War, and the Danish public is likely to be willing to accept considerable casualties if their leaders stick to it.[21]

Permissive legal framework

When the Cold War ended, Danish participation in peace operations was regulated by the parliamentary decision establishing the standby force for use in UN peacekeeping operations in 1964, which was described in Chapter 2. It restricted Danish participation to UN-commanded peace-keeping operations based on Chapter VI mandates and gave the government the power to commit troops without asking parliament for consent. All it had to do was to consult the Foreign Affairs Committee before making a decision. The deployments in Namibia in 1989 and Croatia in April 1992 were consequently decided without a vote in parliament.

From December 1993 onwards a number of legal adjustments have been made in order to facilitate the participation of Danish troops in international missions. The first took place in December 1993 when the 1964 parliamentary decision was repealed as a result of the decision to establish the Danish Reaction Brigade (DRB). This decision and the new laws accompanying it made it possible for Danish forces to participate in operations mandated by the OSCE, operations conducted by NATO with either OSCE or UN mandates, and in peace operations involving the use of force beyond self-defence.[22] In addition, international service was made compulsory for the regulars in the Danish armed forces as of 1 January 1994.[23]

The decision to permit Danish participation in enforcement operations involving the use of force beyond self-defence changed the decision-making process slightly as the government is constitutionally obliged to ask parliament for consent whenever Danish forces are deployed on military operations involving the use of force beyond self-defence.[24] The blurring of the distinction between peacekeeping operations limited to self-defence and enforcement operations with wider mandates led to a new political practice in the 1990s, which saw the government asking for consent from parliament for all major troop contributions regardless of the mission type. Major deployments without a vote in parliament are consequently no longer conceivable.

Another important change easing Danish participation in peace operations followed in 2001 when another modification of the Act on the Aims, Tasks and Organization of the Armed Forces removed the legal require-ment for UN and OSCE mandates. This change resulted from a desire to avoid the controversy generated by the participation in NATO's Opera-tion Allied Force, which was conducted against Serbia in 1999 without a

UN mandate,[25] as well as the decisions by the EU and NATO reserving their right to use force without UN mandates in the future should the need arise.[26]

As a result, the only restriction in domestic law preventing full Danish participation in peace operations is the defence opt-out, one of four, forced upon the government and a majority in parliament by the rejection of the Maastricht Treaty in the June 1992 referendum. The defence opt-out presently prevents Danish participation in EU-led peace operations, and although opinion polls had begun to show stable majority support for repealing the defence opt-out,[27] and the principal parties supporting the opt-outs had reassessed their positions by late 2004, the timing of a new referendum remained unclear at the time of writing.

Financing

Financial considerations have thus far not been an important constraint on Danish participation. The Ministry of Defence (MoD) expenditures on international operations have grown significantly since 1988 when they amounted to DKK 91 million.[28] As is clear from Table 4.4, the expenditures have exceeded the amounts allocated in the defence agreements for international operations in every single year since 1996, when a separate account for this item was created in the defence budget. Until then military participation in peace operations had been financed on an *ad hoc* basis outside of the defence budget.[29] Special reserves totalling DKK 750 million (2002 prices) were established for 2002 and 2003 to cover expenditures in excess of the amounts appropriated for international operations in the

Table 4.4 Ministry of Defence budgets and expenditures on peace operations (current prices; DKK million[a])

	1996	1997	1998	1999	2000	2001	2002	2003[c]	2004[c]
UN, OSCE and NATO operations[b]	700.5	622.2	594.3	979.8	1,134.7	912.5	1,037.4	1,187.0	702.5
EU and OSCE observers	13.9	15.8	15.1	18.3	11.2	6.7	7.8	5.7	5.7
Total expenditures	714.4	638	609.4	998.1	1,145.9	919.2	1,045.2	1,192.7	708.2
Budgets[d]	581	545	557	572	586	600	616	631	643

Source: Danish MoD.

Notes
a DKK 100 = EUR 13.45.
b Gross amounts including storage figures.
c Estimates.
d Net amounts meaning that the figures are not directly comparable with the costs. Still the differences are so large that the expenditures clearly exceed the budget figures.

defence budget,[30] but they were quickly exhausted. In August 2002 Svend Aage Jensby, the defence minister, thus estimated the total deficit for the 2000–04 period covered in the defence agreement to at least DKK 800 million.[31]

On top of the military expenditures come the expenditures on civilian and humanitarian operations, which are covered by the MFA. They have also risen sharply in the 1990s. The cost of running of the IHS, the rapid reaction arrangement for civilian experts, has risen from DKK 15 million in its first year of operation in 1995 to over DKK 50 million from 1998 onwards.[32]

Even though the expenses have continued to exceed the amounts agreed to in the defence agreements, the deficits have, surprisingly perhaps, not become a serious political issue or resulted in calls for reducing the military involvement from the parties behind the defence consensus. The willingness of the defence parties to continue to break the budget to enable Danish forces to participate in new missions provides yet another indication of the importance that they attribute to the Danish involvement in peace operations.

Explaining the activism

No doubt the single most important factor explaining the activist foreign policy and its flagship, the high profile in peace operations, is the end of the Cold War and the disappearance of the Soviet threat to Danish security. Strategically, the end of the Cold War moved Denmark from the frontline to the backwater. In NATO's collective defence structure Denmark is no longer a receiver of reinforcements, but a provider of them. Today, two-thirds of the Danish Army is tasked to take up positions outside of the country in a crisis.[33] The military threat from the East was officially buried in 1992 in official reports commissioned by the MoD,[34] and this paved the way for the establishment of the DRB in November of that year.

That the end of the Cold War gave Denmark unparalleled freedom of action does not explain why the opportunity to conduct an activist foreign policy was seized. Activism and the involvement of the armed forces in peace operations going beyond self-defence was not a 'natural' choice. It was unexpected and generally seen as a clear break with the past by politicians, foreign policy officials and commentators alike in the early 1990s, and many doubted that it would last.[35] A combination of external and internal factors explains why it did.

External factors

Four external factors determined the form and contents of the Danish activism. The outbreak of war close to home in the Balkans gave Denmark a security interest in preventing the conflict from spreading and stemming the flow of refugees. The nature of the Balkan operations creating the need for a more robust approach forced Danish decision to go beyond traditional peacekeeping. The memberships of the EU and NATO generated external pressures as well as internal desires in the foreign policy establishment for Danish participation. It was seen as necessary in order to maintain and enhance Danish influence in the two organizations, and as an obligation that a responsible member of these organizations had to fulfil. Finally, the growing involvement was facilitated by the strong emphasis placed on democracy and human rights after the end of the Cold War. This made it easy to legitimize the growing involvement in peace operations as a continuation of the support for UN peacekeeping operations that had been one of the 'cornerstones' in Danish foreign policy during the Cold War.[36]

While these factors can explain why Denmark, the other Nordics and most other West European countries became increasingly involved in peace operations in the Balkans, they cannot explain the differences between Denmark and the other Nordic states. Denmark was quicker to embrace operations going beyond traditional peacekeeping, it was quicker to give priority to peace operations in its defence planning, and it was the only one to give its military forces pride of place in its foreign policy. The other Nordic countries thus placed far greater emphasis on civilian crisis management, at least rhetorically. To understand these differences we need to move from the international to the national level.

The dynamic duo

The necessary conditions for the activist policy at the domestic level, the political consensus and the strong public support, did not exist in 1990 when the corvette *Olfert Fischer* was sent to the Gulf. Nor did they exist in 1992 when troops were sent to Bosnia to take part in a peace operation that involved a real risk of combat. They were created by an active effort spearheaded by Foreign Minister Uffe Ellemann-Jensen and Defence Minister Hans Hækkerup, who, ashamed of the role Denmark had played in NATO as 'footnote country' in the 1980s, strongly believed that Denmark should play a more active role in the management of international peace and security.[37]

It has become commonplace within the discipline of international relations to dismiss the importance of individuals in foreign policy,[38] but without the pivotal roles played by Ellemann-Jensen and Hækkerup, then defence spokesman for the Social Democrats, *Olfert Fischer* was unlikely to have been sent to the Gulf. Together they played a key role in persuading the sceptics within the government and the Social Democratic Party to accept the deployment of a naval vessel instead of limiting the Danish contribution to humanitarian and medical support.

Similarly, it is also hard to imagine that Denmark would have sent tanks to Bosnia in 1993 had Hækkerup not been the defence minister. A weaker and less confident minister is unlikely to have stood his or her ground and backed the proposal from General Jørgen Lyng, the chief of defence, in the face of scepticism from the Danish foreign minister and strong opposition from the UN Secretariat in New York, the UN force commander in Bosnia and close friends such as Thorvald Stoltenberg, who at the time was the UN-appointed mediator in Yugoslavia. Unlike his Dutch counterpart, who bowed to the pressure from the UN and deployed troops in the safe area of Srebrenica without heavy weapons (a decision that paved the way for the 1995 massacre), Hækkerup did not yield. Instead, he aligned himself with Anders Björck, his Swedish colleague, to make the tanks a precondition for the deployment of the Danish and Swedish contingents in Tuzla.[39]

The deployment of *Olfert Fischer* to the Gulf got the snowball rolling and the subsequent (from a Danish perspective) successful deployments in Croatia and Bosnia created an avalanche that changed the Danes' understanding of their appropriate role in the world. The result was the political consensus and the strong political support that have underpinned the activist foreign policy and the high profile in peace operations since then. At the turn of the century this profile was no longer a topic of debate, it was an axiom that hardly anyone questioned.

This is not to say that Ellemann-Jensen and Hækkerup did it alone; only that they were instrumental in pushing the armed forces to the forefront of Danish foreign policy at a very early stage when it was considered controversial to do so, and other options more in line with past policies seemed more 'natural'. They were supported by other politicians, officials in the defence and foreign ministries and opinion leaders who shared the view that Denmark should pursue an activist foreign policy.[40] And they were lucky. The Danish involvement has thus far resulted in very few casualties. If the early deployments to the Gulf or the Balkans had resulted in significant casualties before the consensus and the strong public support had been consolidated, the whole enterprise would probably have been called off in favour of the traditional low-key approach emphasizing the virtues of traditional peacekeeping, civilian crisis management and humanitarian assistance. As we shall see in later chapters, this was the approach initially chosen by the other Nordic countries.

Factors determining specific contributions

Of the approximately 62,000 Danish personnel deployed on peace missions in the 1948–2002 period, 60,000 have been deployed in the Middle East, Cyprus and the Balkans.[41] Denmark has, in other words, during and after the Cold War primarily contributed to operations so close to home that they were likely to affect national security or result in refugees arriving on its doorstep. This type of indirect security interest, an interest in showing solidarity with allies in the EU and NATO and especially the USA, and the prospects for Nordic cooperation have been the most important factors determining Danish contributions with sizable contingents after the Cold War.[42] These factors can account for the Balkan deployments and the participation in the war against terrorism, the principal purpose of which is to demonstrate solidarity with the USA, as well as the general lack of interest displayed in operations further away from home without participation of important allies or the Nordic partners. The difficulties and costs associated with deployments in distant corners of the globe serve to reinforce this pattern, but such considerations will usually not prove decisive. The Danish deployments in Afghanistan as part of the war against terror demonstrate that distance loses its importance when the political stakes are perceived to be high. Finally, it should be added that deployments with NATO allies and the Nordics serve to enhance force protection because interoperability is high. The huge and widening quality gap separating Western forces from the armed forces of the Third World is also deterring Denmark from deploying troops in operations with limited Western participation. The lesson Denmark drew from Srebrenica was never to deploy troops in a UN-commanded operation involving a real risk of combat.[43]

The principal exception to this pattern, the Danish participation in the operation in Eritrea and Ethiopia (UNMEE) in 2000, actually confirms it because it can be explained by special circumstances: Hækkerup's burning desire to get his brain child, SHIRBRIG, deployed on a successful mission as quickly as possible after it had been made available to the UN. As he makes clear in his memoirs, Hækkerup feared that SHIRBRIG would become a failure if it did not succeed on its first mission. 'A soufflé only rises once,' as he puts it. His initial attempt to get it deployed in Lebanon failed due to Israel's sudden withdrawal, so SHIRBRIG ended up in Eritrea instead.[44]

The concerns triggered by the prospects of a deployment in Sub-Saharan Africa are illustrative of the limits of the Danish commitment to peace operations. Poul Nyrup Rasmussen, the Danish prime minister, kept delaying the deployment out of concern for the security of the troops, and there was also concern that the public would not support sending troops to Africa.[45] This was despite the fact that UNMEE, without a doubt, was the safest operation the UN has conducted since the end of the Cold War. Prior to deployment everything pointed towards a success and the briefing that the Danish contingent received upon their arrival from their commander said it all: 'The situation is very peaceful. In a short while we will take in your weapons for storage. Only guards will be allowed to carry weapons. The rest of you won't need them'.[46]

Danish troops would never have been sent to Africa had SHIRBRIG not been a Danish prestige project, and the worries surrounding the mission show just how reluctant Danish decision makers are with respect to deploying troops on missions that do not involve indirect security interests, do not enable Denmark to signal solidarity with important allies or enhance

Nordic cooperation. While idealism and humanitarianism will always play a role and be invoked when a mission is contemplated, such considerations will not in themselves be sufficiently powerful to trigger a major Danish deployment.[47]

Civilian and military personnel deployable at short notice

Civilian rapid reaction forces have been established by the MFA, the Danish police and DEMA. The MFA established its rapid reaction arrangement, the IHS, in 1995. The IHS has established a roster of 330 personnel and is constantly deploying 30–40 persons abroad on missions for the UN, the OSCE and other international organizations. While election monitoring is the single most important activity, the IHS has also sent human rights monitors, political scientists and legal advisors abroad.[48] The IHS made experts available to the UNSAS in 1999 and to the OSCE's Rapid Expert Assistance and Cooperation Teams (REACT) the following year.[49]

Danish police officers served in the UNFICYP in Cyprus for ten years in the 1964–74 period but none were involved in peace operations again until 1992. In 2000 the number of man years for international service was increased from 50 to 75, a capacity which has been fully exploited since then. A further expansion of the Danish capacity was announced in November 2001 when Denmark made 125 police officers available for the 5,000-strong EU rapid reaction civilian police force that became operational in 2003. Of the 125 officers, 25 officers are available for deployment at short notice.[50]

DEMA bases its contributions on a service package concept (flexible equipment modules with personnel) that can be applied in connection with responses to disasters and complex emergencies. This concept enables DEMA to deploy a fully equipped operational task force designed according to a specific type of disaster within twelve hours. Examples of the service packages offered for international operations include a mobile hospital, a search and rescue package, a rapid logistic service team, and a logistics advisory and monitor service. DEMA personnel and equipment have been made available to UN rapid reaction arrangements, and a further strengthening of DEMA's capacity for international operations is planned in the 2003–06 period.[51]

The 4,500-strong DRB forms the backbone of the army's rapid reaction capacity. It is organized as a mechanized infantry brigade capable of sustaining longer periods of independent combat to enable it to participate in a warfighting role as part of NATO's reaction forces and the Danish defence forces. The entire brigade can in principle be deployed abroad, but personnel availability problems all but rule out contributions exceeding two battalions at any one time. The DRB was originally intended to give Denmark a capacity to deploy and sustain 1,500 troops abroad on international peace missions on a continuous basis. However, recruitment problems and shortages of regular personnel with specialized skills forced a reduction to the 2003 capacity of 1,000 troops. This number can be increased to 1,500 personnel for a limited period of one to two years.[52] The 2005–09 Defence Agreement significantly enhances Denmark's international capacity through the establishment of a new brigade consisting entirely of regulars, which can be deployed abroad at short notice in 'first-wave' operations. In theory this should give the Danish armed forces the capacity to sustain 2,000 personnel (1,500 army and 500 navy and air force) abroad, but recruitment problems may well prevent the attainment of this objective.

As a general rule, Danish contributions to peace operations will be put together from the forces listed in Table 4.5. Most forces are 'multi-hatted',

Table 4.5 Military rapid reaction forces (2004)

	NATO High Readiness/Response Forces	*NORDCAPS*	*SHIRBRIG*
Army	1 light reconnaissance unit Danish Reaction Brigade 4 patrols from the special forces 1 electronic reconnaissance company	1 mechanized infantry battalion 1 armoured battalion 1 light reconnaissance unit 1 M 109 artillery battalion 1 combat engineer company 1 air defence battery (Stinger) 1 military police detachment	1 HQ staff company 1 light reconnaissance unit 1 military police detachment
Navy	1 corvette 1 ocean patrol vessel with helicopter 5 STANDARD FLEX 300 multi-role vessels 1 command support ship 3 submarines (periodically)	1 ocean patrol vessel 2 mine clearing vessels 1 command support ship	. .
Air force	12 F-16 fighters which may be supplemented with 4 F-16 reconnaissance planes 1 logistics support element 3 C-130 Hercules transport planes 1 air defence battery (Stinger)	1 C-130 Hercules transport plane 1 helicopter	. .

Source: Danish MoD.

having been made available for several rapid reaction arrangements, and they can obviously only be used by one rapid reaction arrangement at a time.

The forces made available to the NATO High Readiness/Response Forces must be ready for deployment in 5–30 days whereas the forces made available for NORDCAPS and SHIRBRIG have to be ready for deployment in 30 days. Since Denmark lacks strategic lift capability, quick deployment outside of Europe will depend on assistance from other nations as was the case with the operation in Afghanistan in 2002 where the Danish special forces were flown to the theatre by the US Air Force. In principle, the Danish reaction forces are available for worldwide deployment apart from the Arctic and various jungle and desert areas requiring specialized training and equipment.[53] In practice, as we have seen, most deployments have occurred in places around the Mediterranean.

Denmark has had difficulty in meeting these readiness levels with respect to battalion-sized army contributions. In the Danish interpretation, NATO's readiness levels do not apply to peace operations, only Article 5 defence missions, and – if asked off the record – few officers believe that Denmark would be capable of mobilizing the entire DRB on time in an Article 5 emergency. Response times will consequently be longer for new and unexpected peace operations. The first unexpected deployment undertaken after the establishment of the DRB demonstrated this, as it took a total of eight weeks to get the KFOR contingent deployed in Kosovo in 1999.[54] This operation also pointed to a potential risk of relying on volunteer conscripts on contract for unexpected operations involving a risk of high-intensity conflict: that they may fail to report for service when called up. Some 59 refused to go to Kosovo when they received their mobilization orders, and although persuasion and threats of law suits eventually reduced the number of 'no-shows' to 29, and more than 200 volunteered to take their places, this episode demonstrated the vulnerability of the current arrangement. If an invasion of Kosovo had proved necessary, the refusals would no doubt have been much higher, and this raised questions about the suitability of the Danish model with respect to generating sizable army contributions for future UN-authorized enforcement operations involving high-intensity combat. The decision to establish a rapid reaction army brigade made up of regulars in the 2005–09 Defence Agreement addresses this weakness and should give Denmark the capacity to provide capable army units for enforcement and warfighting operations at short notice.

Training to prepare the civilian and military personnel for their many new tasks

This requirement is met insofar as new training programmes have been introduced to prepare both civilian and military personnel for the complexities of contemporary peace operations. At the same time, criticism of both these training programmes also suggests the need for further improvements. IHS volunteers have thus been pressing continuously for more training, and a study done by the Institute of Military Psychology of soldiers serving in IFOR in 1997 revealed that 50 per cent were dissatisfied with the pre-mission training they had received.[55]

The training provided for IHS volunteers by the MFA is very limited reflecting the fact that applicants have to be experienced and able to take care of themselves in order to be accepted. The MFA runs two types of weekend courses, an introductory course for new volunteers and courses with relevant topics such as conflict resolution, human rights and democratization. Some experienced IHS members have also been sent on advanced international courses. In 2002 security courses were introduced for all personnel requiring it who go on humanitarian missions.[56]

The Danish police provides its volunteers for international missions with a two-week introduction course providing them with a basic understanding of international operations, international organizations, NGOs, human rights and relevant skills such as radio communications, map reading, security training, first aid, stress management, etc. This course is then supplemented with a 1½-day mission-oriented course before deployment.[57] The fact that some of the courses are held at Vordingborg Barracks ensures close cooperation with the Danish Army. The two-week course is open to foreigners as well.

Since the establishment of the DRB in 1994 until 2004 when the conscription period was reduced to four months, most army personnel serving on international missions were conscripts who had signed a DRB contract.[58] All conscripts who expressed interest in joining the DRB were placed in units intended for international missions at the various army regiments supplying troops to the DRB. They then received the standard conscript training focusing on basic military skills and warfighting for 8–12 months. Volunteers, who signed DRB contracts upon the completion of their basic training, then received a further five weeks of supplementary training in peace operations and two weeks of mission-related training before going on a six-month tour of duty.

The introduction of a new four-month conscription period from August 2004 changed this system significantly and in early 2005 a new programme was still not in place. The basic components will remain the same. The primary function of the four-month period is to find volunteers for international service. The volunteers who sign DRB contracts will then receive basic military training and special training preparing them for peace operations before they are deployed abroad. The training provided by the new system will be more focused and at a higher level than before but the training for peace operations training will remain the same. It will involve the following: specialist training; unit training at platoon level, including live firing; supplementary training in peace operation techniques; and field exercises at battalion and brigade level. This general training is supplemented by mission-related training consisting of courses on mission-specific knowledge, special techniques including riot control, special equipment, live firing exercises and medical checks.

The principal difference between these models and the Cold War one described in Chapter 2 is that most DRB conscripts train in the units they will be deployed with for at least nine months before going on a mission. This change was introduced in order to enhance the ability of the troops to cope with the new complexities and the higher levels of stress that most contemporary missions involve. Most volunteers on DRB contracts will go on a rotation mission after the completion of their training and then remain on standby for four years. During this time they receive 14 weeks of refresher training. Key personnel such as leaders, signallers and artillery observers, are called up two or three times each year to take part in exercises, study periods, etc.

Training in peace operations has become an integrated part of the training of Danish officers, something unheard of during the Cold War. In addition, Danish officers of all ranks also participate in the courses run as part of the Nordic UN peacekeeping training programme described in Chapter 2. The programme has been expanded to meet the challenges of the 1990s and was renamed NORDCAPS in 1997.[59] Joint Nordic peace operations exercises have been conducted under NORDCAPS auspices every year since 1997 within the framework of NATO's Partnership for Peace programme.

A final innovation that deserves mentioning here is the growing number of joint civil–military courses intended to enhance the ability of the military and the civilian actors to cooperate in the mission area. The involvement of military instructors in civilian training programmes and vice versa has also grown significantly.

Interoperability with the most likely partners

Many steps have been taken to meet this requirement since the Danish involvement in the Balkans began. Its importance in peace operations involving a risk of combat was understood immediately, and joint training aimed at enhancing interoperability was thus conducted with the Norwegian and Swedish contingents prior to the deployment in Bosnia in 1993. Today, the Danish armed forces engage in close cooperation and joint training with its most likely partners in a number of different organizational settings in order to meet this requirement: the Nordic countries in NORDCAPS and bilaterally; small- and medium-sized traditional (mainly Western) UN troop contributors in SHIRBRIG; the Baltic states in the BALTBAT project and bilateral arrangements and training programmes; Poland and Germany in the Danish-German-Polish Multinational Corps Northeast, whose head-quarters is tasked to contribute to multinational peace operations; and the NATO members that Denmark is cooperating with in NATO's reaction and response forces. NORDCAPS and SHIRBRIG were both set up with the principal objective of enhancing interoperability and rapid reaction in order to enable the participants to deploy effective multinational forces on peace operations at short notice.

Cooperation conducted within these forums has led to a number of deployments with multinational brigades and units. Examples include the two Nordic battalions (NORDBAT 1 and 2) in UNPROFOR, the Nordic–Polish brigade (NORDPOLBDE) and battle group (NPBG) in NATO's IFOR and SFOR missions, and the SHIRBRIG contribution to UNMEE.

Armaments and ROE permitting use of force beyond self-defence if necessary

In a 1966 article presenting the Danish approach to UN peacekeeping operations Lt Col. L.M.K. Skern, the head of the Danish UN department, proudly informs the world that 'to the credit of the Danes in Cyprus no shots have been fired by a Dane performing his UN duties'.[60] Some 20 years later Danish officers are equally proud of the fact that Denmark was the first nation to deploy and successfully use tanks on a UN peace operation. Contemporary presentations of the Danish approach to peace operations and lessons learned emphasize the need for robustness and heavy weapons,[61] and Danish contingents have earned a reputation for robustness in both Bosnia and Kosovo.[62]

This change in approach is commonly explained with references to the 'lessons of Srebrenica', or '18 September (1995) never again', the latter referring to the day when the Danish UN contingent in Croatia suffered ten casualties (two killed and eight wounded) from hostile fire in a single day.[63] This is a misunderstanding. By 1995 Danish Balkan contingents had been given better protection (improved armoured personnel carriers (APCs) and new fragmentation vests), increased firepower (heavy mortars and tanks), and ROE permitting the use of force beyond self-defence. That the need for a more robust approach was understood very quickly is also clear from the report prepared by Lt Col. Lars Møller, commander of the first tank squadron deployed in Tuzla, following his first reconnaissance trip to Bosnia in December 1993: 'The Danish contingent will be deployed in war. We are not talking about a peacekeeping operation, nor war-like conditions, but war'.[64] The lesson had been learned and the approach changed before the fateful summer of 1995.

The new approach obviously does not mean that ROE and armaments will cease to be tailored to the mission at hand. Danish forces will continue to be deployed lightly armed on peace missions and employ the traditional peacekeeping ROE when threat assessments indicate that it is safe to do so. However, its use of worst-case planning assumptions will ensure that Danish contingents even in best-case circumstances will arrive better armed and protected than was the case during the Cold War. APCs, seldom used by Danish contingents during the Cold War, have become standard today in all types of peace operations. In missions where consent is perceived to be uncertain, Danish contingents will be equipped with some or all of the DRB's heavy weapons, i.e. APCs, heavy mortars, tanks, artillery, surface-to-air missiles and anti-tank helicopters.[65]

The Danish approach, in short, does meet the requirements for flexible ROE and armaments tailored to the mission at hand.

Logistics

Several steps were taken in the 1990s in order to improve the self-sufficiency of the Danish forces in the field as well as the organization supporting them from Denmark. The increased need for providing administrative and logistical support to Danish personnel abroad led to the establishment of an international centre for logistical support (DANILOG) in January 2001. The DRB's transport and logistics battalions are geared to meet the deployment requirements for self-sufficiency set by NATO for warfighting (10 days) and the UN/SHIRBRIG for peace missions (60 days). The transport battalion can establish two clearing stations, and the logistics support battalion can provide field ambulances, and a state-of-the-art field hospital with operations teams, specialist doctors, a dental clinic, etc. The field hospital has the capacity to hospitalize 100 patients in beds, and, in case of emergency, another 100 patients on stretchers. The DRB's armoured engineer company has the capacity to improve infrastructure, build bridges and clear mines. This capacity serves the dual purpose of allowing contingents to operate independently in mission areas ravaged by war and to engage in CIMIC-related construction tasks, which have proved crucial with respect to winning the hearts and minds of local populations.

On NATO peace missions, where logistical support is a national responsibility, Danish forces deploy a National Support Element in the mission area to organize and distribute the supplies from Denmark and buy supplies locally. During the IFOR/SFOR operations, the Danish support element was part of a joint Nordic Supply Group. On UN missions the UN is supposed to provide logistical support after 60 days. However, the UN logistical support system tends to be slow and unreliable due to rigid procedures and a chronic shortage of funds. The Danish support system is therefore capable of supplying Danish UN contingents for longer than 60 days if necessary. During the UNPROFOR mission, the Danish contingents were fully supplied from Denmark for the first nine months of the mission.[66]

Summing up, the requirement for a logistical support capacity is met, as the Danish armed forces have been able to support personnel in the field in the 1990s. They have only done so with difficulty, however. Criticism of insufficient support was widespread especially in the early years of the

Balkan deployment,[67] and while the PfP exercise Strong Resolve conducted in Poland in March 2002 demonstrated that the current concept employed by DANILOG was working, it also revealed serious shortcomings in terms of both materiel and training.[68] That the Danish contingent in the UNMEE in Eritrea to their amazement discovered a snow plough when they opened their containers, and that the Danish contingent deployed after the 2003 war in Iraq had been equipped with snow shovels and road salt also suggest room for improvement.[69]

Medical, psychological and family support

No psychological and family support systems existed in the armed forces when the Danish corvette *Olfert Fischer* departed for the Gulf in 1990,[70] and stories about the lack of attention and priority devoted to such matters in the first half of the 1990s abound.[71] According to the general with overall responsibility for the army personnel in the Balkans in 1993–95, 'a tough battle against bureaucracy and a plain lack of common sense' was required to get a proper debriefing procedure in place for contingents returning home.[72] The commander of the contingent in Croatia suffering 16 casualties in September 1995 complained bitterly in his memoirs about the inadequate crisis support provided to his personnel in the aftermath of the attacks,[73] and the support provided to the wounded and their families also proved insufficient.[74]

Since then improvements have been made across the board (Box 4.1). A comprehensive psychological support system has been put in place by the armed forces, a rapid reaction team of psychologists, doctors and nurses, who can be dispatched to accidents and mission areas on short notice, became operational on 1 January 1998, and a crisis centre staffed 24 hours a day opened on 1 July 1999.[75]

An improved system for the repatriation of wounded personnel was introduced in February 1996. Use of specially designed containers makes it possible to fly out 48 lightly wounded personnel at a time in an emergency.[76] Finally, the army has begun to offer all DRB volunteers professional help with respect to finding jobs or choosing the right education when they return from their deployment abroad.[77]

The assistance provided to families while soldiers are away remains limited, and this has prompted a proposal to establish a 'home support unit' to help families in need of practical assistance.[78] Thus far this has not happened and although family support is probably the most neglected area, it is not the one most criticized. The level of psychological support still draws the most fire in spite of all the improvements. Most recently in 2001 the military was thus criticized for not doing enough to help two private groups set up by veterans in order to provide assistance to soldiers with psychological problems.[79] This problem was remedied in the 2005–09 Defence Agreement which allocated funds to these groups.

Box 4.1 The psychological support system developed by the Institute of Military Psychology

1   Briefings on the stresses of international service and its effects before and after the deployment.
2   Training for officers, doctors and army chaplains in 'psychological debriefing'.
3   Courses for sergeants in 'friend support'.
4   Distribution of leaflets to support the personnel.
5   A team of psychologists offers crisis assistance over the phone seven days a week.
6   Family members are invited to briefings before, during and after the completion of a mission.
7   All regiments are assigned a psychologist who stays in regular contact with the commanding officers before, during and after the completion of a mission.
8   A standby team of psychologists, doctors and nurses available for deployment in mission areas on short notice.
9   All individuals sent home prematurely receive an offer of special assistance.
10 Reunions for all personnel are arranged three months after the completion of the mission.
11 All personnel receive a questionnaire concerning stress reactions six months after the completion of the mission.

Sources: Madsen, J.P. (1995) 'Stresspåvirkning under FN-tjeneste', *Militært Tidsskrift*, Vol. 124, No. 1, pp. 4–10; Damm, Allen and Birgitte Hommelgaard (2002) 'Håndtering af psykiske efterreaktioner hos personel i international tjeneste', *Militært Tidsskrift*, Vol. 131, No. 2, pp. 194–200; and interview, Institute of Military Psychology.

On the civilian side, the police have established the most elaborate support system with standard debriefings and offers of psychological assistance. However, it is clear from a recent evaluation that the existing system suffers from many of the flaws that characterized the one employed by the army in the early 1990s.[80] Thus the police and the other civilian actors in this area have some catching up to do.

Intelligence capacity

Denmark relied on the traditional low-key UN approach to intelligence activities when the Balkan deployment began, but the greater risks and unwillingness from allies to share intelligence with the Danish contingents, unless they got something in return, quickly forced a reassessment of this approach.[81] The result has been a general increase in the intelligence capacity of the Danish contingents in the field and in the level of intelligence support they receive from Denmark. The DRB intelligence section has been expanded with eight interpreters capable of speaking Polish, Russian and

Serbo-Croat. Interpreters capable of speaking other languages can be called upon when the need arises.[82] Unmanned aerial vehicles and artillery-locating radars have been procured and communications with Denmark have been significantly improved by the establishment of a situation centre, which is linked by satellite to forces in the field. This initiative was a direct result of the casualties suffered in September 1995.[83] Finally, the establishment of Nordic intelligence cells in both Bosnia and Kosovo also underlines the increased priority devoted to meeting this requirement for success.

Public information capacity

During the Cold War the Danish armed forces did not employ full-time public information officers on UN peacekeeping operations. Public information was handled by the force commander or a designated officer as part of their normal duties. While this model remains in place, certain innovations have been made to address the challenges posed by the increasing attention from the media to which the Danish contingents in the field are subjected. Danish journalists are invited on tours to visit the troops in the field; a three-day course in self-protection for journalists has been established; more military personnel receive training in public information; the number of public information officers on standby contracts, who can be called up at short notice, has been increased; and the army has begun to assign a full-time public information officer to the staff at the beginning and the end of a peace operation. This practice was used for the first time during Operation Alba in Albania in 1997.[84] There is no standard procedure, however, and the need for public information officers is decided on a case-by-case basis. The SFOR contingent in Bosnia was for instance provided with a permanent, full-time press officer to service the local and international media around the clock.[85]

Training is also approached in the same way as was the case during the Cold War. The core of the national training programme is a four-day course held once a year. This is supplemented with civilian courses, courses run by the armed forces in Norway and Sweden and the public information officer course run under the auspices of NORDCAPS. Finally, a training programme in psychological operations (PSYOPS) was established in 2001 to in order to help Danish contingents improve their relationship with the parties and the population in the mission areas. Future contingents will either have PSYOPS specialists on the staff or be able to draw on PSYOPS teams for this purpose.[86] While, strictly speaking, it is wrong to discuss PSYOPS in connection with public information activities, because they will be conducted separately by different personnel, PSYOPS are still relevant here because they will support the public information activities aimed at increasing the local understanding of the work carried out by the Danish contingents.

Are the adjustments made sufficient in order to meet the increased demands posed by contemporary peace operations? A few officers have made calls for better training and complained that too little is being done in order to inform the Danish public about the accomplishments of the Danish forces abroad.[87] Most officers do not regard public information as a problem area, however, and this view is supported by the generally good relationship between the armed forces and the Danish press, including the Danish correspondents working in the mission areas. The principal sources of tension between the press and the armed forces have been related to a few incidents resulting in Danish casualties,[88] and the high level of secrecy surrounding the use of special forces in peace operations. Information about the latter has usually come from allies rather than the Danish armed forces themselves.[89]

All in all, it seems safe to conclude that the Danish armed forces have been able to meet the requirements for public information demanded by contemporary peace operations.

Coordination and cooperation capacity

The capacity of the Danish armed forces to cooperate with civilian actors (CIMIC) in the field increased markedly in the course of the 1990s. While CIMIC as a concept was new to the Danish armed forces, cooperation with civilians on peace operations was not. During the Cold War Danish UN contingents had a sector humanitarian officer (SHO) on the staff performing tasks that are very similar to the ones that CIMIC officers perform today. The Danish contingents became involved in humanitarian tasks in the Balkans from the start in 1992, and these efforts were significantly expanded after NATO took over from the UN in Bosnia in December 1995.

The Danish Army initiated trials with CIMIC advisors in 1993, and in January 1997 CIMIC sections were established at the Army Operational Command, the Eastern Land Command, the Danish Division and the DRB. CIMIC sections are now standard in all Danish battalions deployed on peace operations, and a CIMIC company was made available for NATO in 2002.

CIMIC training has also been institutionalized. The Army Logistics School began running CIMIC courses for Nordic officers within NORD-CAPS in 1999 and a joint CIMIC course for military, DEMA and NGO personnel was established the following year. Joint civil–military training also takes place on a regular basis during NORDIC Peace and SHIRBRIG exercises.

The MFA set up the Humanitarian Contact Group in 1995 to improve coordination and cooperation among the Danish actors involved in humanitarian activities in the field. The Humanitarian Contact Group is open to all the relevant Danish NGOs and state actors and the composition of the group varies from crisis to crisis depending on the nature of the Danish involvement in the crisis at hand. The coordination efforts were expanded during the Kosovo crisis through the establishment of a local contact group and a coordination office in Pristina. This initiative significantly enhanced the effectiveness of the Danish KFOR contingent by speeding up the allocation of money to projects identified by its CIMIC section.[90]

In March 2004 a new joint planning initiative was launched in order to enhance the cooperation and coordination between the relevant Danish ministries, the armed forces, Danish companies and Danish NGOs involved in peace operations at all levels from the strategic to the tactical and in all phases of a deployment (before, during and after). A new standing civil service committee has been established and the armed forces have been provided with an annual budget of DKK 15 million (EUR 2.2 million) for CIMIC-related projects.[91] The new initiative was in part driven by the experience in Iraq where the security situation made it impossible for humanitarian organizations to operate in the Danish area of responsibility. The Danish government therefore wants a capacity to co-deploy civilian experts from the relevant ministries with the Danish armed forces to support humanitarian and reconstruction activities in situations where the humanitarian organizations either cannot or will not operate. The decision to step up the Danish support for the provincial reconstruction teams (PRTs) in Afghanistan in 2005 exemplifies the new approach.[92]

Public security capacity

The Danish capacity in this area has also been enhanced markedly. As mentioned above, Denmark has made 125 police officers available to the EU's rapid reaction civilian police force. The number of police officers made available for peace operations has more than doubled in the past decade, and it constitutes more than 1 per cent of the total Danish police force, which numbers some 10,500.[93] Danish police officers have participated in the whole spectrum of operations, including executive missions with armed personnel like the one in Kosovo. Moreover, high-ranking Danish police officers have led UN police missions in both Bosnia and Kosovo, and a Danish police officer was also in charge of the EU police mission that took over from the UN in Bosnia on 1 January 2003.

Less headway has been made with respect to the other civilian personnel categories demanded by contemporary peace operations, however. Denmark has only provided a very limited number of judges, jailers, prosecutors and legal advisors for peace operations. This lack of capacity is also reflected in the contributions offered to the EU civilian rapid reaction force: 9 rule of law, 24 civilian administration and 320 civil protection personnel emanating primarily from DEMA.[94]

The military has increased its public security capacity considerably. Like most other Western armies, the Danish Army was not at all pleased by its increased involvement in public security tasks in Bosnia and Kosovo. The army leadership perceived the increased involvement in riot control as 'mission creep' and complained that it was contrary to the Danish tradition to use soldiers against civilians.[95] Riot control and similar tasks, so the argument went, were better left to gendarmes and police officers.[96] The deployment of a Danish contingent in Kosovo in 1999 forced the army leadership to reassess its position. Violent clashes with angry demonstrators in Mitrovica first resulted in the dispatch of extra shields, helmets and batons to the contingent and extra training also proved necessary Box 4.2. Requests for teargas in the spring of 2000 were initially turned down by the Army Operational Command in Denmark but developments on the ground forced through a change of policy a few weeks later.[97]

Box 4.2 ROE guiding the use of force against civilian demonstrators in Kosovo (Autumn 1999)

1   Gendarmes (not Danish)
2   Soldiers without shields with rifles over their shoulders
3   Soldiers with shields without rifles
4   Soldiers with shields
5   Police with batons
6   APCs
7   Military police and soldiers with batons
8   Loading of weapons
9   Warning shots
10 Light rockets
11 Light grenades fired from grenade launchers
12 Shots aimed at the legs of the demonstrators
13 Shots aimed directly at demonstrators
14 Use of hand grenades.

Source: Brøndum, Christian (1999) 'Danske soldater i Kosovo får knipler til selvforsvar', *Berlingske Tidende*, 29 October, p. 8.

Since then new teargas equipment has been procured, and the use of teargas, batons and snatch teams has become part of the standard training programme preparing military police officers for deployment on peace operations.[98] Additional training in riot control, including the use of APCs and tanks for this purpose, was also introduced as a result of the lessons learned in Mitrovica. Finally, military police training became joint in 2002 so that officers from all three services are put through the same programme. The idea behind this new initiative is to make it easier to deploy military police companies on peace operations with officers from all three services.[99]

Denmark has, in short, enhanced its public security capacity markedly. This process continues and this requirement must therefore also be regarded as met.

Table 4.6 Denmark and the requirements for success in contemporary peace operations

Requirements for success	Denmark
1. Political will, legal framework and funds for all types of operations	Yes
2. Civilian and military personnel deployable at short notice	Yes
3. Training to prepare the civilian and military personnel for their many new tasks	Yes
4. Interoperability with most likely partners	Yes
5. Armaments and ROE permitting use of force beyond self-defence if necessary	Yes
6. Logistics	Yes
7. Medical, psychological and family support	Yes
8. Intelligence capacity	Yes
9. Public information capacity	Yes
10. Coordination and cooperation capacity	Yes
11. Public security capacity	Yes

Conclusion

Peace operations became the flagship in the new activist foreign policy pursued by Denmark in the 1990s, and Danish participation in all types of operations has grown significantly with respect to both civilian and military personnel. This increase was underpinned by strong political and public support that shows no signs of weakening. The desire to contribute effectively to all types of peace operations was the principal determinant driving the restructuring of the Danish armed forces since the early 1990s, and this desire is also at the heart of *VISION 2010*, the armed forces' own view of their development in the decade ahead.[100] The post-Cold War era has consequently been characterized by a continuous and ongoing effort to meet the eleven requirements for success. As is clear from the analysis and Table 4.6, this effort has been successful.

The principal constraint on Danish participation in the foreseeable future is neither political nor financial as is usually the case, but levels of recruitment. It remains to be seen whether the armed forces can attract sufficient numbers to maintain 2,000 personnel abroad on international missions on a continuous basis, as the 2005–09 Defence Agreement stipulates.

Notes

1. Cited from Andersen, Simon and Jesper Larsen (1997) 'Høj cigarføring', *Jyllands-Posten*, 2 March. Author's translation from Danish.
2. Petersen, Niels Helveg (1995) 'Address to the UN General Assembly, September 30 1994', in Nikolaj Petersen and Christian Thune (eds) *Dansk Udenrigspolitisk Årbog 1994* (København: Dansk Udenrigspolitisk Institut), p. 233 (233–237).

3. *Lov nr. 909 af 8. December 1993 om forsvarets formål, opgaver og organisation m.v.*, and *Lov nr. 122 af 27. februar 2001 om forsvarets formål, opgaver og organisation m.v.*

4. Petersen, Niels Helveg (2000) 'Fredsbevaring anno 2003', *Jyllands-Posten*, 8 October, p. 8; Klarskov, Kristian and Jens Holsøe (2000) 'Dansk forsvarsprofil udhules', *Politiken*, 12 December, p. 1. This assessment is shared by some analysts. See for instance Holm, Hans-Henrik (2002) 'Danish Foreign Policy Activism: The Rise and Decline', in Bertel Heurlin and Hans Mouritzen (eds) *Danish Foreign Policy Yearbook 2002* (Copenhagen: Danish Institute of International Affairs), pp. 19–45.

5. The doctrine was born in a speech by Foreign Minister Uffe Ellemann-Jensen on 17 April 1989 given to the first meeting of the Foreign Policy Commission, which had been tasked to outline the requirements for an effective Danish foreign policy in emerging the post-Cold War era. See Udenrigskommissionen af 1 april 1989 (1990) *Udenrigstjenesten mod år 2000, Bd. I, Betænkning 1209* (København: Udenrigsministeriet, 1990), p. 40.

6. Krasnik, Martin (2000) 'Magelig magt', *Weekendavisen*, 22 December, p. 6.

7. Forsvarskommandoen (2003) *Dansk deltagelse i internationale operationer 1948–2002* (Vedbæk: Forsvarskommandoens Presse- og Informationsafdeling). An overview of the operations that Denmark has participated in since 1948 can be found in Appendix 4.

8. '2.323 danske soldater i fredsstøttende indsats', *FOV Nyhedsbrev* (1999) No. 26, p. 1; Forsvarskommandoen (2002) *Virksomhedsregnskab 2001* (Vedbæk: Forsvarskommandoen), p. 34.

9. *Agreement regarding Danish Defence from 2005–2009* (Copenhagen: Ministry of Defence, 2004) available at <http://forsvaret.dk/FMN/Temaer/Forsvarsforlig+2005+2009/ENG_forlig20052009.htm> (24 November 2004).

10. Nordland, Rod (1994) 'The Mouse Ate the Cat', *Newsweek*, Vol. 123, No. 20 (16 May), p. 18; Pomfret, John (1994) 'In Bosnia. UN Troops Finally Go to War', *The Washington Post*, 5 May, p. A1. Since then the incident has frequently been hailed as proof that force, properly used, may be key to success in contemporary peace operations. See for instance Luttwak, Edward N. (1999) 'Give War a Chance', *Foreign Affairs*, Vol. 78, No. 4 (July/August), p. 40 (36–44).

11. Viveke, Kristoffer Magnus and Lotte Machon (2002) 'Forebyggelse og bilæggelse af voldelige konflikter: Analysedokument', *DUPI Report*, No. 1 (København: Dansk Udenrigspolitisk Institut), pp. 121–122.

12. Beredskabsstyrelsen (2002) *Virksomhedsregnskab 2001* (København: Indenrigs- og Sundhedsministeriet), para. 3.2.7; Viveke and Machon 'Forebyggelse og bilæggelse af voldelige konflikter', pp. 135–136.

13. Andersen, Stefan Birkebjerg and Lone Hollmann (1993) *Avisårbogen 1991* (Odense: Odense Universitetsforlag), pp. 5–6; Ellemann-Jensen, Uffe (1991) 'Efterskrift', in Uffe Ellemann-Jensen and Sven E. Thiede (eds) *Olfert Fischer i Golfen* (København: Langkjær), p. 59; Hækkerup, Hans (2002) *På skansen* (København: Lindhardt & Ringhof), pp. 94–96; Larsen, Thomas (1997) *Erobreren* (København: Børsen), pp. 182–183; Schlüter, Poul (1999) *Sikken et liv* (København: Aschehoug), p. 248.

14. Off-the-record conversation with military officers involved in the planning of a battalion-sized contribution to the operation. See also Hækkerup, *På skansen*, p. 99.

15. 'Danskere uenige om direkte militær indsats', *Berlingske Tidende*, 19 January 1991; 'Gallup: Vi bør betale til Golfkrigen', *Berlingske Tidende*, 17 February 1991.

16. 'Vælgerne siger ok til FNs udvidede aktion', *Berlingske Tidende*, 4 October 1992.
17. Forsvarsministeren (1995) *Årlig Redegørelse 1994* (København: Forsvarsministeriet), p. 45.
18. Ellemann-Jensen, Uffe (1992) 'Det urolige Europa', *Weekendavisen*, 9 October, p. 18. (My translation.)
19. Brøndum, Christian (1999) 'Hvis det bliver alvor', *Berlingske Tidende*, 29 April, p. 16.
20. A total of 54 Danes have died on peace operations since 1948. The majority have been killed by disease and traffic accidents. In addition three Danish aid workers were killed by hostile fire in Bosnia. See Buhl, Ida (2003) 'Trykket stemning i Camp Eden', *Berlingske Tidende*, 18 August, p. 5. Fridberg, Anders V. (2002) 'Dag Hammarskjöld medalje til faldne i FN-tjeneste', *FOV Nyhedsbrev*, No. 6, p. 4; Langberg, Ida (2003) 'Plyndringer plager Irak', *Politiken*, 18 August, p. 2.
21. For an overview of this research and an in-depth discussion of the Danish sensitivity to casualties see Jakobsen, Peter Viggo (2004) 'Har Danmark et body bag syndrom?', *Militært Tidsskrift*, Vol. 133, No. 1 (April), pp. 94–114.
22. *Lov nr. 909 af 8. December 1993 om forsvarets formål, opgaver og organisation m.v; Folketingsbeslutning nr. B 1 af 25 november 1993 om etablering af en international brigade.*
23. *Lov nr. 910 af 8. December 1993 om ændring af lov om forsvarets personel, lov om hjemmeværnet, lov om statens uddannelsesstøtte og lov om værnepligtsorlov m.v. (Udsendelse af personel til FN-tjeneste m.v., herunder orlov for lønmodtagere og uddannelsessøgende m.v.).*
24. *The Constitutional Act of Denmark of June 5, 1953* (Copenhagen: Folketing, 1996), para 19, 2.
25. For an analysis of the Danish involvement in the Kosovo war see Jakobsen, Peter Viggo (2000) 'Denmark at War: Turning Point or Business as Usual?', in Bertel Heurlin and Hans Mouritzen (eds) *Danish Foreign Policy Yearbook 2000* (Copenhagen: Danish Institute of International Affairs), pp. 61–85.
26. NATO (1999) 'The Alliance's Strategic Concept', *NATO Press Communiqué NAC-S(99)65*, 24 April 1999, paras 15, 22, 31, 48; European Council (1999) 'Helsinki European Council: Presidency Conclusion', *Council of the European Union Press Release*, No. 00300/1/99 (Brussels, 11 December 1999), para. 26.
27. Rostrup, Ask and Jesper Thobo-Carlsen (2002) 'Danskere fortryder alle EU-forbehold', *Berlingske Tidende*, 2 June, p. 1.
28. *Danmarks internationale indsats: Rapport fra et tværministerielt udvalg* (København: Finansministeriet, 1993), p. 120.
29. *Danmarks internationale indsats*, pp. 119–124.
30. *Finanslov for finansåret 2002* (København: Finansministeriet), account no. 35.11.05 (Budget Law).
31. Kongstad, Jesper (2002) 'Jensby: Forsvaret mangler penge', *Jyllands-Posten*, 5 August, p. 5.
32. *Finanslov for 2000, Finanslov for 2002*, and *Finanslov for 2004* (København: Finansministeriet), account nos. 6.37.02 and 6.39.02.
33. Hækkerup, *På skansen*, p. 218.
34. *Rapport om Forsvarets fremtidige struktur og størrelse: Rapport fra det af Forsvarsministeren den 11. april 1991 nedsatte Udvalg vedrørende forsvarets udvikling mv.* (København: Forsvarsministeriet, 2 March 1992); Forsvarsministerens Rådgivnings- og Analysegruppe (1992) *Mulighederne for at opstille en dansk hærenhed af brigadestørrelse til indsættelse i internationale operationer* (København: Forsvarsministeriet, October 1992).

35. Clemmesen, Michael H. (1993) 'Efterkoldskrigstidens danske forsvarspolitik', in Nikolaj Petersen and Christian Thune (eds) *Dansk Udenrigspolitisk Årbog 1992* (København: Jurist- og Økonomforbundets forlag), pp. 41–55; Ellemann-Jensen, Uffe (1990) 'Et historisk gennembrud i dansk udenrigspolitik', in Nikolaj Petersen and Christian Thune (eds) *Dansk Udenrigspolitisk Årbog 1990* (København: Jurist- og Økonomforbundets Forlag), p. 185 (185–191); Schönstadt, Jacob (pseudonym of Ib Faurby) (1991) 'Verdenshavet og Frederiksholms Kanal', *Udenrigs*, Vol. 46, No. 2, pp. 12–13.

36. These factors are discussed in greater detail in Chapter 3.

37. In 1983–87 the deployment of the intermediate-range nuclear forces (INF) in Europe led to a breakdown in the traditional consensus on defence policy in Denmark. The opposition consequently forced the minority government to insert a series of footnotes in NATO communiqués in which Denmark distanced itself from decisions related to deployment. For both Ellemann-Jensen and Hækkerup getting rid of the footnote image and the traditional pacifist, low-profile foreign policy and improving the Danish standing in NATO, and especially in Washington, became ends in themselves. See Hækkerup, *På skansen*, pp. 9–10, 30, 40, 97–98, 167; Larsen, *Erobreren*, pp. 230–235.

38. For a recent call to bring individuals back in see Byman, Daniel L. and Kenneth M. Pollack (2001) 'Let Us Now Praise Great Men: Bringing the Statesman Back In', *International Security*, Vol. 25, No. 4 (spring), pp. 107–146.

39. Andersen and Larsen 'Høj cigarføring'; Hækkerup, *På skansen*, pp. 58, 112; Lyng, Jørgen (ed.) (2000) *Ved forenede kræfter: forsvarets øverste militære ledelse: forsvarschefsembedet og forsvarets udvikling 1950–2000* (Vedbæk: Forsvarskommandoen), p. 213. Stoltenberg, whom Hækkerup in his book refers to as his mentor (p. 147), described his opposition and admitted he had been wrong in his address to the seminar celebrating the 50th birthday of UN peacekeeping held at the UN Information Office for the Nordic Countries in Copenhagen on 20 October 1998.

40. Foreign ministry officials lost no time making the case that Denmark should exploit the opportunity presented by the end of the Cold War to pursue an activist foreign policy. See for instance Federspiel, Ulrik (1991) 'Den internationale situation og Danmarks udenrigspolitik', in Nikolaj Petersen and Christian Thune (eds) *Dansk Udenrigspolitisk Årbog 1991* (København: Jurist- og Økonomforbundets forlag), pp. 12–26; and Hoppe, Christian (1994) 'Danmarks østpolitik', in Nikolaj Petersen and Christian Thune (eds) *Dansk Udenrigspolitisk Årbog 1993* (København: Jurist- og Økonomforbundets forlag), pp. 67–97.

41. Hækkerup, *På skansen*, p. 84.

42. For an official discussion of the conditions shaping the Danish participation in peace operations see Forsvarskommissionen (1998) *Fremtidens Forsvar: Beretning fra Forsvarskommissionen af 1997* (København: Forsvarsministeriet), pp. 99–100.

43. Off-the-record conversations with several Danish defence officials and officers.

44. Hækkerup, *På skansen*, pp. 89–93.

45. Brøndum, Christian and Karl Erik Nielsen (2000) 'Nyrup bremser Etiopienstyrke', *Berlingske Tidende*, 26 October, p. 1; Hækkerup, *På skansen*, p. 84.

46. Brøndum, Christian (2000) 'God start for danskerne i Eritrea', *Berlingske Tidende*, 10 December, p. 8.

47. For a theoretical discussion of how different kinds of interests and normative considerations interact to trigger use of force see Jakobsen, Peter Viggo (1998)

Western Use of Coercive Diplomacy After the Cold War: A Challenge for Theory and Practice (Houndmills: Macmillan), pp. 35–38.

48. Viveke and Machon, 'Forebyggelse og bilæggelse af voldelige konflikter', pp. 121–122.

49. *IHB-Nyt*, Vol. 3, No. 1 (March 1999), p. 1; *IHB-Nyt*, Vol. 4, No. 4 (December 2000), p. 1. The newsletter is available at <http://www.um.dk>.

50. Larsen, Jesper (2001) '5.000 politifolk klar til fælles EU-styrke', *Berlingske Tidende*, 20 November, p. 11; Rich, Bente and Lars Bo Kjær (2000) 'Dansk Politi i International Tjeneste', MPA speciale Copenhagen Business School, p. 49; Viveke and Machon, 'Forebyggelse og bilæggelse af voldelige konflikter', pp. 121–122.

51. *Politisk aftale om redningsberedskabet efter 2002* (København: Indenrigs- og Sundhedsministeriet, 21 June 2001), pp. 6–7.

52. Forsvarskommissionen, *Fremtidens Forsvar Beretning fra Forsvarskommissionen af 1997*, pp. 224–225.

53. Army Operational Command (1998) *Army Operational Command Denmark – At the Millennium Change* (Aarhus: Army Operational Command), p. 47.

54. Statsrevisoratet (2001) *Beretning om forsvarets mål og rapportering vedrørende operativ kapacitet* (København: Statsrevisoratet), pp. 42–43.

55. Jacobi, Barbara (2001) 'Soldier in the Danish International Brigade', paper presented at the 37th IAMS (International Applied Military Psychology Symposium) conference, Prague, 21–25 May, p. 1. The soldiers were particularly interested in improvements in three areas: language training, skills relevant for communicating with the local population and the parties, and the information provided about the political situation in the mission area.

56. *IHB-Nyt*, Vol. 5, No. 3 (September 2001); *IHB-Nyt*, Vol. 6, No. 1 (March 2002); *IHB-Nyt*, Vol. 6, No. 2 (June 2002).

57. Rich and Kjær, 'Dansk Politi i International Tjeneste', pp. 26–27.

58. Volunteers on contract generally make up about 60% of the personnel deployed abroad. The original 20/80 mix of regulars and volunteers set when the DRB was established has never been met. See Forsvarskommandoen (2002) *Virksomhedsregnskab 2001* (Vedbæk: Forsvarskommandoen), p. 81; Statsrevisoratet (1998) *Beretning om aktivitets- og ressourcestyringen ved forsvarets deltagelse i fredsstøttende operationer* (København: Statsrevisoratet), p. 10.

59. For detailed information see the NORDCAPS website <http://www. nordcaps.org/> (6 July 2004).

60. Skern, L.M.K. (1966) 'United Nations Peacekeeping Operations From a Danish Viewpoint', *Revue Militaire Generale*, October, p. 364 (353–367).

61. See for instance Hans Hækkerup's presentation to the UN General Assembly on 29 October 1998 printed in *Beretning til Folketinget vedr. De Forenede Nationers 53. generalforsamling, New York, for perioden 8. september–18. december 1998* (København: Udenrigsministeriet), p. 151; and Jensen, Jørn (1996) 'I fredens tjeneste – en bataljonschefs erfaringer', *Militært Tidsskrift*, Vol. 25, No. 2 (June), p. 96 (92–99).

62. According to numerous officers, who served in the Nordic-Polish brigade in IFOR and SFOR, the Danish contingents operated in far more robust manner than their Finnish, Swedish, Norwegian and Polish partners. See the chapter on Denmark in Frantzen, Henning A. (2004) *NATO and Peace Support Operations, 1991–1999: Policies and Doctrines* (London: Frank Cass). See also Smith, R. Jeffrey (2000) 'French Troops in Kosovo Accused of Retreat: UN Police Cite Lack of Support in Mitrovica

Uprising, Inadequate Aid to Civilians', *The Washington Post*, 9 February, p. A14.

63. This is the highest number of casualties ever suffered by Danish forces on peace operations due to hostile fire. The 'lesson of Srebrenica' came up repeatedly in interviews with Danish officers and officials and was even mentioned to me by a Canadian diplomat at a seminar in New York in 2001. For the '18 September never again' slogan see Schjønning, Eigil (1999) 'Hæren og de fredsstøttende operationer', *Militært Tidsskrift*, Vol. 128, No. 1 (March), p. 84.

64. Møller, Lars R. (2001) *Operation Bøllebank: Soldater i kamp* (København: Høst og Søn), p. 197.

65. The Danish approach is thus in accordance with the more robust approach advocated in the recent Western doctrines discussed in the previous chapter.

66. Hillingsø, K.G.H. (1993) Commander Danish Operational Forces, General K.G.H. Hillingsø, 'Peacekeeping and Peacemaking', presentation to North Atlantic Cooperation Council, 18 November 1993.

67. See for instance Bøggild, Eva (1994) 'Farvel til hyggehæren: det danske forsvar er splittet op mellem de udenrigspolitiske ambitioner og den gamle kasernemaleånd', *Press*, No. 99, pp. 55–59.

68. Flügge, Steen (2002) 'Alle taler om det – men ingen gør noget ved det!', *Militært Tidsskrift*, Vol. 131, No. 3 (July), pp. 358–364; Hesselberg, Bjarne (2002) 'Hærens fremtid', *Militært Tidsskrift*, Vol. 131, No. 3 (July), pp. 353–357.

69. Brøndum, Christian (2003) 'Ørkenkrig: Sneplov er blevet væk i ørkenen', *Berlingske Tidende*, 12 July, p. 3.

70. Brøndum, Christian (2000) 'Olfert Fischer banede vejen', *Berlingske Tidende*, 12 September, p. 4.

71. Jensen, Jørn (1996) *I krydsild: Den Danske bataljon i Kroatien og Bosnien* (Højbjerg: Hovedland), p. 146; Rasmussen, Carsten (1995) 'FN-tjeneste i Bosnien-Herzegovina, oplevelse og stress', *Militært Tidsskrift*, pp. 15–16; Schmidt, Kim (1996) 'FN- og NATO-tjeneste i Kroatien og Bosnien – en kompagnichefs erfaringer', *Militært Tidsskrift*, Vol. 125, No. 2 (June), pp. 100–104.

72. Hillingsø, K.G.H. (1997) 'Bosnien tur-retur', *Information*, 27 November, p. 7.

73. Jensen, *I krydsild*, p. 146; Rasmussen, 'FN-tjeneste i Bosnien-Herzegovina', pp. 108–113.

74. *FOV Nyhedsbrev* (1996) 'Bedre service til sårede danske soldater', No. 13–15, pp. 2–4; Kreiner, John (1995) 'Forsvarsministeren åben overfor øget omsorg for sårede', *Officeren*, No. 11 (November), pp. 4–5.

75. *FOV Nyhedsbrev* (1997) 'Forsvaret opretter psykologisk udrykketeam og krisecenter', No. 49, pp. 7–9; *FOV Nyhedsbrev* (1999) 'Utraditionel aftale med Rigshospitalet', No. 24, pp. 1–3.

76. *FOV Nyhedsbrev*, (1996) 'Hjemtransport af sårede fra ex-Jugoslavien er nu for første gang lagt i faste rammer', No. 2, pp. 2–3.

77. *FOV Nyhedsbrev* (1997) 'DRB-soldaterne får professional hjælp til job og uddannelse', No. 17, p. 6.

78. Skipper, Arne (1999) 'Hjemmefronten til analyse', *Jyllands-Posten*, 13 July, p. 6.

79. Brøndum, Christian (2001) 'Ny hjælp til kriseramte soldater', *Berlingske Tidende*, 23 February, p. 4.

80. Rich and Kjær, 'Dansk Politi i International Tjeneste'; off-the record conversations with several Danish police officers with experience from recent peace operations.

81. Johnsen, Poul Pilgaard (2001) 'Tavse agenter', *Weekendavisen*, 5 October; conversation with General K.G.H. Hillingsø.

82. Interview, DRB, 26 February 1998.
83. Lyng, *Ved forenede kræfter*, p. 241.
84. Knudsen, Søren (1997) 'Den danske indsats i Operation Alba', *Militært Tidsskrift*, Vol. 126, No. 5, p. 540 (524–543).
85. *FOV Nyhedsbrev* (1999) 'Nyt job i Bosnien skal give pressen bedre service', No. 2, pp. 6–7.
86. Huglstad, Allan (2001) 'PSYOPS klar til at gå i luften', *Hærnyt*, No. 1, pp. 32–33.
87. See for instance Hesselberg, Bjarne (1995) 'Stresspåvirkninger under FN-tjeneste', *Militært Tidsskrift*, Vol. 124, No. 1 (March), p. 22 (17–23); Jensen, 'I fredens tjeneste', pp. 92–99; Jönsson, Per H. (1997) 'Forsvaret – medierne og mediepolitik', *Officeren*, No. 8 (August), pp. 4–5.
88. Hvidt, Christian (2002) 'Det menneskelige Forsvar', *Berlingske Tidende*, 9 April, Section 2, p. 6.
89. Leder (2002) 'Den danske indsats', *Jyllands-Posten*, 26 July, p. 6.
90. Jakobsen, Peter Viggo (ed.) (2000) 'CIMIC – Civilt–militært samarbejde under fredsstøttende operationer', *DUPI Report*, No. 6 (København: Dansk Udenrigspolitisk Institut), pp. 5, 33; Ottenheim, Freddie (2000) 'CIMIC: Den danske model skaber resultater', *Danske Officerer*, No. 4.
91. *Joint Planning of Civilian and Military Efforts in International Operations* (Copenhagen: Ministry of Foreign Affairs and Ministry of Defence, 2004), available at < http://forsvaret.dk/NR/rdonlyres/BF50F2AD-A15D-44B4-80D7-88CFE20CB518/0/ENG_samtaenkning.pdf > (22 November 2004).
92. Halskov, Lars (2004) 'Danmark opruster i Afghanistan', *Politiken*, 21 November, p. 1.
93. Rigspolitichefen (2002) *Virksomhedsregnskab for dansk politi 2001* (København: Rigspolitichefen), p. 39.
94. Interview EU Council Secretariat, Brussels, 6 May 2004.
95. In actual fact, the Danish contingent serving in Gaza as part of UNEF I used force against civilian demonstrators in March 1957, and riot control was also listed as a task for the military police in the *Nordic UN Tactical Manual*. See Armstrong, Hamilton Fish (1957) 'The UN Experience in Gaza', *Foreign Affairs*, Vol. 35, No. 4 (July), p. 616 (600–619); Engholm, Carl (1976) 'UNEF United Nations Emergency Force', in L.M.K. Skern (ed.) *Danmark i FNs fredsstyrke*, Vol. I (København: Edvard Henriksen), p. 141 (119–162); and *Nordic UN Tactical Manual. Volume 1* (Helsinki: NORDSAMFN, 1992), pp. 83–85.
96. Brøndum, Christian (2000) 'General: Giv os klar besked', *Berlingske Tidende*, 27 February, p. 9; Dragsdahl, Jørgen (2000) 'Danmark som besættelsesmagt', *Aktuelt*, 18 March, p. 15; Jakobsen, 'CIMIC – Civilt–militært samarbejde', p. 31; Jakobsen, Peter Viggo (ed.) (2000) 'CIMIC – Civil–military Cooperation. Lessons Learned and Models for the Future', *DUPI Report*, No. 9 (Copenhagen: Danish Institute of International Affairs), p. 67.
97. Brøndum, Christian (2000) 'På vagt i en betændt by', *Berlingske Tidende*, 23 February, p. 12; Brøndum, Christian (2000) 'Kosovo-styrke ønsker tåregas', *Berlingske Tidende*, 23 February, p. 1; Brøndum, Christian (2000) 'Tåregas sendes ekspres til Kosovo', *Berlingske Tidende*, 24 February, p. 1.
98. *FOV Nyhedsbrev* (2001) 'Bosnien-Hercegovina i Oksbøl', No. 3, pp. 11–12.
99. Bank Nielsen, Lotte (2002) 'Endnu en værnsfælles militærpoliti uddannelse på vej', *FOV Nyhedsbrev*, No. 14, pp. 2–3.
100. Forsvarskommandoen (2000) *VISION 2010* (Vedbæk: Forsvarskommandoen).

5 The Finnish approach to peace operations after the Cold War

Finland is the largest per capita contributor in crisis management operations in Europe, challenged only by Norway. So I guess I could call my country a superpower in crisis management.

Jan-Erik Enestam,
Finnish defence minister, 2002[1]

While Finns may think of themselves as a 'superpower', the fact remains that Finland was far slower than the other Nordic countries to take up the challenges posed by the new types of peace operations. Finland's initial reaction was to stick with traditional peacekeeping and leave more challenging operations to the great powers. By 1995 this position had become untenable and Finland consequently participated in IFOR together with the other Nordic nations. Enhancing the Finnish capacity to participate in peace operations that go beyond traditional peacekeeping has been a priority since then, and in 2005 a bill paving the way for participation in peace enforcement involving offensive operations was submitted to parliament. Its adoption is unlikely to create the political will required for such participation anytime soon, however.

Political will, legal framework and funds for all types of operations

Political will to provide troops and civilian personnel

As was the case in the previous chapter, the strength, depth and evolution of the political willingness to participate in peace operations will be assessed by the following indicators: the rhetoric employed by decision makers; the number and nature of personnel contributions; the level of domestic support; and finally the role played by the government in mobilizing and sustaining domestic support. In the Finnish case these indicators also reveal a significant increase in political will.

Rhetoric

The importance attributed to the Finnish participation in peace operations grew significantly in the course of the 1990s. In 1993 Finnish participation in NORDBAT 2 in Bosnia was successfully resisted by a large segment of the military and political elite on the grounds that it was too dangerous, too costly and likely to have a detrimental effect on national defence. Finland should consequently restrict its participation to traditional peacekeeping and leave operations involving greater use of force to the great powers.[2] Two years later when participation in NATO's IFOR operation in Bosnia was debated, these arguments no longer prevailed. By then two internationalists, President Martti Ahtisaari and Chief of Defence Gustav Hägglund, both appointed in 1994, had succeeded in persuading the foreign policy establishment that 'free-riding' in European crisis management was impossible for a responsible state wanting to join the EU, and that such participation would have the advantage of strengthening national defence.[3] These arguments have been used ever since in official documents and speeches in order to justify Finland's growing involvement in peace operations, participation in operations beyond traditional peacekeeping as well as the establishment of a modern rapid reaction brigade earmarked for peace operations, the Finnish Rapid Deployment Force (FRDF).[4] The growing importance attributed to peace operations was further underlined by the decision to make the development of the EU's crisis management capacity a principal objective for the Finnish EU presidency in the second half of 1999,[5] and by the designation of peace operations as a main task of Finland's armed forces in the Act on Peace Support Operations passed in 2000.[6]

National defence remains priority number one, however, and the increased involvement in peace operations has to be legitimized as a way of strengthening national defence. As pointed out by President Tarja Halonen, the strong emphasis on national defence sets Finland apart from the other Nordic countries:

> Our point of departure in developing our Defence Forces differs from that of the other Nordic countries. We are not developing our Defence Forces as a whole for international preparedness and NATO compatibility. Finland's Defence Forces are still meant to defend Finland, all of Finland .... Participation in international crisis management also develops and strengthens national defence ... [it] does not take place at the expense of national defence.[7]

Participation on the ground

Finland's military contributions have changed in both nature and number. As mentioned above, Finland abandoned its 'traditional peacekeeping only' stance in 1995 when it provided personnel for NATO's IFOR operation, which was tasked to enforce the Dayton Peace Agreement. Since then three additional enforcement operations enforcing peace agreements have been added to the list: SFOR in Bosnia, KFOR in Kosovo and ISAF in Afghanistan. The number of Finnish personnel involved has grown considerably. By the end of 2002, Finnish contributions totalled some 40,000 personnel, an increase of 20,000 compared to the Cold War (1956–87) total of some 20,000.[8] This means that the average contribution a year had grown from 625 during the Cold War to 1,333 personnel in the 1988–2002 period. Since Finnish personnel generally serve 12-month tours, some 1,300 Finns have on average served abroad on peace operations on a continuous basis since the end of the Cold War.[9]

Like its Swedish neighbour, Finland has consistently refused to participate in offensive enforcement operations directed against specific enemies. Finland did not make military contributions to the UN-authorized operations in Kuwait in 1990–91 and Somalia in 1992–93 and refrained from taking part in the US-led combat operations in Afghanistan in 2002–03. Moreover, the Finnish aversion towards participating in offensive operations meant that the Finnish contingents in IFOR and SFOR operated under very restrictive rules of engagement (ROE), which ruled out participation in offensive activities.[10] This aversion is also evident in the Finnish attempt to carve out niches in softer tasks such as civil–military cooperation (CIMIC), mine-clearing and in the joint efforts with Sweden to promote civilian crisis management within the EU.

Finland's civilian contributions have also increased significantly. The Finnish police became involved in peace operations in 1994, and by 2001 some 150 police officers had served on international operations.[11] The number of other civilian experts, most notably election monitors and human rights monitors, have also grown and some 100 experts are now sent abroad each year.[12] In addition, Finland is strengthening its capacities in civilian administration and rule of law to meet EU demands.[13] The Finnish rescue services also became involved in international operations during the 1990s, and their personnel participated in twelve disaster evaluations and nine rescue operations in the 1994–2001 period.[14]

Domestic support

The policy pursued in the 1990s has enjoyed strong political and public support. If we take a look at the operations voted through the Finnish parliament (Eduskunta/Riksdagen), then the participations in ISAF and SFOR were unanimously approved and overwhelming majorities voted in favour of participation in IFOR (147 yes, 7 no) and KFOR (145 yes, 3 no).[15] Likewise, the 1996 proposal to set up a rapid reaction force for peace operations was passed with 128 votes against 51,[16] and parliament has also approved several revisions of the Act on Peacekeeping as we shall see below.

The influence of public opinion on Finnish foreign and security policy is generally regarded as limited by Finnish experts. During the Cold War security policy was left in the hands of the president, especially during the Kekkonen era (1956–82), and the large majority of the Finnish public still holds the view that foreign policy is best handled by the elite.[17] Opinion polls support this interpretation as they usually endorse official policy. To give a few examples: in 1995, 55 per cent agreed with their president and chief of defence that Finnish troops should be made available for EU peacekeeping and crisis management;[18] the 1999 KFOR deployment was supported by 66 per cent;[19] in another 1999 poll 76 per cent approved the Finnish support for the establishment of an EU crisis management capacity regarding it as a good idea; and 80 per cent supported Finnish participation in crisis management operations such as KFOR in December 1999.[20]

There are clear limits to the domestic consensus on peace operations, however. The parliamentary and public reluctance to abandon Finland's traditional approach to peacekeeping has been and remains strong, and there is no support for sending Finnish troops abroad to participate in offensive operations. Three examples illustrate the strong parliamentary abhorrence for offensive operations: the parliamentary insistence in 1995 that the Finnish troops committed to IFOR should not be allowed to participate in offensive operations; the veto in the spring of 1998 of the procurement of small combat helicopters intended to protect the transport helicopters also being procured on the grounds that they could be used offensively; and the concern triggered in 2003 by the revelation that the Ministry of Defence was considering giving the air force's F/A-18 C/D Hornet fighters the capability to attack targets on the ground.[21]

The parliamentary aversion to offensive operations is shared by the public and President Halonen as well. While a 52 per cent majority of the Finnish public approved the US attack on Afghanistan in 2002, 84 per cent opposed Finnish participation in the war.[22] Halonen reflected the same sentiment in a speech in 2000 when she approvingly noted that: 'A characteristic feature of Finland ever since she gained independence has been a determination to remain uninvolved in international disputes – and especially armed conflicts.'[23]

Mobilizing support for Finnish participation in enforcement or war operations directed against specific enemies is, in short, out of the question in the foreseeable future.

Government role in mobilizing and sustaining domestic support

Finnish governments have been very consensus-oriented in their approach to peace operations. They have been careful to cultivate and sustain broad political support for both troop deployments and changes in policy. Proposals have usually been dropped if they failed to attract broad political support. Examples include the proposal to send troops to Bosnia in 1993 as part of NORDBAT 2; the 1995 proposal to establish a rapid reaction brigade for peace operations, which had to be postponed to the following year; and the protracted efforts (1993–2000) to revise the Act on Peacekeeping in a way that permitted Finnish participation in 'enlarged peacekeeping', but not offensive operations or peace enforcement.

The increased risk of casualties has been an issue in Finnish debate in the 1990s. It was used as an argument by traditionalists in the first part of the 1990s to oppose Finnish involvement in peace operations that went beyond traditional peacekeeping, and it also figured prominently in the debates preceding the Finnish deployments in Bosnia and Kosovo. The risk of losses played less of a role in the debate preceding the deployment in ISAF even though Defence Minister Jan-Erik Enestam characterized the operation in Afghanistan as far riskier than the one in Kosovo.[24] This does not necessarily mean that Finnish politicians and the public have accepted the risks, however. It may reflect the fact that the Finnish contribution was small and relatively low-risk, involving a CIMIC company.

Since the Finnish contingents participating in 'enlarged peacekeeping' operations in the Balkans and in Afghanistan have not suffered any casualties from hostile fire, it is difficult to predict whether significant casualties could lead to withdrawals or even a return to the Cold War approach.[25] That Finnish decision makers have done relatively little to prepare the public for casualties increases the risk that casualties will trigger irresistible calls for a withdrawal and a general change of policy. Three factors suggest such a scenario unlikely, however. The first is the strong political and public support that the current Finnish approach to peace operations enjoys. The second is the Finnish interest in maintaining the confidence of Finland's partners in the EU and NATO. The third is the fact that such calls historically have been ignored. This was the case in 1974 when 17 Finnish troops were wounded during the Turkish invasion on Cyprus,[26] and again in 1985 when the kidnapping of 23 Finnish UN troops in Lebanon caused an uproar in Finland.[27]

Permissive legal framework

Finland has made three legal amendments to facilitate participation in contemporary peace operations. At the beginning of the 1990s, the Finnish Peacekeeping Act of 1984 allowed Finland to make a maximum of 2,000 personnel, including reserves, available for UN peacekeeping operations. Decisions to send troops were made by the president based on a proposal put forward by the government after prior consultation with the Foreign Affairs Committee of parliament. The first amendment came in 1993 when the Act was widened to include OSCE operations as well. The second amendment was more far-reaching and controversial constituting a break with the 'traditional peacekeeping only' approach. It was passed in December 1995 to allow participation in IFOR. To this end, the new Act allowed for participation in peace operations carried out by regional organizations acting on a mandate from the UN or the OSCE, and widened the scope for defensive use of force to permit participation in 'enlarged peacekeeping' operations characterized by limited consent and ROE allowing reactive use of force in defence of the mission and civilians. Participation in 'peace enforcement' involving offensive use of force against designated enemies was explicitly ruled out, however.[28] This distinction was less than clear and created problems for the Finnish commanders who had to clear orders from their superiors in the field with Helsinki, and refuse to carry them out if they were judged to involve 'offensive operations'.

This problem was addressed by a third amendment passed in 2000. As a result of this amendment, the determination as to whether Finnish forces can participate fully in an operation will now be made by the government prior to deployment on the basis of the nature of the operation, the mandate and the ROE. Under the new Act, the government must consult parliament, and not just the Foreign Affairs Committee, if the ROE of the force are wider than in traditional peacekeeping, and this is also the case if the ROE are widened during an ongoing operation.[29] Finally, the new Act also makes it legal for Finnish troops to participate in humanitarian operations on request by a special organization or agency of the UN. This revision was made to prevent a repetition of the situation in 1999 when Finnish peacekeepers in Macedonia had to turn down a request from UNHCR for humanitarian assistance because the operation in question (NATO's AFOR) did not have the UN mandate then required by the Finnish Peacekeeping Act.[30]

A fourth amendment was in the cards in September 2005 as the Finnish government submitted a bill to parliament which, if passed, would permit Finnish participation in peace enforcement operations, involving offensive use of force against designated enemies, as well as participation in peace operations without a UN mandate in exceptional situations. The proposed law on military crisis management would bring Finnish legislation in line with that of the other Nordic countries. The only remaining difference would be that the Finnish govenment still could not order its regulars abroad on peace operations.

The principal factor motivating this comprehensive reform of the Peacekeeping Act was the desire to enable Finland to participate fully in the development of the military crisis management capacity of the EU. The Ministry of Defence (MoD) had been lobbying for a reform since late 2001, but it was the 2004 decision to participate in the establishment of EU battle groups that created the sense of urgency required to move the issue along. The bill, which is based on recommendations proposed by a working group established by the Ministry of Foreign Affairs (MFA), is expected to pass since it enjoys the support of the Minister of Defence, the Minister of Foreign Affairs, the Chief of Defence, the President and the Prime Minister.[31]

The adoption of the new law is unlikely to make much of a difference in practice, however. Finnish participation in enforcement operations involving offensive operations against designated enemies and operations without a UN mandate continue to seem highly unlikely in the foreseeable future. As mentioned above, political and public support for such operations would be very hard to mobilize, President Halonen only supported the new bill reluctantly and the Finnish aversion to offensive operations lacking a UN mandate was illustrated by the strong reaction to the US-led war against Iraq in 2003. The Finnish government characterized it as 'unacceptable',[32] and ruled out contributing to a post-war peacekeeping force unless it had a UN mandate.

Financing

The Finnish costs of participation have increased five-fold since the early 1990s: from EUR 26.9 million (FIM 160 million) in 1993 to EUR 105.8 million in 2004 (Table 5.1).[33] Major General Pertti Nykänen, who participated in a working group established by the MFA in 1993 to consider how Finland should tackle the challenges posed by post-Cold War peacekeeping, was thus on target with his estimate that it would be six times more expensive to participate in 'enlarged peacekeeping' than traditional peacekeeping operations.[34]

The rising costs have not led to changes in the budgetary procedures or policy. Expenditures are split between the MFA and the MoD and the ministries are happy with the current arrangement which was adopted in the late 1980s.[35] The MFA covers payroll and training expenses for both civilian and military personnel, whereas the MoD covers material expenses, administrative costs as well as the participation of military observers. Unexpected costs resulting from new operations that cannot be covered by the appropriations on the regular MFA and MoD budgets are financed by supplementary budgets.[36] This is also true for the procurement of

Table 5.1 MFA and MoD expenditures and estimates on international peace operations 1998–2004 (current prices; EUR million)

	1998[a]	*1999*[a]	*2000*	*2001*	*2002*	*2003*[b]	*2004*[b]
MFA military personnel	43.668	46.932	60.733	52.343	45.808	54.079	51.971
MFA civilian personnel	4.992	9.693	6.191	5.720	7.926	10.288	10.363
MoD	17.927	43.920	31.236	7.318	24.466	59.368	43.424
Total	66.587	100.545	98.160	65.381	78.200	123.735	105.758

Sources: The government proposals to parliament for the state budget 2000–04.

Notes
a   Figures before 2000 have been converted from FIM to EUR at FIM 100 = EUR 16.81.
b   Budget estimates.

special equipment needed for the international operations. A separate appropriation of EUR 67.3 million has thus been allocated for the 2002–06 period for the procurement of special equipment for international activities.[37]

The growing costs have not served as a major constraint on the Finnish deployments either. Financing has not become a political issue or a source of disagreement between the politicians and the military leadership. This is not to say that economic considerations have been unimportant. Financing was a recurring problem during the Cold War,[38] and the need to find money to pay for the growing involvement in the Balkans also influenced the decisions to turn down UN requests for deployments in Belgrade (replacement for a French logistic battalion) and Bosnia (NORDBAT 2) in the first half of 1993, and to withdraw the Finnish battalion from UNDOF by the end of that year.[39] Still, it is important not to exaggerate the importance played by financial considerations in these decisions. Even if the Finnish economy had not been in deep recession, the Balkan deployments would probably have been turned down due to the strong opposition to Finnish involvement in operations going beyond traditional peacekeeping by President Mauno Koivisto and several prominent members of the political and military elites. That economic considerations were less than decisive is also suggested by the fact that they played very little role in the debate preceding the decision to participate in IFOR two years later.

Explaining the changes of the 1990s

The changes in the Finnish approach in many ways mirror the changes found in the other Nordic countries: peace operations are seen as far more important than before, the contributions are higher in terms of both civilian and military personnel, the traditional approach to peacekeeping operations has been abandoned, participation is no longer restricted to the UN, legal adjustments have been made to facilitate participation and the costs have increased dramatically.

These similarities are not surprising as Finland was subjected to the same external forces as the other Nordic countries. The end of the Cold War made the changes possible, the wars in the Balkans gave Finland a security interest in stemming the spread of violence and refugees, the operations in the Balkans created a need to go beyond traditional peacekeeping, pressures from the EU and NATO increased the political costs of non-involvement and finally the new normative climate resulting from the end of the Cold War meant that the changes could be legitimized as a logical continuation of the UN policy pursued during the Cold War.[40]

These external forces cannot explain the two main differences that set Finland apart from the other Nordic countries: the slow pace of reform and the strong reluctance to go beyond traditional peacekeeping. Two national factors explain these differences: threat perceptions and the historical relations with Russia.

Threat perceptions

Unlike the other Nordic countries, Finland has still not buried the military threat from the East. Although the likelihood of a large-scale attack on Finland is now regarded as low, an attack on Finland is still not ruled out, and Finnish defence planning is consequently focused on preventing and, if need be, repulsing a 'strategic strike intended to force the state leadership into taking desired decisions by paralysing central institutions and functions of society and the defence system'.[41] This priority is also reflected in the force structure which continues to be based on general conscription.

The priority attached to national defence has slowed down the process of reform and left less room for the internationalization that characterizes the armed forces of the other Nordic countries. Instead of engaging in fundamental restructuring, Finland has sought to meet the challenges of contemporary peace operations by establishing the FRDF, but it is telling that even this modest step of internationalization was opposed by 51 of the 200 members of parliament on the grounds that it would weaken national defence.[42] This argument has also been used to oppose Finnish participation in operations going beyond traditional peacekeeping.

While Finland's geopolitical location next to Russia helps to explain why Finland remains unwilling to bury the threat from the Russian bear completely, geographic proximity holds no explanatory power in itself. To understand the Finnish threat perceptions and the aversion to war, which plays a strong role in the reluctance to go beyond traditional peacekeeping, one has to look at the historical relationship with the Russian neighbour.[43]

Relations with Russia

The Finnish parliament exploited the Russian Revolution in 1917 to declare Finland independent from Russia, and the remaining part of the century was spent defending this status in the face of Soviet pressure. Finland fought two wars against the Soviet Union during the Second World War to preserve her independence,[44] and the Cold War was one long struggle to keep the Soviets at arms length while convincing the rest of the world that Finland was an independent state and not a Soviet satellite.[45] The two principal components in the Finnish policy was a credible defence capability, the importance of which was underlined by the two wars, and a policy of non-involvement in international conflicts reflecting a deeply held aversion to the use of force for offensive purposes.

The latter aversion is not hard to understand considering that more than 80,000 Finns lost their lives in the two wars against the Soviet Union, and that 30,000 Finns died in the course of the Finnish Civil War in 1918.[46] Thus, Finland always stayed neutral in armed conflicts as well as disputes involving the superpowers during the Cold War. Instead, Finland sought to promote peaceful conflict resolution and the rule of law in international relations. In the words of President Urho Kekkonen, Finland saw its role on the international scene as that of 'physician rather than a judge',[47] and this view remains relevant as a guide to understanding Finnish foreign policy today. One indication is found in the controversy triggered by the Finnish vote in favour of UN resolution 678 authorizing the war against Iraq in 1990. This was seen in some quarters as a violation of Finnish neutrality even though this war enjoyed near universal support because it was fought to uphold the cardinal principle in the UN Charter: the ban on interstate aggression.[48]

Another indication is the concern often expressed in the first part of the 1990s that participation in operations involving the use of force beyond self-defence would undermine the Finnish reputation for neutrality and impartiality and make it impossible for Finland to play its favourite role as a mediator on the international scene.[49] A final indication can be found in President Halonen's quote of 2000 mentioned above in favour of Finnish non-involvement in the armed conflicts of others.[50]

Factors determining specific contributions

Two factors have served to make the Finnish deployment pattern different from that of the other Nordic countries. The first is a stronger public and political desire to support UN-commanded peace operations with large contingents.[51] This factor explains why Finland as the only Nordic country continued to provide a battalion for an ongoing UN peacekeeping operation outside of Europe throughout the 1990s (UNIFIL).[52] While Finland, as mentioned above, did withdraw its battalion in Golan in 1993, the 500-strong Finnish battalion in UNIFIL in Lebanon stayed in place until the end of 2001. It also explains the decision taken in December 2000 to provide 200 personnel to UNMEE in Eritrea.[53]

This support for UN operations is also related to the second factor that distinguishes Finland from the other Nordic states: a greater reluctance to go beyond traditional peacekeeping. The UNIFIL commitment obviously made it easier for Finland to resist pressures for more personnel to the operations in the Balkans. The Finnish contributions to these 'enlarged peacekeeping' operations were not only considerably smaller than the other Nordic contributions, but the Finnish contingents were also softer (construction and CIMIC) and operating under more restrictive ROE. Until 1999 when some 800 personnel were made available for KFOR, Finland essentially tried to stick to its traditional peacekeeping approach. While the large contribution to KFOR, which involved infantry and employed wider ROE than was the case in IFOR/SFOR, may be seen as an indication that the aversion to 'enlarged peacekeeping' may be easing, Finland remains unwilling to participate in enforcement operations involving offensive operations against designated enemies.

A third factor shaping Finnish deployment decisions is the requirement for OSCE or UN mandates. Like Sweden, Finland has consistently turned down requests for contributions to operations without such mandates,[54] and the requirement for a mandate was emphasized again in 2003 when the Finnish government, as mentioned above, made participation in a peacekeeping force in Iraq contingent upon the existence of a UN mandate.

A fourth, and very important, factor has been the interest in improving the Finnish standing within the EU and NATO, which is seen as crucial for Finland's national security and international position. While the UN continues to be a priority in Finnish policy, improving relations with the EU and NATO has become more important in the course of the 1990s. The growing Finnish involvement in NATO's operations in the Balkans, and more recently the EU's, is a reflection of this. Whereas MFA officials tone down the shift in priorities by emphasizing that the UN continues to be just as important as the EU and NATO,[55] the Finnish military makes no bones about its priorities: 'The EU provides the most important framework for Finland's Defence Forces' international activities... Our first priority is to take part in EU-led PSO-operations in the Nordic framework.'[56] NATO's Partnership for Peace (PfP) programme is viewed as equally important because it offers 'the only environment to develop cooperation capabilities and to make national capabilities compatible for both EU-led and NATO-led crisis-management operations.'[57] The interest in developing closer relations with NATO through the PfP programme thus played an important role in the 1996 decision to establish the NATO-compatible FRDF.[58]

The interest in enhancing the Finnish standing within the EU became an important driver of deployment decisions because Finland like Sweden had to fight suspicions that it would free-ride and hamper the efforts to give the EU a security dimension after it handed in its EU application in 1992. These concerns were expressed by the Commission and several EU members during the application process, and they surfaced again on the eve of the Finnish EU presidency in the first half of 1999.[59] Finland's growing involvement in the peace operations in the Balkans and especially the decision to move beyond traditional peacekeeping and participate in IFOR was strongly motivated by the desire to dispel these concerns and prove Finnish trustworthiness and reliability, not just in the EU but also in NATO where Finland has participated in the PfP programme since 1994. In addition, it is also a principal motivation behind Finland's strong support for the establishment of an EU crisis management capacity.

A fifth and final factor worth mentioning is the emphasis placed on Nordic cooperation. Finland prefers to work together with the other Nordic countries in the field. When asked to rank Finland's partners of choice,

Finnish MFA officials placed the Nordic countries at the top of the list followed by Great Britain, the EU and the USA.[60] The importance of Nordic cooperation is visible both at the rhetorical level and on the ground where Finnish contingents often cooperate with contingents from the other Nordic countries. Finnish contributions thus tend to be legitimized with reference to Nordic cooperation as this has a special resonance with the public and parliament. The IFOR deployment – the first that formally went beyond traditional peacekeeping – was greatly facilitated by the fact that the Finnish contingent was going to serve in a Nordic–Polish brigade. The same was true for the Finnish decision to establish a joint EU battle group with Sweden in October 2004 and invite Norway to join in.[61] The need to catch up with the other Nordic countries was also a forceful argument for change in the course of the 1990s. The Danish Reaction Brigade served as an inspiration and helped legitimize the establishment of the FRDF, and the decision to go beyond traditional peacekeeping was greatly facilitated by the decisions taken in the other Nordic countries to do so. The Finnish military did clearly not appreciate being left behind and feared marginalization when NORDBAT 2 went to Bosnia in 1993.[62] The military has also used Nordic cooperation to legitimize its closer cooperation with the EU and NATO.

Civilian and military personnel deployable at short notice

Civilian crisis management became a priority area in Finnish foreign and security policy in the second half of the 1990s, and rapid reaction capacities have been mushrooming since then. Finland has made 75 police officers available for the EU's rapid reaction police force, approximately 1 per cent of the national force,[63] and 52 Finnish police officers participated in international operations under the auspices of the EU, the OSCE and the UN in 2002.[64]

Rapid reaction registers have also been established for election monitors, human rights monitors and other types of civilian experts. These registers were merged into one in 2001 by the MFA and the new register was made compatible with the REACT system employed by the OSCE to enhance rapid reaction.[65] In early 2004 the register held details of 608 experts.[66]

The Ministry of Justice has assembled a register of Finnish experts to assist in the administration of civil and criminal justice, development of basic rights and legislation, improvement of the judiciary and prison system, planning and development of the electoral system, and election monitoring. The register includes circuit judges, prosecutors, advocates and experts from the Ministry of Justice and it will be added to the register of experts established by the MFA. The ambition is to be able to dispatch up to ten judicial administration experts simultaneously for civilian crisis management tasks.[67] As of May 2004, Finland had made 25 rule-of-law and civil administration experts available to the EU civilian crisis management rapid reaction force.[68]

Finally, Finland's rescue services have established a rapid reaction force, the Finn Rescue Force (FRF), for disaster evaluations and rescue missions abroad. The FRF comprises personnel from Finland's five largest emergency centres, with a combined total strength of about 200 professional rescue personnel and other experts. Eight experts were available to the UN Disaster Assessment and Coordination (UNDAC) team in January 2004,[69] and 196 personnel had been committed to the EU rapid reaction force.[70] Readiness for departure can be achieved in anything from a few hours to one or two days, depending on the number of personnel needed.

The military rapid reaction capacity has also been strengthened considerably. A major step was taken with the establishment of the FRDF, giving Finland the capacity to deploy a battalion abroad at any given time. The first FRDF battalion became operational in 1998 and went to Kosovo the following year.[71] Since then additional units have been added to the rapid reaction pool, and Finland now offers a wider variety of army personnel for international service than ever before. Navy units have also been included for the first time and air force units may be included after 2006.[72] Until then the Finnish air force can only participate in international exercises.[73] All the rapid reaction forces (2,000 personnel) listed in Table 5.2 have been made available to the EU, NATO, NORDCAPS and the UN, and they are supposed to be ready for deployment 30 days after a political decision has been taken. In reality, this may not be possible for larger contributions. Although the Finnish infantry battalion in Kosovo was the first non-NATO contingent to take operational control in KFOR,[74] assembling the force had taken nearly two months or twice as long as it

Table 5.2 Military rapid reaction forces with a readiness of 30 days or less (2004)

	Forces	EU	NATO/PARP	NORDCAPS	SHIRBRIG	UNSAS
Army	Military observers	X	X	X	. .	X
	Staff officers	X	X	X	. .	X
	Brigade C3I; framework nation and brigade HQ logistical capability	X	. .	X	. .	. .
	1 infantry battalion	X	X	X	X	
	1 engineer battalion	X	X	X	X	X
	1 transport company	X	X	X	X	X
	1 CIMIC company	X	X	X	. .	X
	CIMIC group framework	X	X	X	. .	X
Navy	1 minelayer	X	X	X	. .	. .

Source: Finnish MoD.

was supposed to.[75] Deploying 300 personnel on 10 days' notice as part of the Finnish–Norwegian-Swedish EU battle group will therefore be quite a challenge for the Finnish armed forces.

Although the Finnish government legally can commit up to 2,000 personnel for peace operations at a time, this has never happened in practice and such a deployment could only be maintained for a short period of time.[76] As mentioned above, the deployments since the end of the Cold War indicate a sustainable capacity of some 1,300 personnel a year. The Finnish participation in peace operations is based entirely on volunteers who have made a commitment to report for international service with seven days' notice. No personnel, including regulars, can be ordered abroad and the commitment made to go on an international mission is not legally binding. Volunteers can thus renege on their commitment until they board the plane taking them abroad. This has occasionally caused problems. As many as 25 per cent of the officers in a contingent have said no after training had been completed and it was time to go, and the increased need for personnel with specialized skills is beginning to take its toll on the regulars.[77] The recruitment of privates has so far not been a major problem, however. Some 5,000–6,000 apply for international service each year and an impressive 98 per cent of the volunteers for the FRDF make a commitment to go on an international mission upon the completion of their training.[78] Moreover, the personnel requirement is also eased by the fact that most volunteers serve 12-month tours in order to qualify for attractive tax breaks. It has been possible to serve six-month tours since 1999.[79]

In developing its rapid reaction capacity, Finland has made a conscious decision to specialize in areas where it believes that its peacekeeping tradition and its technical know-how give it a comparative advantage. Priority has thus been given to CIMIC and high-tech capabilities such as command, control and communications systems and protection against weapons of mass destruction.[80]

Training to prepare the civilian and military personnel for their many new tasks

Finland claims to be among 'the leading countries in the EU and the OSCE in the training of civilian crisis management experts',[81] and this is also correct in the sense that Finland is one of nine countries involved in the development of the EU's civilian crisis management training programme.[82] A pilot project, which eventually may lead to the establishment of an EU centre for civilian crisis management, was initiated in 2002,[83] and the Ministry of Justice also plans to arrange special training for the personnel in its rapid reaction register for judicial experts.[84] However, by early 2004 the training provided for the civilian personnel other than the police, who receive a UN Police Officer Course,[85] remained rather limited.

Some mission-oriented training has been provided by the Finnish Defence Forces International Centre (FINCENT), but the efforts have thus far been hampered by a lack of money. To reduce the need for pre-mission training, the MFA, which recruits most of the civilian personnel, has recruited highly qualified personnel only and teamed up first-timers with experienced personnel. Most training has been provided on the job in the mission areas.[86]

The need for improved military training was underlined immediately by Defence Minister Elisabeth Rehn when Finnish participation in 'enlarged peacekeeping' was first debated in 1993,[87] and this requirement was one of the factors that eventually led to the establishment of the rapid reaction brigade earmarked for peace operations (FRDF). FINCENT has also been beefed up to meet the training requirements of the 1990s.

Since 1996 when training for the FRDF began, Finnish volunteers for peace operations have been trained in two ways. Volunteers, who have already completed their military training as conscripts, join the traditional way by responding to advertisements. They then receive 3–4 weeks of training at FINCENT before they are deployed in the field or put on standby for peacekeeping service for a year, during which time they must be ready to report for mission-oriented training with seven days' notice. At the end of the mission-oriented training programme, the actual selection of personnel takes place and approved volunteers then sign up for a 6- to 12-month tour, which may be extended for an additional 6 months. This training programme is essentially the same as the one employed during the Cold War.

Conscripts interested in international service have the additional option of joining the FRDF, whose personnel are put through a specialized training programme. The selected volunteers are first trained for warfighting in a national defence role and assigned to a wartime unit. It is followed by three months of training in international crisis management and peace-keeping. The aim of this training is to create coherent units capable of functioning in a multinational force. The training language is therefore often English, in particular in communications and close order exercises. In addition to the three-month programme in peace operations, some volunteers participate in an international crisis management exercise such as Nordic Peace. At the end of their training volunteers are asked to sign a standby contract involving a willingness to report for international service at an unknown location with seven days' notice. The standby contract lasts for a year and can be extended for a year at a time.[88] Prior to deployment the personnel receive mission-oriented training.

The Finnish regulars volunteering for international service also receive basic training in peace operations, and this training is supplemented with specialized training within the PfP and NORDCAPS programmes. In addition to training their own nationals, Finland is also offering training to foreigners within these frameworks. At FINCENT Finland offers PfP partners peacekeeping courses, and Finnish personnel are also involved in peace operations planning, training and consulting abroad.

Interoperability with the most likely partners

Achieving interoperability with NATO countries has been a main priority for the Finnish defence forces ever since Finland joined PfP in 1994, and for good reason. Language proved to be a major problem when Finland provided personnel to NORDBAT 1 in Macedonia in 1993 as only half the personnel according to Norwegian officers spoke proper English.[89] Language problems also reduced the operational effectiveness of the first Finnish contingents in IFOR.[90] On top of this came problems related to lack of knowledge of NATO procedures, materiel and so on. These problems have now been overcome as a result of an energetic effort to meet the interoperability goals set by NATO in the Planning and Review Process (PARP). Finland has gone out of its way to achieve interoperability, adopting NATO map marking symbols, NATO procedures, staff organization and NATO interoperable equipment.[91]

Annually, more than 1,000 Finnish soldiers participate in about 400 PfP events and exercises, NATO courses and meetings.[92] These efforts have paid off. The Finnish KFOR battalion deployed in Kosovo in 1999 did not experience any interoperability problems related to equipment, procedures or language.[93] By 2001 Finland's reaction forces met the goals required for NATO interoperability,[94] and this was further underlined when Finland in May 2003 became the first non-NATO member ever to command a multinational brigade in a NATO-commanded peace operation (KFOR).[95]

In addition to the efforts undertaken within the PfP, Finland has used its involvement in NORDCAPS, SHIRBRIG and UNSAS to enhance its interoperability, and it is also deeply involved in the establishment of the EU crisis management capacity. Finland has thus assumed the framework nation responsibility for the development of command, control, communications and information system for the NORDCAPS brigade, and it is involved in the establishment of two EU battle groups, one involving Norway and Sweden and another set up by Germany and The Netherlands.[96]

Armaments and ROE permitting use of force beyond self-defence if necessary

The unwillingness to participate in peace enforcement left Finnish decision makers with the challenge of defining a workable middle ground option between traditional peacekeeping and peace enforcement.

The solution became 'enlarged peacekeeping', a concept clearly modelled on the situation in Bosnia. Enlarged peacekeeping has the following hallmarks:

1 The situation or its perpetuation poses a threat to international peace and security.
2 Use of force is authorized in a UN resolution, whereas in conventional peacekeeping this authorization is expressly given by the Secretary-General and endorsed by the Security Council.
3 Use of force is authorized under Chapter VII of the UN Charter, without particular emphasis on self-defence.
4 One or more of the conflicting parties has not given its consent or active commitment to fulfilling the goals of the operation.

A sharp distinction is drawn between enlarged peacekeeping and peace enforcement, which is defined as an operation undertaken without consent and involving the use of full-scale force in order to avert or repel an attack as was the case in Operation Desert Storm.[97] While this distinction is easy to make at the theoretical level, it will often be difficult in the field. A withdrawal of consent may necessitate a shift from enlarged peacekeeping to enforcement as was the case in Bosnia, and full-scale use of force has as a rule been permitted in defence of the mandate on enlarged peacekeeping operations. The Finnish solution to this problem until 1999 was to issue their contingents deployed on enlarged peacekeeping operations (IFOR and SFOR) with very restrictive ROE ruling out Finnish involvement in any tasks that might involve use of force beyond self-defence. If there was a risk that this might happen, Finnish commanders had to check with Helsinki before carrying out their orders. The result was frustrating not just for the Finnish commanders but also their partners in the NORDPOL brigade since the Finnish contingent was unable to contribute fully in the tasks at hand.[98]

To avoid this problem, the Finnish KFOR contingent was provided with wider ROE, and a lasting solution was found in the Act on Peace Support Operations passed in 2000. Under this Act, the government determines whether an operation should be classified as enlarged peace-keeping or peace enforcement before committing troops, so that Finnish contingents can participate fully when deployed.

There was consensus from the start in 1993 when the debate began that Finnish participation in peace operations going beyond traditional peace-keeping would require better protection in the form of armoured vehicles and mine clearing equipment and more firepower to enable effective defence. Mortars, grenade launchers, heavy machine guns and antitank missiles were seen as essential from the beginning,[99] and tanks and artillery were added to the list of recommended equipment later as a result of the lessons learned in Bosnia.[100]

One could actually argue that the Finnish military already had learned this lesson the hard way in Lebanon in the 1980s. The Finnish contingent in UNIFIL was thus equipped with APCs and heavier weapons once it was realized that consent and cooperation from the parties could not be taken for granted. Moreover, prominent Finnish officers with experience from UNIFIL such as Ensio Siilasvuo and Gustav Hägglund had already made the case for equipping peacekeeping forces with APCs and heavy weapons, including artillery and tanks, before the Balkan operations were launched.[101] The Finnish armed forces in other words participated in 'enlarged peacekeeping' before they invented the term.

That the lesson has been acted on is evident from a look at the equipment of the Finnish KFOR battalion. It had 70 SISU APCs, a combat support company equipped with 120 and 81 mm mortars and tube-launched, optically tracked, wire-guided (TOW) missiles, night vision equipment, secure communications and an explosive ordnance disposal (EOD) team with modern equipment.[102]

Logistics

Providing for the Finnish contingents deployed in enlarged peacekeeping operations proved a challenge, as they required better and more equipment and supplies than the traditional UN contingents. Gearing up for the new challenges took time. Some of the equipment used by the defence forces proved inadequate for the conditions abroad (the supposedly best field kitchens in the world were worn out after just three months in Kosovo),[103] and it initially proved difficult to get the equipment ready in time as was the case with the construction unit in IFOR.[104] To address these problems FINCENT was put in charge of supplying all the Finnish contingents abroad and provided with full-time staff to handle logistics.[105] In addition to enhancing its national support capacity Finland also intensified its cooperation with its Nordic partners, first in the Balkans, where the Nordic Support Group in SFOR was considered one of the most successful examples of multilateral cooperation in the operation,[106] and Finland subsequently established a joint flight service with Norway and Sweden in order to supply their contingents in Afghanistan.[107]

Medical, psychological and family support

Post-mission stress and other psychological problems were quite small during the Cold War and there has not been any significant change in the 1990s even though the stress levels in some operations may have been higher. This can in part be explained by the increased emphasis placed on psychological support. The support provided to the personnel has been enhanced and the Finnish system is similar to the one employed in the other Nordic countries. Personnel are briefed on psychological stress reactions and ways to deal with them prior to departure; openness about possible problems is encouraged and personnel are urged to talk with the trained personnel in the mission area about any problems they might have; the psychological status of personnel is monitored by trained personnel in the mission areas; standard procedures exist for the provision of additional assistance when required; and debriefing sessions are carried out by trained personnel after stressful incidents.[108]

The support provided to the families has also been enhanced. Information is available on websites, and situation reports from the mission areas are updated on a weekly basis. The families are given a contact number at FINCENT to call if they encounter problems, and the Finnish Blue Berets Association runs a special project to help the families. The Finnish defence forces have also made it much easier for the families to get hold of their loved ones in the field in real time. The personnel serving abroad can be contacted via e-mail and phone, and a deal with a Finnish mobile phone operator allows families to contact personnel in Afghanistan at almost the same rate as domestic calls in Finland. The most important feature of the support programme is without doubt the leave arrangement, which is much envied in the other Nordic countries. All Finnish personnel get six days leave a month. Most personnel go home for a week after four weeks' service, but it is also possible to work eight weeks and then spend two weeks at home. All flights from and to Finland are free of charge.[109] This liberal leave system not only reduces the hardship for the families, but it also makes international service more attractive for personnel and serves to reduce the risk of psychological problems.

The medical support provided for personnel has not changed markedly, except for the procurement of new equipment such as the armoured SISU ambulances. Finnish battalions are provided with field hospitals, doctors, dentists and medics. Training in first aid is a priority and conducted frequently during missions, and arrangements for the repatriation of wounded or injured personnel are made in each mission.[110]

Intelligence capacity

Intelligence had traditionally not been a priority on the UN-led operations due to the restrictions on such activities by the UN. Things changed when Finland began to take part in NATO-led operations where intelligence played a much bigger role. The Finnish construction battalion in IFOR did not have its own intelligence section and it proved difficult for the Finns to obtain intelligence from other contingents, including the Nordics. The intelligence personnel from the other Nordic countries started holding informal meetings on a regular basis in Sarajevo in 1995, but Denmark and Norway initially opposed Finnish participation. Lack of trust was part of the explanation but the main factor was concern that Great Britain and the USA would put a stop to further intelligence sharing if they found out that it was shared with Finland. The situation gradually improved but the process was slow and it was only in KFOR that Finland was finally allowed to participate fully on an equal footing with the others in the Nordic intelligence cells in which the informal cooperation eventually resulted.[111]

Finland reacted by beefing up its own intelligence capacities considerably. The SFOR and KFOR contingents both had intelligence sections (ten personnel) and electronic warfare sections (ten personnel). Additional personnel were deployed in the Nordic intelligence cells in Bosnia and Kosovo, and in KFOR Finland also established a Finnish Intelligence Organization consisting of six personnel.[112]

Public information capacity

In an article published in 1990, Gustav Hägglund, the future Finnish chief of defence, argued that the importance of public relations had been underestimated on UN peacekeeping operations and that the handling of the press required a professional spokesperson.[113] Ten years later Colonel Arto Tuomas Räty, who commanded the first Finnish KFOR contingent, reiterated the call for putting more emphasis on media operations, which he identified as an area in need of further improvement.[114] The Finnish defence forces have made progress in the intervening years, however. Finnish battalions now have two public information officers who are trained journalists, and information campaigns are devised prior to deployment as a matter of policy. Once in the field the public information officers cooperate closely with the CIMIC personnel to make the information campaigns for the local population as effective as possible. Full-time information officers are only deployed on battalion-size deployments. In smaller deployments public information is handled by an officer as part of normal duties.[115]

Coordination and cooperation capacity

CIMIC is a priority and seen as something that Finnish peacekeepers do better than other countries. The following remarks by Foreign Minister Erkki Tuomioja are typical in this respect:

> Whereas the peacekeepers of a superpower army prefer to stay heavily armed in their vehicles, without any dialogue with the locals other than that which is based on orders, Finnish peacekeepers try, whenever possible and without compromising their military capability, to build up cooperation with the local inhabitants, based on confidence, and to establish bridges – sometimes literally – between mutually suspicious, mutually hostile and sulky population groups.[116]

While this is also true of the peacekeepers from Britain and the other Nordic countries, Finland does have something to brag about. Its UNIFIL contingent in Lebanon was substantially involved in civilian projects and this has continued in the 1990s[117] where CIMIC personnel have played an important role in the Finnish contributions to SFOR, KFOR and ISAF. The CIMIC contribution to SFOR was substantial. Finland was put in charge of the multinational CIMIC company established in the Nordic–Polish Battle Group (NPBG) in 2000 and provided most of the personnel and the funds for its work. In 2001 the entire Finnish contribution to SFOR (105 personnel) consisted of CIMIC personnel.[118] The Danish and Swedish CIMIC units were quite envious of the Finnish unit's annual budget of more than FIM 1 million (EUR 168,000) but it also created an imbalance in the work carried out in the NPBG's area of responsibility since the Danes and the Swedes were unable to provide the same level of assistance as the Finns.[119]

The Finnish KFOR battalion had a CIMIC section of five to six personnel plus liaison officers for each company. Their work was facilitated by the hiring of 50 local interpreters, a high number for a battalion.[120] In ISAF Finland contributed the largest CIMIC unit (50 personnel).

The Finnish CIMIC units have a good reputation. A Swedish study published in 1998 comparing the Danish, British, Finnish and Swedish CIMIC contingents in Bosnia concluded that the Finnish rotation system was superior to the one used by the other nations, which rotated all personnel every six months. In contrast, the Finnish CIMIC personnel serve for twelve months, only a third of the unit is rotated at a time, and the rotation is carried out with an overlap period of two weeks. The Finnish model ensures both greater continuity and less loss of local knowledge than the models employed by the other nations.[121] A weakness identified in the Finnish model at the time, the need to have CIMIC projects approved by the MFA in Helsinki, was remedied in Kosovo, where the MFA had a local representative in Pristina approving the CIMIC projects proposed by the Finnish battalion.[122] The MFA had given the battalion an annual CIMIC budget of EUR 150,000.[123]

The coordination between the MFA and the MoD is close and has a long tradition going back to the Cold War. The coordination with the other relevant ministries is now being improved as the growing Finnish involvement in civilian crisis management has created a need for closer cooperation with the Ministry of the Interior and the Ministry of Justice. Working groups with representatives from these ministries were established in 2002 and 2003, and the establishment of central registers with the civilian personnel will also facilitate overall coordination.

The MFA has not established close partnerships with national NGOs, in contrast to the case in Denmark and Norway. While the MFA is in favour of establishing a closer working relationship, the Finnish NGOs have thus far been rather unwilling to do so. However, it is not a major priority for the MFA since the number of relevant Finnish NGOs is rather limited. Establishing partnerships with international NGOs is therefore seen as more important.[124]

Public security capacity

As mentioned already, Finland has enhanced its civilian capacity in this area. The pool of civilian personnel and rule-of-law personnel that is available for deployment on international operations has been enhanced, and the number of personnel actually deployed has increased. The military capacity has also been enhanced, but not much. The Finnish defence forces are not exactly keen on public security tasks and prefer to leave them to civilians. The Finnish defence forces do not carry out such tasks at home, although they may act in support of the police and other civilian authorities in emergencies, and they would consequently like to limit their involvement in such tasks as much as possible. However, the Finnish defence forces have also put increased emphasis on riot control in its training programmes and procured new equipment for this task. All personnel are given a basic introduction to riot control, whereas special units such as quick reaction forces are given more comprehensive training. The exact nature of the training programme obviously depends on the mission at hand. Finnish personnel are equipped with batons, shields and personal armour and are trained in the use of APCs for riot control. The Finnish KFOR contingent was equipped with teargas following the riots in March 2004.[125]

Conclusion

Although Finland remains the most 'traditionalist' of the Nordic countries, it has moved beyond traditional peacekeeping in the 1990s. The Finnish willingness and capacity to meet the new requirements of contemporary peace operations have grown considerably, and Finland now participates fully in enforcement operations aimed at enforcing ceasefires and peace agreements. The unwillingness to participate in enforcement operations that lack a UN mandate and/or involve offensive operations against a designated enemy is the only factor preventing Finland from meeting all the conditions for success (Table 5.3). Both the MFA and the Finnish defence forces continue to enhance their capacity for international operations, and indications are that the Finnish involvement will continue to grow in the decade ahead. The domestic support for the Finnish involvement in peace operations is strong, and the political desire to enhance the Finnish profile within the EU and NATO and maintain a good relationship with the USA is likely to result in a stronger commitment abroad. The principal constraint on increased involvement is numbers of personnel as all Finnish personnel still have to volunteer for international service. It remains to be seen whether the regulars will continue to volunteer for international operations in the

Table 5.3 Finland and the requirements for success in contemporary peace operations

Requirements for success	Finland
1. Political will, legal framework and funds for all types of operations	No, not peace enforcement that either lacks a UN mandate or involves large-scale offensive operations against designated enemies
2. Civilian and military personnel deployable at short notice	Yes
3. Training to prepare the civilian and military personnel for their many new tasks	Yes
4. Interoperability with most likely partners	Yes
5. Armaments and ROE permitting use of force beyond self-defence if necessary	Yes
6. Logistics	Yes
7. Medical, psychological and family support	Yes
8. Intelligence capacity	Yes
9. Public information capacity	Yes
10. Coordination and cooperation capacity	Yes
11. Public security capacity	Yes

numbers required for Finland to further enhance its military involvement in peace operations abroad. The increased professionalism of the other Nordic and European armies and the premium placed on professional rapid reaction forces capable of enforcement at short notice in both the EU and NATO will put pressure on Finland to develop such capabilities as well. To participate in the joint Finnish–Norwegian–Swedish battle group Finland thus had to enhance its initial contribution from some 40 special forces to 300 personnel. The latter was seen as the absolute minimum in Brussels, and this contingent will be made up of primarily professionals and enlisted personnel.[126]

Notes

1. Enestam, Jan-Erik (2002) 'New Threats, New Challenges: A Finnish View', remarks at the CSIS, Washington, DC, 11 April (Ministry of Defence of Finland).
2. See Bruun, Staffan (1993) 'Finland bör kunna delta i militära FN-operationer', *Hufvudstadsbladet*, 16 September, p. 4; Ledere (1993) 'Vad vill FN i Bosnien?', *Hufvudstadsbladet*, 23 June 1993, p. 2; 'Finlands roll i kriget i Bosnien', *Hufvudstadsbladet*, 12 June 1993, p. 2; 'Omstritt förslag om FN-trupperna läggs på is', *Hufvudstadsbladet*, 29 October 1993, p. 1.

3. Ahtisaari, Martti (1994) 'Finnish Foreign and Security Policy in the 1990s', address by President Martti Ahtisaari at the annual meeting of the National Defence Courses; Stenström, Bo (1994) 'Finland – Fripassagerare?', *Internationella Studier*, No. 4 (winter), pp. 14–17 (14–20). Ahtisaari was president of Finland from 1994 to 2000; Hägglund was chief of defence from 1994 to 2001.

4. See for instance the three white papers on defence: *Security in a Changing World: Guidelines for Finland's Security Policy* (Report by the Council of State to parliament on 6 June 1995); *European Security Development and Finnish Defence* (Report by the Council of State to parliament on 17 March 1997); *Finnish Security and Defence Policy 2001* (Report by the government to parliament on 13 June 2001). See also: Ahtisaari, 'Finnish Foreign and Security Policy in the 1990s'; Ahtisaari, Martti (1996) 'Speech by President of the Republic Martti Ahtisaari at the 30th Anniversary Celebrations of the Central Finland Ideological National Defence Association in Keuruu on 18.12.1996' (Helsinki: Ministry for Foreign Affairs of Finland); Halonen, Tarja (2001) 'Speech by President of the Republic Tarja Halonen at the 40th anniversary celebration of the National Defence Course Association on 21 May 2001' (Helsinki: Office of the President of the Republic of Finland).

5. *Prime Minister's Report to Parliament Concerning European Security and Defence Policy: Crisis Management During the Finnish Presidency* (Helsinki: Council of State, 25 November 1999).

6. *Finland's Participation to Peace Support Operations, Legal Framework*, FSC.DEL/227/01 (Helsinki: Ministry of Defence of Finland, 12 June 2001).

7. Halonen, 'Speech by President of the Republic Tarja Halonen at the 40th anniversary Celebration of the National Defence Course Association on 21 May 2001'. The Finnish chief of defence agrees. See his rejection of a suggestion that Finland should copy Sweden's more internationally oriented defence model: 'Chief of Defence: Swedish Military Model Not Applicable to Finland', *Helsingin Sanomat International Edition*, 9 March 2004.

8. Figures obtained from the Finnish MoD. The total in this material is 43,000 and this is also the number generally employed in official statements and statistics. However, this figure appears to be mistaken. If one adds up the totals provided for each year since 1956 the total comes to 40,330.

9. Finnish personnel can choose between 6- and 12-month tours but most serve 12 months to earn the right to a tax break.

10. Fjell, Trond and Bård Lien (2001) 'Internasjonale og nasjonale engagementsregler (ROE) i samme multinasjonale operasjon', *Norsk Militært Tidsskrift*, Vol. 171, No. 6/7, p. 17 (12–18).

11. *Finnish Security and Defence Policy 2001*, p. 74 (internet version). The white paper is available at < http://www.defmin.fi/index.phtml/page_id/13/topmenu_id/7/menu_id/13/this_topmenu/7/lang/3/fs/12 >.

12. *Finnish Security and Defence Policy 2001*, p. 73. Interview with MFA official, 24 May 2002.

13. *Finnish Security and Defence Policy 2001*, pp. 76–77.

14. *Finnish Security and Defence Policy 2001*, pp. 76–77.

15. Aro, Miia (2000) 'Finland's Peacekeeping Operations from 1991 to 1999: Transitions and Readjustment', in *Northern Dimensions 2000* (Helsinki: Finnish Institute of International Affairs), pp. 55–58 (50–62); 'Parliament Endorsed Finnish Participation in ISAF', *Diplomatic Diary*, 11 January 2002 (Ministry for Foreign Affairs of Finland).

16. 'Beredskapstrupper grundas', *Nordisk Kontakt*, Vol. 41, No. 5–6 (1996), p. 60.

17. Eliasson, Johan L. (2002) 'The European Security and Defense Policy Process and Non-Allied Members Finland and Sweden', paper for the 43rd Annual ISA Convention, New Orleans, 24–27 March, pp. 15, 17–18. See also Forsberg, Tuomas and Tapani Vaahtoranta (2001) 'Paradoxes of Post-Neutrality: Finnish and Swedish Views of NATO and the ESDP', *European Security*, Vol. 10, No. 1 (spring), p. 84 (68–93).

18. Nokkala, Arto (1996) 'Finland's Security Policy 95: Consolidation and Main Discussion', in *Yearbook of Finnish Foreign Policy* (Helsinki: Finnish Institute of International Affairs), p. 11 (6–15).

19. Forsberg, Tuomas (2000) 'Finland and the Kosovo Crisis: At the Crossroads of Europeanism and Neutrality', in *Northern Dimensions 2000* (Helsinki: Finnish Institute of International Affairs), p. 46 (41–49).

20. 'Finnish Foreign Policy 1999, December', *Virtual Finland* (Finnish Institute of International Affairs for the MFA). < http://virtual.finland.fi/finfo/english/chronology/chrono1999_12.html >.

21. Skogberg, Lena (2003) 'Finland utreder: Hornet utrustas med bomber?', *Hufvudstadsbladet*, 15 February, p. 5; Törnudd, Klaus (2001) 'The Makers of Finnish Security Policy', in Bo Huldt, Teija Tiilikainen, Tapani Vaahtoranta and Anna Helkama-Rågård (eds) *Finnish and Swedish Security – Comparing National Policies* (Stockholm: Swedish National Defence College and the Programme on the Northern Dimension of the CFSP conducted by the Finnish Institute of International Affairs and the Institut für Europäische Politik), p. 272 (259–278).

22. '52% of Finns Polled Approve of US Military Action in Afghanistan', *Helsingin Sanomat International Edition*, 2 January 2002.

23. Halonen, Tarja (2000) 'At the Core of Europe as a Non-Participant in Military Alliances – Finnish Thoughts and Experiences', Guest lecture by President of the Republic Tarja Halonen at the University of Stockholm 2 May 2000 (Helsinki: Office of the President of the Republic of Finland).

24. 'Parliament Must Decide on Possible Finnish Peacekeeping Role in Afghanistan', *Helsingin Sanomat International Edition*, 18 December 2001; 'All Parties Approve Finnish Participation in Afghanistan Peacekeeping Effort', *Helsingin Sanomat International Edition*, 10 January 2002.

25. As of 2001, only one Finnish peacekeeper had been killed in combat, and that was in Cyprus in 1964. The remaining 41 deaths resulted from suicides (10), traffic accidents (11), disease (9), and other types of accidents such as plane crashes and mines (11). See *Statsrevisorernas berättelse för 2001* (Helsingfors: Statsrevisorerna, 2002), p. 105.

26. Siilasvuo, Ensio (1992) *In the Service of Peace in the Middle East* (London: Hurst/New York: St Martin's Press), p. 94.

27. Urquhart, Brian (1987) *A Life in Peace and War: Memoirs* (New York: Harper & Row), pp. 372, 374.

28. For attempts to clarify these terms see Aro, 'Finland's Peacekeeping Operations from 1991 to 1999', pp. 52–53; Höglund, Kari (1998) 'Finnish Contribution to Peacekeeping', *Virtual Finland*, < http://virtual.finland.fi/finfo/ english/peace.html >.

29. For English version see *Finland's Participation to Peace Support Operations*; Government proposition, 20/2000.

30. 'Finnish Foreign Policy 1999, April', *Virtual Finland* (Finnish Institute of International Affairs for the MFA). < http://virtual.finland.fi/finfo/english/chronology/chrono1999_04.html >.

31. 'New legislation would ease restrictions governing peacekeeping operations', *Helsingin Sanomat International Edition*, 11 May 2005; *Regeringens proposition*

till Riksdagen med förslag till lag on militär krishantering och vissa lagar som har samband med den, RP 110/2005 rd.

32. *Finland's Position on the War on Iraq* (Helsinki: Office of the President of Finland, 20 March 2003).
33. *Yearbook of Finnish Foreign Policy 1993* (Helsinki: Finnish Institute of International Affairs), p. 85.
34. Bruun, 'Finland bör kunna delta i militära FN-operationer'.
35. *Statsrevisorernas berättelse för 2001*, p. 108.
36. 'Finlands deltagande i det militära genomförandet av fredsöverenskommelsen för Bosnien-Hercegovina', *SRR* 3/*1995*, 18 December, p. 2.
37. Defence Committee Report 2/2001 vp, 14 December 2001, p. 20. <http://www.eduskunta.fi/efakta/vk/puv/puvm0201.pdf>.
38. Kronlund, Jarl and Juha Valla (1996) *Suomi rauhanturvaajana, 1956–1990* (Porvoo: WSOY), p. 454.
39. Eknes, Åge (1995) 'The Nordic Countries and UN Peacekeeping Operations', in Åge Eknes (ed.) *The Nordic Countries in the United Nations: Status and Future Perspectives* (Copenhagen: Nordic Council), p. 80 (65–83); 'Norden berett gå in i Bosnien', *Hufvudstadsbladet*, 5 May 1993, p. 1; *Yearbook of Finnish Foreign Policy 1994* (Helsinki: Finnish Institute of International Affairs), p. 73.
40. See Chapter 3 for a discussion of these factors.
41. *Finnish Military Defence 2002* (Helsinki: Information Division of the Defence Staff, 2002), p. 7.
42. 'Beredskapstrupper grundas'; Glogan, Tim (1996) 'Finland Gives Go-Ahead to Form Standby Force', *Jane's Defence Weekly*, Vol. 25, No. 20 (15 May), p. 8.
43. *Finnish Defence and the Challenge of International Crisis Management* (Helsinki: Ministry of Defence of Finland, 2001), p. 3.
44. The Winter War 1939–40 and the Continuation War 1941–44.
45. Jakobson, Max (1998) 'Finland in the New Europe', *The Washington Papers*, No. 175 (Westport, CT: Praeger for Center for Strategic and International Studies, Washington, DC), p. 74.
46. Kuoppamäki, Pasi (2000) *A Web History of Finland* <http://ky.hkkk.fi/~k21206/finhist.html#war> (12 May 2003); *Finland – A Country Study, 'The Finnish Civil War'* (Library of Congress, Federal Research Division Country Studies): <http://lcweb2.loc.gov/frd/cs/fitoc.html> (21 July 2004).
47. Kekkonen, Urho (1982) *A President's View* (London: Heinemann), p. 131. That this was indeed the guiding star of Finnish foreign policy is evident from Törnudd, Klaus (1969) 'Finland in the United Nations in the 1960s', in Ilkka Heiskanen, Jukka Huopaniemi, Keijo Korhonen and Klaus Törnudd (eds) *Essays on Finnish Foreign Policy* (Helsinki: Finnish Political Science Association), pp. 50–59; and Vesa, Unto (1980) 'Determining Finland's Position in International Crises', in *Yearbook of Finnish Foreign Policy 1979* (Helsinki: Finnish Institute of International Affairs), pp. 2–19.
48. Paasio, Pertti (1991) 'Finland and Regional Conflicts', in *Yearbook of Finnish Foreign Policy 1991* (Helsinki: Finnish Institute of International Affairs), pp. 3–5.
49. See the statement by Defence Minister Elisabeth Rehn from October 1992 in *Yearbook of Finnish Foreign Policy 1993* (Helsinki: Finnish Institute of International Affairs), p. 87. For an overview of the Finnish debate see Nokkala, 'Finland's Security Policy 95'.
50. This policy of military non-involvement is not universally supported in the Finnish debate. For a critique see Archer, Toby (2003) 'Keeping Out of It: The Hangover of Finnish Neutralism and the Limits of Normative Commitments',

Yearbook of Finnish Foreign Policy 2003 (Helsinki: Finnish Institute of International Affairs), pp. 57–70.

51. Interviews with MFA officials, 24 May 2002.
52. Denmark withdrew from Cyprus in 1993 and Sweden and Norway withdrew from Lebanon in 1994 and 1998, respectively.
53. 'Finland to Begin Withdrawing From Peacekeeping Operation in Bosnia', *Helsingin Sanomat International Edition*, 4 December 2002.
54. Examples include Operation Provide Comfort in 1991 and AFOR in 1999.
55. Interviews conducted with MFA officials, 24 May 2002.
56. *Finnish Defence and the Challenge of International Crisis Management*, pp. 1–2.
57. *Finnish Military Defence 2002*, p. 7.
58. Möttölä, Kari (2001) 'Finland, the European Union and NATO – Implications for Security and Defence', in Erich Reiter and Heinz Gärtner (eds) *Small States and Alliances* (Heidelberg: Physica-Verlag), p. 136 (113–144).
59. *Finnish Defence and the Challenge of International Crisis Management*, p. 1; Jopp, Mathias (1998) 'Introduction', in Mathias Jopp and Riku Warjovaara (eds) *Approaching the Northern Dimension of the CFSP: Challenges and Opportunities for the EU in the Emerging European Security Order* (Helsinki: Finnish Institute of International Affairs; Bonn: Institut für Europäische Politik), p. 14 (11–23).
60. Interviews with Finnish MFA officials, 24 May 2002.
61. Kirk, Lisbeth (2004) 'Sweden and Finland Announce Joint EU Battle Group', *EUobserver.com*, 25 October, <http://euobserver.com/?aid=17443&sid=13> (27 October 2004).
62. Stenström, 'Finland – Fripassagerare?'
63. Hansen, Jens Jørgen (2002) 'De nordiske lande og ESFP. De nordiske landes indflydelsesmuligheder på udviklingen af ESFP', *DUPI Report*, No. 9 (København: Danish Institute of International Affairs), p. 41.
64. *Berättelse om regeringens åtgärder under år 2002* (Helsingfors: Riksdagen, 2003; B4/2003), p. 79.
65. *Finland's Development Cooperation 2000* (Helsinki: Ministry for Foreign Affairs, 2001), p. 185.
66. *Finland's Development Cooperation 2003* (Helsinki: Ministry for Foreign Affairs, 2004), p. 171.
67. *Finnish Security and Defence Policy 2001*, p. 75.
68. Interview EU Council Secretariat, 6 May 2004.
69. See the UNDAC website <http://www.reliefweb.int/undac/undac_members_list.html> (31 June 2004).
70. Interview EU Council Secretariat, 6 May 2004.
71. Räty, Arto Tuomas (2000) 'Finnish Battalion's Motto Is: Firm, Fair and Friendly', *NATO's Nations and Partners for Peace*, No. 1, p. 34 (32–34).
72. *Finnish Security and Defence Policy 2001*.
73. *Finnish Military Defence 2002*, p. 28.
74. Heikka, Henrikki (2003) 'Maintaining a Balance of Power that Favors Human Freedom: The Finnish Strategic Experience', paper prepared for the Annual ISA Convention, Portland, OR, 25 February–1 March, p. 50.
75. 'Finnish Foreign Policy 1999, September', *Virtual Finland* (Finnish Institute of International Affairs for the MFA) <http://virtual.finland.fi/finfo/english/chronology/chrono1999_09.html>.
76. Finland did come close to the limit in 1989 when 1,912 personnel were deployed simultaneously. In 1999 the figure was 1,823 personnel.
77. Interview with Finnish MoD official, 24 May 2002.

78. 'Finnish Troops and Aircraft to Take Part in NATO-Led Exercise in Poland', *Helsingin Sanomat International Edition*, 21 February 2002. This commitment to go on an international operation is not legally binding, however, and the volunteers can still say no when they are asked to honour it.
79. E-mail communication to author from Advisor Marko Hynninen, Peace Support Operations Branch, MoD, 16 June 2003.
80. Enestam, Jan-Erik (2003) *Assessment of the International Activities of Defence Administration. Speech to the Paasikivi Society 10 March* (Helsinki: Ministry of Defence of Finland), p. 3.
81. *Finland's Development Cooperation 2001* (Helsinki: Ministry for Foreign Affairs, 2002), p. 154.
82. For this project see: < http://www.aspr.ac.at/euproject/main.htm >.
83. 'Ekenäs vill ha center för krishantering', *Hufvudstadsbladet*, 5 March 2002.
84. *Finnish Security and Defence Policy 2001.*
85. *Finnish Security and Defence Policy 2001.*
86. Interviews with MFA officials, 24 May 2002.
87. Bruun, 'Finland bör kunna delta i militära FN-operationer'.
88. *Beväringstjänsten 2002* (Helsinki: Huvudstabens informationsavdelning), pp. 46–48.
89. Holmen, Bengt and Ståle Ulriksen (2000) 'Norden i felt: På oppdrag for FN og NATO', *NUPI*-rapport, No. 257 (Oslo: Norsk Utenrikspolitisk Institutt), pp. 21–22.
90. Hägglund, Sami (1998) 'Krishantering med militära medel', *SI Serie*, S: 3 (Stockholm: Försvarshögskolan, Strategiska Institutionen), p. 99.
91. 'The Jane's Interview: Finland's Chief of Defence, General Gustav Hägglund', *Jane's Defence Weekly*, Vol. 29, No. 13 (1 April 1998).
92. *Cooperation in Nato's Partnership for Peace Programme* (Ministry of Defence of Finland, 6 March 2002); Sivonen, Pekka (2001) 'Finland and NATO', in Huldt *et al.*, *Finnish and Swedish Security*, p. 97 (92–104).
93. Räty, 'Finnish Battalion's Motto Is: Firm, Fair and Friendly', p. 34.
94. Heikka, Henrikki (2003) 'Maintaining a Balance of Power', pp. 49–50.
95. FNB (2002) 'Finland vill ha fredlig Irak-lösning', *Hufvudstadsbladet*, 21 September; Väistö, Pentti (2003) 'Finsk FN-trupp tar över i Kosovo', *Hufvudstadsbladet*, 13 February, p. 6.
96. Agence France-Presse, Helsinki (2004) 'Finland Ready to Join Dutch–German EU Battle Group', 3 November.
97. Höglund, 'Finnish Contribution to Peacekeeping'.
98. Fjell and Lien 'Internasjonale og nasjonale engagementsregler (ROE) i samme multinasjonale operasjon', p. 17; Holmen and Ulriksen, 'Norden i felt', pp. 32–33.
99. Bruun, 'Finland bör kunna delta i militära FN-operationer'.
100. Hägglund, 'Krishantering med militära medel', pp. 98–99.
101. Hägglund, Gustav (1990) 'Peace-keeping in a Modern War Zone', *Survival*, Vol. 32, No. 3 (May/June), pp. 233–240; Siilasvuo, *In the Service of Peace in the Middle East*, pp. 351–353.
102. Räty, 'Finnish Battalion's Motto Is: Firm, Fair and Friendly', p. 33.
103. Grüne, Yrsa (2000) 'Amiral Juhani Kaskeala om Kfors framtid Nordisk brigad helt möjlig', *Hufvudstadsbladet*, 16 December, p. 6.
104. Hägglund, 'Krishantering med militära medel', p. 101.
105. E-mail communication to author from Advisor Marko Hynninen, Peace Support Operations Branch, MoD, 16 June 2003.
106. Holmen and Ulriksen, 'Norden i felt', pp. 27–28.

107. Andersen, Bjørn Christian (2002) 'Felles nordisk flytransport til Afghanistan', *Forsvarsnett* (www.mil.no), 21 March.
108. E-mail communication to author from Advisor Marko Hynninen, Peace Support Operations Branch, MoD, 16 June 2003.
109. E-mail communication to author from Advisor Marko Hynninen, Peace Support Operations Branch, MoD, 16 June 2003; Räty, 'Finnish Battalion's Motto Is: Firm, Fair and Friendly', p. 33.
110. E-mail communication to author from Advisor Marko Hynninen, Peace Support Operations Branch, MoD, 16 June 2003.
111. Interviews with Swedish MoD official, 22 May 2002, and Finnish MoD official, 24 May 2002.
112. E-mail communication to author from Advisor Marko Hynninen, Peace Support Operations Branch, MoD, 16 June 2003.
113. Hägglund, 'Peace-keeping in a Modern War Zone', p. 240.
114. Räty, 'Finnish Battalion's Motto Is: Firm, Fair and Friendly', p. 34.
115. E-mail communication to author from Advisor Marko Hynninen, Peace Support Operations Branch, MoD, 16 June 2003.
116. Tuomioja, Erkki (2001) 'Non-military Crisis Management as A Part of Foreign and Security Policy', address at TAPRI, Tampere Peace Research Institute, 20 April.
117. Eriksson, Pär (1998) *Civil-militär samverkan på taktisk nivå i fredsfrämjande operationer. Motiv, metoder och förutsättningar* (Stockholm, FOA, FOA-R-98-00968-170-SE), p. 35.
118. *Verksamhetsberättelse 2001* (Helsinki: Försvarsministeriet, 2002), p. 18.
119. *FOV Nyhedsbrev* (2000) 'CIMIC-house på handelsstrøg i Maglaj', No. 14, pp. 3–4; Madsen, Kai (2000) 'Manglende dansk bidrag stopper processen', *FOV Nyhedsbrev*, No. 14, p. 6. The same problem also occurred in UNIFIL in the 1980s because the poorer battalions were unable to match the level of support provided to the civilian population by the Finnish battalion. See Eriksson, *Civil-militär samverkan på taktisk nivå i fredsfrämjande operationer*, p. 35.
120. Räty, 'Finnish Battalion's Motto Is: Firm, Fair and Friendly', p. 34; Wulff, Maria Broberg and Karin Ströberg (2001) *Utvärdering av svenska bataljonens humanitära insatser i Kosovo* (Stockholm: Totalförsvarets Forskningsinstitut, FOI-R-0171-SE), p. 21.
121. Eriksson, *Civil-militär samverkan på taktisk nivå i fredsfrämjande operationer*, p. 28.
122. Wulff and Ströberg, *Utvärdering av svenska bataljonens humanitära insatser i Kosovo*, p. 14.
123. Wulff and Ströberg, *Utvärdering av svenska bataljonens humanitära insatser i Kosovo*, p. 22.
124. Interview with Finnish MFA official, 24 May 2002.
125. 'Finnish peacekeepers permitted to use tear-gas in Kosovo', *Helsingin Sanomat International Edition*, 11 April 2004.
126. *Finnish Security and Defence Policy 2004* (Helsinki: Prime Minister's Office, Government report 6, 2004), p. 96; 'Finnish Special Forces Could Be Used in NATO Operations', *Helsingin Sanomat International Edition*, 7 April 2004.

6   The Norwegian approach to peace operations after the Cold War

The participation in international military operations has grown considerably, both in volume and in its share of the defence budget. International operations, and their demands for mobility, protection, readiness and interoperability, are increasingly determining the development of the Norwegian armed forces, not least the army. This has to a large extent influenced procurement and training and exercise patterns. Such decisions have often been implemented at short notice, but with considerable consequences for the long term defence plans.

Norwegian Defence Policy Commission: final report, 2000[1]

The Norwegian case presents an interesting combination of civilian activism and military foot-dragging. On the civilian side, Norway was a frontrunner, being the first country in the world to develop a civilian standby capacity for peace operations as part of its 'model' for peace diplomacy in the early 1990s.[2] The Norwegian standby systems have served as a source of inspiration, not just for the other Nordic countries but for many other countries as well. In contrast, the Norwegian efforts to meet the new military requirements for success in post-Cold War peace operations have been slow, reluctant and plagued by financial problems. The reform process only started in earnest after the Kosovo conflict which served as a painful wake up call for the Norwegian armed forces and their political masters. In spite of these problems Norway has managed to meet our eleven requirements for success, but it has had to rely on *ad hoc* solutions to do so.

Political will, legal framework and funds for all types of operations

The strength, depth and evolution of the political willingness to participate in peace operations will once again be assessed by the following indicators: the rhetoric employed by decision makers, the number and nature of personnel contributions, the level of support these contributions enjoy in the government, parliament and in the public at large, and finally the role played by the government in mobilizing and sustaining domestic support. The Norwegian case reveals the same pattern as the other Nordic countries: a significant increase in political will.

Rhetoric

Peace operations have gradually taken centre stage in Norwegian defence and security policy. This was not the case during the Cold War when peace operations were considered 'idealistic' foreign policy and financed in part by the development budget. Today, peace operations are officially treated as an integral part of the Norwegian defence policy and even promoted as a prerequisite for effective national defence. Enhancing the Norwegian capacity for peace operations has been a priority in each and every defence white paper produced since 1992.[3] Governments and especially the defence ministers have fought a long and hard battle since the mid-1990s to convince sceptics that the distinction between national defence and international operations has become meaningless, and that national defence does not suffer as a result of Norway's increased international involvement. The following passage from a 1998 address by Defence Minister Dag Jostein Fjærevoll is typical of the arguments employed:

> Norwegian participation in international peace operations contributes to fulfilling our national security and defence policy by taking a responsibility to provide security outside our immediate surroundings. It is of crucial importance to a small country that international norms and legal principles are upheld. Norwegian international participation clearly visualizes our contribution. A major international military involvement has also become necessary for Norway to compensate for the reduced attention and interest in and around our near abroad. The international situation, marked by regional and ethnic conflicts, is characterized by reciprocity between national and international security. If we contribute actively to maintaining international peace and security, we may feel more confident if Norway in the future should need military assistance from others. This is particularly important for a country which has traditionally imported security. To Norway it becomes instrumental to see the participation in peace operations through NATO, UN, OSCE and other organizations as a continuation of the purely national effort to secure our own security. Against this background, the government seeks to maintain a considerable military involvement abroad. Norwegian contributions to international military operations have too often been marked by *ad hoc* solutions seeking to adapt to a given operation.[4]

Participation on the ground

Norway's military contributions have increased significantly since the end of the Cold War. As of 1 January 1988, a total of 32,000 Norwegians had served on UN operations.[5] By May 2002 the total had almost doubled to 61,824.[6] The annual average contribution has thus risen from 780 during the Cold War (1947–87) to a post-Cold War average of 2,130. In qualitative terms the changes have been equally significant. The peacekeeping-only policy has been abandoned, and Norway now provides personnel for all types of operations, including offensive enforcement. The Norwegian government decided in principle to make personnel available for peace enforcement in 1993,[7] but contributions were initially limited to support services such as logistics, medical personnel, military police and transport. Norway did not contribute infantry to an enforcement operation until NATO initiated SFOR in December 1996. Since then Norwegian infantry have participated in KFOR, and Norwegian F-16 fighters and special forces have taken part in offensive operations in NATO's Operation Allied Force and the US-led Operation Enduring Freedom in Afghanistan.[8] Both the Norwegian Air Force and Navy became involved in peace operations in the 1990s, and today all services are involved in international operations on a continuous basis.

The changes in the number and nature of the military contributions are mirrored on the civilian side as well. The Norwegian police got their debut on peace operations in the UN operation in Namibia in 1989 and by December 2003 some 700–800 Norwegian police officers had participated in peace operations abroad.[9] The number of other civilian experts such as relief workers, human rights advisers, peace mediators and observers, election monitors and supervisors and rescue personnel on international missions has also increased following the establishment of three civilian rapid reaction systems: the Norwegian Standby Arrangements of Professionals (NORSTAFF) (1991), the Norwegian Resource Bank for Democracy and Human Rights (NORDEM) (1995), and Norwegian Support Teams (NST) (1998). NORSTAFF had sent an estimated 4,000 personnel abroad by July 2003,[10] NORDEM had sent more than 1,000 personnel abroad by 2000,[11] and NST rescue personnel had been on missions in Albania, Guinea, Sierra Leone and Tajikistan by the end of 2002.[12]

Domestic support

Norway's growing involvement in peace operations has been based on strong political and public support. Deployments are usually supported unanimously and only a handful of exceptions to this rule can be identified in the post-Cold War era. The first was the participation in the naval embargo imposed upon Iraq following its invasion of Kuwait in 1990, which was opposed by the Socialist Left Party (Socialistisk Venstreparti) on the grounds that it was not a UN-led operation.[13] The second was the reinforcement of the Norwegian contingent in Somalia in September 1992, which was opposed by the Conservative Party (Høyre) and the Progressive Party (Fremskrittspartiet) arguing that Somalia differed too much from Norway in terms of climate and culture, and that the 70 soldiers in question should be held in reserve for operations in the Balkans instead.[14] The third was the continued involvement in UNIFIL in Lebanon that the Conservative Party and the Progressive Party began to oppose in the mid-1990s because they wanted to use the troops in the Balkans instead.[15] The fourth exception was the 1998 decision to make a transport plane available for a possible attack on Iraq, which was opposed by the Socialist Left Party because it lacked an explicit UN mandate.[16] Finally, the Socialist Left Party also opposed Norway's participation in Operation Enduring Freedom because it was not led by the UN, and because it did not want Norway to participate in warfighting.[17]

The strong political support has translated itself into strong public support for Norwegian participation in peace operations, including controversial operations that either lack clear UN mandates or involve offensive use of force. Some 62 per cent of the Norwegian population thus supported Norway's participation in NATO's Operation Allied Force in Kosovo when the operation began (23 per cent were opposed),[18] and a subsequent poll in early April 1999 had 61 per cent supporting a Norwegian contribution to an eventual NATO invasion of Kosovo with ground forces.[19] Later in April the supporters of this proposal had fallen to 43 per cent but they still outnumbered the opponents (36 per cent).[20] The decision to send forces to Afghanistan in December 2001 was also endorsed by a slight majority of the population (54 per cent),[21] even though the US bombing campaign preceding it had divided the Norwegians and induced Norwegian bishops to demand that the bombing be stopped.[22] Finally, polls showed 70–79 per cent support for the government's decision not to participate in the US-led war against Iraq in 2003.[23] All the opinion polls preceding it had shown clear majorities opposed to the war,[24] a factor that undoubtedly influenced the government's decision to say no to the US request for military support.

The high level of support has not crowded out criticism and debate. The most persistent criticism of Norway's growing international involvement since the early 1990s has been the concern voiced by retired officers and members of the Norwegian parliament (Stortinget) of the Cold War generation, that the preoccupation with peace operations was undermining national defence. While these protests have succeeded in slowing down the pace of military reform, they have not been able to prevent the internationalization of Norway's security and defence policy. This process has accelerated in recent years and although it is too early to write off the old guard, its influence is clearly on the wane. The internationalization of the Norwegian armed forces is now irreversible.

Government role in mobilizing and sustaining domestic support

Norwegian governments have consistently sought to build a consensus for the growing international involvement. It has been an uphill battle persuading the sceptics that it is both desirable and necessary to give priority and money to international operations at a time when the national defence structure is being cut dramatically. While the need for consensus has slowed down the process of reform, the overall picture is one of success. The governments have succeeded in mobilizing and sustaining support for Norway's involvement in enforcement operations in the Balkans and, most recently, participation in warfighting operations in Afghanistan. The latter is no mean achievement in a nation that takes pride in describing itself as a 'humanitarian great power',[25] and traditionally has been opposed to the use of force for purposes other than self-defence. The participation in offensive operations in Kosovo and Afghanistan was very controversial and the government consequently tried to make it as palatable to the public as possible. Operation Allied Force in Kosovo was portrayed to the public as a 'limited military operation',[26] and the Norwegian role in Afghanistan (which involved offensive actions by special forces and F-16s) was characterized by Prime Minister Kjell Magne Bondevik as 'preventive', 'deterrent' and 'defensive' in nature.[27]

The sensitivity of operations going beyond traditional peacekeeping has induced Norwegian governments to downplay the increased risks of casualties. When the decision to participate in enforcement operations was taken in 1993, Chief of Defence Torolf Rein sounded the alarm warning that the Norwegian public was unprepared for the possibility that attempts to enforce peace in far-away conflicts might result in Norwegian troops returning home in coffins.[28] Such warnings and calls for a debate have been made regularly since then.[29] Most recently, Major Hallgeir Mikalsen, who was shot and nearly killed in Afghanistan in May 2003, called for a debate wondering: 'What would happen if ten Norwegians came home in body bags?'[30]

His question is difficult to answer with certainty. The death of a Norwegian soldier in Afghanistan in May 2004 did not result in calls for a withdrawal or a change of policy. On the contrary, Norwegian politicians and the major newspapers recognized the risk for further losses but stressed the need for continued involvement in Afghanistan.[31] Their reaction is likely to have been the same if ten soldiers had been killed by hostile fire for three reasons. First, Norway has some experience with taking casualties. Twenty-one Norwegians lost their lives in UNIFIL (1978–98) and seven died in Bosnia (1992–99).[32] In all, a total of 38 Norwegians died on peace operations between 1947 and 2000. Second, the political consensus on peace operations makes it unlikely that casualties would generate a strong political demand for a major change in policy.[33] Third, improvements in both training, equipment and medical support (see below) have been made in order to enhance the safety of the Norwegian personnel deployed abroad, and the emphasis placed on personnel safety is further underlined by the recent Joint Doctrine, which states that forces deployed on peace support operations require better protection than forces engaged in a battle for national survival.[34] The attention paid to personnel security and recent efforts to prepare the public and parliament for losses will make it easier for the government to stay the course if significant casualties are taken.[35]

Permissive legal framework

In accordance with constitutional practice, Norwegian governments consult with the parliament's Enlarged Foreign Affairs Committee before international deployments of military units or major personnel increases in ongoing operations are made.[36] Deployments of observers and individuals are usually made without parliamentary involvement.[37] At the end of the Cold War, a parliamentary decision of 1964 limited the Norwegian involvement to 1,330 personnel in traditional peacekeeping and observer missions mandated by the UN only.[38] Since then the scope for participation has been widened considerably in a number of parliamentary decisions and legal revisions. The first was made in 1993 when the parliamentary approval of a government white paper led to the expansion of the Norwegian standby force to 2,022 personnel and allowed for participation in enforcement operations and participation in peacekeeping operations conducted by regional organizations such as NATO and the Conference on Security and Cooperation in Europe (CSCE, now OSCE). The white paper made clear that Norway could participate in peacekeeping operations mandated by either the UN or the CSCE, but that participation in peace enforcement would require a UN mandate.[39]

The following year the government published a white paper calling for a revision of the law to make it possible to order professional officers abroad on peace operations.[40] This proposal was fiercely resisted by the officer corps and their professional associations arguing that it was wrong to force officers, who had joined the armed forces to defend their homeland, to participate in operations abroad. They were supported by pacifists opposed to Norwegian involvement in 'offensive operations' abroad and four of the smaller parties in parliament.[41] Supporters of the proposal argued that the government should be able to use the military in pursuit of Norwegian interests both at home and abroad.[42] The proposal was finally approved in 1996, and the new law entered into force on 1 January 1999. It only allowed the government to order professional officers abroad when impossible to find enough volunteers. Moreover, it did not apply to officers who entered service before 1 January 1999 unless they signed a statement accepting the new law.[43]

Neither the government nor the chief of defence was satisfied with this law as it made it difficult to deploy forces abroad at short notice. They pressed for further changes and finally got their way in June 2004 when parliament passed another revision of the law which made it possible to order all professional officers abroad when required.[44] This revision was adopted by parliament with 46 votes to 24 in spite of strong protests from the officers' trade unions. The Centre Party (Senterpartiet), the Progressive Party and the Socialist Left Party voted against it.[45]

The requirement for an explicit UN or OSCE mandate has also been waived. The first step in this direction was taken as early as 1994 when a parliamentary majority consisting of the Centre Party, the Conservative Party and the Labour Party (Arbeiderpartiet) decided that 'possible Norwegian participation in humanitarian operations, rescue operations or peace operations without a formal mandate from the UN or CSCE, but in accordance with the principles of the UN Charter and the principles in the Helsinki Final Act and the Paris Charter, must be decided on a case-by-case basis and be submitted to parliament'.[46]

The second step was taken in February 1998 when Norway made a transport plane available for a possible US-led attack on Iraq in February 1998 which did not have an explicit UN mandate.[47] The plane was never used, however, so it was not until Norwegian forces participated in NATO's Operation Allied Force the following year that Norway took active part in a military operation without a UN mandate. The new policy was subsequently formalized in a white paper approved by parliament, which stated that Norway, in situations where it proved impossible to obtain an explicit UN mandate, would have to determine for itself whether a 'legal basis' for the use of force still existed. The 'legal' requirement for Norwegian participation in peace operations lacking an explicit UN mandate was defined as 'the highest degree of political and legal legitimacy possible'.[48] The US-led war against Iraq in 2003 failed to meet this condition and the Norwegian government refused to participate because it lacked 'a clear basis in international law'.[49]

Norway's legal framework is, in short, very permissive. Participation in all types of peace operations is permitted, a UN or OSCE mandate is not required, and professional officers can be ordered abroad at short notice when necessary.

Financing

The increase in military expenditures on international operations from NOK 335 million in 1990 to a peak of NOK 2,041.4 million in 2000 speaks for itself (Table 6.1).[50] Finding the funds has been a struggle because the armed forces throughout the period have been mired in a deep structural and economic crisis due to constant under-funding and an inability to adapt to the realities of the post-Cold War era.[51] Since 1988 the military costs have

Table 6.1 MoD expenditures on international operations 1995–2003 (current prices; NOK million[a])

	1995	1996	1997	1998	1999	2000	2001	2002	2003[b]	2004[b]
Expenditure	856.8	1,257.5	985.7	1,180.6	2,000	2,041.4	1,578	1,823.5	1,019	700

Sources: Liland, Frode with Kirsten Alsaker Kjerland (2003) *Norsk utviklingshjelps historie 3: 1989–2002: På bred front* (Bergen: Fakbogforlaget), p. 98; Budget Item 1792: Norwegian forces abroad, St. prp. nr. 1 (2001–02)–(2003–04).

Notes
a   NOK 100 = EUR 12.28.
b   Budget estimates.

been financed by a budget appropriation for peace operations on the regular defence budget.[52] This appropriation has usually been too small to cover the actual costs and *ad hoc* solutions have therefore been employed to finance the resulting deficits. They have been covered by a combination of savings (often terminations and reductions of ongoing operations), by the expropriation of funds initially earmarked for other purposes on the regular budget (typically investments) and by the adoption of supplementary budgets. In 1995 unused funds on the development budget were expropriated to pay part of the bill for IFOR, but this proved so controversial that it has not been done since.[53] By 1997, the government felt that the financing of peace operations by appropriations on the defence budget earmarked for other purposes had gone too far. It therefore decided in principle to finance all costs exceeding the budget appropriation for peace operations through the adoption of supplementary budgets.[54] This model was by and large employed until the budget year 2002 when a four-year budget cycle was introduced for the first time.[55] The result was increased flexibility as excesses in one year can be covered by the appropriations for the following years, but it does not remove the need for supplementary funding if the annual costs continue to exceed the NOK 900 million initially budgeted for each year in the period. NOK 776 million was thus required in supplementary funding to cover the excess resulting from the involvement in Afghanistan in 2002.[56] The struggle for funds thus continues and the proposed NOK 700 million budget for 2004 does not appear realistic even though the number of Norwegian troops abroad has been reduced considerably.

The economic difficulties have repeatedly forced Norway to either terminate or reduce its involvement in ongoing operations in order to finance the involvement in new ones. In 1994 the deployment of a 370-strong logistics battalion in Bosnia led to the termination of the Norwegian contributions to UNMOGIP in Kashmir, UNIKOM in Kuwait and UNOSOM II in Somalia as well as a gradual reduction of the contribution to UNPROFOR/UNPREDEP in Macedonia.[57] The following year the Norwegian UN contingent in Lebanon was reduced by 200 personnel to help finance the involvement in Bosnia.[58] In 1998 the contribution to the Lebanon operation was terminated in order to help maintain and reinforce the Norwegian contribution to the Nordic–Polish brigade in SFOR. In 1999 Norway withdrew completely from SFOR in order to be able to deploy a battalion in Kosovo.[59] The following year the participation in KFOR forced the termination of the Norwegian participation in UNAMSIL in Sierra Leone,[60] and in 2003 the KFOR contingent was cut with 260 personnel and the remaining ten Norwegian UN observers in Africa were withdrawn to help finance the involvement in Afghanistan.[61] These reductions led to repeated clashes between the Ministry of Defence (MoD) and the Ministry of Foreign Affairs (MFA) as the latter opposed the resulting reduction in the number of Norwegian contributions to UN-commanded operations. Further reductions in 2004 meant that the number of Norwegian military personnel deployed abroad by 1 July of that year had declined to 600, the lowest figure since the involvement in UNIFIL in Lebanon began in 1978.[62] The economic difficulties plaguing the Norwegian armed forces since the end of the Cold War have, in short, been a major determinant of their international involvement.

The cost of participating in peace operations with civilian personnel, which is covered by the MFA, has also increased significantly. The cost of running NORDEM rose from NOK 13 million to NOK 24 million in the 1995–2000 period,[63] and the total bill for the 1993–2002 period came to NOK 136 million.[64] The expenditures on civilian police deployments are much higher. Sustaining the deployment abroad of the 73 police officers as of May 2003 for a year would cost NOK 51.1 million, or approximately NOK 700,000 a head.[65] The total spent on civilian personnel is difficult to determine since it does not figure separately in the MFA's budget, but the total expenditures on peace, democracy and human rights have exploded during the 1990s, as is clear from Table 6.2.

Explaining the changes

Norway's increased willingness to participate in peace operations can in part be explained by the same external factors that pushed the other Nordic countries in the same direction. The disappearance of the Soviet threat

Table 6.2 MFA expenditures on peace, democracy and human rights 1991–2001 (NOK million[a])

	1991	*1993*	*1995*	*1997*	*1999*	*2001*
Expenditure	58.3	217.3	521	573.4	1,234	1,407.6

Source: Liland. Frode with Kirsten Alsaker Kjerland (2003) *Norsk utviklingshjelps historie 3: 1989–2002: På bred front* (Bergen: Fakbogforlaget), p. 105.

Notes
a   NOK 100 = EUR 12.28.

made the changes possible, the wars in the Balkans gave Norway a security interest in stemming the spread of violence and refugees, the nature of the operations in the Balkans created a need to go beyond traditional peace-keeping, pressures from the EU and NATO increased the political costs of non-involvement, and the new normative climate resulting from the end of the Cold War made it easy to legitimize the increased involvement as a logical and desirable continuation of the UN policy pursued during the Cold War.[66]

The Norwegian reform process has its own distinct characteristics, however. The pace of military reform has been much slower than in Denmark, even though both countries have been subjected to the same pressures from NATO to establish effective rapid reaction forces. As was the case in Sweden, it took a major embarrassment in Kosovo to convince the armed forces to make rapid reaction a real priority. Like its Swedish neighbour, Norway waited until the turn of the century to embark on fundamental defence reforms. Only Finland is slower in this respect. In contrast, Norway was quickest off the mark in the civilian field. It was the first country in the world to establish a civilian rapid reaction capability for humanitarian and peace operations, and it directly inspired the arrangements subsequently set up by the other Nordic countries and Canada, the OSCE and the UN.[67]

We have to take a look at the domestic level to understand these differences as well as the civilian activism and the military foot-dragging. The activism in the civilian and humanitarian field grew out of Norway's humanitarian tradition and the work of a small network of dedicated visionaries spearheaded by Jan Egeland. The military foot-dragging can be explained by a combination of the '9 April Never Again' defence culture and successful societal resistance to defence reform at the local and regional levels.

The rise of the Norwegian model

The MFA views the increased involvement in peace diplomacy in the 1990s as an expression of the values and norms embodied in two Norwegian traditions and popular movements: the Christian missionaries and the labour movement, both of which emphasized values such as equality, peace, democracy, solidarity, safety and a duty to assist people in need.[68] These traditions underpinned Norway's traditional support for mediation, humanitarian assistance and development assistance, and they also gave rise to the close cooperation between the MFA and development NGOs, which served as a principal source of inspiration for the Norwegian model that emerged in the 1990s.[69] While these traditions without a doubt con-stitute the historical preconditions for the activism of the 1990s, they cannot explain its timing. To do so three additional factors must be considered. The first is the increased revenue from Norway's production of oil and gas,[70] without which it would have been very difficult to pay for the increased activism (it is not cheap – the budget allocation for humanitarian assistance alone rose from NOK 685 million in 1988 to over NOK 2 billion in 1999).[71] The second is the end of the Cold War which led to 'new thinking' in the MFA. The result was a white paper, the so-called bible of Norwegian foreign policy, which was presented to parliament in 1989. It argued that Norway had to be 'active' and 'creative' and seek to make a real difference on the international scene.[72] The final piece of the puzzle is Jan Egeland, a humanitarian visionary, who had the will and the ability to realize the ambitions expressed in the white paper for a more activist and creative foreign policy. Before joining the MFA first as an advisor (1990–92) and then as state secretary (1992–97), he had held leading positions in Amnesty International (1982–86) and the Norwegian Red Cross (1988–90) and written a book advocating a more active Norwegian human rights policy.[73] He joined the MFA with a clear ambition to give Norway a more active role on the international scene, and his NGO background gave him the contacts and credibility required to establish the close and informal cooperation between the MFA and the humanitarian NGOs that forms the institutional basis of the Norwegian model. He was the architect behind the establishment of NORSTAFF and NORDEM and played an important part in the negotiations that led to the Oslo agreement in 1993 that 'put Norway on the map as an international peace mediator'.[74] This success consolidated the Norwegian model and paved the way for further expansion.

Other people also deserve credit for the creation of the model. Egeland enjoyed the support of the three foreign ministers he worked for (Thorvald Stoltenberg, who brought him into the MFA, Johan Jørgen Holst and Bjørn Tore Godal), and he also benefited from the pioneering work carried out in the 1980s by another foreign minister, Knut Frydenlund, as well as established tradition for close cooperation between the MFA and the NGOs in the development field. That said, Egeland was the pivotal figure in the policy network behind the creation of the model that he came to personify.[75]

Military foot-dragging

Unlike the civilians, the armed forces were slow to seize the opportunity for reform presented by the end of the Cold War. It took more than ten years before Norwegian force planning finally took the collapse of the Soviet Union into account. Although 'uncertainty' replaced an immediate military attack from Russia as the new threat in official documents as early as 1993,[76] invasion defence against a comprehensive attack from Russia remained the dominant factor structuring the development and activities of the armed forces until June 2001, when the Long Term Defence Plan for 2002–05 was adopted by parliament. According to this plan Russia did not constitute a military threat and any comprehensive military operation against Norwegian territory was considered 'highly unlikely within the next ten years.'[77]

Geographic proximity provides a first-cut explanation as to why it took so long to bury the threat from the East. Norway reacted quicker than Finland, which shares a much larger border with Russia, more or less simultaneously with Sweden, whose position is similar, and much slower than Denmark, which is further away. But geography cannot in itself explain why Norway failed to adjust its threat perceptions so long after the military threat from the East had vanished. To understand the slow pace of military reform we need to take its defence culture and the resistance at the local and regional levels into account.

'9 April Never Again' defence culture

Denmark and Norway were both attacked by Germany on 9 April 1940 but this experience played very different roles in the defence debates of the 1990s in the two countries. In Denmark it played no role whatsoever; in Norway it dominated the debate. Every attempt to internationalize the armed forces was met with the argument that it would undermine the capacity for invasion defence and result in a new 9 April.[78] The proponents of invasion defence regarded international operations as a luxury that Norway could not afford at a time when the armed forces were facing major budget cuts. In their view, the Norwegian armed forces should spend less time abroad and focus on the defence of the homeland. Norwegian officers should not be forced to participate in international operations, and to ensure a proper defence capacity general conscription, a large army and a large home guard had to be preserved.[79]

Until the mid-1990s the military leadership and most of the officer corps held this view. In 1996 Chief of Defence Arne Solli made clear that the involvement in international operations was creating an imbalance in the defence structure and weakening national defence,[80] and this view was also reflected in the lack of priority given to the rapid reaction forces, which repeatedly failed to meet their readiness targets, and in the fact that invasion defence continued to be the focus of the curriculum in the War College in Oslo until 1997.[81]

The increasing involvement of NATO in peace operations (NATO, unlike the UN, had a high status in the eyes of the officer corps),[82] the professional desire to be able to participate effectively in operations alongside the other NATO partners and the shock provided by the readiness problems revealed by the Kosovo deployments all helped to change the tide in favour of internationalization. As a result, the military leadership as well as younger officers with direct experience from the Balkans are now coming out in favour of both professionalization and internationalization of the armed forces.[83] The military leadership did not get its way in the negotiations resulting in the formulation of the 2002–05 Defence Plan. The white paper proposed by the government, which was based on a recommendation from the chief of defence, was defeated by a majority in parliament, who thought it would result in an unacceptable weakening of national defence.[84] This outcome demonstrates that the 9 April Never Again lobby remains a force to be reckoned with – a fact also illustrated by the way in which MoD officials and the military leadership constantly go out of their way to make the case that the international involvement does not undermine national defence, and that it actually is required to avoid a new 9 April.[85] However, without the support of the military leadership and the younger generation of officers, the 9 April Never Again argument cannot be sustained. This does not mean that the opposition to internationalization will cease. This opposition has never been based solely on military grounds. It also has strong roots in political and business interests at the regional and local levels, and it was the alliance between the military elite and these interests that made it so powerful throughout the 1990s.

Resistance at the local and regional levels

It is an iron law of defence politics that proposals to close or move military bases trigger local protests. That Norway is no exception is evident from the following comment by Brigadier Erik Ianke:

> We have the impression that our bases have become the main employer in many districts. The moment we begin reducing or closing, the local politicians react and are supported in the parliament...the armed forces have in many respects become enmeshed in local politics. We do not even dare to consider closing the defence commands in Bodø and Stavanger. Here we encounter built-in and self-imposed political barriers.[86]

What is unusual about Norway is the extent to which local and regional interests have been successful in slowing down the restructuring of the armed forces. The explanation provided by Norwegian defence experts is that the armed forces traditionally have been seen as an instrument of local and regional development, and that defence politics as a consequence has focused more on local and regional development than military effectiveness.[87] The importance attached to such development issues is also visible in the Long Term Defence Plan for 2002–05:

> The government has high ambitions concerning the development of our districts and regions. Our ambition to preserve current settlements and develop viable regions in all parts of the country remains. This has been a central factor shaping the recommendations for reductions in the peacetime organization of the armed forces that are put forward in this white paper.[88]

These reductions were met by a storm of protests, and a parliamentary majority forced the minority government to cancel some of the reductions and accept the procurement of a new generation of fast patrol boats, the building of which would secure a lot of jobs.[89] Thus, local and regional interests once again succeeded in slowing the process of defence reform, but their victory is bound to be short-lived. The proposals forced upon the government lacked adequate funding, and additional cuts will hence be required in order to balance the budget in the next agreement. A further professionalization of the armed forces and a reduction in the size of the home guard are thus bound to be approved then.[90] This said, the influence of local and regional interests on Norwegian defence politics will remain strong as long as a majority in parliament remains content to impose defence agreements without adequate funding upon the government and the chief of defence. Thus far, every defence agreement since the end of the Cold War has been underfunded, suggesting that the problem is likely to remain for some time.

Factors determining specific contributions

Norway's military deployment pattern changed in the course of the 1990s. National security, military relevance and personnel security became determinants of Norway's force deployments in the 1990s and as a result the UN lost out to NATO, the EU and US-led operations,[91] which today receive the lion's share of Norway's military contributions. A fear of marginalization in Europe has prompted Norway to pursue a 'troops-for-influence' strategy, as Nina Græger has coined it, in relation to the EU and NATO,[92] and this strategy has also been employed vis-à-vis the USA since the 'war on terror' began in 2001.

The UN has been marginalized. Norway has only been willing to provide observers to UN-commanded operations since the pull-out from UNIFIL in 1998, and these symbolic contributions have been the first to go when money was required to fund new operations elsewhere. The abandonment of the UN has triggered some domestic criticism and the MFA is very unhappy about it.[93] The MFA's concern that the lack of support for UN-commanded operations will damage Norway's reputation at the UN has fallen on deaf ears in recent years, however.[94] Instead, the MoD's insistence that Norway should concentrate on a few but important conflicts to save money and maximize influence and force protection has carried the day.

Nordic cooperation plays much the same role as it has always done in Norwegian deployment decisions. Nordic cooperation enhances legitimacy, force protection, interoperability and cost-effectiveness, but it is not decisive. It is nice but not necessary. Still, Nordic cooperation has gained a new importance as a back door to the EU. NORDCAPS is thus seen as a way of giving Norway a greater say in EU-led operations. The Norwegian decision in November 2004 to provide 300 personnel to the EU battle group that Finland and Sweden decided to establish one month earlier may reduce the value attributed to NORDCAPS in this respect, however.[95]

Civilian and military personnel deployable at short notice

The number of civilian personnel has increased significantly due to the establishment of five rapid reaction arrangements: NORSTAFF, NORDEM, NST, one for police officers and one for rule-of-law personnel (judges, prosecutors and jailers). NORSTAFF, the world's first civilian standby force, was set up after the humanitarian crisis in northern Iraq in 1991 to enhance the UN's capacity to help and protect refugees and internally displaced persons in humanitarian emergencies. In mid-2004 it was made up of roughly 300 experienced professionals from 25 different job categories, and approximately 100 persons are out on assignments in the field at any given time. NORSTAFF supplies personnel to fill positions ranging from headquarters staff to mechanics in the field. All personnel hold regular civilian jobs when on standby but are available for deployment at 72 hours' notice. NORSTAFF has emergency response agreements with eight UN organizations but has also made personnel available for other humanitarian organizations and regional organizations such as the OSCE.[96]

NORDEM is made up of a Resource Bank and a Standby Force. The Resource Bank established in 1993 consists of approximately 120 persons with expertise in the areas of election assistance, democratic organizations, news media, minority protection, constitutional reform, rule of law, good governance and human rights education. As of 2003, the Standby Force included 200 members available for international assignments of up to six months' duration at one to three weeks' notice. The Standby Force covers the following categories: election observers, technical election support, election experts, political analysis, local governance, free media, good governance, legal reform, human rights monitors, and investigators of gross violations of human rights. In the 1995–2000 period 70 per cent of the assignments fell within the areas of election observation and election assistance.[97] In 2003 NORDEM completed 38 assignments involving 111 individuals for a total period of 360 work-months.[98]

The NST standby teams were established in 1997 by Norway's Directorate for Civil Defence and Emergency Planning to provide assistance in connection with international disasters at short notice. The Directorate has established two support teams on standby, consisting of nine members each. The size and specific composition of the teams are flexible and may be adapted to the mission in question. The teams are on 24-hour standby and will be deployed fully equipped. A mission normally lasts up to six weeks but can in certain situations be extended by another six weeks.[99] By mid-2004, the NST had a pool of 53 personnel.[100] The NST teams were made available to the EU's civilian rapid reaction force in February 2003.[101]

The Directorate is also responsible for seven persons that Norway has made available for the UN Disaster Assessment and Coordination (UNDAC) standby arrangement.[102]

The Norwegian police have established a standby capacity for international operations of some 80 personnel, the equivalent of 1 per cent of the national police force. This capacity has been made available for both the EU and the UN. As of 1 May 2004, 54 Norwegian police officers were participating in operations around the world.[103]

Finally, the Ministry of Justice established a rapid reaction arrangement for rule-of-law personnel in the autumn of 2003. Thirty experts from this arrangement were made available to the EU, the OSCE and the UN for international missions on 1 March 2004.[104]

The military rapid reaction capacity has also been enhanced significantly. The initial attempts to establish rapid reaction forces for NATO were not very successful. These forces proved anything but rapid when activated, and the Kosovo crisis revealed serious problems with both the air force and army units earmarked as NATO reaction forces. The Norwegian contingent for KFOR was the last to arrive in Kosovo three months after the deployment had begun. The British KFOR commander, General Michael Jackson, was not amused and greeted it with the following remark: 'What took you so long? Have you been walking?'[105] This embarrassment led to the establishment of an Armed Forces Task Force for International Operations.[106] The task force consists of units from all branches of the armed forces and is designed with a capability to conduct both warfighting and peace operations.

When fully organized in the summer of 2005, the force will include approximately 2,300 army personnel, 440 navy personnel and 1,000–1,500 from the air force (see Table 6.3 for a breakdown of the units that had been made available for international rapid reaction arrangements by mid-2004).[107] The new force is thus considerably larger than the old standby force which totalled 2,022 personnel. The establishment of the new force is more or less on schedule. The 450-strong Telemark Battalion, part of the Norwegian Army High Readiness Force (NOA HRF) with a response time of 3–7 days, was declared operational on 1 July 2003 as planned,[108] and in mid-July its 150-strong engineering company departed for Iraq.[109]

Training to prepare the civilian and military personnel for their many new tasks

The personnel serving in Norway's reaction forces, civilian and military, all receive specialized training. If we look at the civilian standby forces first, then all selected volunteers for the NORSTAFF standby force receive a three-day basic course to enable them to function effectively in an emergency situation. Specialized courses are also provided in areas such as security, logistics, protection and communications, and new courses are

Table 6.3 Military rapid reaction forces with a readiness of 30 days or less (July 2004)

	Forces	EU	NATO RF	NATO NRF	NORDCAPS	SHIRBRIG
Army	1 mechanized infantry	X	X	..	X	..
	1 tank squadron	..	..	..	..	..
	1 engineer company	X	..	..	..	..
	1 HQ and service support squadron	..	..	..	..	..
	1 military police detachment	X	..	..	..	..
	1 CIMIC team	X	..	..	..	..
Air force	12 fighter planes	X	X	(6)	X	..
	1 maritime patrol aircraft	X	X	..	X	..
	2 transport aircraft	(1)	X	..	X	..
	4 helicopters	X	X	..	X	X
	1 DA-20 jet (electronic warfare)	..	X	X	..	..
	1 anti-aircraft unit	X	X	..	X	..
Navy	1 frigate	..	X	X	X	..
	1 submarine	X	X	X	X	..
	4 fast patrol boats + 1 support ship	(1)	X	X	X	..
	1 mine countermeasures vessel	X	X	X	X	..
	1 mine command ship	X	X	X	X	..
	1 unit mine clearance divers	X	X	X	X	..
	Special forces	..	..	X	..	..

Source: Norwegian MoD.

continuously being developed. In addition, a limited number of volunteers are sent on courses run by the UN.[110]

NORDEM personnel are required to attend a basic six-day course consisting of three components: a general knowledge part focusing on international and regional mechanisms for the protection of human rights, the UN mandate, structure and human rights operations; skills training in the field of election observation or human rights monitoring and investigation; and a third section focusing on practical aspects of international fieldwork. In addition to the basic course election observers and election supervisors receive a three-day course on elections. Before going on a mission they receive written information materials and a briefing about the assignment and the situation in the mission area. After the completion of a mission, debriefings are organized and the personnel submit a written after-action report.[111]

NST personnel receive courses tailored to their missions that have been planned and carried out in cooperation with the UN Disaster Management Training Programme. The courses include information and practical training on subjects such as humanitarian organizations, cultural awareness, stress management, security, radio procedures, media relations, English language and the establishment and running of a base.[112]

The police only accept volunteers with a minimum of six years' experience from active service who fulfil the basic UN requirements for civilian police. Accepted volunteers receive a two-week basic UN course, which includes training in English, human rights and international standards for police work. In addition, the police officers receive one week of mission-oriented training before being deployed abroad. Six to eight weeks after the completion of their mission, the officers are summoned to an after-mission briefing and evaluation.[113]

The training provided by the military was inadequate during most of the 1990s. The mechanized infantry battalions that Norway contributed to SFOR in 1997–99 were incapable of conducting offensive operations at the battalion level when they were deployed in the field.[114] The need to correct this and a host of other shortcomings led to a considerable delay in the deployment of the Norwegian KFOR contingent in 1999, and this experience resulted in the adoption of a new training programme in the army. The new programme recognizes that it takes four to six months to create the effective combat-capable units that contemporary peace operations require.[115]

Conscripts who are interested in international operations are placed in special units commanded by officers who have also volunteered for such service. They then train together for a full year before going abroad on an international mission. The training programme is divided in two. The first part focuses on basic military skills and warfighting. The second part is a two- to four-month specialization in peace operations, and volunteers for peace operations who have already completed their basic military training join the programme at this stage.[116] When training is complete the volunteers either go directly on a rotation mission in a known location or go on standby for possible deployment with the army's response unit (the Telemark Battalion). The battalion (KFOR III) deployed in Kosovo in the summer of September 2000 was the first to go through this system, and it was also the first in which the personnel were asked to sign up for a

12-month tour (two 6-month contracts). Until then the normal tour of duty had lasted six months and this remains the case for the personnel in the response unit. The 12-month tour in the rotation missions was introduced to enhance continuity in the field and to reduce recruitment problems. The first rotation contingent primarily consisting of personnel on 12-month contracts was the KFOR battalion deployed in the summer of 2002.[117]

In addition to this general programme, Norwegian officers receive training in peace operations at the war colleges and go on the specialized training programmes offered by NATO, NORDCAPS and the UN.

Interoperability with most likely partners

A high degree of interoperability with other nations is a requirement for success in Norwegian peace operations doctrine, and interoperability with allies has been a priority since the early 1990s.[118] The importance attributed to interoperability was reflected in the decision to engage in joint training prior to the deployment of NORDBAT 2 in Tuzla in 1993,[119] and it is also clear in the way the need for interoperability has been one of the key drivers of the internationalization of the Norwegian armed forces. The Norwegian policy has to a large extent been driven by the interoperability requirements established by NATO, but it has also been pursued in other multinational settings such as NORDCAPS, which resulted from a Norwegian initiative.[120] The participation in SHIRBRIG and the EU rapid reaction force also serves to enhance Norway's interoperability with its partners, as does its efforts to reform the UN system in accordance with the recommendations presented in the *Brahimi Report*.[121] Most recently, the Norwegian government has launched the so-called North Sea Strategy which aims at deepening military cooperation and interoperability with its NATO partners Denmark, Germany, The Netherlands and the UK to facilitate joint contributions to the NATO Response Force.[122] It has also accepted the invitation to join the joint battle group established by Finland and Sweden in October 2004. The 300-strong Norwegian contribution will be ready from 2008.

Armaments and ROE permitting use of force beyond self-defence if necessary

It was understood immediately that the involvement in peace operations going beyond traditional peacekeeping would require forces with better training, better protection, better equipment and heavy weapons. Indeed, it was the inability of the Norwegian Army to meet these requirements that forced Norway to limit its participation in UNPROFOR and IFOR to support units.[123] The participation in these operations led to the procurement of new equipment in order to enhance force protection,[124] and the adoption of a new doctrine which tailored the force package and the

ROE to the situation in the mission area. It reflected the lessons learned that operations going beyond traditional peacekeeping called for highly trained and heavily armed contingents with robust mandates and ROE, and that the dispatch of traditional peacekeepers to war zones was a recipe for failure.[125]

Norway generally places limitations on the use of its forces in peace operations,[126] and the practice is even recommended in the Norwegian doctrine.[127] The nature of these limitations is determined on a case-by-case basis depending on the nature of the operation and the Norwegian contribution to it. In KFOR Norway placed few restrictions on its personnel and made a 200-strong rapid reaction force (Task Force Viking) available for the force commander as a strategic reserve for use in emergencies throughout the KFOR theatre of operations. In Iraq a far more restrictive approach was employed for the deployment of an engineer company in 2003–04. The Norwegian ROE were stricter than those of other contributors as the Norwegian contingent was only allowed to use force in self-defence.[128]

Logistics

The Norwegian Air Force was not geared for international operations when it was told to deploy a helicopter wing in Bosnia in August 1993. On the contrary, it came as a great surprise that the wing was actually going abroad, even though it was listed as a reaction unit on seven-day readiness. When the order came the logistical support system had to be created from scratch. It took almost two months to get it ready to go, and effective supply lines between Norway and the mission area were not established until six months after the deployment had begun. Almost a year passed before a reliable communications system was in place.[129]

The Norwegian chief of staff in the Nordic–Polish brigade in IFOR, Kjell Grandhagen, characterized logistics as a comparative handicap for Norway,[130] and the Kosovo operations in 1998–99 demonstrated that logistics remained an Achilles' heel for both the air force and the army.[131] The joint doctrine published in 2000 called for the establishment of a logistics base in Norway responsible for coordinating and transporting all supplies to and from the mission areas,[132] the need for improvements was further underlined in a defence white paper in early 2001,[133] and the chief of defence subsequently made international logistical support a priority.[134] The results have begun to show. The logistical support provided to the army's response unit has been beefed up, all army personnel including observers are now supported from the same base, Terningmoen,[135] and the naval and air force deployments undertaken as part of the war against terrorism in 2002–03 also reveal marked improvements, suggesting that the logistical support system has become a help rather than a hindrance as was often the case during the 1990s.[136]

Another indication of progress is provided by the fact that Norway became lead nation in the joint flight service established together with Finland and Sweden to supply their contingents in Afghanistan in 2002.[137]

Medical, psychological and family support

Improvements have been made across the board but they have been rather slow in coming. The first step was taken in 1993 when the life insurance of UN personnel was doubled,[138] but the efforts undertaken to enhance the psychological support system were severely criticized in an evaluation in 1998. It demanded improvements in the selection procedures, introduction of standard procedures for the psychological support provided during operations in the field, improved monitoring of the psychological status of personnel in the field, better reporting procedures during and after deployment, an enhanced presence of psychologically trained personnel in the field, the introduction of standard psychological debriefings following stressful incidents in the field, strengthened follow-up after demobilization, and a strengthening of the existing networks of UN veterans.[139] Moreover, the evaluation also called for improvements in the information and service provided to families during the deployments.

Most of these recommendations have now been acted upon. The selection process, the pre-mission training in stress management, the debriefing procedures employed on the missions following incidents, the demobilization programme and the follow up have all been improved.[140] In its budget proposal for 2005 the government proposed that psychologically damaged veterans should be entitled to compensation, and the new law entered into force on 1 January 2005.[141] Veterans with psychological problems caused by their international service have long struggled for this right, and the proposal was probably triggered by a number of lawsuits launched against the government to obtain compensation.[142]

A proper family support system is also in the making. The 6th Division, which trains most of the army personnel going abroad, has started a pilot project, 'Military families in Troms', offering comprehensive support packages to the families staying at home.[143] In spite of recent improvements, most Norwegian officers remain unconvinced of the capacity of the armed forces to provide their families with the necessary support while they serve on international operations. Only 20 per cent believed this to be the case in a poll published in June 2004.[144] To make international service more attractive and ease the hardship it imposes on family life, the officer union has called for more home leave. It wants an introduction of the Finnish system, which grants personnel one week's home leave for every four weeks served abroad. In contrast, Norwegian personnel are only granted home leave twice a year.[145]

The medical support system has also been improved. An agreement with a civilian airline ensures that Norwegian personnel can be evacuated quickly from mission areas throughout the world,[146] and modern equipment has also been procured for the response forces. The container-based surgical unit which entered into service in 2003 is the most advanced in the world and far safer both for personnel and patients than the tent-based field hospitals in use until then.[147]

Intelligence capacity

The Norwegian armed forces have recognized that the need for intelligence on contemporary peace operations is high, and their joint doctrine thus emphasizes the importance of effective cooperation with other intelligence services, international organizations and NGOs before and during operations, as well as the importance of getting a precise understanding of the mission area and the nature of the conflict prior to deployment.[148] A Norwegian battalion deployed on peace operations has a relatively high intelligence capacity. It will usually have an intelligence section with five to six trained intelligence personnel as well as special forces engaged in security and intelligence at the tactical level to enhance force protection. In addition, Norwegian contingents will also be supported with strategic intelligence from national and allied sources.[149] The Norwegian contingents in Bosnia and Kosovo also benefited from the establishment of Nordic intelligence cells. In the years ahead the intelligence capacity of the Norwegian forces deployed abroad will be enhanced even further through the establishment of an intelligence battalion, which is being set up following a request from NATO. The battalion is expected to become operational at the start of 2006.[150]

Public information capacity

Public information was not a priority during the Cold War and not much of a priority in the first part of the 1990s either. This has now changed in response to the increased demands from the media. The Telemark Battalion, the army's high readiness force, has been equipped with a small public information section staffed with an officer and a private. In addition, Norwegian battalions participating in peace operations all have a public information section consisting of one to three personnel on their staff. The public information section in the Norwegian KFOR contingent was thus initially staffed with three personnel. An additional officer was added in July 2002 until budget cuts and a reduction in the size of the Norwegian contingent reduced it to only one in the spring of 2003.[151]

Norwegian information officers have traditionally been recruited for one operation at a time from a relatively large pool (approximately 160) of conscript officers in the reserves, who are journalists by trade or have a similar media-related background. Most information officers continue to be recruited in this way. Since most information officers are professional journalists, the media training provided by the Norwegian armed forces is limited to a day or two.[152]

Coordination and cooperation capacity

The Norwegian armed forces are no stranger to civil–military cooperation (CIMIC). The Norwegian battalions in UNIFIL cooperated closely with the local authorities and carried out a variety of civil tasks such as refuse collection, and CIMIC cells have been standard on all the Norwegian Balkan battalions since 1996. CIMIC was never a priority, however, and remained a speciality limited to the contingents deployed on international operations. Only the battalions earmarked for international operations and the 6th Division responsible for training the army contingents going abroad have established CIMIC sections.[153]

This approach came under increased fire by the end of the 1990s. Lessons learned reports called for more resources and better training of the Norwegian contingents and proposed the establishment of CIMIC sections in all Norwegian units down to the battalion level. The level of coordination among the Norwegian organizations involved in peace operations was found wanting both at home and in the mission areas, and the remedies proposed were: more joint training between the military, police and the NGOs; enhanced concentration and coordination of the overall Norwegian contribution to peace operations; more co-deployment of Norwegian military, police and NGOs; tying of Norwegian assistance to areas where the Norwegian military is deployed; enhanced coordination between the MFA and the MoD; and a streamlining of the procedures used to assess proposals for CIMIC projects submitted by the Norwegian CIMIC contingents in the field.[154]

The degree of coordination has subsequently been enhanced, especially between the MFA and the MoD, and funds are now released quicker by the MFA for use by Norwegian military contingents for CIMIC projects. Thus, the Norwegian battalion in Kosovo was granted NOK 3 million for such projects in 2002–03.[155] Still, the military remains ambivalent about its involvement in CIMIC. The joint doctrine wants to leave non-military tasks to the civilian experts in the mission areas,[156] and a Norwegian soldier interviewed on a social patrol in Kosovo in 2003 was not exactly thrilled about it either. In his view: '[t]alking to people is not really something soldiers should spend their time on.'[157]

Public security capacity

Norway has, as already mentioned, strengthened its civilian public security capacity for international operations significantly. The same cannot be said about the military capacity, even if progress has been made. The Norwegian armed forces view public security as one of the 'non-military tasks' that are best left to civilian experts. According to their joint doctrine, '[i]t is not natural that our forces serving abroad should carry out tasks that we as a matter of principle will not allow our forces to carry out at home (e.g. public security).'[158] It is hardly surprising then, that a lessons learned seminar in 2000 recommended that the army units' capacity for civilian policing should be improved and that a civilian police unit should be attached to the army's high readiness force.[159]

'Natural' or not, the Norwegian Army has also been forced by developments in the mission areas to accept public security tasks as part of its duties on peace operations. Since 1996–97 Norwegian peace operations contingents have been trained and equipped for public security tasks, including riot control. Norwegian contingents have been employed for such tasks in Kosovo since 1999 and in Afghanistan since December 2003 on a regular basis, and all infantry contingents now receive extensive training in public security tasks before going abroad on peace missions. They are provided with special equipment for riot control such as helmets, pads, shields and batons, and instructed in the use of water cannons and teargas.[160] On 1 August 2002 a joint military police education for all the services was established to make it easier to deploy military police from all three services abroad on peace operations.[161]

The Norwegian contingents trained for public security tasks have been put to the test on several occasions in recent years in Kosovo where Norwegian troops have been forced to use teargas and fire warning shots to disperse demonstrators on several occasions.[162] Unlike some NATO contingents which either fled or stayed in their barracks, the Norwegians were among the ones who stood their ground during the riots in Kosovo in March 2004.[163] Twenty Norwegians were wounded in these operations.[164]

Conclusion

The Norwegian efforts to modernize their approach to peace operations have been uneven but ultimately successful. While Norway was first out of the starting block with respect to setting up civilian rapid reaction forces, it was slow to gear up its military forces for the requirements of post-Cold War peace operations. These efforts were generally characterized by last-minute improvisations throughout the 1990s and officially pronounced a failure in 2000. Since then a complete overhaul of the Norwegian approach has succeeded in bringing the Norwegian armed forces up to speed so that they now meet the eleven requirements for success (Table 6.4). Their capacity for peace operations will continue to grow in the decade ahead as the internationalization of the armed forces continues, and the strong political and public support underpinning the growing commitment to peace operations suggests that it is likely to be fully exploited. The troops-for-influence strategy employed by Norway vis-à-vis the EU, NATO and the USA, and the desire by the MFA to increase the number of Norwegian

Table 6.4 Norway and the requirements for success in contemporary peace operations

Requirements for success	Norway
1. Political will, legal framework and funds for all types of operations	Yes
2. Civilian and military personnel deployable at short notice	Yes
3. Training to prepare the civilian and military personnel for their many new tasks	Yes
4. Interoperability with most likely partners	Yes
5. Armaments and ROE permitting use of force beyond self-defence if necessary	Yes
6. Logistics	Yes
7. Medical, psychological and family support	Yes
8. Intelligence capacity	Yes
9. Public information capacity	Yes
10. Coordination and cooperation capacity	Yes
11. Public security capacity	Yes

troops serving in UN-led operations both point towards increased involvement. At the same time, the economic difficulties plaguing the armed forces serve as a real constraint on further expansion. These difficulties contributed to the significant NOK 200 million reduction in the budget for international operations for 2004 and the drop in the number of troops deployed abroad to 600 in mid-2004, the lowest level since 1978. All things considered, it seems unrealistic to expect Norway to be able to sustain more than 1,000 personnel abroad on a continuous basis in the near term.

Notes

1. NOU 2000: 20, section 1.7.
2. The Ministry of Foreign Affairs defines the model in the following way: 'The "Norwegian model" refers to the close, but informal and flexible form of cooperation that has developed between the authorities and NGOs. The concept refers not only to humanitarian assistance, but also to the close cooperation on peace and reconciliation processes, where the local knowledge and contacts of the organizations can be utilized.' See Minister of International Development and Human Rights Johnson, Hilde F. (1999) 'Norwegian Humanitarian Assistance', statement to parliament on humanitarian assistance, 21 January.
3. St. meld. nr. 14 (1992–93) led to an increase in the size of the Norwegian standby force for UN operations, but the efforts to enhance the Norwegian capacity for peace operations was officially deemed a failure by 1999. See St. meld. nr. 38 (1998–99).
4. Fjærevoll, Dag Jostein (1998) 'Challenges for Norwegian Defence into Year 2000. Address by Mr Dag Jostein Fjærevoll, Norwegian Minister of Defence, Oslo Military Society, 5 January 1998' (Oslo: Forsvarsdepartementet).
5. Skar, Harald Olav (ed.) (1989) *Norsk utenrikspolitisk årbok 1988* (Oslo: Norsk Utenrikspolitisk Institut), p. 132.

6. *Norsk deltagelse i internasjonale fredsoperasjoner* <http://www.mil.no/intops/ start/historie/> (16 July 2004). For an overview of Norway's participation in peace operations, see Appendix 6.

7. St. meld. nr. 14 (1992–93), p. 59.

8. NTB (1999) 'Norsk specialstyrke samarbejdede med UCK', *Aktuelt*, 21 June; Solholm, Rolleiv (2002) 'Afghanistan: Norwegian Forces in Action', *The Norway Post*, 4 March; Solholm, Rolleiv (2003) 'Norwegian F-16s on Afghanistan Bombing Mission', *The Norway Post*, 30 March. The Norwegian F-16 did not take part in bombing missions in Allied Force because they were not equipped to hit targets on the ground. See NTB (1999) 'Norge skal ikke delta i bombeangrep', *Aftenposten*, 28 May.

9. Politidirektoratet (2003) 'CIVPOL – Norsk politideltagelse i fredsoperasjoner', <www.politi.no/tema/civpol.shtml> (25 July 2004). For an overview of the missions conducted between 1989 and 2000 see Chapter 6 in St. meld. nr. 18 (1999–2000).

10. Estimate e-mailed to author by Jannicke Storm, Norwegian Refugee Council, 24 July 2003.

11. Olesen, Gunnar, Ole Espersen, Birthe L. Nautrup, Lisbeth Pilegaard, Ulrik Sørensen Rohde, and Eilís Ward (2002) *Evaluation of the Norwegian Resource Bank for Democracy and Human Rights (NORDEM)* (Copenhagen: T&B Consult), factsheet, <http://odin.dep.no/ud/engelsk/publ/rapporter/ 032181-220006/index-hov002-b-n-a.html>.

12. Skarbomyr, Odd (2002) 'DSB søker fagfolk til beredskapsstyrken for internasjonal innsats', <www.dsb.no>, 9 April; *Årsrapport 2002 Direktoratet for sivilt beredskap* (Tønsberg: Direktoratet for sivilt beredskap).

13. Nustad, Knut and Henrik Thune (2003) 'Norway: Political Consensus and the Problem of Accountability', in Charlotte Ku and Harold K. Jacobson (eds) *Democratic Accountability and the Use of Force in International Law* (Cambridge: Cambridge University Press), pp. 166–167 (154–175).

14. Nustad and Thune, 'Norway: Political Consensus and the Problem of Accountability', p. 158.

15. Bonde, Aalak (1997) 'Fortsatt FN-styrker i Libanon', *Aftenposten*, 29 December; B.innst.S.nr.7 (1997–98). Norway eventually withdrew from UNIFIL in 1998.

16. Saure, Kjell Erik (1998) 'Norge sender Hercules-fly', *Aftenposten*, 19 February.

17. Innst.S.nr.6 (2002–03).

18. Jones, Gerald (1999) 'Norwegians Support NATO Bombing', *The Norway Post*, 28 March.

19. Jones, Gerald (1999) 'Majority Back Ground Offensive', *The Norway Post*, 7 April.

20. Ellingsen, Lajla (1999) 'Fire av ti for norske bakkestyrker', *Dagbladet*, 20 April.

21. Leder (2001) 'Støtte i folket', *Aftenposten*, 7 December.

22. Solholm, Rolleiv (2001) 'Norwegians Divided on the Bombing of Afghanistan', *The Norway Post*, 26 October; Solholm, Rolleiv (2001) 'Norwegian Bishops: Stop the Bombing', *The Norway Post*, 29 October.

23. Narum, Håvard (2003) 'Klart norsk nei til krig i Irak', *Aftenposten*, 19 March; Narum, Håvard (2003) 'Stort flertall bak Norges nei til krig', *Aftenposten*, 28 March; Narum, Håvard (2003) 'økende krigsmotstand i Norge', *Aftenposten*, 10 April; Solholm, Rolleiv (2003) 'Majority Supports Government's Iraq Policy', *The Norway Post*, 28 March.

24. Narum, Håvard (2003) 'Flertallet mot krig blir mindre', *Aftenposten*, 13 February; Narum, Håvard (2003) 'Fortsatt norsk flertall mot Irak-krig',

Aftenposten, 13 March; NTB (2003) 'Økt norsk motstand mot krig i Irak', *Aftenposten Nettutgaven*, 19 January; NTB (2003) 'Annenhver nordmann mot krig i Irak', *Aftenposten Nettutgaven*, 6 February.

25. Bondevik, Kjell Magne (1998) 'Demokrati og stabilitet i en globalisert økonomi', *Aftenposten*, 27 October; Matlary, Janne Haaland (1998) 'Soft Power', *Aftenposten*, 18 August; Lunde, Leiv (1998) 'Høyres Sjømenn', *Dagbladet*, 11 August.

26. Elvik, Halvor and Ann-Magrit Austenå (1999) 'Norge er i krig', *Dagbladet*, 25 March.

27. Bondevik, Kjell Magne (2002) 'Norge er i krig mot internasjonal terror', *Vårt Land*, 2 October.

28. Hegna, Liv and Erik Berglund (1993) 'Ola ikke klar til å krige for FN', *Aftenposten*, 20 June.

29. Alteskjær, Torgrim and Petter Jamissen (2000) 'Fredsstøtteoperasjoner – Nye utfordringer for Forsvaret', *Norsk Militært Tidsskrift*, Vol. 170, No. 2, p. 19 (16–21); Brekke, Sigve and Bjørn Olav Knutsen (1997) 'Politiske rammebetingelser for norsk deltagelse i internasjonale militære operasjoner', *FFI Rapport*, No. 96/04008 (Kjeller: Forsvarets Forskningsinstitutt), p. 19; Børresen, Jacob (1993) 'Fredsoprettende operasjoner – bør Norge deltag?', *Norsk Militært Tidsskrift*, Vol. 163, No. 8–9, pp. 3–4 (1–4); Diesen, Sverre (2000) 'Forsvarspolitiske aspekter ved det norske kandidaturet til FNs sikkerhetsråd', presentation at the seminar *Norway and the UN Security Council*, Norwegian Institute of International Affairs, 17 August.

30. Hagen, Gunnar (2003) 'Skutt i Afghanistan', *Dagbladet*, 25 June.

31. Leder (2004) 'Farlig oppdrag i Afghanistan', *Aftenposten*, 25 May; Fyhn, Morten (2004) 'Faren øker for NATO-soldater i Afghanistan', *Aftenposten*, 25 May; NTB (2004) 'Bondevik: Vil fortsette som planlagt i Afghanistan', *Aftenposten*, 24 May.

32. Rosvoll, Frank (2003) 'FN-veteraner minnes falne i Libanon', Forsvarsnett (www.mil.no), 14 May; Johansen, Per Anders (1999) 'Militærinnsats for 4,3 milliarder kroner', *Aftenposten*, 25 November.

33. Jakobsen, Peter Viggo (2004) 'Har Danmark et body bag syndrom?', *Militært Tidsskrift*, Vol. 133, No. 1 (April), pp. 94–114.

34. *Forsvarets Fellesoperative Doktrine Del B – Operasjoner* (Oslo: Forsvarets Overkommando, 2000), p. 129.

35. The increased risk of casualties and the need for force protection was thus emphasized by Defence Minister Kristin Krohn Devold in her presentation to parliament on 15 December 2003: 'Norway's Participation in Multinational Operations Abroad During 2004', available at <http://www.odin.dep.no/fd/ engelsk/aktuelt/taler/ statsraad_a/010011-090091/dok-bu.html>.

36. The Enlarged Foreign Affairs Committee consists of the ordinary members of the Foreign Affairs Committee, the president and the vice-president of the parliament (if not already members) together with the chairman of the Defence Committee and up to 11 members appointed by the Elections Committee with due regard to the strength of the political parties. The deliberations in the enlarged committee are secret and this has been criticized by a number of parties believing that the Norwegian public is entitled to a plenary debate in parliament before Norwegian troops are sent abroad on warfighting operations. The secrecy and lack of public debate characterizing the decision-making process preceding Norway's participation in Operation Allied Force was criticized heavily, and three parties subsequently forced a public debate on the participation in Operation Enduring Freedom in Afghanistan in December 2001. Two of the parties vowed to force another

plenary debate if the government wanted to make Norwegian forces available for the war against Iraq in 2003 (which it did not), so a new practice may be in the making. See Narum, Håvard (2001) 'Carl I. Hagen og statsmaktkampen', *Aftenposten*, 9 December; Hegtun, Halvor (2002) 'SV og Sp. krever åpen debatt om krig', *Aftenposten*, 31 December; Hegtun, Halvor og Per Anders Johansen (1999) 'Med rett til å bombe', *Aftenposten*, 17 April.

37. Kristiansen, Rolf (1970) *Norsk militær innsats for de Forente Nasjoner 1949–1970* (Oslo: Forsvarets Krigshistoriske Avdeling), pp. 209–210; and the first statement by Foreign Minister Jan Petersen in the parliamentary debate on Norwegian force contributions to Afghanistan, 5 December 2001 <http://www.stortinget.no/stid/ 2001/s011205-01.html>.

38. St. prp. nr. 61 (1963–64).

39. St. meld. nr. 14 (1992–93); Innst. S. nr. 135 (1992–93).

40. St. meld. nr. 46 (1993–94).

41. Eide, Espen Barth (1996) 'Norsk multilateralt militærsamarbeid i en ny epoke', in Iver B. Neumann and Ståle Ulriksen (eds) *Sikkerhetspolitikk – Norge i makttriangelet mellom EU, Russland og USA* (Oslo: Tano), p. 326 (308–335); Innst. S. nr. 23 (1994–95).

42. For the debate see Brekke, Sigve (1995) 'Internasjonal fredstjeneste', *Arbeiderbladet*, 27 June, p. 7; Christie, Werner (1996) 'Tvangsbeordring til FN-tjeneste?', *Aftenposten*, 23 February; Christie, Werner (1996) 'Beordret til å drepe. Ny lov om internasjonale militære operasjoner', *Arbeiderbladet*, 15 May; Eide, Espen Barth (1995) 'Forsvarets internasjonale rolle', *Aftenposten*, 18 April; Eide, Kjell (1996) 'Tvangsbeordring til krigsinnsats', *Dagbladet*, 19 April; Folkvord, Erling (1996) 'Kva slags krig er det befalet vil nekte å delta i?', *Dagbladet*, 16 January; Plahte, Jens (1996) 'Tvangsbeordring til krigføring utenlands', *Dagbladet*, 22 January.

43. *Pressemelding*, 055/98 'Nytt regelverk for tjenestegjøring i internasjonale fredsoperasjoner', 11 September 1998 (Oslo: Forsvarsdepartementet).

44. Ot. prp.nr. 60 (2003–04).

45. See Stortinget <http://www.stortinget.no/otid/2003/ov040610.html#sak1>.

46. See Innst. S. nr. 23 (1994–95). Author's translation.

47. Salvesen, Geir and Olav Trygge Storvik (1998) 'Bare SV er imot militær-aksjon', *Aftenposten*, 17 February; Saure, Kjell Erik (1998) 'Norge sender Hercules-fly', *Aftenposten*, 19 February.

48. St. meld. nr. 38 (1998–99).

49. *Press Release*, No. 38/2003 'A Day of Sadness and Grief, Norway's Prime Minister Says', 20 March 2003 (Oslo: Office of the Prime Minister).

50. Liland, Frode with Kirsten Alsaker Kjerland (2003) *Norsk utviklingshjelps historie 3: 1989–2002: På bred front* (Bergen: Fakbogforlaget), p. 98.

51. On these problems see Otterlei, Jonny M. (2002) 'Norwegian Defence Reforms of the 1990s', *FFI/Rapport*, No. 2002/01206 (Kjeller: Norwegian Defence Research Establishment); and *Norway's Future Defence* (Oslo: Ministry of Defence, 2001).

52. Magne, Holter and Eilert Struknes (1988) (eds) *Norsk Utenrikspolitisk Årbok 1987* (Oslo: Norsk Utenrikspolitisk Institutt), p. 210.

53. B. innst. S. nr. 7 Tl.01 (1995–96); Lægreid, Turid (1996) 'Den 'nye' utanrikspolitikken: humanitær assistanse som realpolitikk?' in Neumann and Ulriksen, *Sikkerhetspolitikk – Norge i makttriangelet mellom EU, Russland og USA*, pp. 302–303 (287–307). During most of 1980s, the use of development funds to cover part of the costs for the UNIFIL contingent was standard.

54. Fjærevoll, 'Challenges for Norwegian Defence into Year 2000; St. prp. nr. 1 (1997–98), p. 9.
55. NATO Review (2002) 'Interview: Kristin Krohn Devold: Norwegian Defence Minister', No. 4 (winter), <http://www.nato.int/docu/review/2002/issue4/english/interview.html> (21 November 2004).
56. St. prp. nr. 39 (2001–02); St. prp. nr. 80 (2001–02); Innst. S. nr. 119 (2001–02); Innst. S. nr. 6 (2002–03).
57. Innst. S. nr. 139 (1993–94).
58. Lægreid, 'Den 'nye' utanrikspolitikken', pp. 298–299.
59. Thune, Henrik and Ståle Ulriksen (2002) 'Norway as an Allied Activist – Prestige and Penance Through Peace', *NUPI Notat*, No. 6 (Oslo: Norwegian Institute of International Affairs), pp. 6–7.
60. Johansen, Per Anders and Elisabeth Randsborg (2000) 'FO vil ofre Sierra Leone for norsk innsats i Kosovo', *Aftenposten*, 22 August.
61. Johnsen, Gunnar (2002) 'Kutter FN-oppdrag i Afrika for å betale Afghani-stan-krig', *Aftenposten*, 26 November; Solholm, Rolleiv (2003) 'Norwegian forces in Kosovo to be Reduced in Number', *The Norway Post*, 8 April.
62. Fyhn, Morten (2004) 'Bunnrekord for norske fredsoppdrag', *Aftenposten*, 4 July.
63. Olesen *et al.*, *Evaluation of the Norwegian Resource Bank for Democracy and Human Rights (NORDEM)*.
64. Liland, *Norsk utviklingshjelps historie 3: 1989–2002*, p. 115.
65. St. meld. nr. 18 (1999–2000), chapter 10.
66. See Chapter 3 for a discussion of these factors.
67. Olesen *et al.*, *Evaluation of the Norwegian Resource Bank for Democracy and Human Rights (NORDEM)*.
68. *Norge i fredens tjeneste – Norske bidrag til fred og forsoning* (Oslo: Utenriksdepartementet, 1999). Analyses of the Norwegian model reach the same conclusion. See Bucher-Johannessen, Bernt (1999) 'Den norske modellen: bruken av ikke statlige aktører i norsk utenrikspolitikk. Et mulig svar på utenrikspolitiske utfordringer for Norge etter den kalde krigen', hovedoppgave i statsvitenskap, Universitetet i Oslo, pp. 4–5; Nygaard, Hege Cecilie (2002) 'Norway's Role in Conflict Resolution: An Examination of the Norwegian Model', unpublished MA thesis, University of Bradford, pp. 14–18.
69. On this cooperation see Bucher-Johannessen, 'Den norske modellen', pp. 41–57.
70. Nygaard, 'Norway's Role in Conflict Resolution', pp. 9–12; Tamnes, Rolf (1997) *Norsk utenrikspolitikks historie. Bind 6: Oljealder 1965–1995* (Oslo: Universitetsforlaget), p. 444.
71. Bucher-Johannessen, 'Den norske modellen', p. 69; *The Norwegian Strategy for Humanitarian Assistance* (Oslo: Ministry of Foreign Affairs), p. 1.
72. St. meld. nr. 11 (1989–90).
73. Bucher-Johannessen, 'Den norske modellen', p. 90. The book in question was: Egeland, Jan (1985) *Impotent Superpowers – Potent Small States: Potentials and Limitations of Human Rights Objectives in the Foreign Policies of the United States and Norway* (Oslo: International Peace Research Institute). Since 1997 Egeland has served as special advisor to the Norwegian Red Cross (1998–99), UN envoy for Cyprus (1999), special UN envoy for Colombia (1999–2002), secretary-general of the Norwegian Red Cross (2002–03) and UN under-secretary-general for humanitarian affairs and emergency relief coordinator (2003–).
74. *Norge i fredens tjeneste.*

75. This conclusion is based on Bucher-Johannessen, 'Den norske modellen', pp. 88–95.
76. St. meld. nr. 16 (1992–93), p. 24.
77. St. meld. nr. 45 (2000–01).
78. See Godal, Ingvald (1997) 'Forsvaret svekkes', *Aftenposten*, 8 September; Waaler, Tor (1994) 'Hvem er ansvarlig for forsvaret', *Norsk Militært Tidsskrift*, Vol 164, No. 6/7, pp. 31–34.
79. For a more thorough analysis of the 9-April-Never-Again defence culture see Heier, Tormod (2000) 'Forsvarets utvikling etter den kalde krigen – den vanskelige veien', *Norsk Militært Tidsskrift*, Vol. 170, No. 3, pp. 20–23; and Ulriksen, Ståle (2002) *Den norske forsvarstradisjonen – militærmakt eller folkeforsvar?* (Oslo: Pax Forlag).
80. Solli, Arne (1996) 'Nytt forsvar for nye omgivelser', *Norges Forsvar*, No. 1 (January), pp. 20–26. See also Neumann, Iver B. and Ståle Ulriksen (1996) 'Norsk forsvars- og sikkerhedspolitik', *Militært Tidsskrift*, Vol. 124, No. 5 (January), pp. 317–319 (298–327).
81. Græger, Nina and Halvard Leira (2003) 'Globalisation vs. Localisation, Norwegian Strategic Culture After World War Two', paper prepared for the 44th Annual Convention of the International Studies Association, Portland, OR, 25 February–1 March, p. 19; Løwer, Elbjørg (2000) 'Vårt forsvar i internasjonalt perspektiv', *Norsk Militært Tidsskrift*, Vol. 170, No. 2, p. 9 (4–11); Ramberg, Leif Morten (1998) 'Luftforsvaret en læringsorganisasjon?: logistiske utfordringer ved NORAIRs deployering til Bosnia 1993', *IFS Info*, No. 1 (Oslo: Institutt for forsvarsstudier).
82. Kosmo, Jørgen (1995) 'Norsk forsvars internasjonale engasjement, foredrag av forsvarsminister Jørgen Kosmo, Bergen Militære Samfunn 31 oktober 1995', *FD info*, No. 9/10 (September/October), pp. 7–16.
83. Mood, Robert (2000) 'Erfaringer fra KFOR I', *Norsk Militært Tidsskrift*, Vol. 170, No. 6/7, pp. 12–13 (6–13); Tangen-Olsen, Dag (2002) 'Lærdommen fra Afghanistan', *Norges Forsvar*, No. 2 (March).
84. Skogrand, Kjetil (2001) 'Forliket som forsvant. Refleksjoner omkring behandlingen av langtidsproposisjonen for Forsvaret', *Norsk Militært Tidsskrift*, Vol. 171, No. 8/9, pp. 15–17.
85. Devold, Kristin Krohn (2002) 'Omstillingen av Forsvaret – noen perspektiver: Foredrag av forsvarsminister Kristin Krohn Devold i Institutt for Forsvarsopplysning 26. februar 2002', <http://odin.dep.no/fd/norsk/aktuelt/taler/p10001326/010011-090056/dok-bn.html>; Diesen, Sverre (2001) 'Upresise påstander om endringene i Forsvaret', *Aftenposten*, 4 March; Heløe, Gunnar (2002) 'Norsk sikkerhetspolitikk – i omgivelser i forandring: Foredrag ved Folk og Forsvars årsmøte 28. februar 2002 av statssekretær Gunnar Heløe', <http://odin.dep.no/fd/norsk/aktuelt/taler/p10001333/010011-090058/dok-bn.html>.
86. 'Treg omstilling av Forsvaret', *Aftenposten*, 10 August 1998. My translation.
87. Græger and Leira, 'Globalisation vs. Localisation, Norwegian Strategic Culture After World War Two'; Heier, 'Forsvarets utvikling etter den kalde krigen'.
88. St. meld. nr. 45 (2001–02), section 5.8.2. The previous Long Term Plan held an identical passage: St. meld. nr. 22 (1997–98), p. 43.
89. Ulriksen, *Den norske forsvarstradisjonen*, p. 233.
90. Leknes, Knut (2003) 'Debatten om Heimevernet', Forsvarsnett (www.mil.no), 7 April; Leknes, Knut (2003) 'Forsvarets behov må styre', Forsvarsnett (www.mil.no), 18 June.

91. For the formulation of these determinants see St. prp. nr. 46 (1993–94); St. meld. nr. 22 (1997–98); and St. meld. nr. 38 (1998–99).
92. Græger, Nina (2002) 'Norway and the EU Security and Defence Dimension: A "Troops-for-Influence" Strategy', in Nina Græger, Henrik Larsen and Hanna Ojanen (eds) *The ESDP and the Nordic Countries. Four Variations on a Theme* (Helsinki: Finnish Institute of International Affairs; Berlin: Institut für Europäische Politik), pp. 33–89.
93. Eliassen, Ingeborg (2003) 'Kongo trenger norske offiserer', *Stavanger Aftenblad*, 6 June; Moe, Ingeborg (2003) 'Norsk Folkehjelp: Soldater i Irak er sløseri', *Dagbladet*, 11 June; Thomassen, Carsten (2003) 'Bondeviks FN-politikk er pinlig', *Dagbladet*, 11 June; Nordstrøm, Mariann (2003) 'Flyktningerådet: Send soldater til Kongo', *Aftenposten*, 3 June.
94. Johansen and Randsborg, 'FO vil ofre Sierra Leone for norsk innsats i Kosovo'; Johnsen, 'Kutter FN-oppdrag i Afrika for å betale Afghanistan-krig'.
95. *Pressemelding* No. 24/2004 'Regjeringen går inn for deltagelse i nordisk innsatsstyrke for EU fra 2008', 18 November 2004 (Oslo: Forsvarsdepartementet).
96. 'Personnel', NOREPS website <http://www.noreps.com/public/personnel.htm>; and 'Emergency Roster', NRC website <http://www.nrc.no/NRC/eng/frames/preparedness.htm> (both 24 August 2004).
97. NORDEM website: <http://www.humanrights.uio.no/english/nordem/index_ny.html> (30 July 2004); and Olesen *et al.*, *Evaluation of the Norwegian Resource Bank for Democracy and Human Rights (NORDEM)*, factsheet and chapter 4.
98. *Norwegian Resource Bank for Democracy and Human Rights Annual Report 2003* (Oslo: Norwegian Centre for Human Rights/NORDEM, 2004), p. 1.
99. *The Norwegian Support Teams* (Oslo: Directorate for Civil Defence and Emergency Planning, 1997), p. 5.
100. E-mail communication from Direktoratet for sivilt beredskap, 17 August 2004.
101. *DSBs årsberetning 2003* (Tønsberg: Direktoratet for samfundssikkerhet og beredskab, 2004), p. 40.
102. Data valid as of 27 January 2004. <http://www.reliefweb.int/undac/undac_members_list.html> (31 July 2004).
103. St. meld. nr. 39 (2003–04), p. 32.
104. St. meld. nr. 39 (2003–04), p. 32.
105. Devold, Kristin Krohn (2004) 'Fra snuoperasjon til transformation: Foredrag av Forsvarsminister Kristin Krohn Devold i Oslo Militære Samfund 5. januar 2004', <http://odin.dep.no/fd/norsk/aktuelt/taler/p10001326/010011-090092/dok-nn.html>.
106. St. prp. nr. 38 (1998–99).
107. *Adapting Norway's Armed Forces to the Requirements of International Operations* (Oslo: Ministry of Defence, 1999); Rønne, Jahn (2003) 'Innsatsstyrkene er fremtidens forsvar', Forsvarsnett (www.mil.no), 6 June.
108. For a detailed presentation of the NOA HRF see their brochure: *Strength in Action!* (Elverum: NOA HRF, 2002).
109. Rønne, Jahn (2003) 'Army Response Unit Reaches Objectives', Forsvarsnett (www.mil.no), 26 June.
110. NORSTAFF website: <http://www.nrc.no/NRC/FR/frames/beredskap2.htm> (31 July 2004).

111. NORDEM website: <http://www.humanrights.uio.no/english/nordem/index_ny.html> (31 July 2004); *Norwegian Resource Bank for Democracy and Human Rights Annual Report 2003* (Oslo: Norwegian Centre for Human Rights/NORDEM, 2004), p. 6.
112. *The Norwegian Support Teams* (Oslo: Directorate for Civil Defence and Emergency Planning, 1997), p. 6.
113. St. meld. nr. 18 (1999–2000), para. 6.2.5.
114. Hagtvedt, Arne O. (2001) 'Minneord om NORBN/SFOR', *Norsk Militært Tidsskrift*, Vol. 171, No. 1, p. 49 (48–51).
115. *Forsvarets Fellesoperative Doktrine Del B – Operasjoner*, pp. 131, 146.
116. Ingebrigtsen, Andreas, Kim H. Bjorheim and Jan Harald Tomassen (2003) 'Foran åttende runde i Kosovo', Forsvarsnett (www.mil.no), 23 May; e-mail communication from Military Advisor Vegard Valther Hansen, Norwegian Institute for International Affairs, 25 June 2004.
117. *Folk og Forsvar*, No. 1 (February 2003), p. 3; *KFOR (5) – Norway's role as Lead Nation* (Oslo: Norwegian Ministry of Defence, 2001), p. 9; Solholm, Rolleiv (2000) 'Officers Withdraw From KFOR Service', *The Norway Post*, 18 October.
118. *Forsvarets Fellesoperative Doktrine Del B – Operasjoner*, 2000, p. 132.
119. Gustafsson, Bengt (1994) 'Testimony by Supreme Commander Bengt Gustafsson to the Swedish parliament on the Swedish effort in Bosnia, 24 February 1994' printed in *Försvarsutskottets betänkande1993/94:FÖU09*.
120. *Pressemelding* No. 025/97 'Styringskomite for multinasjonal fredsbrigade opprettes', 23 May 1997 (Oslo: Forsvarsdepartementet).
121. *Norsk strategi for oppfølging av Brahimi-rapporten* (Oslo: Utenriksministeriet, 2001), <http://odin.dep.no/ud/norsk/generell/fn/032001-990426/dok-bn.html>.
122. St. prp. nr. 42 (2003–04), p. 32.
123. Brekke and Knutsen, 'Politiske rammebetingelser for norsk deltagelse i internasjonale militære operasjoner', p. 15; Grandhagen, Kjell (1997) 'Med IFOR til Bosnia-Herzegovina. Erfaringer fra den Nordisk-Polske brigade', *Norsk Militært Tidsskrift*, Vol. 166, No. 2, p. 46 (17–19, 42–46); Nordbø, Toralv (1992) 'Norske militære i fredsoperasjoner', *Forsvarsstudier*, No. 7 (Oslo: Institutt for Forsvarsstudier).
124. B.innst.S.nr.7 Tl.01 (1995–96).
125. Grandhagen, 'Med IFOR til Bosnia-Herzegovina. Erfaringer fra den Nordisk-Polske brigade', p. 19; St. meld. nr. 38 (1998–99).
126. For a discussion of the need for national ROE on peace operations see Fjell, Trond and Bård Lien (2001) 'Internasjonale og nasjonale engagementsregler (ROE) i samme multinasjonale operasjon', *Norsk Militært Tidsskrift*, Vol. 171, No. 6/7, pp. 12–18.
127. *Forsvarets Fellesoperative Doktrine Del B – Operasjoner*, p. 135.
128. *Pressemelding* No. 3/2004 'Feil om norsk Irak-engasjement', 26 January 2004 (Oslo: Forsvarsdepartementet).
129. Ramberg, 'Luftforsvaret en læringsorganisasjon?'
130. Grandhagen, 'Med IFOR til Bosnia-Herzegovina', p. 46.
131. Alteskjær and Jamissen, 'Fredsstøtteoperasjoner – Nye utfordringer for Forsvaret', p. 21; *Kosovo-krisen: Nasjonal rapport* (Oslo: Forsvars-departementet, 2001), p. 9. For the problems in the air force see Ramberg, 'Luftforsvaret en læringsorganisasjon?: logistiske utfordringer ved NORAIRs deploytering til Bosnia 1993'.
132. *Forsvarets Fellesoperative Doktrine Del B – Operasjoner*, p. 141.
133. St. prp. nr. 45 (2000–01), section 5.5.1.

134. FFI (2002) 'LOGIKK: Logistikk i krise og krig', Forsvarsnett (www.mil.no), 22 March.
135. Aas, Vegard Nygårdshaug (2003) 'Klar for innsats - og avreise', Forsvarsnett (www.mil.no), 17 June.
136. Johnson, Eirik Espolin (2002) 'Til krigen med samband på boks', Forsvarsnett (www.mil.no), 20 March; Opland, Marit (2003) 'Surgical Unit Just What the Doctor Ordered', Forsvarsnett (www.mil.no), 3 April; Wangberg, Marita I. and Stian Solum (2003) 'Støttespillere ved Gibraltar', Forsvarsnett (www.mil.no), 15 May.
137. Andersen, Bjørn Christian (2002) 'Felles nordisk flytransport til Afghanistan', Forsvarsnett (www.mil.no), 21 March.
138. *Pressemelding* No. 051/93 'Doblet livsforsikring til FN-soldater', 14 May 1993 (Oslo: Forsvarsdepartementet).
139. Statens helsetilsyn (1998) *Oppfølging av personell som har tjenestegjort i internasjonale fredsoperasjoner* (Oslo: Statens helsetilsyn, Utredningsserie, 7-98).
140. Dølør, Jens Schanche (2002) 'Oppsummering av observasjoner og inntrykk', in Jon Christian Laberg, Bjørn Helge Johnsen, Jarle Eid and Wibecke Brun (2002) *Mental beredskap under internasjonale operasjoner. KFOR undersøkelsen. Rapport 1* (Bergen: Sjøkrigsskolen, Universitet i Bergen), pp. 85–90; Mood, Robert (2000) 'Erfaringer fra KFOR I', p. 12; TV2.NO Nyhetene (2003) 'Norsk pilot bombet opprørere', *TV2.NO Nyheter*, 28 January; Næss, Tomas Kothe (2003) 'Svært vellykket bombing', *Adresseavisen*, 29 January.
141. *Pressemelding* No. 25/2004 'Erstatning for psykiske belastningsskader', 3 December 2004 (Oslo: Forsvarsdepartementet).
142. Opland, Egil M. (2002) 'Var FN-soldat på 80-tallet', *Adresseavisen*, 30 September; Rapp, Ole Magnus (1999) 'FN-soldat får ikke erstatning for psykisk skade', *Aftenposten*, 21 March; Skjerve, Erik (2003) 'Klar til strid mot staten', *www.fofo.no*, 19 May (8 August 2003); Summetonen (2003) 'Psykisk skadet', *Bergensavisen*, 7 June.
143. Aas, Vegard (2002) 'International Efforts', Forsvarsnett (www.mil.no), 1 August. See also Løvhaug, Geir (2003) 'Familien i fokus', Forsvarsnett (www.mil.no), 25 June.
144. NTB (2004) 'Offiserer skeptiske til Forsvaret', *Aftenposten nettutgaven*, 2 June.
145. Solholm, Rolleiv (2001) 'KFOR Troops Want More Home Leave', *The Norway Post*, 27 May.
146. Wangberg, Marita I. (2003) 'Skal evakuere norske soldater', Forsvarsnett (www.mil.no), 11 July.
147. Opland, Marit (2003) 'Advanced Medical Surgery Unit to Norway', Forsvarsnett (www.no.mil), 18 February.
148. *Forsvarets Fellesoperative Doktrine Del B – Operasjoner*, pp. 137–138.
149. E-mail communication from Military Advisor Vegard Valther Hansen, Norwegian Institute for International Affairs, 25 June 2004.
150. Myrseth, Bjørn (2003) 'Flere fakta-finnere i felt', Forsvarsnett (www.mil.no), 18 February.
151. Skjerve, Erik (2003) 'Kraftig norsk info-kutt', *Forsvarets Forum*, No. 8 (May), p. 10.
152. E-mail communication from Military Advisor Vegard Valther Hansen, Norwegian Institute for International Affairs, 25 June 2004.
153. Ruset, Bjørn Inge (2001) 'Utfordringer for sivilt-militært samarbeid i et fremtidig forsvar', in Bjørn Inge Ruset (ed.) *Militærmaktseminaret 2000*

Forsvaret ved et veiskille (Oslo: Norsk Utenrikspolitisk Institutt), p. 104 (95–110).

154. Dølør, 'Oppsummering av observasjoner og inntrykk', pp. 89–90; *Forsvarets Fellesoperative Doktrine Del B – Operasjoner*, p. 136; Mood, 'Erfaringer fra KFOR I', *Norsk Militært Tidsskrift*, p. 12; Pharo, Per Fredrik Ilsaas (2000) 'Norge på Balkan 1990–1999. "Lessons learned"', *IFS Info*, No. 3 (Oslo: Institutt for Forsvarsstudier), p. 10; Ruset, 'Utfordringer for sivilt-militært samarbeid i et fremtidig forsvar', pp. 104–109.
155. Pettersen, Jim (2003) 'Hjelp for tre millioner', Forsvarsnett (www.mil.no), 25 June.
156. *Forsvarets Fellesoperative Doktrine Del B – Operasjoner*, p. 136.
157. Høydalsvik, Eva (2003) 'Kosovo – her er så underligt', *Forsvarets Forum*, No. 8 (May), p. 13.
158. *Forsvarets Fellesoperative Doktrine Del B – Operasjoner*, p. 137.
159. Pharo, 'Norge på Balkan 1990–1999, p. 10.
160. E-mail communication from Military Advisor Vegard Valther Hansen, Norwegian Institute for International Affairs, 25 June 2004.
161. Kristoffersen, Torgrim (2001) 'Det nye Forsvaret 2001–2005', *Folk og Forsvar*, No. 4 (November), p. 13 (4–17).
162. Gjendem, Rebecca (2000) 'Norwegian Troops Help Quiet Protest in Kosovo', *The Norway Post*, 4 March.
163. Kluge, Lars and Reidun J. Samuelsen (2004) 'Nordmenn skjøt varselskudd – NATO sender flere soldater', *Aftenposten Nettutgaven*, 19 March; Nilsen, Kjell Arild (2004) 'Norske soldater i kamp i Kosovo', *Aftenposten Nettutgaven*, 17 March.
164. Solholm, Rolleiv (2004) 'Kosovo: 20 Norwegian Soldiers Wounded in Serious Disturbances', *The Norway Post*, 18 March.

7 The Swedish approach to peace operations after the Cold War

> The establishment of military units and personnel for international activities and operations has changed from being a sideshow for the Swedish armed forces to a main task...and this 'revolution' is affecting most of the armed forces.
>
> Brigadier General Michael Moore[1]

The internationalization of the Swedish armed forces is better characterized by the word 'evolution' than revolution. The process has been slow and although Sweden spends twice as much on defence as Denmark and Finland, the Swedish armed forces are not capable of deploying and sustaining more personnel abroad.[2] Progress with respect to meeting our success conditions has nevertheless been continuous since the Swedish involvement in the Balkans began in 1992, and Sweden now meets ten of our eleven requirements for success.

Political will, legal framework and funds for all types of operations

Taken together all our indicators demonstrate a considerable increase in the Swedish willingness to participate in peace operations in the course of the 1990s.

Rhetoric

Peace operations have moved from the periphery to the centre in official documents and statements related to foreign policy and defence. Peace operations were for the first time officially designated as a main task of the Swedish armed forces in 1996,[3] and the need to improve the capacity for peace operations has become one of the principal arguments employed to legitimize the current restructuring of the armed forces, which began in earnest with the passing of the defence bill *The New Defence* in 2000.[4] The new importance attached to peace operations was underlined by the fact that Defence Minister Björn von Sydow justified his appointment of Johan Hederstedt, a strong supporter of internationalization, as supreme commander later that year on the grounds that peace operations had become the main task of the Swedish armed forces.[5]

Participation on the ground

In numerical terms Sweden's military contribution to peace operations has increased considerably. Whereas the Cold War contribution (1948–89) totalled approximately 55,000 personnel,[6] the post-Cold War total had already climbed to approximately 30,000 personnel by the spring of 2002,[7] meaning that the average contribution a year had grown from 1,341 during the Cold War to 2,143 personnel in the 1989–2002 period. Since the lion's share of Sweden's contributions has consisted of military personnel serving six-month tours, an average of 1,072 Swedes have served abroad on peace operations on a continuous basis since the end of the Cold War.

Although the traditional peacekeeping-only policy has been abandoned, Sweden has not been prepared to go all the way, stopping short of participating in offensive enforcement operations directed against designated enemies in order to restore peace or enforce compliance with UN resolutions. Sweden refused to make military contributions to the UN-authorized operations in Kuwait in 1990–91 and Somalia in 1992–93, and it refrained from taking part in the US-led combat operations in Afghanistan in 2002–03 and in Iraq in 2003.

Swedish policy has been consistent on this point: Defence Minister Thage G. Peterson adamantly refused to allow Swedish soldiers participating in IFOR to take part in offensive operations in 1995 and the IFOR bill explicitly ruled it out.[8] The bills authorizing the Swedish participation in IFOR/SFOR, KFOR, ISAF and Operation Artemis all stressed the importance of consent from the parties and the existence of a peace agreement, and a 2001 proposal from an analyst with the Swedish Defence Research Agency that Sweden should make its reaction forces available for offensive operations was greeted with complete silence.[9] The Swedish ambivalence towards the use of force for offensive purposes is also evident in the importance attached to the distinction between civilian and military crisis management in the EU, and the high priority given to the development of the EU civilian crisis management capacity.[10] Nothing, in short, suggests that this restriction on Swedish participation is about to be lifted in the near future.

In the longer term the Swedish position is untenable. The line between enforcement of fragile ceasefires and offensive operations is blurred as the EU-led Operation Artemis in Democratic Republic of Congo in 2003 demonstrates. The ceasefire that Operation Artemis was mandated to uphold only existed on paper and the Swedish special forces deployed as part of this operation killed over 20 militia soldiers.[11] The distinction is thus academic on the ground, and it will also come under increased pressure politically as the EU establishes a capacity for offensive (enforcement) operations. The establishment of up to nine 1,500-strong battle groups will give the EU such a capacity by 2007,[12] and the Swedish ambition to play a role in this process can only be realized if the self-imposed ban on offensive enforcement operations is lifted.[13]

Sweden's civilian contributions have also changed in both number and nature. The Swedish International Development Agency (SIDA) has established a database with 2,400 personnel with expertise in the following areas: administrative support, democratization, human rights, elections, media and rule of law.[14] These experts can go abroad at short notice and have been made available to the EU, the OSCE and the UN. Swedish civilian police have participated in peace operations since 1964 when 20 officers participated in UNFICYP in Cyprus, and by 2000 approximately 2,000 personnel had participated in international missions.[15] The Swedish Rescue Services Agency (SRSA) also makes civil protection personnel available for international operations. It can draw from a pool of 1,700 personnel and has sent some 1,200 personnel on more than 100 international rescue operations since the beginning in 1988.[16]

Domestic support

Political and public support for the Swedish policy has been remarkably strong. The personnel contributions discussed in the Swedish parliament (Riksdagen) in the 1989–2002 period have all been supported by a large majority in both parliament and the public at large. If we look at parliament first, then the decisions to participate in peace operations have been supported by all the parties represented. The two parties on the Left, the Left Party (Vänsterpartiet) and the Green Party (Miljöpartiet), have objected in principle to Swedish participation in operations led by NATO (IFOR and KFOR) on the grounds that it served to compromise Swedish neutrality and weaken the standing of the UN and international law.[17] As a consequence they have demanded that participation in NATO-led operations be seen as the exception to the rule. However, both parties still supported Swedish participation in both operations. No party, in other words, has questioned the Swedish commitment to peace operations as such, but judging from the reservations expressed by some parties the consensus on peace operations would collapse if Sweden widened its participation to include offensive enforcement operations as well.

Public support has, not surprisingly given the political consensus, been very strong also. Surveys conducted by the National Board of Psychological Defence in the 1993–2002 period show 68–78 per cent support for the decisions to deploy troops in former Yugoslavia/make troops available for UN peace operations involving a risk of combat. The opposition to these decisions have fluctuated between 17 and 28 per cent.[18] In addition, the proportion of the public viewing international operations as the principal task of the armed forces has grown considerably in recent years. A total of 13 per cent rated international operations as the single most important task for the armed forces in the next 10 years when asked in 1998 and 1999. In 2000 this proportion jumped to 38 per cent, and two years later it had climbed to 43 per cent and was by far the top scorer among the four main tasks.[19]

The consensus has not prevented the Swedish participation from generating a number of controversies, but their impact on policy has been very limited. The decision to go beyond traditional peacekeeping met with some resistance from traditionalists believing that it would undermine Sweden's ability to act as an impartial mediator on the international scene.[20] However, this debate was confined to a limited number of academics and experts, and it never became a major political issue. It did, however, help to ensure that the government portrayed both UNPROFOR and IFOR as traditional peacekeeping operations entailing greater risks than usual.[21] The decision to participate in IFOR did generate a heated public debate, but the issue was not the participation itself. Instead, the debate was triggered by the restrictions placed on the Swedish contingent by Defence Minister Thage G. Peterson. His insistence that Swedish troops should not be allowed to participate in offensive operations caused an uproar since it was interpreted to mean that Swedish soldiers were incapable of participating in IFOR on the same terms as the other contributors. Peterson, however, stuck to his guns and made sure that the restriction was inserted in the IFOR bill.[22]

Government role in mobilizing and sustaining domestic support

Swedish policy has been shaped by concern that the 'militarization' of the Swedish approach to peace operations, i.e. the movement from traditional peacekeeping towards peace enforcement, would trigger opposition, and Swedish governments have consequently sought to portray it as a continuation of Sweden's traditional support for UN peacekeeping. This strategy has been highly successful in maintaining the political consensus on peace operations, but it has come at a cost. The increased risks that contemporary peace operations pose to the personnel have been downplayed. Although government representatives on a number of occasions have made clear that the Swedish policy may result in a loss of lives,[23] such warnings have been the exception rather than the rule, and the commander of the first Bosnia battalion is consequently of the opinion that Swedish politicians have failed to prepare the public adequately for casualties.[24]

So far this has not become a problem since Swedish losses have been very low and caused exclusively by accidents. Whether a significant number of Swedish casualties resulting from hostile action would be sufficient to trigger a change in policy or a withdrawal from the operation in question is debatable. Former Swedish ambassador to the UN Anders Ferm, the only one to have looked at the issue in some detail, concludes that the answer is yes and recommends that Sweden be careful about deploying troops in internal conflicts.[25] His analysis is not based on any evidence and strongly influenced by the US withdrawal from Somalia which was trigged by the loss of 18 US servicemen and 73 wounded in October 1993. The Somalia experience is not applicable in the Swedish context for two reasons, however. The Clinton administration did not regard the operation in Somalia as a priority, and there was only limited domestic support for the operation when the soldiers were killed.[26] Neither is true in Sweden where the government accords a high priority to peace operations and the domestic support is strong. These differences make it hard to believe that even a considerable number of combat-related casualties in themselves would be sufficient to produce a major shift in the Swedish support for peace operations. Recent research suggests that casualties have little impact on policy when the operation in question is supported by a united political elite, has a worthwhile objective, a reasonable chance of success and the government has prepared the public for possible losses.[27] The Swedish involvement in peace operations has always met all these conditions except the last one, and this may explain why the loss of 18 soldiers did not have an impact on the Swedish participation in the UN operation in Congo in the early 1960s.

Permissive legal framework

As has been the case in the other Nordic countries, Sweden has also adjusted its laws related to peace operations in the course of the 1990s. When the Berlin Wall came down Swedish personnel were only allowed to participate in UN-commanded peace operations based on Chapter VI mandates and no one could be ordered to serve abroad. These restrictions no longer apply. The passing of a new law in 1992 gave the government the right to make forces available for peacekeeping activities on request by the UN and the CSCE (now the OSCE), and it also raised the ceiling on the number of armed personnel serving abroad to 3,000.[28]

The 1992 law only applies to traditional peacekeeping operations, however. Operations involving the use of force beyond self-defence require parliamentary approval by simple majority according to the Swedish constitution. The Swedish participations in UNPROFOR, IFOR, SFOR, KFOR and ISAF have therefore all been based on government bills approved by parliament. In practice the blurring between Chapter VI and Chapter VII mandates means that the government will ask for parliamentary approval whenever armed personnel are sent on missions that are likely to involve the use of force beyond self-defence.

Three additional changes have served to create a more permissive legal framework. In 1994 a new law authorized the government to send Swedish personnel abroad to participate in training within the framework of NATO's Partnership for Peace (PfP),[29] in 1996 parliament approved a defence bill designating peace operations as one of the main tasks of the Swedish armed forces,[30] and in 2003 a new law made international service compulsory for all officers joining the armed forces after 1 June 2003.[31] This did not satisfy the Swedish Defence Commission which wants international service to be compulsory for all officers. Its 2004 report strongly urged the political authorities to make international operations compulsory for all officers unless the armed forces solved the problem by making international service a precondition for promotion.[32] A legal revision making international service compulsory for officers is hence to be expected if the armed forces fail to do so.

Another legal revision is also on the cards. The creation of an EU capacity for military crisis management is likely to produce an expansion of the existing government authority inherent in the 1992 law to make armed personnel available for EU-led peace operations as well. Such a revision was proposed by the Swedish Defence Commission in 2001,[33] and all indications are that it will be adopted when the need arises. It follows logically from the Swedish support for the decision taken at the Helsinki summit in June 1999 that the EU should be able to conduct peace operations 'in accordance with UN principles', it enjoys the support of the liberal-conservative Moderate Party (Moderaterna),[34] and it is unlikely to generate much controversy as it would be in keeping with the UN Charter and current Swedish policy.

However, the Helsinki decision also opened up the possibility of EU-led peace enforcement operations conducted without a UN mandate,[35] and Swedish participation in such operations would be a different story altogether because they would violate the UN Charter. An EU decision to launch such an operation would present Swedish decision makers with a difficult dilemma: a refusal to participate would damage Sweden's influence and standing in the EU, but participation would create problems at home because the strong domestic support for peace operations to a large extent rests on the desire to strengthen the UN and international law.

Sweden faced a similar dilemma when NATO initiated its bombing campaign against Yugoslavia in 1999 without a UN mandate. The Swedish public was deeply divided on the issue and the government opted for a middle course between outright condemnation and support of NATO.[36] Rhetorically, the Swedish government expressed its regret that NATO's operation lacked 'unequivocal support in international law' but it also described the operation as 'necessary' and 'inevitable'.[37] With respect to troop contributions, the government stuck to traditional Swedish policy: it said no in April to a NATO request for troops to AFOR, the humanitarian operation conducted by the alliance in Albania, on the grounds that the operation did not have a UN mandate, but it also made clear its intention to participate in KFOR if it obtained a UN mandate.[38]

Interestingly, Foreign Minister Anna Lindh took a position that does not rule out Swedish participation in future enforcement operations that lack a formal UN mandate. She characterized NATO's operation as a necessary response to an 'exceptional' situation,[39] and her 1998 argument that military force can be used legitimately in situations of 'duress' without a UN mandate suggests that Sweden might be willing to support an EU enforcement operation without a UN mandate in an 'exceptional' situation.[40]

There are, in sum, no longer any legal restrictions at the national level preventing Sweden from participating in the full spectrum of peace operations.

Financing

Sweden's growing involvement in peace operations has not surprisingly resulted in a dramatic rise in costs. The average annual cost in the period 1960–61 to 1991–92 amounted to SEK 278 million (1990 prices).[41] The figure for 1992–93 was almost twice as high, SEK 500 million (current prices), and a look at Table 7.1 shows that this figure had more than doubled by the end of the decade. Finding the money has been a constant struggle resulting in political disagreements and bureaucratic infighting.[42] This was the case with respect to the Bosnia deployment in 1993,[43] and again in 1999 with respect to Kosovo. In the latter instance, the lack of clear procedures and disagreements between the Ministry of Foreign Affairs (MFA) and the Ministry of Defence (MoD) served to delay the deployment of the Swedish KFOR contingent, which was the last to arrive in theatre.[44]

Financial considerations provide part of the explanation as to why Sweden has never come close to the maximum deployment level (3,000 armed personnel) established by law. The involvement in the Balkans resulted in the termination of the contributions to UNFICYP, UNIFIL and UNOSOM II in order to save money,[45] and the Kosovo deployment led to a significant reduction in the Swedish contribution to SFOR from 500 to 40 personnel.

Table 7.1 MFA and MoD expenditures and estimates on peace operations 1996–2004 (current prices; SEK million[a])

	1996	1997	1998	1999	2000	2001	2002	2003	2004[b]
MFA	1047.9	94.8	74.8	173.1	202.2	119.5	128.5	130.9	127.1
MoD	..	451.3	472.1	675.0	986.7	1075.2	1050.8	1185.9	1200.0
Total	1047.9	546.1	546.9	848.1	1188.9	1194.7	1179.3	1316.8	1327.1

Sources: Budget proposals 1996–97 to 2003–04 and Swedish Armed Forces Headquarters.
Notes
a   SEK 100 = EUR 11.08.
b   Budget estimates.

Several attempts have been made to solve the recurring problems in the course of the 1990s. An attempt by the Social Democrats, then in opposition, to establish one budget allocation for peace operations to avoid the scramble for funds each time a new UN operation was established failed in 1992.[46] However, a step in that direction was taken in budget year 1993–94 when the MFA took over the financial responsibility from the MoD.[47] This arrangement only lasted until 1997 when the appropriation for peace operations was split between the MoD and the MFA, so that contributions with armed personnel were financed by the defence budget and contributions with unarmed personnel, including military observers, were financed by the MFA budget.[48] In the wake of the problems experienced in connection with the Kosovo deployment, the Defence Committee in parliament and the Defence Commission urged the government to establish clearer procedures for the financing of peace operations. The government's solution in its defence budget proposal for 2002 was to combine the budget allocations for peace promoting activities and training and preparedness in order to achieve a greater flexibility within the existing budget.[49] Needless to say, this 'solution' will only work if it generates sufficient funds to cover the costs of peace operations. If not, the need to finance peace operations with funds initially earmarked for other activities in the budget will remain together with all the problems to which this practice gives rise. Helpful though they are, improved procedures cannot solve problems emanating from a lack of earmarked funds and unwillingness within the armed forces to give sufficient priority to peace operations.[50]

Explaining the changes of the 1990s

Sweden was pushed by the same external forces that pushed the other Nordic countries in the same direction: the end of the Cold War permitted a greater involvement in peace operations, the outbreak of war in the Balkans created a security interest in stemming the spread of violence and refugees, the nature of the Balkan operations necessitated a shift from peacekeeping to peace enforcement, pressures from the EU and NATO, and it helped that the increased involvement in peace operations could be legitimized as a continuation of the traditional UN policy pursued during the Cold War.[51]

These external factors cannot account for the distinct features of the Swedish approach, however. Unlike the NATO members Denmark and Norway, Sweden has not been willing to make personnel available for combat operations, and the pace of reform has been similar to Norway's, slower than Denmark's, but faster than Finland's. To understand this we need to take a look at three domestic factors: threat perceptions, the strong opposition to reform within the armed forces and the successful tradition of neutrality which has served to keep Sweden out of wars since the end of the Napoleonic wars in 1814.

Threat perceptions

It took ten years before the collapse of the Soviet Union made a real difference to Swedish defence planning. The risk of an armed attack upon Sweden was not considered 'unlikely' in official documents until the Swedish government presented its defence bill in the autumn of 1995.[52] This threat perception notwithstanding, the defence agreement covering the 1997–2001 period effectively set the warning time for the 'unlikely' attack to one year, the time accorded the armed forces to put all its units on a war footing.[53] It took another four years before the threat of invasion officially ceased to be seen as 'the dominant motive for the total defence resources structure'.[54] This change reflected a new threat assessment made by the Defence Commission in the spring of 1999 according to which 'an invasion attempt aiming at the occupation of Sweden does not seem feasible in the coming 10 years provided that Sweden has a basic defence capability'.[55] This assessment set the stage for the passing of the 2000 defence bill which was the first to give real priority to the creation of reaction forces earmarked for international operations.[56]

A look at a map goes some way towards explaining why it took so long. Sweden reacted quicker than Finland, which is closer to Russia, much slower than Denmark, which is further away, and more or less simultaneously with Norway, which has a similar geostrategic location. Geography has no explanatory power in its own right, however, so to understand the process we need to move on to our second explanatory factor.

Opposition within the armed forces

The armed forces acted as a brake upon defence reform and internationalization during most of the 1990s. Owe Wictorin, then supreme commander, fought hard to minimize budget cuts and structural change prior to the passing of the 1997–2001 defence agreement. He even launched a public campaign against the government's defence bill denouncing its threat assessment as far too optimistic and complaining that the proposed budget cuts went too far.[57] His protests enjoyed widespread support within the armed forces and in the light of such opposition it is not hard to understand why the reforms undertaken in 1996 were modest.[58]

More generally, the officer corps has not been enthusiastic about the growing involvement of the Swedish armed forces in peace operations. According to a prominent Swedish defence analyst, most Swedish officers continued to view international operations as a sideshow compared to the 'real' task, invasion defence, in 1997,[59] and two years later unwillingness to give sufficient priority to peace operations was considered one of the main reasons why it took so long to deploy the Swedish KFOR contingent in Kosovo.[60] A final and more recent indication of their lack of enthusiasm is provided by the strong opposition within the officer corps to making international operations compulsory for them. Only 12 per cent supported the proposal in a 2000 poll, while 87 per cent opposed it.[61]

The tradition of neutrality

If the officer corps had been the only actor in Sweden resisting internationalization, the decisive shift would undoubtedly have come earlier than 2000. However, their 'Sweden first' approach resonated well with the belief in neutrality that remained strong in Swedish society throughout most of the 1990s, and the shift towards internationalization in the 2000 defence bill was opposed by 125 members in parliament (180 voted in favour) in part because they feared it would make it impossible for Sweden to defend itself.[62] The neutrality tradition not only made it natural to continue to think of defence issues in national terms, it also generated a number of additional obstacles slowing down the process of internationalization. Neutrality during the Cold War in the Swedish understanding gave pride of place to peaceful conflict resolution, mediation, support for the UN, non-use of force except in self-defence and bridge-building between the East and the West. These principles were not easily reconciled with Swedish participation in peace enforcement operations, cooperation with NATO and support for the establishment of the EU capacity for military crisis management. The need to mobilize and sustain public and political support for new policies, which were clearly at odds with the neutrality doctrine, dictated a slower pace of reform than would otherwise have been the case.

Factors determining specific contributions

The principal factors determining the Swedish personnel contributions are similar to the ones identified in the other Nordic countries: a link to national security, capacity, costs, the actions of the other Nordic partners, the interest in enhancing the Swedish standing within the EU and NATO, and finally a desire to signal support for the UN.[63] As a result, the vast majority of Swedish personnel have served in the Balkans in the post-Cold War era. No Swedish battalion has served outside of Europe since the contribution to UNIFIL was terminated in 1994, and the priority attached to the European continent is also clear from the fact that the involvement in the Balkans led to a termination of the Swedish participation in UN operations in Cyprus, Lebanon and Somalia.

The focus on the EU and NATO is a feature of the 1990s and it has become a key determinant. There is unanimous agreement among Swedish analysts that the interest in bolstering the application for EU membership played an important role in the Swedish decision to provide troops for UNPROFOR in 1993,[64] and Sweden has subsequently used its substantial involvement in peace operations in the Balkans as a means of positioning itself as close to NATO as possible without actually becoming a member, and as a means of enhancing its influence within the EU. Participation in peace operations has proved an effective way to silence critics such as Britain, who expressed scepticism as to whether Sweden and the other new neutral EU members would contribute to the construction of a new European security order.[65] Sweden's use of troop contributions to enhance its European credentials was also demonstrated during its EU presidency when it was the first state to respond to a NATO request for additional troops to Kosovo in the spring of 2001.[66] Troop contributions have also been used to cultivate strategic partnerships in Europe as the operational cooperation between Swedish and British intelligence units in Kosovo and subsequently Afghanistan show. Finally, the European focus is also visible in the way Sweden sees closer Nordic cooperation within NORDCAPS as a means of enhancing its influence within the EU.[67] The importance attached to the EU is further underlined in the supreme commander's 2004 planning proposal for the 2005–14 period which by and large is based on the demands posed by the emerging EU military crisis management capacity.[68]

The Europeanization of the Swedish approach to peace operations does not mean that the UN has been forgotten. A UN mandate is still a prerequisite for Swedish participation, Sweden has worked hard to ensure that the establishment of the EU reaction forces takes place in close coordination with the UN and it has also played an active role in the implementation of the recommendations made in the *Brahimi Report*.[69] The number of Swedish personnel serving on UN-commanded operations has also increased slightly since May 2003 due to the contributions to MONUC in Democratic Republic of Congo (80 personnel) and UNMIL in Liberia (230 personnel).[70] These contributions cannot hide that the experience in the Balkans made Sweden wary of contributing personnel to UN-commanded operations going beyond traditional peacekeeping. Concern for the safety of Swedish personnel and the fact that the political benefits as a rule will be higher and the risks lower in UN-delegated operations led by NATO, the EU and Western lead nations than in UN-commanded operations suggest that Swedish decision makers will continue to give priority to the former type of operations.

Civilian and military personnel deployable at short notice

The Swedish capacity to deploy both civilians and military personnel on peace operations has grown considerably. As mentioned above, Sweden's civilian contributions come from three main sources: SIDA, the Swedish police and SRSA. SIDA has made 35 civilian experts available to the OSCE REACT teams, but the 2,400 experts in its database are also available for other organizations.[71] The Swedish police have increased its international capacity to 170 personnel, amounting to a little more than 1 per cent of the size of the national police force. The full capacity has been made available for the EU police force and 50 officers are placed on 30 days' standby.[72] The contributions to international civilian rapid reaction forces are summarized in Table 7.2.

The civil protection personnel provided by the SRSA is organized in specialized teams and service packages and can go abroad with 3–12 hours' notice depending of the nature of the response required.[73] SRSA personnel have been made available for the EU and the UN's UNDAC teams.[74]

Finally, a rapid reaction arrangement for judges and prosecutors is currently being established following the recommendations of a report prepared by the Ministry of Justice in 2002. It recommended the establishment of a personnel pool of 60–80 judges and 40–50 prosecutors and a contribution of 10 personnel to the rule-of-law component of the EU rapid reaction force.[75] By mid-2004, the latter contribution had been made and work on the rapid reaction arrangement was due to begin in earnest in the autumn of 2004.[76]

Military personnel

Sweden has increased its capacity for rapid reaction significantly since 1996 when the decision to establish SWERAP (Swedish Rapid Reaction Unit) was taken.[77] 500-strong SWERAP was declared operational on 1 July 1998, but the first attempt to deploy it in Kosovo the following year was not particularly successful. The unit proved too small as it had to be supplemented with 300 personnel, and it also took too long to deploy. The Kosovo embarrassment, the EU decision in 1999 to establish a military reaction force and the establishment of a force register within NATO's PARP (Planning and Review Process) in 2000 set the stage for a significant

Table 7.2 Swedish contributions to international civilian rapid reaction forces (spring 2004)

EU	OSCE (REACT)	UN (UNDAC)	UN (UNSAS)
170 civilian police	35 (human rights,	8 disaster	100 civilian
262 civil protection	elections, media,	management	police
10 rule of law	rule of law and	experts	
30 civil administration	democratization)		
	3 civilian police		

Sources: EU Council Secretariat, SIDA.

strengthening of the Swedish rapid reaction capacity, which was expanded to include units from the Swedish Air Force and Navy as well.[78]

The new reaction forces, totalling some 2,000 personnel, are based on NATO standards and are all placed on 30 days' readiness or less. Most of the existing units became operational on 1 January 2001 and they have been made available for EU, NATO and UN service on peacekeeping and peace enforcement operations (see Table 7.3).[79] Currently, deployments of 1,000 personnel can be sustained abroad on a continuous basis, a number that can be increased to 1,500 personnel for shorter periods provided that units from the Air Force and Navy are involved.[80] The new reaction forces have been successfully activated for deployments in Kosovo in March 2001 (mechanized company), in Afghanistan in January 2002 (intelligence platoon), in Democratic Republic of Congo in June 2003 (special forces) and in Liberia in March 2004 (mechanized company).

Table 7.3 Military forces with a readiness of 30 days or less made available to international rapid reaction arrangements (July 2004)

	Forces	EU	NATO – PARP	NORDCAPS	SHIRBRIG	UNSAS
Army	50 staff officers, including CIMIC personnel	X	X	X	X	X
	60 military observers	X	..	..	..	X
	HQ staff officers	..	..	X	..	..
	HQ company	..	..	X	..	X
	Special forces	X	X	..	..	X
	1 CIMIC company	X	X			X
	1 mechanized battalion	X	X	X	X	..
	1 logistics battalion	..	..	X	..	X
	1 military police company	X	X	X	X	X
	1 engineer company	X	X	X	X	X
	1 intelligence platoon	X	X	X	..	..
	NBC detachment	X	..	..	..	..
Air force	4–8 reconnaissance/ fighter planes	X	X	X	..	X
	4 transport planes	X	X	X	..	X
	1 plane for electronic intelligence missions	X	..	..	..	..
Navy	2 corvettes + 1 supply ship	X	X	X	..	X
	2 mine clearance vessels + 1 support ship	X	X	X	..	X
	1 submarine	X	..	X	..	X

Sources: NORDCAPS, SHIRBRIG and Swedish Armed Forces Headquarters.

The ambition is to enhance this capacity even further so that by 2009 Sweden can deploy a 1,500-strong battle group with 300 personnel backup that meets EU standards,[81] but the question remains whether volunteers in sufficient numbers can be persuaded to sign up for international service. A lack of volunteers may become a significant problem as the current proportion of conscripts (7–10 per cent) volunteering for international service needs to be increased to 30 per cent in order to fill the existing rapid reaction forces.[82] Moreover, it is already proving difficult to recruit personnel to ongoing missions.[83] Since the vast majority of the regular personnel cannot be ordered abroad, finding officers in sufficient numbers may also become a problem.

Training to prepare the civilian and military personnel for their many new tasks

Two of the main suppliers of civilian personnel, SIDA and SRSA, limit their training programmes to the bare essentials such as security training, first aid, communications and information about the mission area. This is possible because only highly trained experts are admitted into their reaction arrangements.[84] The Swedish police, in contrast, have an elaborate training programme. All police officers go through a two-week UN Police Officer Course, which is arranged by the Swedish National Police Board in coopera- tion with the Swedish Armed Forces International Centre (SWEDINT). This is supplemented by four days of mission-oriented training immediately prior to departure. In addition to this general programme, the Swedish National Police Board and SWEDINT also run a specialized course for senior police officers, the UN Police Commander Course.[85]

The military runs several specialized training programmes in order to prepare its personnel for peace operations. Swedish contributions to peace operations are based almost exclusively on volunteers who are individually recruited through recruitment campaigns. Privates signing up to serve in army units receive different training depending on whether they volunteer for service in a rotation unit for a mission whose location and deployment period is known in advance, or for the new rapid reaction standby units where the mission is unknown.[86] Training for the rotation units is limited to three weeks of mission-oriented training, whereas basic training for the standby units lasts six weeks in order to enhance unit cohesion and effectiveness. This training is supplemented with mission-oriented training prior to departure.[87] The personnel volunteering for the standby units in the Air Force and Navy receive similar training.

Additional training is available for volunteers, who have not received basic military training, specialists and officers. The priority attached to peace operations has been increased in the training of Swedish officers at all levels during the 1990s,[88] language training has been improved, and officers of all ranks also participate in multinational courses and exercises conducted within NORDCAPS and NATO's PfP programme.

Whereas these training programmes are generally seen as effective, the training for enforcement operations has been criticized as insufficient. A study of the first rapid reaction company, which was declared operational in January 2001 and subsequently deployed in Kosovo in April of that year, concluded that the training was deficient in several respects and that the company was inadequately prepared for peace enforcement when deployed.[89] Critics have also pointed out that Swedish officers lack the ability to lead troops in war-like situations because unit training has been neglected.[90]

Interoperability with most likely partners

Achieving the level of interoperability required to cooperate effectively on the ground with Sweden's most likely partners, the Nordic countries and selected NATO countries such as Great Britain, has been a priority for the Swedish armed forces since their involvement in the Balkans began. The realization that the Bosnia deployment would be harder and riskier than traditional peacekeeping thus resulted in joint training with the Danish and Norwegian units in NORDBAT 2 prior to the deployment in Tuzla in 1993.[91] The increased need for interoperability has also been a key factor driving Sweden's cooperation with NATO since 1995, and it has had a profound influence on training, procurement, staff procedures and doctrinal thinking.[92] These efforts culminated with the order given by the Swedish supreme commander in December 1999 that both organization and procedures should be fully adapted to NATO's.[93]

To achieve this objective Sweden has cooperated closely with the Nordic NATO members, Denmark and Norway, played an active role in the PfP training programme and participated in the establishment of multinational forces earmarked for peace operations such as the EU reaction force, SHIRBRIG and NORDCAPS. Among the reaction forces, NORDCAPS is regarded as a priority not only because it represents an effective way of enhancing interoperability among the Nordic countries, but also because it is seen as a way of obtaining a greater influence in the EU and NATO and as a way of improving relations with Great Britain.[94]

Finally, Sweden has also participated in the multinational Nordic battalions in the Balkans. However, Sweden remains reluctant to participate in multinational forces below the battalion level in peace enforcement operations for security reasons. Concern for the security of the personnel hence induced the Swedish High Command to fight a decision by the MoD to deploy a joint Finnish–Swedish battalion in Kosovo in May 1999. The plan was finally dropped at a time when the Finnish troops were engaged in joint training with Swedish troops at SWEDINT.[95] The EU decision to set up rapid reaction battle groups led to a similar proposal in April 2004, when the Swedish defence minister, Leni Björklund, suggested that Finland and Sweden should make a joint battle group (1,500 strong) available for EU-led peace operations on 15 days' notice.[96] The supreme commander's reaction was predictable; he expressed scepticism and proposed the establishment of a Swedish battle group instead, which could be operational by 2009.[97] Leni Björklund prevailed, however, and the decision to establish a Finnish–Swedish battle group was announced in October 2004.

Armaments and ROE permitting use of force beyond self-defence if necessary

The Bosnia deployment effectively changed the Swedish approach to peace operations. Colonel Ulf Henricsson, the first commander of the Bosnia battalion, simply refused to go to Bosnia with traditional peacekeeping equipment, and he had his way.[98] In his view, an operation like the one in Bosnia, situated somewhere between Chapter VI and Chapter VII, required a force equipped and trained for 'worst case Chapter VII'. Drawing on the lessons learned by the Danish battalion in Croatia, he also interpreted the old peacekeeping adage 'firm, fair and friendly' with a greater emphasis on 'firm' than was the norm.[99] His robust approach impressed his UNPROFOR commander Michael Rose, the press corps, his Danish colleagues in NORDBAT 2 and, most importantly, the local parties.[100] Rose later described Henricsson's approach in his memoirs:

> Although Sweden has not been at war for 300 years, it was plain that they had lost nothing of the martial quality that allowed them to dominate northern Europe in the seventeenth century. They could be extremely bloody-minded and always returned fire immediately with their heavy weapons if they were fired upon...Henricsson had personally led their first convoy across the conflict line. At a Bosnian Serb roadblock, he was confronted by an aggressive soldier who told him he had orders not to allow him to pass. Henricsson immediately put a loaded pistol to the soldier's head and informed him that he had just received a new set of orders...Because of their tough-minded approach, the Swedes were respected by all of the warring parties.[101]

At home, his robust approach did not go down well with the traditionalists, who accused the Swedish contingent of being trigger-happy and too aggressive.[102] The results on the ground proved the critics wrong, however, and Henricsson's approach was eventually codified in the Swedish peace support operations doctrine published in 1997.[103]

The new doctrine tailors armaments and ROE to the mission at hand. If consent is perceived as genuine the traditional approach to peacekeeping is employed, but if there is a risk that consent may be withdrawn or the mandate contains Chapter VII authorization, then a peace enforcement force with a warfighting capability should be deployed.[104]

The new approach and Sweden's increased involvement in peace operations have had a profound impact on procurement policies. When the Balkan deployments began the Swedish army first had to borrow armoured personnel carriers (APCs) from Finland for the Macedonia operation. Additional APCs subsequently had to be procured rapidly from Germany to meet the demands generated by the Bosnia deployment.[105] Since then the involvement in peace operations has led to the development and procurement of modern equipment especially suited for such operations, including equipment that did not exist in the Swedish defence organization such as armoured wheeled vehicles and communications equipment.[106] That all the new equipment such as the infantry fighting vehicle CV 90 goes to the new reaction forces provides another indication of the way in which procurement and modernization is driven by the international operations.[107]

Logistics

The deployment of the first battalion in the Balkans was a struggle as the Swedish logistics organization was not geared to supporting battalions operating abroad. According to one member of the battalion, problems generated by the lack of logistical and other forms of support were so severe that they wore out key members of the leadership even before the battalion had left Swedish soil.[108] The Bosnia deployment served as a shock to the system and efforts to improve the logistical support provided to Swedish forces serving abroad have continued since then. Organizational changes such as the establishment of a new centralized logistics organization (FMLOG) in 2002, procurement of new equipment, participation in the PARP process aimed at achieving logistical interoperability with NATO, cooperation with the other Nordic nations as well as the establishment of a rapid reaction engineer company have all served to enhance the Swedish capacity for supporting its forces abroad.

In spite of the progress made, it is generally acknowledged that the logistical support system remains in need of further improvement.[109] Setting up the support system for the new reaction forces that became operational in 2001–03 proved quite a challenge,[110] and recent exercises abroad also have demonstrated the need for further improvement, a situation also underlined by the fact that full interoperability with NATO logistical standards will not be a reality before 2008 at the earliest.[111] This said, the need for improvement does not alter the fact that the Swedish armed forces have been able to support and sustain the forces they have deployed abroad since the early 1990s.

Medical, psychological and family support

Swedish policymakers realized as early as May 1992 that participation in the peace operation in Bosnia would require better medical and psychological support for the armed personnel (Box 7.1).[112] An improved system including a standby crisis support team and a new demobilization programme designed to deal with psychological after-effects was therefore already in place the following year when the first Swedish battalion went to Bosnia.[113] Since then lessons learned have led to further improvements, and the Swedish system is now similar to the one established in Denmark. In 2003 the first Bosnia battalion was united again in order to determine whether the soldiers where suffering from psychological after-effects as a result of their service in Bosnia 10 years earlier.[114]

The police and the rescue services have established similar psychological and medical support systems for their personnel and they all appear to be working quite well.[115] This, however, cannot be said to be the case about the family support provided by the military. It is a major source of frustration and practical assistance with snow clearing and similar tasks is therefore seen as crucial in order to increase the number of volunteers for international service.[116] More leave for personnel serving abroad is also seen as important, and a comparison with the Finnish system makes it easy to see why. Whereas Finnish personnel earn the right to six days of leave at

---

Box 7.1 The military psychological support system

1   Briefings for all personnel on stress reactions prior to deployment.
2   Training for officers, doctors and army chaplains in stress monitoring and management.
3   Standard debriefings following the completion of each assignment.
4   Monitoring of the psychological status of the personnel in the field.
5   Database on the personnel to facilitate support in crises.
6   Crisis support procedures to deal with incidents, deaths and injuries during the mission (debriefings, handling of deaths or injuries).
7   Debriefing personnel available in Sweden for rapid dispatch to mission areas in emergencies.
8   Family support in the form of briefings and information.
9   Demobilization programme including psychological debriefings and briefings on post-mission stress symptoms.
10 Reunions for all personnel 4–12 months after the mission; more if necessary.

Source: Ödlund, Ann (2001) Psykisk stress i samband med internationella insatser. En översiktlig beskrivning av problemområdet (Stockholm: Totalförsvarets Forskningsinstitut, FOI-R–0044–SE), p. 17.

home for every four weeks they serve abroad, Swedish personnel get less than half: 2.5 days of leave per month and are only allowed one trip home during their six-month tour.[117]

Intelligence capacity

While the importance of gathering and analysing intelligence information was understood by Swedish UN commanders during the Cold War, it was usually done in a haphazard way without proper equipment or trained personnel.[118] The Bosnia deployment forced a reassessment of this practice. It was realized that timely intelligence was essential for force protection and mission success, and that the Swedish battalions by and large would have to produce it themselves. The UN was not capable of providing the information required during UNPROFOR, and the situation did not change markedly after NATO took over.

Sweden's status as a non-NATO member goes some way towards explaining why it proved difficult to get access to the intelligence gathered at higher command levels during IFOR and SFOR. Equally, if not more important, however, was the fact that the Swedish battalions had very little to offer in return. The situation gradually improved as the Swedish contingents beefed up their intelligence capacity and a Nordic intelligence cell was established in Bosnia, but the real breakthrough only came once the introduction of specialized intelligence platoons during the KFOR operation gave the Swedish battalions quality information with which to trade.[119] Sweden, in other words, learned rule number one of international intelligence cooperation the hard way: you only get access to information if you have something to offer in return.

Intelligence is now a priority. The Swedish doctrine regards it as an 'essential element' in peace operations and as 'vital' for mission success,[120] and the need to further enhance the Swedish intelligence capacity is officially acknowledged.[121]

Public information capacity

> [I]t is of paramount importance to be aware, organized and active in all information matters. General information operations should be integrated into the day-to-day conduct of operations in all PSO, and coordination has to take place at every level.
>
> *Joint Military Doctrine, Peace Support Operations*[122]

As this quote illustrates, the Swedish armed forces acknowledge the importance of information operations in contemporary peace operations, and more time and resources are now devoted to this aspect of peace operations than was the case in the past. Today, Swedish battalions are deployed with four full-time press and information officers who are responsible for devising a coherent information strategy directed at both the local and international community. Relations with the press are usually handled by the press and information officers rather than the force commander.

Press and information officers are usually recruited among either civilians or officers in the reserves with relevant civilian training. The press and information training provided for regular officers remains limited, although SWEDINT since the mid-1990s has run an international press and information officer course to prepare officers for assignments as press and information officers in multinational HQs in peace operations.[123] Finally, it is also worth mentioning that the Swedish armed forces have run survival courses for Swedish journalists once a year since 1997.[124]

Coordination and cooperation capacity

Confronted with the need to cooperate closely with local civilian actors as well as international humanitarian organizations in the mission areas, Sweden has also enhanced its CIMIC capacity in the field.[125] The Swedish efforts to enhance its CIMIC capability began in earnest in 1997 when it became part of the new doctrine and the army's new reaction force was provided with a CIMIC section.[126] Since then it has been a major focus of Swedish training and exercise activities (Nordic Peace, Viking and international courses arranged by SWEDINT),[127] CIMIC staff personnel have been made available for rapid reaction (see Table 7.3), a CIMIC handbook was published in 2002, and CIMIC personnel have played an increasingly prominent role in the military contributions that Sweden has made in recent years. The Swedish contribution to the Nordic–Polish battle group in 1999–2002 consisted primarily of CIMIC (20–25) personnel, and a Swedish CIMIC company (45 personnel) participated in ISAF in Afghanistan from September 2002 to February 2004.

Steps to strengthen civil–military coordination and cooperation among Swedish actors have been taken at both at home and in the mission areas. Representatives from the ministries of Defence, Foreign Affairs and Justice meet on a weekly basis in two information working groups (Beredningsgruppen and Operationsgruppen) to discuss strategic and operational issues related to the Swedish participation in peace operations. They function mainly as forums for sharing information, however, and the MoD has therefore proposed the establishment of a body with higher-level representation and decision-making authority.[128]

During 2000 SIDA entered in direct cooperation with the Swedish armed forces using the Swedish CIMIC personnel in Kosovo as an implementing partner.[129] The experiment was successful,[130] and SIDA subsequently provided the Swedish CIMIC contingents in Bosnia and Kosovo with SEK 1 million each for humanitarian projects.[131]

Public security capacity

As Table 7.2 illustrates, Sweden has enhanced its civilian capacity in this area significantly in recent years, and strengthening the EU capacity for civilian crisis management was one of the principal objectives pursued when Sweden held the rotating EU presidency in the spring of 2001. The Swedish armed forces have the same cautious approach to the use of its personnel for public security tasks as other Western forces. Swedish military forces are as a matter of doctrine only allowed to work in support of the police. They cannot conduct police work as such and their training in public security tasks is restricted to riot control. Instead, the Swedish armed forces have chosen to prepare their military police contingents better for the challenges presented by the breakdown in law and order in the mission areas. Whereas Swedish military police traditionally were used for traffic control they are now trained to be able to carry out other functions such as:

- escort and VIP protection
- coordination and cooperation with local police forces
- investigation of violations of international law
- criminal investigations
- support for riot control.[132]

These changes proved their worth in March 2004, when Swedish military police successfully prevented Albanian demonstrators from entering a Serb town in Kosovo. A total of 14 Swedish troops were injured in the clashes.[133]

Conclusion

Sweden has been adjusting its approach to peace operations since 1992 when the deployments in the Balkans began. In qualitative terms, these efforts have been successful as Sweden now meets all our operational requirements for success (Table 7.4). A political unwillingness to make military contributions to offensive enforcement operations is the only restriction preventing Swedish participation in the full range of peace operations. Political and public support for a strong Swedish involvement in all other types of operations remains strong, and a continuation of the strong Swedish involvement in peace operations is therefore to be expected. The ongoing efforts to enhance both the civilian and military capabilities for peace operations all but guarantee a growing involvement. The defence reforms initiated in 2000 should at the very least lead to a doubling of the number of military personnel (1,000) that Sweden currently can sustain abroad on a continuous basis. This objective had not been achieved by 2005 and major reforms, especially with respect to recruitment and increased professionalism, will be required to achieve the longer-term goal involving the

Table 7.4 Sweden and the requirements for success in contemporary peace operations

Requirements for success	Sweden
1. Political will, legal framework and funds for all types of operations	No, not peace enforcement involving large-scale offensive operations against designated enemies
2. Civilian and military personnel deployable at short notice	Yes
3. Training to prepare the civilian and military personnel for their many new tasks	Yes
4. Interoperability with most likely partners	Yes
5. Armaments and ROE permitting use of force beyond self-defence if necessary	Yes
6. Logistics	Yes
7. Medical, psychological and family support	Yes
8. Intelligence capacity	Yes
9. Public information capacity	Yes
10. Coordination and cooperation capacity	Yes
11. Public security capacity	Yes

deployment of a 1,500-strong battle group on 15-day notice with 300 personnel backup.[134]

Notes

1. Moore, Michael (2000) *Revolution i det svenska försvaret* (Stockholm: Försvarsberedningen, Försvarsdepartementet), p. 7.
2. See appendix 7.
3. Government Defence Bill 1996/97:4.
4. Government Bill 1999/2000:30.
5. Ledare (2000) 'Vilken uppgift har det militära försvaret?', *Vårt Försvar*, Vol. 111, No. 4 (December).
6. Sköld, Nils (1990) *United Nations Peacekeeping after the Suez War. UNEF I: The Swedish Involvement* (London: Hurst), p. 2.
7. Utrikesdepartementet, Försvarsdepartementet, Justitiedepartementet (2002) 'Svensk syn på den fredsfrämjande verksamheten – några huvudlinjer', Promemoria, draft, spring, p. 18. An overview of Sweden's participation in peace operations can be found in Appendix 8.
8. Peterson, Thage G. (1999) *Resan mot mars: Anteckningar och minnen* (Stockholm: Albert Bonniers Förlag AB), p. 550; Government Bill 1995/96:113.
9. Eriksson, Pär (2001) 'Vi måste kunna anfalla', *Dagens Nyheter*, 12 November, p. A04.
10. On the Swedish efforts to promote conflict prevention and civilian crisis management within the EU see Björkdahl, Annika (2002) *From Idea to Norm: Promoting Conflict Prevention*, Lund Political Studies 125 (Lund: Department of Political Science, Lund University); Ojanen, Hanna (2002) 'Sweden and

Finland: What Difference Does It Make to be Non-aligned?', in Nina Græger, Henrik Larsen and Hanna Ojanen (eds) *The ESDP and the Nordic Countries. Four Variations on a Theme* (Helsinki: Finnish Institute of International Affairs; Berlin: Institut für Europäische Politik), pp. 168–173 (154–217).

11. Johansson, Gunnar (2003) 'Svenskar i blodig strid. Fientlig milis öppnade eld i Kongo', *Expressen*, 22 November, p. 20.
12. AFP (2004) 'EU Approves Rapid-Reaction Battlegroups', *The Australian*, May 18.
13. Both the Swedish defence minister, Leni Björklund, and the Swedish Defence Commission wanted Sweden to contribute to the establishment of EU battle groups. See Hedström, Ingrid (2004) 'Björklund vill ha svensk-finsk trupp', *Dagens Nyheter*, 7 April, p. A15; Swedish Defence Commission (2004) 'Försvar för en ny tid', Ds 2004:30, pp. 72–73. The Swedish supreme commander, Håkan Syrén, proposed that Sweden should make a complete battle group with 300 personnel backup available for the EU after 2008. See *ÖB alternativ till utformning av Försvarsmakten* (Stockholm: Försvarsmakten, Högkvarteret; 30 April 2004), bilag 3, p. 38.
14. *Att verka för fred – ett gemensamt fredscentrum i Sverige* (SOU 2000:74), pp. 81–82.
15. *Att verka för fred*, p. 77.
16. Myhlback, Lennart (1998) 'Internationella insatser – ett medel för vår säkerhetspolitik? Ett civilt perspektiv', presentation at Kungl. Krigsvetenskapsakademien Höstsymposium, *Internationella insatser – ett medel för vår säkerhetspolitik?*, 22 October.
17. 1995/96: UU04 Svenskt deltagande i fredsstyrka i f.d. Jugoslavien; 1998/99:UFöU2 Svenskt deltagande i fredsstyrka i Kosovo.
18. Stütz, Göran (2002) *Opinion 2002 – Den svenska allmänhetens syn på samhället, säkerhetspolitiken och försvaret hösten 2002* (Stockholm, Styrelsen för psykologisk försvar), p. 42.
19. Stütz, *Opinion 2002*, p. 52.
20. Gunnar Jervas has been the most vocal proponent of this view: Jervas, Gunnar (1994) 'Övergripande reflektioner och rekommendationer', in Gunnar Jervas and Rutger Lindahl (eds) 'Skall Sverige tvinga fram fred?', *Research Report*, No. 19 (Stockholm: Utrikespolitiska Institutet), pp. 121–125; and Jervas, Gunnar (2000) '"Fredsfrämjande insatser" i kritisk belysning', *Internationella Studier*, No. 3, pp. 45–54. Jervas's 1994 writings were countered by three of his colleagues: Dalsjö, Robert, Lennart Johansson and Hans Zettermark (1994) 'FN måste kunna bruka våld – och Sverige medverka', *Vårt Försvar*, Vol. 105, No. 3 (June), pp. 33–35.
21. See for instance Svenonius, Camilla and Anders Hellner (1994) 'Fredsbevarande styrka av ny typ: NORDBAT 2', in Jervas and Lindahl, 'Skall Sverige tvinga fram fred?', pp. 34–35 (25–36).
22. On this debate see Göranson, Sverker (1996) 'Svensk bataljon under NATO-befäl', *Vårt Försvar*, Vol. 107, No. 3 (June), p. 7 (6–9); Peterson, *Resan mot mars*, pp. 514, 550.
23. Svenonius and Hellner, 'Fredsbevarande styrka av ny typ: NORDBAT 2', p. 25.
24. Heimerson, Staffan (1995) 'En vinjett från fältet: Med adrenalin upp till hårfästet. En samtal mellan översten Ulf Henricsson och reportern', in Bo Huldt, Gustaf Welin and Torsten Örn (eds) *Bevara eller skapa fred. FNs nya roll* (Stockholm: Norsteds förlag), p. 27 (15–29). This impression is generally shared by the Swedish officers and political analysts to whom I have spoken.

25. Ferm, Anders (1995) 'Fredsbevarande operationer, inrikespolitiken och opinionen – hur starkt är stödet och när sviktar det?', in Huldt et al., *Bevara eller skapa fred. FNs nya roll*, pp. 344–362.

26. Burk, James (1999) 'Public Support for Peacekeeping in Lebanon and Somalia: Assessing the Casualties Hypothesis', *Political Science Quarterly*, Vol. 114, No. 1 (spring), pp. 53–78.

27. For an overview of this research see Jakobsen, Peter Viggo (2004) 'Har Danmark et body bag syndrom?', *Militært Tidsskrift*, Vol. 133, No. 1 (April), pp. 94–114.

28. *Lag om väpnat styrka för tjänstgöring utomlands* 1992:1153.

29. *Lag om utbildning för fredsfrämjande verksamhet* 1994:588.

30. Proposition 1996/97:4. *Totalförsvar i förnyelse – etapp 2.*

31. *Lag om väpnad styrka för tjänstgöring utomlands* 2003:169.

32. *ÖB alternativ till utformning av Försvarsmakten*, bilag 3, p. 38.

33. *Gränsöverskridande sårbarhet – gemensam säkerhet* (Stockholm: Försvarsdepartementet, Försvarsberedningen, 2001; Ds 2001:14), p. 190.

34. Representatives from the Moderate Party effectively support such a revision in the defence committee report on the government bill proposing Swedish participation in KFOR: 1998/99:UFÖU2.

35. This was strongly resisted by the Swedish government who in vain tried to insert an explicit requirement for a UN mandate in the declaration. The Swedish efforts were defeated by a majority preferring the vaguer formulation identical to the one used by NATO 'in accordance with UN principles'. See Ojanen, Hanna with Gunilla Herolf and Rutger Lindahl (2000) *Non-Alignment and European Security Policy* (Helsinki: Finnish Institute of Foreign Affairs; Bonn: Institut für Europäische Politik), p. 132.

36. The government as a result became caught in the crossfire between critics who thought it was doing either too much or too little to support NATO. One prominent critic in the former camp was Ingvar Carlson, former Swedish prime minister and member of the governing Social Democratic Party, who strongly condemned NATO's attack on Serbia as a violation of international law. See Carlson, Ingvar and Shridath Ramphal (1999) 'NATO's Vigilante Warfare Gives a Bad Example to the World', *International Herald Tribune*, 1 April, p. 4. The internal divisions were illustrated in an opinion poll taken at the start of the air campaign which showed 27% in favour of Swedish participation in the war, 52% against and 21% who did not know: Wendel, Per (1999) 'Svenskar ska inte vara med i bombanfallen', *Expressen*, 25 March, p. 12.

37. Hall, Thomas (1999) 'Lindh mycket oroad över utvecklingen', *Dagens Nyheter*, 26 March, p. A5; TT (1999) 'Bombningarna är en europeisk tragedi', *Dagens Nyheter*, 25 March, p. A05.

38. Hellberg, Anders (1999) 'Nato ber Sverige delta militärt i Albanien', *Dagens Nyheter*, 8 April, p. A8.

39. Lindh, Anna (2000) 'Natos flyginsats mot Jugoslavien var nödvändig', *Svenska Dagbladet*, 6 July.

40. Lindh, Anna (1998) 'Sweden in Europe', address at the Swedish Institute of International Affairs, Stockholm, 16 December. This interpretation of international law is very controversial and clearly at odds with the UN Charter which bans all use of force without a UN mandate except in self-defence.

41. Didner, Henrik (1994) 'Kostnader för svenskt deltagande i FN-styrkor', in Jervas and Lindahl, 'Skall Sverige tvinga fram fred?', p. 74 (73–80).

42. This was also the case during the Cold War. See Ferm, 'Fredsbevarande operationer, inrikespolitiken och opinionen', pp. 356–357.

43. Svenonius and Hellner, 'Fredsbevarande styrka av ny typ: NORDBAT 2', p. 28; Utrikesutskottets betänkande 1992/93:UU35 Svenskt deltagande i av FN:s säkerhetsråd beslutade insatser för säkerställande av fred i f.d. Jugoslavien.
44. Granholm, Niklas (2000) 'Tar vi internationella insatser på tillräckligt allvar? Implikationer för svenska internationella fredsfrämjande insatser av Kosovo-kriget', in Bo Ljung *et al.* (eds) *Aspekter på Kosovo-operationen mars–juni 1999* (Stockholm: FOA; FOA-R–00-01488-170-SE, April), pp. 75–85.
45. *Sveriges deltagande i internationella fredsfrämjande insatser* (Stockholm: Utrikesdepartementet, 1995, Ds 1995:25), p. 107.
46. Svenonius, and Hellner, 'Fredsbevarande styrka av ny typ: NORDBAT 2', p. 26.
47. Lindholm, Krister (1996) 'Svensk säkerhetspolitik i praktiken', *Arménytt*, No. 5, p. 23.
48. *Budgetproposition 1996/97:1, utgiftsområde 5, Utrikesförvaltning och internationell samverkan* (Stockholm: Finansdepartementet), p. 18.
49. *Internationella fredsfrämjande insatser och hjälpinsatser* (Stockholm: Riksdagens Revisorer, Rapport 2001/02:9), pp. 75–77.
50. On the unwillingness within the armed forces to give priority to peace operations see: Dalsjö, Robert (1999) 'Internationellt engagemang; säkerhetspolitisk nödvändighet och militärt måste', *Försvar i Nutid*, No. 1 (Stockholm: Centralforbundet Folk och Försvar), p. 5; Granholm, 'Tar vi internationella insatser på tillräckligt allvar?', p. 82.
51. See Chapter 3 for a discussion of these factors.
52. Government Bill 1995/96:12.
53. *The Renewal of Sweden's Defence: Phase 2*, unofficial shortened version of the Government Defence Bill 1996/97:4 passed by parliament on 20 November and 13 December 1996 (Stockholm: Ministry of Defence, 1996), p. 16.
54. Ministry of Defence (1999) *Summary of the Government Bill the New Defence* (Government Bill 1999/2000:30), p. 4.
55. *Summary of the Government Bill the New Defence*, p. 4.
56. Government Bill 1999/2000:30.
57. Björeman, Carl, Cronenberg, Arvid and Gard, Helge (1996) 'Ett försvar med anpassningsstruktur: Vision eller realitet?', *Försvar i Nutid*, No. 4–5, pp. 61, 66; Rapp, Johan (1995) 'Swedish Chiefs Criticize Budget Cut Proposals', *Jane's Defence Weekly*, Vol. 24, No. 12 (23 September), p. 8; Rapp, Johan (1996) 'Cuts "Premature", Says Swedish Defence Chief', *Jane's Defence Weekly*, Vol. 25, No.11 (13 March), p. 10.
58. For a vivid account of Wictorin's clashes with his defence minister see the memoirs of the latter: Peterson, *Resan mot mars*, pp. 517–523.
59. Dalsjö, 'Internationellt engagemang; säkerhetspolitisk nödvändighet och militärt måste', p. 5.
60. Granholm, 'Tar vi internationella insatser på tillräckligt allvar?'.
61. Ullbors-Hägg, Ingrid (2001) 'Försvarsmaktens ökade internationalisering: kan beslutet genomföras?' (Stockholm: Institutionen för Civil Beredskap, Försvarshögskolan; Uppsala: Statsvetenskapliga institutionen, Uppsala universitet), pp. 28–29.
62. TT (2000) 'Sveriges forsvar trimmes til fremtiden', *Aktuelt*, 31 March 2000, p. 15.
63. For an official discussion of determinants see 'Svensk syn på den fredsfrämjande verksamheten – några huvudlinjer'.

64. Dalsjö, Robert (1995) 'Sweden and the Balkan Blue Helmet Operations', in Lars Ericson (ed.) *Solidarity and Defence: Sweden's Armed Forces in International Peace-keeping Operations during the 19th and 20th Centuries* (Swedish Military History Commission, Stockholm), p. 105 (95–118); Granholm, 'Tar vi internationella insatser på tillräckligt allvar?', p. 82; Huldt, Bo (1995) 'Working Multilaterally: The Old Peacekeepers' Viewpoint', in Donald C.F. Daniel and Bradd C. Hayes (eds) *Beyond Traditional Peacekeeping* (New York: St Martin's Press), pp. 112 (191–119); Pellnäs, Bo (1998) 'Internationella operationer i ett säkerhetspolitiskt perspektiv', *Royal Swedish Academy of War Sciences Proceedings and Journal*, Vol. 202, No. 1, p. 12 (6–14).

65. Walter, Tor Egil (2001) 'Nordiske militære utfordringer i et svensk perspektiv', in Bjørn Inge Ruset (ed.) *Militærmaktseminaret 2000 Forsvaret ved et veiskille* (Oslo: Norsk Utenrikspolitisk Institutt), p. 42 (37–61).

66. Ritzau/TT (2001) 'Sverige sender flere tropper til Kosovo', *Aktuelt online*, 22 March.

67. Rosenius, Frank (2000) 'Sveriges försvarsmakt – under radikal förandring', *Norsk Militært Tidsskrift*, Vol. 169, No. 6/7, p. 46 (42–46).

68. *ÖB alternativ till utformning av Försvarsmakten.*

69. Improving coordination between the EU and the UN was thus a priority for Sweden during its presidency of the EU the spring of 2001: Ojanen, 'Sweden and Finland', pp. 170, 190–191; interview in the MFA, May 2002. It was also one of the key objectives of the *Partners in Prevention* conference hosted by the Ministry of Foreign Affairs in August 2002.

70. The contribution to MONUC lasted a year and was terminated in June 2004. The contribution to UNMIL began in March 2004 and it was extended until March 2006 in January 2005.

71. *Samverkanscenter i Kramfors för katastrof- och fredsinsatser* (Stockholm: Utrikesdepartementet; SOU 2001:104), p. 7.

72. *Domare och åklagare i internationella insatser* (Stockholm: Justitie-departementet; Ds 2002:1, January 2002), p. 103.

73. For detailed information on the teams and the service packages see: < http:// www.srv.se/ >.

74. See the UNDAC homepage < http://www.reliefweb.int/undac/undac_ members_list.html >; Ministry of Defence (2002) 'Sverige anmäler resurser till EU-krishantering', press release, 12 September.

75. *Domare och åklagare i internationella insatser*, p. 114.

76. Interview with official from the Ministry of Justice, 23 June 2004.

77. *The Renewal of Sweden's Defence: Phase 2*, p. 8.

78. 'Oacceptabelt långsam process', *Försvarets Forum*, No. 6 (1999); 'Swerap ersätts med nytt koncept', *Försvarets Forum*, No. 7 (1999); Government Bill 1999/2000:30, pp. 47–48.

79. For detailed information about the units see: < http://www.mil.se/int/ article.php?id=274 > (2 September 2004).

80. *Budgetproposition 2002/03:1, utgiftsområde 6, Försvar samt beredskap mot sårbarhet* (Stockholm: Finansdepartementet), p. 68.

81. *ÖB alternativ till utformning av Försvarsmakten.*

82. Christensen, Fhlemming (2001) 'Försvarsmakten genomgår en radikal omstrukturering', *Royal Swedish Academy of War Sciences Proceedings and Journal*, Vol. 205, No. 6, p. 134 (128–136). See also Pellnäs, Bo (1998) 'Deltagande i internationella operationer: konsekvenser för det nationella försvarets utformning', *Strategiskt Forum*, No. 4, November (Stockholm: FOA).

83. Brännström, Anders (2001) 'Kontinuitet i internationella operationer', *Royal Swedish Academy of War Sciences Proceedings and Journal*, Vol. 205, No. 1, p. 11 (3–13); Ullbors-Hägg, 'Försvarsmaktens ökade internationalisering: kan beslutet genomföras?', p. 29.
84. SRSA does participate in international training exercises within the International Humanitarian Partnership organization. See the SRSA website: <http://www.srv.se/funktioner/frameset/default.asp?om_id=17> (22 June 2004).
85. For course information see the SWEDINT website: <http://www.swedint.mil.se/?lang=eng> (22 June 2004).
86. Volunteers for the rapid reaction units sign a contract involving an obligation to report for service for a six-month deployment with seven days' notice in the standby period (12–42 months depending on the contract).
87. See: <http://www.armen.mil.se/article.php?id=6793> (22 June 2004).
88. Neretnieks, Karlis (2000) 'The Swedish Approach to Peace Support Operations', in *Challenges of Peacekeeping and Peace Support into the 21st Century: The Doctrinal Dimension* (Carlisle, PA: US Army Peacekeeping Institute, Center for Strategic Leadership), p. 23 (22–30); Tornberg, Claes (1997) 'Advanced Training of Officers within the Diplomatic Environment', *Royal Swedish Academy of War Sciences Proceedings and Journal*, Vol. 201, No. 3, pp. 51–57.
89. Westerdahl, Fredric (2004) 'Beredskapsförband till Kosovo – värderingar av stridsförmågan', *Royal Swedish Academy of War Sciences Proceedings and Journal*, Vol. 208, No. 1, pp. 94–111.
90. Andersson, Lars (2001) *Militärt ledarskap – när det gäller: svenskt militärt ledarskap med fredsfrämjande insatser i fokus* (Stockholm: HLS förlag), p. 161; Eriksson, 'Vi måste kunna anfalla'; Santesson, Olof (2002) 'Världens bästa soldater', *Royal Swedish Academy of War Sciences Proceedings and Journal*, Vol. 206, No. 3, pp. 107–112.
91. Gustafsson, Bengt (1994) 'Testimony by Supreme Commander Bengt Gustafsson to the Swedish parliament on the Swedish effort in Bosnia', 24 February 1994 printed in Försvarsutskottets betänkande1993/94:FÖU09.
92. *Joint Military Doctrine, Peace Support Operations* (Stockholm: Swedish Armed Forces, 1997), p. 6–3.
93. Walter, 'Nordiske militære utfordringer i et svensk perspektiv', p. 57.
94. Sydow, Bo von (1999) *Sweden's Security in the 21st Century* (Stockholm: Ministry of Defence), p. 16; Hederstedt, Johan (2001) Presentation by Supreme Commander Johan Hederstedt 'Sveriges nya försvar – Leaner but Meaner', at the Swedish embassy in Copenhagen, 26 September 2001; interviews with Swedish officers and defence officials, May 2002.
95. Hellberg, Anders and Stefan Lisinski (1999) 'Strid om Kosovostyrka. Militären: Politikerna väljer alltid det sämsta och billigaste alternativet', *Dagens Nyheter*, 18 March, p. A05. The Finnish High Command shared the concerns expressed by their Swedish colleagues but consented to the establishment of the joint force. *Virtual Finland* 'Finnish Foreign Policy 1999: May', (Finnish Institute of International Affairs for the MFA). <http://virtual.finland.fi/finfo/english/chronology/chrono1999_05.html>.
96. Hedström, 'Björklund vill ha svensk-finsk trupp'. The Defence Commission also wanted Sweden to contribute to the establishment of battle groups in cooperation with other countries. See Defence Commission (2004) 'Försvar för en ny tid', Ds 2004:30, pp. 72–73.
97. *ÖB alternativ till utformning av Försvarsmakten.*
98. Walter, 'Nordiske militære utfordringer i et svensk perspektiv', pp. 42–43.

99. Henricsson, Ulf (1995) 'CO NORDBAT 2:01 Erfarenheter från uppdraget i Bosnien i september 1993–6 april 1995', in Anders Kjølberg, Bjørn Olav Knutsen, Wegger Strømmen (eds) *Konfliktløsning i Europa, FFI/Rapport*, No. 95/00759, (Kjeller: Forsvarets Forskningsinstitutt, 24 March), p. 78.
100. Møller, Lars R. (2001) *Operation Bøllebank: Soldater i kamp* (København: Høst og Søn), pp. 191–193; Rieff, David (1995) *Slaughterhouse. Bosnia and the Failure of the West* (London: Vintage), p. 168.
101. Rose, Michael (1998) *Fighting for Peace* (London: Harvill Press), p. 34. Contrary to Rose's claim the Swedish contingent did not always return fire. By February 1994 the Swedish battalion had come under fire 100 times, but only returned fire on approximately 10 occasions. See Görsjö, Alf (1994) 'Testimony by NORDBAT chief of staff Lt Col Alf Görsjö to the Swedish parliament' on the Swedish effort in Bosnia, 24 February 1994 printed in Försvarsutskottets betänkande 1993/94:FÖU09.
102. Dalsjö, 'Sweden and the Balkan Blue Helmet Operations', p. 108.
103. Henricsson's view of grey area operations is thus reproduced: *Joint Military Doctrine, Peace Support Operations* (Swedish Armed Forces, 1997), pp. 2–7.
104. *Joint Military Doctrine, Peace Support Operations*, Chapter 2.
105. Stjernfelt, Bertil (1993) 'UN Peacekeeping Expanding, Accelerating – If Not Exploding', *Royal Swedish Academy of War Sciences Proceedings and Journal*, Vol. 197, No. 6, p. 600 (587–606); Walter, 'Nordiske militære utfordringer i et svensk perspektiv', p. 43.
106. Neretnieks, Karlis (1998) 'En armé för såväl nationelle som internationella uppgifter, går det?', *Royal Swedish Academy of War Sciences Proceedings and Journal*, Vol. 202, No. 1, pp. 15–27. See also the special issue on the equipment developed and procured to enhance the protection of the Swedish troops serving abroad: 'Tema Skydd', *FMV aktuellt*, No. 2 (2002) (Stockholm: Försvarets Materielverk).
107. Neretnieks, 'En armé för såväl nationelle som internationella uppgifter, går det?'.
108. Andersson, *Militärt ledarskap – när det gäller*, p. 127.
109. Brännström, 'Kontinuitet i internationella operationer', p. 45.
110. Larsson, Henrik (2001) 'Logistikaspekten i SWAFRAP och motsättningar i utvecklingsprocessen' (Stockholm: Managementinstitutionen, Försvarshögskolan); Lövgren, Christian (2002) 'Knepigt pussel at utrusta insatsstyrkorna', *Logistiknytt*, No. 3, pp. 7–8. For a discussion of the logistical problems facing the first Swedish battalion in Bosnia see Görsjö, Testimony by NORDBAT chief of staff Lt Col Alf Görsjö to the Swedish parliament.
111. Grohp, Joachim (2002) 'Försörjningsdivisionen – Logistik under internationella övningar', *Logistiknytt*, No. 3, pp. 6–7.
112. Försvarsutskottets yttrande, 1992/93: FöU11y, 28 May 1992.
113. Lundin, Tom and Ulf Otto (1996) 'Swedish Soldiers in Peacekeeping Operations: Stress Reactions Following Missions in Congo, Lebanon, Cyprus, and Bosnia', *NCP Clinical Quarterly*, Vol. 6, No. 1 (winter), pp. 9–11; Svenonius and Hellner, 'Fredsbevarande styrka av ny typ: NORDBAT 2', p. 28.
114. TT (2003) 'Bosnienbataljon återförenas', *Dagens Nyheter*, 6 August, p. A05.
115. For a detailed description see Ödlund, Ann (2001) *Psykisk stress i samband med internationella insatser. En översiktlig beskrivning av problemområdet* (Stockholm: Totalförsvarets Forskningsinstitut, FOI-R–0044–SE), pp. 17–19.

116. Boëne, Bernard, Christopher Dandeker, Jurgen Kuhlmann and Jan van der Meulen (2000) *Facing Uncertainty. Report 2: The Swedish Military in International Perspective* (Stockholm: National Defence College, Department of Leadership), pp. 29–30; Ullbors-Hägg, 'Försvarsmaktens ökade internationalisering: kan beslutet genomföras?', pp. 28–29; interviews at SWEDINT and the MoD, May 2002.

117. Brännström, 'Kontinuitet i internationella operationer', p. 11; *Internationella fredsfrämjande insatser och hjälpinsatser*, p. 14; interviews with Swedish officers and defence officials, May 2002.

118. Ahliny, Anders (2001) 'Underrättelsetjänst vid internationella insatser', *Vårt Försvar*, Vol. 111, No. 2 (May); Welin, Gustaf and Christer Ekelund (1999) *FN på Cypern. Den svenska fredsbevarande insatsen 1964–1993* (Stockholm: Probus Förlag), pp. 87–88, 310; Wærn, *Katanga*, pp. 54, 62–63, 67–68.

119. Ahliny, 'Underrättelsetjänst vid internationella insatser'; Rawlinson, Michael (2002) 'Specialförband vara eller inte vara i PSO?: En fallstudie av svenska Bosnien- och Kosovobataljoner' (Stockholm: Krigsvetenskapliga institutionen, Försvarshögskolan. C-uppsats 19 100:2002), pp. 30–48; interviews with Swedish intelligence officers and defence officials, May 2002.

120. *Joint Military Doctrine, Peace Support Operations*, pp. 5-8 and 5-9.

121. *Ny struktur för ökad säkerhet – nätverksförsvar och krishantering* (Stockholm: Försvarsdepartementet, Försvarsberedningen; DS: 2001:44, 31 August 2001), pp. 231–233.

122. *Joint Military Doctrine, Peace Support Operations*, p. 5-4.

123. Interview SWEDINT, May 2002.

124. Sjöden, Anders (2002) 'Försvaret lär journalister överlevnadsteknik', *Arménytt*, No. 2 (July), pp. 30–31.

125. The gradual enhancement of the CIMIC capacity in the Swedish UNPROFOR battalions is described in Almén, Anders, Pär Eriksson and Fredrik Lindgren (1997) *Militära och civila uppgifter vid internationella insatser. Problem och möjligheter vid samverkan och koordinering* (Stockholm: FOA, FOA-R–96-00364-1.1–SE), pp. 5-7.

126. *Joint Military Doctrine, Peace Support Operations*, pp. 5-3, 5-4.

127. SOU 1999: 29, pp. 42–43; SOU 2001: 23, pp. 131–133.

128. *Internationella fredsfrämjande insatser och hjälpinsatser* (Stockholm: Riksdagens Revisorer, Rapport 2001/02:9), pp. 42–43, 72; interviews at the MoD and the MFA, May 2002. A coordination body with higher-level representation between the three ministries was established in 1995 but it ceased functioning in 2001.

129. Until then SIDA had been sceptical about the value of such cooperation. See: Eriksson, Pär (1998) *Civil–militär samverkan på taktisk nivå i fredsfrämjande operationer. Motiv, metoder och fööruts ättningar* (Stockholm: FOA, FOA-R–98-00968-170–SE), pp. 37–39.

130. Alberoth, Jonas (2000) 'Närbilder från en fredsfrämjande insats – Samverkan och civil–militärt samarbete i Kosovo', in *Att verka för fred – ett gemensamt fredscentrum i Sverige* (SOU 2000:74, 31 August), pp. 145–146 (127–148); Wulff, Maria Broberg and Karin Ströberg (2001) *Utvärdering av svenska bataljonens humanitära insatser i Kosovo* (Stockholm: Totalförsvarets Forskningsinstitut, FOI-R–0171–SE).

131. Försvarsmakten (2001) 'Bosnien, juli 2001 (SFOR)', < http://www.mil.se/int/index.php?lang=S&c=news&id=3374 > (30 July 2001); Försvarsmakten (2002) 'SIDA-pengar till Kosovobataljonen', < http://www.swedint.mil.se/index.php?c=news&id=7633 > (20 April 2002).

132. Eriksson, Pär (2000) *Polisiärt och militärt i fredsfrämjande operationer – analys av en gråzon* (Stockholm: FOA; FOA-R–99-01305-170–SE, December), pp. 69–70; *Joint Military Doctrine, Peace Support Operations*, pp. 5-15, 5-16; interview SWEDINT, May 2002.
133. Liedholm, Jesper (2004) 'Påfrestande dygn för de svenska soldaterna i Kosovo', <http://www.mil.se/int> (19 March).
134. *ÖB alternativ till utformning av Försvarsmakten.*

8   A new Nordic model in the making?

> There is...uncertainty regarding whether or not the Nordic countries
> will retain their special "Nordic profile" [in peace operations] in the future,
> or whether they will be integrated into a larger network of states within
> the EU, PfP etc.
>
> Åke Eknes[1]

The preceding chapters have shown that all the Nordic states individually
meet the requirements for success in post-Cold War peace operations, so
the potential for the establishment of an effective new model clearly exists.
This chapter determines whether this potential can be realized. To be
effective, a new model must have the relevant civilian and military capacity
available for rapid deployment, an institutional capacity for joint rapid
strategic decision making and planning, and finally a common strategic
culture enabling the Nordics to agree when, how and where their crisis
management capacities should be used.[2]

This chapter evaluates whether the new framework for Nordic cooperation established since the end of the Cold War meets these requirements.
Each of the three requirements are addressed in turn and the final section
discusses the strengths and weaknesses of the new Nordic model and
outlines a number of policy recommendations that the Nordics must
consider if they want their new model to be as influential as the old one.

Military capacity: forces for the post-Cold War era

NORDCAPS

NORDSAMFN (Nordic cooperation group for military UN matters)
established to coordinate the deployment of the Nordic standby forces for
UN peacekeeping operations during the Cold War was terminated in 1997.
NORDSAMFN's focus on UN peacekeeping operations was by then no
longer relevant in a world where the Nordics increasingly and predomi-
nantly participated in operations going beyond traditional peacekeeping led

by other international organizations. NORDCAPS (Nordic Coordinated Arrangement for Military Peace Support) was therefore set up in its place to provide the Nordics with military capabilities covering the full spectrum of peace operations, which could be made available to all the relevant international organizations.

NORDCAPS like its predecessor only involves military forces, but the numbers have grown. All three services are now involved and the level of integration is higher than before (Table 8.1). The size of the force register has doubled from some 6,000 to 12,000 personnel: 9,200 army, 1,200 navy and 1,600 air force. The army component serves as the basis for a 5,000-strong multinational brigade-size unit that the Nordics made available for deployment at 30–60 days' notice on EU, OSCE, NATO and UN-led

Table 8.1 NORDCAPS force pool (2004)

	Forces	Denmark	Finland	Sweden	Norway	Total
Army	Staff officers, including CIMIC personnel	..	25	30	..	55
	Military observers	..	30	..	..	30
	Brigade C3I, framework nation and brigade HQ logistics capability	..	1	..	..	1
	HQ staff officers	..	36	19	..	55
	HQ companies	..	..	1	..	1
	Armoured battalions	1	..	..	..	1
	Artillery battalions	1	..	..	..	1
	Engineer battalions	..	1	..	..	1
	Mechanized battalions	1	1	2	2	6
	Military police companies	1	..	1	..	2
	Engineer companies	1	..	1	..	2
	Logistics companies	..	..	1	..	1
	Transport companies	..	1	..	..	1
	Reconnaissance units	1	..	..	..	1
	CIMIC companies	..	1	..	..	1
Air force	Fighter planes	..	..	12	12	24
	Transport planes	1	..	4	2	7
	Maritime patrol aircraft	..	..	..	1	1
	Helicopters	1	..	..	4	5
	Air defence units	1	..	..	1	2
Navy	Corvettes	..	..	2	..	2
	Frigates	..	..	..	1	1
	Fast patrol boats	..	..	..	4	4
	Ocean patrol vessels	1	..	..	..	1
	Mine clearance and support vessels	2	1	2	2	7
	Support ships	1	..	..	1	2
	Mine clearing diving team	..	..	..	1	1
	Submarines	..	..	1	1	2

Source: NORDCAPS.

peace operations on 1 July 2003.[3] It is not yet geared for offensive peace enforcement, but it is supposed to be available for the full spectrum of peace operations when it is fully developed in 2006. Plans for the naval and air force components are being developed, but their levels of ambition have yet to be decided upon.

Most of the brigade units are national and non-integrated, but steps to establish multinational solutions have been taken in areas where the national capabilities are insufficient. Finland has taken the lead in the development of brigade-level communication and information systems, Norway is in charge of combat support and Sweden heads the establishment of a multinational logistics battalion.

A small step towards giving NORDCAPS a civilian capacity was taken in 2003, when Iceland, the fifth Nordic nation, made its Iceland Crisis Response Unit (ICRU) available for the force register. ICRU consists of some 100 civilian personnel (police, engineers, legal experts, medical experts, and search and rescue personnel), who are available for international operations at short notice.[4] The civilian rapid reaction capacities in the other four Nordic countries have thus far not been made available for NORDCAPS. The civilian involvement in NORDCAPS has been limited to training activities, primarily civil–military cooperation (CIMIC) courses and civilian participation in peace operations exercises.

As was the case in the old model, basic training of individuals and units remains a national responsibility, but the training cooperation has been expanded significantly. The old Nordic peacekeeping manuals (the Blue books) have been replaced by a *NORDCAPS Peace Support Operations Manual* covering the full spectrum of peace operations,[5] and the number of peace operations courses offered to individual officers has grown. A total of 25 courses involving some 850 students were arranged at training centres in the four Nordic countries during 2003. The new courses added to the programme in the 1990s include: CIMIC, press and information, NATO/Partnership for Peace (PfP) logistics and staff officers, and engineering and mine-clearing.[6] In addition, a number of joint training programmes have been established such as the Nordic UN Senior Management Seminar (UNSMAS), preparing civilian and military personnel for top leadership positions in UN peace operations. This course is held once a year and rotates among the four Nordic countries.

Finally, a programme of joint peace operations exercises held within the NATO PfP framework has been in existence since 1997, when the first Nordic Peace exercise took place. The Nordics take turns hosting these annual exercises.

SHIRBRIG

The Nordics also cooperate in SHIRBRIG (UN Standby High Readiness Brigade), which since 2000 has made forces available for UN peace operations at short notice (15–30 days) for a period of up to six months. SHIRBRIG deployed a headquarters (all member countries), an infantry battalion (The Netherlands and Canada) and a headquarters company (Denmark) to UNMEE in November 2000 (1,964 personnel). In addition, SHIRBRIG has provided a planning team to assist the Economic Community of West African States (ECOWAS) in the planning of a peace operation in Côte d'Ivoire in March 2003 and 20 personnel to assist the UN in setting up the core of the interim UN headquarters in Liberia (UNMIL) in September 2003.[7] In 2005 SHIRBRIG made a contribution for the UN operation in Sudan (UNMIS). SHIRBRIG had provided seven personnel to the 14-strong advance team authorized by the Security Council in 2004 and subsequently deployed the nucleus of the force headquarters and the headquarters support elements (some 200 personnel).[8] In addition to these operational deployments, SHIRBRIG has begun to assist the regional and sub-regional organizations in Africa in their efforts to establish multinational standby forces.

As is the case with NORDCAPS, SHIRBRIG cannot be used for offensive enforcement operations; enforcement of ceasefires/peace agreements constitutes the upper limit of the brigade's capacity. SHIRBRIG was originally conceived for traditional peacekeeping operations only and had still not deployed infantry on an enforcement mission by early 2005. The principal differences between NORDCAPS and SHIRBRIG are related to readiness and membership. SHIRBRIG has a higher level of readiness and 16 members (+ 5 observers).[9] Like NORDCAPS it involves military forces only (Table 8.2).

Table 8.2 Nordic SHIRBRIG contributions (2004)

Forces	Denmark	Finland	Sweden	Norway	Total
HQ company	1	. .	. .	. .	1
Engineer battalion	. .	1	. .	. .	1
Infantry battalion	. .	1	1	. .	2
Military police company	1	. .	1	. .	2
Engineer company	. .	. .	1	. .	1
Transport company	. .	1	. .	. .	1
Reconnaissance unit	1	. .	. .	. .	1
Transport helicopters company	. .	. .	. .	1	1

Source: SHIRBRIG.

BALTBAT and BALTRON

The Baltic Battalion (BALTBAT) is a multinational 674-strong battalion consisting of multinational units and national infantry companies from each of the three Baltic states, Estonia, Latvia and Lithuania, which is earmarked for peace operations (Table 8.3). It is relevant in this context

Table 8.3 BALTBAT organization

Unit	Personnel
Baltic support group	8
Staff	19
HQ and supplies company	136
Logistics company	109
Estonian company (infantry)	134
Lithuanian company (infantry)	134
Latvian company (infantry)	134
Total	674

because it has been set up with Nordic assistance, and because its officers and units have been co-deployed with Nordic contingents on a more or less continuous basis since 1994 in various peace operations. By 2002, more than 2,000 Baltic soldiers had been co-deployed with Danish forces.[10] 54 Lithuanian soldiers went with the Danish contingent to Iraq in October 2003,[11] and in the spring of 2004 a joint Baltic contingent (97 strong) was co-deployed with the Danish KFOR contingent. Some 200 soldiers have been co-deployed with Norwegian and Swedish units, and a small number has been co-deployed with the Finnish contingent in KFOR.[12] This practice and the continuing close military cooperation between the Nordics and the Baltic states make it is reasonable to regard BALTBAT as part of the force pool on which the Nordics can draw. Military cooperation was further intensified in 2003 when the Baltic and Nordic defence ministers decided to hold annual meetings to discuss issues related to military cooperation, and Denmark became lead nation on a new brigade project, which will give each of the Baltic states a capacity to make a battalion available to NATO.[13]

The Nordics are also involved in the establishment of a Baltic Naval Squadron (BALTRON). This project will in time give the Baltic states a capability to provide minelayers for international operations. Logistical support for such operations will have to be provided by others, however, making co-deployment with the Nordic navies an obvious option.

Institutional capacity: rapid joint decision making and planning

The principles of cooperation and decision making in NORDCAPS are the same as in NORDSAMFN. Cooperation is based on consensus, and decisions to commit troops are made on a case-by-case basis in each capital. The organizational set-up is similar to the old one, but more comprehensive. At the top level, the defence ministers meet twice a year. The NORDCAPS steering group (NSG), meeting two to three times a year, translates the decisions taken by the ministers into overall guidelines and policies. The NORDCAPS Military Coordination Group (NMCG), which meets four to six times a year, carries out the tasks formulated by the NGS and coordinates operational command. A multinational planning element was established in 2000 to deal with the practical tasks related to the establishment and the maintenance of the new force register. The planning element was supplemented with a multinational nucleus staff in 2002, which meets on a regular basis to plan and carry out training for the staff and the other multinational formations within the brigade. The working language is 'Scandinavian' but all documentation is produced in English, and NATO procedures are used when feasible. Working groups are also used in order to solve specific tasks.[14] The staff and planning capacity to keep the force register updated and ready for action is thus in place.

The capacity for rapid decision making has been demonstrated repeatedly over the years both during and after the Cold War. The long tradition of joint consultation and coordination with respect to deployments suggests that NORDCAPS will work as well as its predecessor. Rapid joint decision making is facilitated by the tradition of cooperation, very similar national decision-making procedures, and the high level of domestic support that NORDCAPS missions can count on in all four countries. Domestic support can be taken for granted because the NORDCAPS brigade only has been declared ready for uncontroversial missions such as enforcement of peace agreements (KFOR in Kosovo), conflict prevention (UNPREDEP in Macedonia) and assistance to civilians (ISAF in Afghanistan) that do not involve offensive use of force.[15]

Strategic culture: agreement on when, where and how to use NORDCAPS

NORDCAPS is only relevant to the extent that the Nordics can agree to use it. NORDCAPS has still not been used as a basis for deploying a joint Nordic unit, and all the Nordic governments have alternative joint options in the other rapid reaction arrangements they belong to in the EU, NATO and the UN. The million dollar question is, in other words, how often will the Nordics be willing to use NORDCAPS to generate joint contributions?

Agreement on when NORDCAPS should be used?

This is basically a question about threat perceptions, interests and values. On this the Nordics have always agreed. During the Cold War the threat of escalation was central to all four countries. Fearing that a local conflict might escalate into a superpower confrontation, they all supported UN peacekeeping as a way of reducing this risk. Likewise, they all saw UN peacekeeping as an important tool for strengthening the UN, international law and peaceful conflict resolution in the international system.

The Nordic consensus on interests, values and threat perceptions was maintained after the Cold War ended. The normative foundation remained the same. The Nordics still participate in peace operations in order to strengthen the UN, international law and peaceful conflict resolution, but the normative changes resulting from the end of the Cold War have meant that they have added democracy and human rights to the list of fundamental values that they want peace operations to promote and protect.[16]

The threat of escalation has been replaced by a host of new threats that the Nordics also agree on. Three events have been crucial in shaping Nordic threat perceptions in relation to peace operations. The first was the disappearance of the Soviet threat which made it possible for the Nordics to give peace operations a higher priority. The second was the outbreak of war in the Balkans which gave them a security interest in doing so. The perceived need to prevent the armed conflicts in the Balkans from spreading and an interest in influencing the construction of the new security architecture in Europe made the Balkans the central theatre of operations for all the Nordic countries in the 1990s. The third event shaping the Nordic threat perceptions and subsequent force deployments was the September 11 attacks on the World Trade Center and the Pentagon. As was the case in other Western countries, the Nordics reacted by giving priority to the international fight against terrorism. Military personnel from all four Nordic states quickly became involved in operations related to the fight against terrorism, and it will remain a key determinant of Nordic deployment decisions in the foreseeable future.[17]

Agreement on where NORDCAPS should be used?

The Nordic consensus on threats and values has not surprisingly translated itself into a strong convergence in their post-Cold War deployment patterns (see Table 8.4). The number of peace operations with only one Nordic participant (not shown) is very small indeed. Most operations have either none or two or more Nordic participants. The two NATO members Denmark and Norway usually participate in the same operations and this is also true for Finland and Sweden. The increased willingness of the latter pair to participate in NATO-led operations will undoubtedly increase the number of operations with participation from all four countries, and the growing number of EU-led operations is likely to have the same effect.[18] Supporting EU-led operations is a priority in all four countries, and the Danish government is actively trying to get rid of its EU defence opt-out so that Denmark can play its 'rightful' role in these operations. Since the UN is less of a priority than it used to be, the prospects for joint Nordic action seem less bright in UN-led operations. SHIRBRIG should obviously enhance the scope for such action, but both Finland (200 personnel to UNMEE) and Sweden (80 personnel to MONUC in Democratic Republic of Congo and 230 personnel to UNMIL in Liberia) have made contributions to UN-led operations outside this framework in 2003 and

Table 8.4 Peace operations initiated after 1987 involving troops from two or more Nordic countries[a]

Area	Mission	Organization/ Lead nation	Duration	DK	SF	N	S
Namibia	UNTAG	UN	1989–90	X	X	..	..
The Gulf	UN naval embargo	USA	1990–91	X	..	X	..
Somalia	UNOSOM	UN	1992–94	..	..	X	X
Macedonia	UNPROFOR/ UNPREDEP	UN	1993–99	X	X	X	X
Adriatic Sea	Sharp Guard	NATO	1993–96	X	..	X	..
Bosnia	Deny Flight	NATO	1993–95	X	..	X	..
Bosnia	UNPROFOR	UN	1993–95	X	..	X	X
Bosnia	IFOR/SFOR	NATO	1996–	X	X	X	X
Serbia/ Kosovo	Allied Force	NATO	1999	X	..	X	..
Albania	AFOR	NATO	1999	X	..	X	..
Kosovo	KFOR	NATO	1999–	X	X	X	X
Ethiopia/ Eritrea	UNMEE	UN	2000–01	X	..	..	X
Macedonia	Amber Fox	NATO	2001–02	X	..	X	..
Mediterranean	Active Endeavour	NATO	2001–03	X	..	X	..
Afghanistan	Enduring Freedom	USA	2002–03	X	..	X	..
Afghanistan	ISAF	UK, TR, D, NATO	2002–	X	X	X	X
Macedonia	Allied Harmony	NATO	2002–03	X	..	X	..
Macedonia	Concordia	EU	2003	..	X	X	X
Iraq	Iraqi Freedom (post-war)	USA	2003–	X	..	X	..
Liberia	UNMIL	UN	2003	X	..	X	..
Sudan	UMIS	UN	2005–	X	X	X	X

Notes
a   Military observers are not included.

2004. Denmark and Norway, in contrast, relied on SHIRBRIG to make their contributions (20 personnel) to UNMIL in 2003.

In sum, the Nordic deployment record since 1987 gives some reason for optimism concerning the future of NORDCAPS. The scope for joint deployments is considerable since the Nordics tend to participate in the same missions. Agreement on the choice of missions is no guarantee that the NORDCAPS option will be chosen, however. This will also require agreement on how it should be used.

Agreement on how NORDCAPS should be used?

This question has both operational and strategic dimensions. At the operational level, the question is related to mission types and the legal requirements for using force beyond self-defence (how NORDCAPS should be used in actual missions). At the strategic and political level, the question is related to the priority and role NORDCAPS is assigned in the foreign and security policy of the four principal members (how NORDCAPS should be used as a policy instrument).

At the operational level, the four Nordic countries have already made a brigade-size force available for traditional peacekeeping as well as enforcement of ceasefires/peace agreements. By 2006 the ambition is to make NORDCAPS available for the full spectrum of peace operations which, if taken literally, must include offensive enforcement operations as well. The current ambition is realistic. Peacekeeping and ceasefire/peace agreement enforcement is business as usual for the Nordics who have all committed troops to such operations since the mid-1990s. The same cannot be said for the 2006 ambition, however. This ambition does not seem realistic in light of the Finnish and Swedish unwillingness to participate in enforcement operations involving offensive use of force. Denmark and Norway have participated in such operations in Kosovo and Afghanistan, but there is absolutely no political support for such endeavours in Finland and Sweden.

A Nordic consensus to go beyond enforcement of peace agreements by 2006 consequently does not seem likely. It cannot be completely ruled out, however, as the joint EU battle group that Finland, Norway and Sweden announced their intention to establish in the autumn of 2004 could pave the way for Finnish and Swedish participation in offensive enforcement operations. The new battle group is expected to become operational in 2008.[19]

The requirement for a UN mandate in operations with Chapter VII authority presents another complication for the 2006 ambition. Only Denmark and Norway have thus far been willing to use force beyond self-defence without a UN mandate, and nothing suggests that Finland and Sweden will be willing to do so in the foreseeable future. Thus, a Nordic consensus on using NORDCAPS for such operations is not around the corner either. A final complication is presented by the Danish defence opt-out that prevents Denmark from participating in all EU-led peace support operations with military personnel. As mentioned above, this has not prevented the other three Nordic countries from establishing a joint EU battle group.

The answer to the question of how NORDCAPS should be used at the operational level is, in short, that the Nordics can agree on using NORDCAPS for operations mandated by the UN that do not go beyond enforcement of peace agreements. This consensus does not necessarily mean that NORDCAPS will be used as the framework for organizing such deployments, however. Contributions can also be organized within the EU, NATO or the UN, or *ad hoc* as part of a coalition of the willing, and, as Table 8.5 demonstrates, the alternatives have generally been

Table 8.5 Joint Nordic military deployments in peace operations initiated after 1987[a]

Joint units	Duration
Nordic Battalion in UNPROFOR/UNPREDEP (NORDBAT 1)	1993–99
Nordic Battalion in UNPROFOR (NORDBAT 2)	1993–95
Nordic–Polish Brigade in IFOR and SFOR (NORDPOLBDE)	1995–99
Nordic–Polish Battle Group in SFOR (NPBG)	2000–02
Swedish mine clearing unit in the Finnish battalion in Lebanon	2000
Joint Norwegian (lead nation)–Danish HQ in Kosovo	2001

Notes
a   Observer missions are not included.

preferred to joint Nordic options in the post-Cold War era. The joint Nordic option has only been chosen in six of the twenty cases in which two or more Nordic states have participated in the same operation since 1987. If we count the joint contributions to IFOR/SFOR as one, the total is down to five. While this represents a clear improvement compared to the Cold War, when only one joint deployment was made (the Danish–Norwegian battalion (DANOR) in UNEF I), there is no escaping the conclusion that joint Nordic deployments remain rather exceptional.

The failure to deploy a joint Nordic unit in KFOR in 1999 is especially noteworthy. A joint deployment seemed an obvious choice at the time since the Nordics could have built on the successful experiences from the joint deployment in IFOR/SFOR. Although the initial experience with the Nordic–Polish Brigade in IFOR was marred by many problems related to communications, language, logistics, national restrictions and different national ROE,[20] the situation gradually improved as a result of lessons learned, and in a number of areas the joint deployment in SFOR evolved into a real success story. The Nordic (logistical) support group in SFOR is thus considered one of the most successful examples of multilateral cooperation in the entire operation. All national support elements, except the Norwegian, were co-located in Pecs, and economies of scale were achieved in the administration and in the procurement and distribution of 'common use items' such as water, fresh food and petrol.[21] Intelligence was another area where successful cooperation eventually led to the establishment of a joint Nordic intelligence cell.[22]

Yet in spite of these positive experiences the Nordics refrained from deploying a joint unit in KFOR. Denmark wanted to build on the success in Bosnia and continue the cooperation in Kosovo,[23] but these plans collapsed in part because Finland and Sweden gave higher priority to securing a place in the British sector. The end result was that the Finnish, Norwegian and Swedish contingents went to serve in the British sector whereas the Danish contingent was deployed in the French sector.[24] A plan to deploy a joint Finnish–Swedish battalion in KFOR also came to naught. The Swedish High Command fought the plan vigorously arguing that it would compromise the security of the personnel. Their argument, also used on other occasions when joint Nordic units have been contemplated, was that it is too dangerous to form multinational units below the battalion level.[25] As a result, the plan was finally dropped at a time when the two contingents were engaged in joint training at SWEDINT.[26]

In theatre, it is clear that Finland, Sweden and Norway benefited from their co-deployment in the British sector. Their cooperation is universally praised by officers from all three nations, and one of the KFOR commanders, Juan Ortuño Such, joined the choir hailing the Nordic intelligence cell in Kosovo as an example of intelligence integration for others to follow.[27] The problems with communications, language, national restrictions and differences in the national ROE largely appear to be a thing of the past. In spite of this, Finland, Norway and Sweden decided not to make a joint contribution through NORDCAPS to KFOR, an option they discussed in late 2003.[28] A proposal for deploying a joint NORDCAPS provincial reconstruction team (PRT) in Afghanistan in the summer of 2004 suffered the same fate.[29]

The Nordic deployment pattern since 1987 consequently does not provide any firm clues about the prospects for joint NORDCAPS deployments in the future. One the one hand, the number of joint deployments has increased. On the other hand, joint deployments remain very much the exception. To get a better idea about the future of NORDCAPS, it is therefore necessary to examine how the NORDCAPS option is viewed in the Nordic capitals.

In Copenhagen the answer is 'vaguely, if at all'. Speaking off-the-record, senior officers and MoD officials make no bones about the fact that they regard NORDCAPS as a waste of time. At best, NORDCAPS is seen as a way of helping Finland and Sweden into NATO and Norway into the EU. At worst, it is viewed as a duplication of capacities established within NATO, or as unwelcome competition to SHIRBRIG.[30] For the military NATO is the only game in town. NATO standards and procedures are regarded as the key to operational effectiveness regardless of the institutional setting employed (coalitions of the willing, EU, NATO or UN).[31] NORDCAPS is not viewed as very attractive because it is not 100 per cent NATO-interoperable and not up to NATO standards. Unlike their Nordic colleagues, Danish officers do not view NORDCAPS as a way of enhancing Danish influence in NATO. This is in their view best done inside the alliance itself. Thus, it is no coincidence that Denmark has refrained from taking the lead in developing any of NORDCAPS's multinational units.

The current Danish government (from November 2001) shares the military's lack of enthusiasm for Nordic cooperation. Danish ministers stayed away from at least four meetings with their Nordic colleagues in 2003, the Danish prime minister decided not to join the other Nordic prime ministers on a trip to thank the Thai government for its efforts to help the Nordic victims of the tsunami in January 2005,[32] and Nordic cooperation, traditionally one of the four cornerstones in Danish foreign policy, was conspicuous by its absence in the foreign policy white paper, *A Changing World*, published in June 2003.[33] NORDCAPS is, in short, not really seen as an option in Copenhagen at the moment. The reason is that the foreign and security policy establishment in Denmark views NATO, the EU and *ad hoc* coalitions with the USA as the best avenues for promoting Danish interests, and that SHIRBRIG (a Danish prestige project) is the preferred option for UN-led operations. This does not rule out Danish participation in joint NORDCAPS deployments, but it does mean that NORDCAPS rarely will be seen as the first option of choice.

It is not just in Denmark that Nordic cooperation is seen as less important than it used to be, however. This is also true in the other Nordic countries. In Finland as Hanna Ojanen has noted:

> [I]nterest in Nordic issues has declined following EU membership: the EU has rapidly become central both in practical politics and as a factor of identification. Finland channels its policies primarily through the EU, adapting goals to what is already on the agenda.[34]

This observation is supported by Finnish President Tarja Halonen's unsentimental approach to Nordic cooperation within the EU. In her view, it is simply one option among many: 'There are no permanent alliances; instead coalitions of countries vary from one issue to the next'.[35] That cooperation with Britain was given a higher priority than Nordic cooperation in KFOR serves as a further illustration of this point. At the same time, NORDCAPS is clearly a priority in Helsinki. According to the Finnish Ministry of Defence: 'The EU provides the most important framework for Finland's Defence Forces' international activities ... Our first priority is to take part in EU-led peace operations in the Nordic framework'.[36]

Their colleagues in the Ministry of Foreign Affairs agree. When asked to rank Finland's partners of choice for peace operations, the Nordic countries top the list followed by Britain, the EU and the USA.[37] A major reason for this enthusiasm is that it is much easier to legitimize Finnish participation in peace operations when it takes place within a Nordic setting. The Finnish rapprochement to NATO would have been extremely difficult to legitimize at home, had it not been couched within Nordic cooperation. Helsinki was an early supporter of expanding the Nordic cooperation on peace operations before the NORDCAPS initiative was taken,[38] and Finnish officials have no difficulty in envisaging the use of NORDCAPS. To give but one example, in 2000 the Finnish chief of defence Admiral Juhani Kaskeala (wrongly) envisaged the deployment of a NORDCAPS brigade in Kosovo by 2003.[39]

Norway is equally positive. Norway proposed the establishment of NORDCAPS and has played an important role in its development.

NORDCAPS has become an important instrument in the Norwegian 'troops-for-influence' strategy pursued in relation to the EU and NATO,[40] and in the Norwegian efforts to maintain the high Nordic profile in peace operations. In Oslo's reading of the situation, the Nordic position is under threat because the increased involvement of the great powers effectively has made brigade-size contributions the minimum requirement for operational influence and autonomy. Oslo regards NORDCAPS as a cost-effective solution to this problem since none of the Nordics have the capacity to field such contributions on their own.[41] NORDCAPS is, in short, a priority in Oslo both in its own right and as a way of enhancing Norwegian influence in the EU, NATO and the UN.

Cost-effectiveness and the need to field brigade-size contributions in order to obtain a higher profile and greater influence in operations led by the EU, NATO and the UN are also seen as NORDCAPS advantages in Stockholm.[42] NORDCAPS is seen as a counterweight to great power dominance within the EU,[43] and as a way of facilitating Swedish participation in NATO-led operations. Military cooperation with NATO would be hard to legitimize outside the Nordic framework, and the cooperation with the Nordic NATO members within NORDCAPS is seen as crucial for the Swedish efforts to enhance NATO interoperability. Thus, Stockholm has no trouble envisaging the use of NORDCAPS in future operations. Indeed, for former Swedish Supreme Commander Johan Hederstedt NORDCAPS is the preferred option when Sweden's armed forces are deployed abroad,[44] and former Swedish Defence Minister Bjørn von Sydow concurs: 'The long-term objective should be to be able to send a joint Nordic peace-promoting brigade whenever the need arises'.[45]

In sum, the analysis of the 'how' question suggests joint NORDCAPS deployments involving Finnish, Norwegian and Swedish troops to be feasible, both technically and politically, in operations mandated by the UN that do not go beyond enforcement of peace agreements. All three nations regard NORDCAPS as a useful instrument to enhance their profile and influence in peace operations led by the EU, NATO and the UN. For Finland and Sweden, NORDCAPS serves as a back door to NATO, whereas Norway can use it as a back door to the EU. It is also seen as a way of saving money in all three capitals, and their cooperation within NORDCAPS also led to the establishment of their joint aerial supply of their contingents in Afghanistan and Africa.[46] Although NORDCAPS is not a priority in Copenhagen, Danish participation in a joint NORDCAPS brigade participating in a NATO-led operation cannot be ruled out. The same will be true for EU-led operations if the Danish defence opt-out in the EU is overturned in a future referendum. As has been the case in the past, Copenhagen is likely to take a pragmatic attitude towards the Nordic option and employ it when useful.

A new model in the making?

A new effective model has emerged with NORDCAPS as its core. The expanded and updated NORDCAPS training programme and the publication of new training manuals allow the Nordics to continue to influence training standards and peace operations doctrine at the international level. This influence is evident in the increased training assistance provided to the Baltic states and African regional organizations with respect to establishing multinational forces for peace operations.

With respect to force generation, the new NORDCAPS model is more comprehensive and more integrated than its predecessor. It enables the Nordics to provide sizable military contingents to peacekeeping and enforcement operations, not involving offensive operations, as well as critical enablers in high demand such as logistics, headquarters staff, combat support services and communications. This is sufficient to give the Nordics a greater say in the planning and running of EU- and NATO-led operations and a commanding influence in UN operations where they could provide the largest contingents and act as lead nations. NORDCAPS might even provide a tri-service force package if the plan for air and sea components goes ahead. This would give the Nordics a capacity that only the great powers provide for peace operations at present.

Finally, NORDCAPS enjoys a number of advantages compared to some of the other force pools and rapid reaction arrangements in which the Nordic countries take part. It is cost-effective due to its multinational logistics, combat support and communication and information systems; it will make participation in peace operations easier to legitimize, especially in Finland and Sweden; the similarities in the Nordic strategic cultures facilitates its use; and the lessons learned and positive operational experiences that the Nordic cooperation has resulted in since the end of the Cold War makes it a well-tested and trustworthy option.

All these improvements may not be sufficient to ensure that Nordic will remain a 'brand name' in the field of peace operations, however. The possibility pointed to by Eknes in 1995 that the Nordic profile might be dissolved in a larger network is still very real. Nordic cooperation does not enjoy the same level of support in all the Nordic governments that it used to. Although, Finland, Norway and Sweden, as we have seen, regard Nordic cooperation within NORDCAPS as a useful instrument for enhancing their influence within the EU, NATO and the UN, it is no longer is the only game in town. In the post-Cold War era, influence and prestige within the field of peace operations can also be obtained through other channels such as bilateral cooperation with the great powers or through informal alliances within the EU and NATO. Indeed, Denmark has all but abandoned Nordic cooperation in favour of these new channels. The problem for NORDCAPS is, in short, that the Nordic countries individually can use several other options to maintain a high national profile in peace operations.

Denmark has arguably succeeded in doing so by pursuing a very activist policy within the UN and NATO in the post-Cold War era. Moreover, the most notable 'Nordic' successes in the post-Cold War era, SHIRBRIG which the *Brahimi Report* held up as a model for others to follow, BALTBAT and the multinational Baltic Defence College which served as the model for the defence college established in Bosnia-Herzegovina, all included non-Nordic countries. This suggests that the old Nordic profile may be difficult to preserve. It would at a minimum require new initiatives enabling the Nordic countries to make high-profile contributions which set them apart from the other players in the field.

Enhancing the Nordic profile: proposals for strengthening the new Nordic model

Establishing a fully fledged civilian rapid reaction component within NORDCAPS would be the most cost-effective way to give the Nordic brand name a longer shelf life. As pointed out in Chapter 3, it remains a challenge for the international community to get qualified civilian experts deployed in the right place at the right time in the right numbers. It was a problem in Kosovo and East Timor in 1999 and the problem repeated itself in Afghanistan in 2002 and again in Iraq the following year. These were all high-profile operations enjoying the support of Western great powers, and if it is a problem on such operations, it is a problem in all operations.[47] The civilian rapid reaction arrangements established by the EU, the OSCE and the UN remain works in progress and their effectiveness is limited by a lack of capacity and a lack of political will on the part of the member states.

The Nordics have responded to the 'civilian' challenge by establishing their own civilian rapid reaction arrangements, and they are all providing personnel for the rapid reaction arrangements set up by the EU, the UN and the OSCE. However, besides the establishment of a joint Nordic police commanders course held once a year in Stockholm and some joint training between the Nordic rescue services,[48] surprisingly little cooperation is taking place at the Nordic level. Part of the reason is no doubt that the establishment of civilian capacities to a large extent has been driven by the EU. Influencing the establishment of the EU capacity has been a priority in all the Nordic capitals, and proposals to establish a joint Nordic capacity have thus been dismissed as a wasteful duplication of the efforts undertaken within the EU.[49] While the interest in influencing the EU capacity – by far the most comprehensive and ambitious in the world – is obvious, the lack of interest in the establishment of a Nordic capacity is not. The existence of alternative military arrangements has not led to the termination of NORDCAPS. On the contrary, NORDCAPS is seen as a very useful instrument for influencing developments in the EU, NATO and the UN in all the Nordic capitals, except Copenhagen; and even here few would go so far as to recommend its termination.

The argument that the existence of alternative arrangements renders a Nordic civilian arrangement superfluous is therefore less than compelling. It goes without saying that a Nordic civilian arrangement should use the same standards and procedures as the EU, the UN and the OSCE in order to ensure interoperability with personnel from other nations. Developing a Nordic capacity that is not 100 per cent interoperable with the principal international organizations involved in civilian operations would indeed be a waste of time and resources. However, a Nordic civilian rapid reaction capacity that was interoperable with the principal players would give the Nordic countries a number of political and operational advantages.

The combined Nordic civilian capacity (see Table 8.6) makes it possible to develop indispensable niche capabilities in short supply that would enhance their political profile and give the Nordic countries a lead-nation capacity. Civilian rule-of-law teams (judges, jailers, prosecutors and correctional staff), civilian administration teams, and police mission leadership teams are examples of such capabilities. These capabilities can also be established within other multinational settings but Nordic teams would be easier to deploy and more effective. If we compare a joint Nordic capacity to that of the EU, which is the most advanced in the world, then it would be far easier for the Nordic countries to agree on swift action. The similarities in their strategic cultures and national decision-making procedures are far greater than is the case in the EU at large, and it is far easier for five than 25 states to agree on joint action at short notice. The establishment of the EU civilian rapid reaction force is hampered by heavy bureaucratic infighting over turf between the Commission and the Council Secretariat, and lack of political will from EU member states. Although the EU members have committed a total of 5,000 police to the EU rapid reaction capacity, they were not able to find the 650 police required for the EU Police Mission in Bosnia and the Proxima police mission in Macedonia in 2003. Financing and procurement also emerged as major problems preventing rapid reaction that had not been overcome in mid-2005.[50]

Table 8.6 Nordic civilian contributions to the EU (May 2004)

	Police	Rule of law	Civil protection	Civil administration
Denmark	125	9	320	24
Finland	75	25	196	16
Norway	80	30	18	. .
Sweden	170	10	262	30
EU total	5,000	282	2083	248

Sources: EU Council Secretariat, Norwegian Ministry of Justice.

Nordic teams would also be more effective than EU teams due to their shared cultural and educational background. To give an example, the northern members of the EU take a different view of policing in peace operations than the southern members.[51]Moreover, effective cooperation and coordination between the civilian and military rapid reaction forces will also be easier to achieve within the smaller and more homogenous Nordic setting than within the EU, where this has proved very difficult.[52]

A joint Nordic civilian capacity would also make political sense from a Nordic perspective as it would enable the Nordics to offer specialized force packages in high demand that would enhance their influence and prestige in the EU, NATO and the UN. The usefulness of such packages would be further enhanced if they were modelled on the SHIRBRIG 'first in, first out' concept. This concept has at least three advantages: it enhances the Nordic profile as the first wave gets the most attention, the problem of sustainability that the Nordics are facing due to their limited personnel pool is removed as one only has to deploy for a limited period of time (six months if the SHIRBRIG model is employed), and it will be easier to attract volunteers since the adventurous prefer to go in on the first wave.

The establishment of a joint Nordic civilian rapid reaction capacity would not only enable the Nordics to offer much sought after civilian capacities at short notice. It would also enable them to establish unique joint civil–military force packages with a higher degree of integration than is the case in the existing rapid reaction arrangements. Effective civil–military coordination and cooperation have been a problem on all the major peace operations conducted since the end of the Cold War, so the Nordics could really add value in this area.

CIMIC would be the best place to start such a process for two reasons. The first is that the Nordic armies and the Nordic civilian organizations already have established a habit of cooperation and coordination in this area. The second is that it is a high priority in Finland and Sweden. While this is not the case to the same extent in Denmark and Norway, CIMIC units have also played an increasing role in their contributions to peace operations in recent years. All four Nordic nations have thus contributed CIMIC personnel to the ISAF operation in Afghanistan suggesting that it should be possible to extend Nordic cooperation to this area as well.[53]

The case for establishing a civilian counterpart to NORDCAPS is, in sum, overwhelming. It would allow the Nordics to reassert themselves as leaders within the field of peace operations by setting examples for others to follow. It would be cost-effective and enhance the Nordic standing and influence within the EU, NATO and the UN as well as operational effectiveness. A new Nordic model with rapid reaction civilian and military capacities would enable the Nordics to preserve the traditional high Nordic profile in peace operations. Without such a model this profile is in danger of being lost.

Notes

1. Quoted from Eknes, Åge (1995) 'The Nordic Countries and UN Peacekeeping Operations', in Åge Eknes (ed.) *The Nordic Countries in the United Nations: Status and Future Perspectives* (Copenhagen: Nordic Council), p. 81 (65–83).
2. This definition of strategic culture is inspired by Alfred Van Staden *et al.* who define their key term 'strategic concept' in a similar way. See Van Staden, Alfred, Kees Homan, Bert Kreemers, Alfred Pijpers and Rob de Wijk (2000) *Towards a European Strategic Concept* (The Hague: Netherlands Institute of International Relations, Clingendael), p. 5.
3. The defence opt-out prevents Denmark from participating in EU-led operations.
4. *Pressemelding* No. 33/2003 'Island inn i nordisk forsvarssamarbeid', 3 September 2003 (Oslo: Forsvarsdepartementet).
5. *Nordcaps PSO Tactical Manual Vol. I and II* (Helsinki: NORDCAPS, 2002).
6. For an overview of NORDCAPS courses see the NORDCAPS website: <www.nordcaps.org/pages/courses>. These courses are all open to non-Nordic nationals.
7. See the SHIRBRIG website: <www.shirbrig.dk>; and Jakobsen, Peter Viggo (2002) 'UN Peace Operations in Africa Today and Tomorrow', in Michael Bothe and Boris Kondoch (eds) *The Yearbook of International Peace Operations, Volume 7, 2001* (The Hague: Klüwer Press International), p. 167 (153–180).
8. UN News Service (2004) 'Press Briefing by UN Readiness Brigade', 23 June. <http://www.un.org/News/briefings/docs/2004/SHIRBIRG.brf.doc.htm> (15 September 2004).
9. As of mid-2005, the 16 members were: Argentina, Austria, Canada, Denmark, Finland, Italy, Ireland, Lithuania, Netherlands, Norway, Poland, Portugal, Romania, Slovenia, Spain and Sweden. Argentina had temporarily suspended its membership. The fiev observers were: Chile, Czech Republic, Hungary, Jordan and Senegal. See the SHIRBRIG website: <www.shirbrig.dk>.
10. Brett, Julian Elgaard (2002) *No New Dividing Lines. Danish Defence Support to the Baltic States* (Copenhagen: Danish Institute of International Affairs), p. 23.
11. HOK Presse (2003) 'Det danske kontingent i Irak DANCON/IRAK hold 2', <www.hok.dk>, 30 September.
12. Gustafsson, Håkan (2001) 'Nordiskt bistånd till balterna men med vilken ambition?' (Stockholm: Strategiska institutionen, Försvarshögskolan; C-uppsats 19 100:1030), p. 57; Ministry of Defence, Republic of Latvia 'Participation in Peace-keeping Mission in Kosovo', <http://www.mod. gov.lv/index.php?pid=13169> (30 November 2004).
13. See *Baggrundsnotat vedrørende brigadeprojekter i Estland, Letland og Litauen*, CHODO3, 20 June 2003; Ministry of Defence (2003) 'Nordic Defence Ministers Plan Joint Contribution to Kosovo', press release, 24 November.
14. NORDCAPS website: <www.nordcaps.org> (21 November 2003).
15. Fridberg, Anders V. (2002) 'NORDCAPS tager form', *FOV Nyhedsbrev*, No. 23, p. 9.
16. Løwer, Elbjørg (1999) *Humanitær intervensjon. Indlæg ved militær etisk fagseminar 14–15 september i Oslo Militære Samfund* (Oslo: Forsvars-departementet); Halonen, Tarja (2000) *Crises and Crisis Management. Lecture by President of the Republic Tarja Halonen at the Norwegian Institute of International Affairs (NUPI) in Oslo on 26 October* (Helsinki: Office of the President of the Republic of Finland); Lindh, Anna (1998) *Sweden in Europe.*

Address at the Swedish Institute of International Affairs, Stockholm 16 December (Stockholm: Ministry of Foreign Affairs); Petersen, Niels Helveg (1996) *Statement by the Minister for Foreign Affairs at the 51st session of the General Assembly on September 24th, 1996* (New York: Permanent Mission of Denmark to the United Nations).

17. Heløe, Gunnar (2003) *Norges deltagelse i internasjonale militære operasjoner: Hvorfor, hvor og hvordan. Foredrag på høstseminar på Forsvarets høyskole 19 November* (Oslo: Forsvarsdepartementet); Enestam, Jan-Erik (2002) *New Threats, New Challenges: A Finnish View. Remarks at the CSIS, Washington, DC, 11 April* (Helsinki: Ministry of Defence, 2002); Lindh, Anna and Erkki Tuomioja (2002) 'Gemensamt EU-förslag från Sveriges och Finlands utrikesministrar: Kontrakt tvingar alla agera mot terror', *Dagens Nyheter*, 18 December, p. A04; Rasmussen, Anders Fogh (2003) *Danmark i verden. Tale ved Forsvarsakademiets årsdag fredag den 31. oktober 2003* (København: Statsministeriet).

18. For a list of EU- and NATO-led peace operations see Appendixes 9 and 10, respectively.

19. Kirk, Lisbeth (2004) 'Sweden and Finland Announce Joint EU Battle Group', *EUobserver.com*, 25 October, < http://euobserver.com/?aid=17443&sid=13 > (27 October 2004); *Pressemelding* No. 24/2004 'Regjeringen går inn for deltagelse i nordisk innsatsstyrke for EU fra 2008', 18 November 2004 (Oslo: Forsvarsdepartementet).

20. Grandhagen, Kjell (1997) 'Med IFOR til Bosnia-Herzegovina. Erfaringer fra den Nordisk-Polske brigade', *Norsk Militært Tidsskrift*, Vol. 166, No. 2, pp. 17–19, 42–46; Holmen, Bengt and Ståle Ulriksen (2000) 'Norden i felt: På oppdrag for FN og NATO', *NUPI-rapport*, No. 257 (Oslo: Norsk Utenrikspolitisk Institutt), pp. 27–28; and conversations with Nordic officers serving in the Nordic–Polish Brigade in IFOR.

21. Holmen and Ulriksen, 'Norden i felt: På oppdrag for FN og NATO', pp. 27–28; Kochanowski, Franciszek (2000) 'Participation of the Polish Armed Forces in Peacekeeping Missions in the Nineties', in *Yearbook of Polish Foreign Policy 2000* (Warsaw: Ministry of Foreign Affairs), < http://msz.gov.pl/warecka/yearbook/2000/2000.html >.

22. Interviews with Swedish MoD official, 22 May 2002 and Finnish MoD official, 24 May 2002.

23. Hækkerup, Hans (2002) *På skansen* (København: Lindhardt & Ringhof), pp. 58–59.

24. One Danish officer involved in the process later likened the Nordic competition for places in the British sector to the Second World War race for Berlin in an off-the-record conversation with the author.

25. The Swedish supreme commander also used this argument to reject a proposal for a joint Nordic battalion in SFOR when the initial contributions were reduced. See Hækkerup, *På skansen*, pp. 58–59.

26. Hellberg, Anders and Stefan Lisinski (1999) 'Strid om Kosovostyrka. Militären: Politikerna väljer alltid det sämsta och billigaste alternativet', *Dagens Nyheter*, 18 March, p. A05. The Finnish High Command shared the concerns expressed by their Swedish colleagues but consented to the establishment of the joint force. *Virtual Finland* 'Finnish Foreign Policy 1999: May' (Ministry for Foreign Affairs of Finland). < http://virtual.finland.fi/finfo/english/ chronology/chrono1999_05.html >.

27. Valpolini, Paolo (2000) 'Interview with Lt Gen Juan Ortuño Such, Commander Kosovo Force and Commander Eurocorps', *Jane's Defence Weekly*, Vol. 3, No. 1 (2 August).

28. Ministry of Defence, 'Nordic defence ministers plan joint contribution to Kosovo'.
29. The proposal is discussed in Grüne, Yrsa (2004) 'Finland med i nordisk Afghanistanoperation', *Hufvudstadsbladet*, 11 January, p. 4.
30. This conclusion is based on several off-the-record conversations with senior officers and Ministry of Defence officials in recent years.
31. *De sikkerhedspolitiske vilkår for dansk forsvarspolitik* (København: Udenrigsministeriet, 2003), p. 18.
32. Eriksson, Göran (2005) 'Statsministrar får audiens', *Dagens Nyheter*, 14 January, p. A07; Moll, Jakob (2003) 'Tomme danske sæder i Norden', *Fyens Stiftstidende*, 18 August.
33. *A Changing World: The Government's Vision for New Priorities in Denmark's Foreign Policy* (Copenhagen: Ministry of Foreign Affairs, 2003), p. 8.
34. Ojanen, Hanna (2000) 'Participation and Influence: Finland, Sweden and the Post-Amsterdam Development of the CFSP', *Occasional Papers*, No. 11 (Paris: Institute for Security Studies Western European Union, January), p. 4.
35. Halonen, Tarja (2001) *A Finnish Solution – Active Membership of the European Union. Speech by President of the Republic Tarja Halonen to Dansk Udenrigspolitisk Selskab (Danish International Affairs Society) at Christiansborg on 4 April 2001.* (Helsinki: Office of the President of Finland).
36. *Finnish Defence and the Challenge of International Crisis Management* (Helsinki: Ministry of Defence of Finland, 2001), pp. 1–2.
37. Interviews with Finnish MFA officials, 24 May 2002.
38. Hækkerup, *På skansen*, p. 59.
39. Grüne, Yrsa (2000) 'Admiral Juhani Kaskeala om Kfors framtid: Nordisk brigad helt möjlig', *Hufvudstadsbladet*, 16 December, p. 6
40. Græger, Nina (2002) 'Norway and the EU Security and Defence Dimension: A "Troops-for-Influence" Strategy', in Nina Græger, Henrik Larsen and Hanna Ojanen (eds) *The ESDP and the Nordic Countries. Four Variations on a Theme* (Helsinki: Finnish Institute of International Affairs; Berlin: Institut für Europäische Politik), pp. 33–89.
41. *NORDCAPS* (Oslo: Ministry of Foreign Affairs, 2002).
42. Hederstedt, Johan (1999) *Internationalisera försvaret!* (Stockholm: Försvarsdepartementet), pp. 18–20; Rosenius, Frank (2000) 'Sveriges försvarsmakt – under radikal förandring', *Norsk Militært Tidsskrift*, Vol. 69, No. 6/7, p. 46 (42–46); interview at SWEDINT, 21 May 2002.
43. Interviews with Swedish MFA officials, 21 May 2002.
44. Johan Hederstedt made this remark at an information lunch at the Swedish embassy in Copenhagen on 26 September 2001.
45. Sydow, Bo von (1999) *Sweden's Security in the 21st Century* (Stockholm: Ministry of Defence), p. 16.
46. Devold, Kristin Krohn (2002) *Forsvarspolitisk redegjørelse ved forsvarsminister Kristin Krohn Devold. Nordisk råds 54. sesjon, Helsingfors 31 October* (Oslo: Forsvarsdepartementet); Rønne, Jahn (2003) 'Saving Money on Nordic Transport', Forsvarsnett (www.mil.no), 20 March.
47. de Mello, Sergio Vieira (2000) 'How Not to Run a Country: Lessons for the UN from Kosovo and East Timor', unpublished manuscript.
48. *The Nordic Countries and International Peace-keeping Operations* (Oslo: Ministry of Foreign Affairs, 1999).
49. For one such proposal see the report from the Nordic Council *Presidiets rapport om konfliktförebyggande och civil krishantering* (København: Nordisk Råd, ANP 2001:737), pp. 20, 32.

50. Jakobsen, Peter Viggo (2004) 'The Emerging EU Civilian Crisis Management Capacity – A 'Real Added Value' for the UN?', background paper for the *Copenhagen Seminar on Civilian Crisis Management* arranged by the Royal Danish Ministry of Foreign Affairs, 8–9 June, p. 10.
51. Interview at the National Police Board in Stockholm, 22 May 2002.
52. Bloom, Frida (2001) 'Sweden Still Struggling for Civilian Aspects of EU Crisis Management', *PENN Newsletter*, No. 14 (May) (Berlin: Project on European Nuclear Non-Proliferation), pp. 4–5; Hansen, Kenneth Smith and Casper Klynge (2001) *EU og civil krisestyring* (København: Dansk Udenrigspolitisk Institut), pp. 67–69, 73, 77–78; interviews with EU officials, 6 May 2004.
53. For a proposal to include CIMIC in NORDCAPS see Eriksson, Pär (1998) *Civil–militär samverkan på taktisk nivå i fredsfrämjande operationer. Motiv, metoder och förutsättningar* (Stockholm: FOA, FOA-R–98-00968-170–SE), pp. 46–47.

Appendix 1

UN mission acronyms

DOMREP	Mission of the Representative of the Secretary-General in the Dominican Republic
MICIVIH	International Civilian Mission in Haiti
MINUCI	United Nations Mission in Côte d'Ivoire
MINURCA	United Nations Mission in the Central African Republic
MINURSO	United Nations Mission for the Referendum in Western Sahara
MINUSTAH	United Nations Stabilization Mission in Haiti
MIPONUH	United Nations Civilian Police Mission in Haiti
MONUA	United Nations Observer Mission in Angola
MONUC	United Nations Organization Mission in Democratic Republic of Congo
ONUB	United Nations Operation in Burundi
ONUC	United Nations Operation in the Congo
ONUCA	United Nations Observer Group in Central America
ONUMOZ	United Nations Operation in Mozambique
ONUSAL	United Nations Observer Mission in El Salvador
ONUVEN	United Nations Observer Mission in Nicaragua
UNAMET	United Nations Mission in East Timor
UNAMIC	United Nations Advance Mission in Cambodia
UNAMIR	United Nations Assistance Mission for Rwanda
UNAMSIL	United Nations Mission in Sierra Leone
UNASOG	United Nations Aouzou Strip Observer Group
UNAVEM I	United Nations Angola Verification Mission I
UNAVEM II	United Nations Angola Verification Mission II
UNAVEM III	United Nations Angola Verification Mission III
UNCRO	United Nations Confidence Restoration Organization in Croatia

UNDOF	United Nations Disengagement Observer Force
UNEF I	First United Nations Emergency Force
UNEF II	Second United Nations Emergency Force
UNFICYP	United Nations Peacekeeping Force in Cyprus
UNGCI	United Nations Guards Contingent in Iraq
UNGOMAP	United Nations Good Offices Mission in Afghanistan and Pakistan
UNIFIL	United Nations Interim Force in Lebanon
UNIIMOG	United Nations Iran–Iraq Military Observer Group
UNIKOM	United Nations Iraq–Kuwait Observation Mission
UNIPOM	United Nations India–Pakistan Observation Mission
UNMEE	United Nations Mission in Ethiopia and Eritrea
UNMIBH	United Nations Mission in Bosnia and Herzegovina
UNMIH	United Nations Mission in Haiti
UNMIK	United Nations Mission in Kosovo
UNMIL	United Nations Mission in Liberia
UNMIS	United Nations Mission in Sudan
UNMISET	United Nations Mission of Support in East Timor
UNMOGIP	United Nations Military Observer Group in India and Pakistan
UNMOP	United Nations Mission of Observers in Prevlaka
UNMOT	United Nations Mission of Observers in Tajikistan
UNOCI	United Nations Operation in Côte d'Ivoire
UNOGIL	United Nations Observation Group in Lebanon
UNOMIG	United Nations Observer Mission in Georgia
UNOMIL	United Nations Observer Mission in Liberia
UNOMSA	United Nations Observer Mission in South Africa
UNOMSIL	United Nations Observer Mission in Sierra Leone
UNOMUR	United Nations Observer Mission Uganda–Rwanda
UNOSOM I	United Nations Operation in Somalia I
UNOSOM II	United Nations Operation in Somalia II
UNOVER	United Nations Observer Mission to Verify the Referendum in Eritrea
UNPREDEP	United Nations Preventive Deployment Force
UNPROFOR	United Nations Protection Force
UNPSG	United Nations Police Support Group
UNSCOB	United Nations Special Committee on the Balkans
UNSF	United Nations Security Force in West New Guinea (West Irian)
UNSMIH	United Nations Support Mission in Haiti
UNTAC	United Nations Transitional Authority in Cambodia
UNTAES	United Nations Transitional Administration for Eastern Slavonia, Baranja and Western Sirmium
UNTAET	United Nations Transitional Administration in East Timor

UNTAG	United Nations Transition Assistance Group in Namibia
UNTEA	United Nations Temporary Executive Authority in West New Guinea (West Irian)
UNTMIH	United Nations Transition Mission in Haiti
UNTSO	United Nations Truce Supervision Organization
UNYOM	United Nations Yemen Observation Mission

Appendix 2

Non-UN mission acronyms

ECOFORCE	ECOWAS Peace Force for Côte d'Ivoire
ECOMIL	Economic Community of West African States Mission in Liberia
ECOMOG	Economic Community of West African States Ceasefire Monitoring Group
IFOR	Implementation Force
INTERFET	International Force for East Timor
ISAF	International Security Assistance Force in Afghanistan
KFOR	Kosovo Force
MISAB	Inter-African Mission to Monitor the Implementation of the Bangui Agreements
SFOR	Stabilization Force

Appendix 3

UN peace operations 1948–2005 (March)

UN-commanded peacekeeping and observer (Chapter VI) missions

Mission	Duration	Authorized strength/maximum deployment[a]
UNTSO – United Nations Truce Supervision Organization in the Middle East	June 1948–	572 M
UNMOGIP – United Nations Military Observer Group in India and Pakistan	January 1949–	109 M
UNEF I – First United Nations Emergency Force (Middle East)	November 1956– June 1967	6,073 M
UNOGIL – United Nations Observation Group in Lebanon	June–December 1958	591 M
UNSF – United Nations Security Force in West New Guinea (West Irian)	October 1962– April 1963	1,576 M
UNYOM – United Nations Yemen Observation Mission	July 1963– September 1964	189 M
UNFICYP – United Nations Peacekeeping Force in Cyprus	March 1964–	6,411 M
DOMREP – Mission of the Representative of the Secretary-General in the Dominican Republic	May 1965– October 1966	2
UNIPOM – United Nations India–Pakistan Observation Mission	September 1965– March 1966	96 M
UNEF II – Second United Nations Emergency Force (Middle East)	October 1973– July 1979	6,973 M
UNDOF – United Nations Disengagement Observer Force (Golan Heights)	June 1974–	1,450

(*continued*)

Mission	Duration	Authorized strength/maximum deployment[a]
UNIFIL – United Nations Interim Force in Lebanon	March 1978–	7000
UNGOMAP – United Nations Good Offices Mission in Afghanistan and Pakistan	May 1988– March 1990	50
UNIIMOG – United Nations Iran–Iraq Military Observer Group	August 1988– February 1991	400 M
UNAVEM I – United Nations Angola Verifications Missions I	January 1989– June 1991	70 M
UNTAG – United Nations Transition Assistance Group in Namibia	April 1989– March 1990	7,500
ONUCA – United Nations Observer Group in Central America	November 1989– January 1992	1,098 M
UNAVEM II – United Nations Angola Verifications Missions II	June 1991– February 1995	710
ONUSAL – United Nations Observer Mission in El Salvador	July 1991– April 1995	1,159
MINURSO – United Nations Mission for the Referendum in Western Sahara	April 1991–	2,800
UNAMIC – United Nations Advance Mission in Cambodia	October 1991– March 1992	1,124
UNPROFOR – United Nations Protection Force (former Yugoslavia)	February 1992– March 1995	45,870
UNTAC – United Nations Transitional Authority in Cambodia	March 1992– September 1993	21,089
UNOSOM I – United Nations Operation in Somalia I	April 1992– March 1993	4,269
ONUMOZ – United Nations Operation in Mozambique	April 1992– December 1994	9,378
UNOMUR – United Nations Observer Mission Uganda–Rwanda	June 1993– September 1994	81
UNOMIG – United Nations Observer Mission in Georgia	August 1993–	200
UNOMIL – United Nations Observer Mission in Liberia	September 1993– September 1997	458
UNMIH – United Nations Mission in Haiti	September 1993– June 1996	7,130
UNAMIR – United Nations Assistance Mission for Rwanda	October 1993– March 1996	5,640
UNASOG – United Nations Aouzou Strip Observer Group (Chad/Libya)	May 1994– June 1994	15
UNMOT – United Nations Mission of Observers in Tajikistan	December 1994– May 2000	62
UNAVEM III – United Nations Angola Verifications Missions III	February 1995– June 1997	8,030

(*continued*)

Mission	Duration	Authorized strength/maximum deployment[a]
UNCRO – United Nations Confidence Restoration Organization in Croatia	March 1995– January 1996	15,522 M
UNPREDEP United Nations Preventive Deployment Force (Former Yugoslav Republic of Macedonia)	March 1995– February 1999	1,187
UNMIBH – United Nations Mission in Bosnia and Herzegovina	December 1995– December 2002	2,105
UNMOP – United Nations Mission of Observers in Prevlaka Peninsula (southern border between Croatia and the Federal Republic of Yugoslavia)	January 1996– December 2002	28
UNSMIH – United Nations Support Mission in Haiti	July 1996– July 1997	1,700
MONUA – United Nations Observer Mission in Angola	July 1997– February 1999	3,568
UNTMIH – United Nations Transition Mission in Haiti	August– November 1997	300
MINUGUA – United Nations Verification Mission in Guatemala	January– May 1997	155
MIPONUH – United Nations Civilian Police Mission in Haiti	December 1997– March 2000	372
UNPSG – United Nations Police Support Group (Croatia)	January– October 1998	114
MINURCA – United Nations Mission in the Central African Republic	April 1998– February 2000	1,488
UNOMSIL – United Nations Observer Mission in Sierra Leone	July 1998– October 1999	352
UNMIK – United Nations Mission in Kosovo	June 1999–	3,580
UNMEE – United Nations Mission in Ethiopia and Eritrea	July 2000–	4,200

Notes

a Authorized strength includes troops, military observers, civilian police and international civilian staff. Where authorized strength was not available maximum deployment of troops, military observers, civilian police and international civilian staff during the mission is used. Maximum deployment is marked M.

UN-commanded peace operations beyond Chapter VI: de facto/de jure

Mission	Duration	Authorized strength[a]
ONUC – United Nations Operation in the Congo	July 1960– June 1964	19,828
UNIKOM – United Nations Iraq–Kuwait Observation Mission	February 1993– October 2003	3,645
UNOSOM II – United Nations Operation in Somalia II	May 1993– March 1995	30,800
UNTAES – United Nations Transitional Administration for Eastern Slavonia, Baranja and Western Sirmium	January 1996– January 1998	6,017
UNMIK – United Nations Mission in Kosovo	June 1996–	3,657
UNTAET – United Nations Transitional Administration in East Timor	October 1999– May 2002	10,790
UNAMSIL – United Nations Mission in Sierra Leone	October 1999–	17,500
MONUC – United Nations Organization Mission in Democratic Republic of Congo	November 1999–	17,175
UNMISET – United Nations Mission of Support in East Timor	May 2002–	970
UNMIL – United Nations Mission in Liberia	September 2003–	16,115
UNOCI – United Nations Operation in Côte d'Ivoire	April 2004–	7,025
MINUSTAH – United Nations Stabilization Mission in Haiti	June 2004–	8,870
ONUB – United Nations Operation in Burundi	June 2004–	6,204
UNMIS – United Nations Mission in Sudan	March 2005–	11,733

Notes
a   Includes troops, military observers, civilian police and international civilian staff.

UN-delegated Chapter VII enforcement operations

Mission	Lead nation/ organization	Duration	Strength
Unified Command (Korea)	USA	July 1950– July 1953	341,628
ECOMOG – ECOWAS Ceasefire Monitoring Group (Liberia)	ECOWAS	August 1990–1997	11,000
Desert Storm (Kuwait)	USA	January– February 1991	540,000
Operation Restore Hope (Somalia)	USA	December 1992– May 1993	37,000

(*continued*)

Mission	Lead nation/ organization	Duration	Strength
Operation Turquoise (Rwanda)	France	June–August 1994	2,500
Operation Restore Democracy (Haiti)	USA	September 1994–March 1995	20,000
Operation Deliberate Force Bosnia	NATO	August–September 1995	278 aircraft
IFOR – Implementation Force (Bosnia)	NATO	December 1995–December 1996	60,000
SFOR – Stabilization Force (Bosnia)	NATO	December 1995–	20,000
Operation Alba (Albania)	Italy	April–August 1997	7,000
MISAB – Inter-African Mission to Monitor the Implementation of the Bangui Agreements (Central African Republic)	Gabon	January 1997–April 1998	800
ECOMOG – ECOWAS Cease-fire Monitoring Group (Sierra Leone)	ECOWAS	March 1998–May 2000	12,000
ECOMOG – ECOWAS Ceasefire Monitoring Group (Guinea-Bissau)	ECOWAS	February 1998–1999	712
KFOR – Kosovo Force	NATO	June 1999–	50,000
INTERFET – International Force for East Timor	Australia	September 1999–February 2000	8,000
Operation Palliser (Sierra Leone)	Great Britain	May–June 2000	4,500
ISAF – International Security Assistance Force in Afghanistan	1. Great Britain 2. Turkey 3. Germany 4. NATO	December 2001–	8,000
Operation Licorne (Côte d'Ivoire)	France	September 2002–	3,900
Operation Artemis (Democratic Republic of Congo)	France/EU	May–September 2003	1,500
ECOMICI – Economic Community of West African States Mission in Côte d'Ivoire	ECOWAS	September 2002–April 2004	1,400
ECOMIL – Economic Community of West African States Mission in Liberia	ECOWAS	August–September 2003	3,563
Multinational Force (Iraq)	USA	October 2003–	156,654

Source: United Nations.

Appendix 4

Danish military personnel in peace operations 1958–2003

UN-commanded Chapter VI peacekeeping and observer missions

Mission	Duration	Total personnel
UNTSO – United Nations Truce Supervision Organization in the Middle East	1948–	554
UNMOGIP – United Nations Military Observer Group in India and Pakistan	1949–	312
UNEF I – First United Nations Emergency Force (Middle East)	1956–1967	11,000
UNOGIL – United Nations Observation Group in Lebanon	1958	6
UNYOM – United Nations Yemen Observation Mission	1963–1964	11
UNFICYP – United Nations Peacekeeping Force in Cyprus	1964–1994	22,623
UNIPOM – United Nations India–Pakistan Observation Mission	1965–1966	4
UNDOF – United Nations Disengagement Observer Force (Golan Heights)	1974	4
UNIFIL – United Nations Interim Force in Lebanon	1978–	2
UNGOMAP – United Nations Good Offices Mission in Afghanistan and Pakistan	1988–1990	8
UNIIMOG – United Nations Iran–Iraq Military Observer Group	1988–1991	40
UNTAG – United Nations Transition Assistance Group in Namibia	1989–1990	258
UNIKOM – United Nations Iraq–Kuwait Observation Mission	1991–1996	74
UNPROFOR – United Nations Protection Force (former Yugoslavia)	1992–1995	8,044
UNCRO – United Nations Confidence Restoration Organization in Croatia	1995–1996	900

(continued)

Mission	Duration	Total personnel
UNPREDEP United Nations Preventive Deployment Force (Former Yugoslav Republic of Macedonia)	1993–1999	469
UNOMIG – United Nations Observer Mission in Georgia	1993–	53
UNMOT – United Nations Mission of Observers in Tajikistan	1994–	20
UNMIBH – United Nations Mission in Bosnia and Herzegovina	1995–2002	39
UNMOP – United Nations Mission of Observers in Prevlaka Peninsula (southern border between Croatia and the Federal Republic of Yugoslavia)	1996–2002	1
UNPSG – United Nations Police Support Group (Croatia)	1998	7
UNMIK – United Nations Mission in Kosovo	1999–	10
UNMEE – United Nations Mission in Ethiopia and Eritrea	2001–	333

UN-delegated Chapter VII enforcement operations

Mission	Lead nation/ organization	Duration	Total personnel
Naval embargo against Iraq (Gulf)	USA	1991–92	304
IFOR – Implementation Force (Bosnia)	NATO	1996	1,616
SFOR – Stabilization Force (Bosnia)	NATO	1997–	7,442
Operation Alba (Albania)	Italy	1997	59
KFOR – Kosovo Force	NATO	1999–	5,762
INTERFET – International Force for East Timor	Australia	1999–2000	2
ISAF – International Security Assistance Force in Afghanistan	1. Great Britain 2. Turkey 3. Germany 4. NATO	2001–	196
Multinational Force (Iraq)	USA	2003–	934

UN-commanded operations beyond Chapter VI: de facto/de jure

Mission	Duration	Total personnel
ONUC – United Nations Operation in the Congo	1960–1964	1,000
MONUC – United Nations Organization Mission in Democratic Republic of Congo	2000–	8

(*continued*)

Mission	Duration	Total personnel
UNTAET – United Nations Transitional Administration in East Timor	1999–2002	2
UNAMSIL – United Nations Mission in Sierra Leone	1999–	12
UNMISET – United Nations Mission of Support in East Timor	2003–	4
UNMIL – United Nations Mission in Liberia	2003	2

Appendix 5

Finnish military personnel in peace operations 1956–2003

UN-commanded Chapter VI peacekeeping and observer missions

Mission	Duration	Total personnel
UNEF I – First United Nations Emergency Force (Middle East)	1956–57	437
UNOGIL – United Nations Observation Group in Lebanon	1958	8
UNMOGIP – United Nations Military Observer Group in India and Pakistan	1961–	165
UNFICYP – United Nations Peacekeeping Force in Cyprus	1964–	7,410
UNTSO – United Nations Truce Supervision Organization in the Middle East	1967–	628
UNEF II – Second United Nations Emergency Force (Middle East)	1973–79	4,604
UNDOF – United Nations Disengagement Observer Force (Golan Heights)	1979–93	5,995
UNIFIL – United Nations Interim Force in Lebanon	1992–2001	10,650
UNGOMAP – United Nations Good Offices Mission in Afghanistan and Pakistan	1988–90	11
UNIIMOG – United Nations Iran–Iraq Military Observer Group	1988–91	55
UNTAG – United Nations Transition Assistance Group in Namibia	1989–90	968
UNIKOM – United Nations Iraq–Kuwait Observation Mission	1991–	69
UNOSOM I – United Nations Operation in Somalia I	1992–93	10
UNPROFOR – United Nations Protection Force (former Yugoslavia)	1992–95	571
UNPREDEP United Nations Preventive Deployment Force (Former Yugoslav Republic of Macedonia)	1993–98	2,154

(*continued*)

Mission	Duration	Total personnel
UNTAES – United Nations Transitional Administration for Eastern Slavonia, Baranja and Western Sirmium	1996–98	8
UNMOP – United Nations Mission of Observers in Prevlaka Peninsula (southern border between Croatia and the Federal Republic of Yugoslavia)	1996–2002	6
UNMEE – United Nations Mission in Ethiopia and Eritrea	2000–	226

UN-commanded beyond Chapter VI: de facto/de jure

Mission	Duration	Total personnel
UNMIK – United Nations Mission in Kosovo	1999–	10

UN-delegated Chapter VII enforcement operations

Mission	Lead nation/ organization	Duration	Total personnel
IFOR – Implementation Force/SFOR – Stabilization Force (Bosnia)	NATO	1996–2003	2,111
KFOR – Kosovo Force (Kosovo)	NATO	1999–	4,100
ISAF – International Security Assistance Force in Afghanistan	1. Great Britain 2. Turkey 3. Germany 4. NATO	2002–	100

Appendix 6

Norwegian military personnel in peace operations 1956–2003

UN-commanded Chapter VI peacekeeping and observer missions

Mission	Duration	Total personnel
UNTSO – United Nations Truce Supervision Organization in the Middle East	1956–	605
UNEF I – First United Nations Emergency Force (Middle East)	1956–1967	10,989
UNMOGIP – United Nations Military Observer Group in India and Pakistan	1949–94	140
UNOGIL – United Nations Observation Group in Lebanon	1958	54
UNYOM – United Nations Yemen Observation Mission	1963–64	7
UNIPOM – United Nations India–Pakistan Observation Mission	1965–66	2
UNIFIL – United Nations Interim Force in Lebanon	1978–99	34,166
UNIIMOG – United Nations Iran–Iraq Military Observer Group	1988–91	35
UNAVEM I, II, III – United Nations Angola Verifications Missions I, II, III	1988–97	69
UNIKOM – United Nations Iraq–Kuwait Observation Mission	1991–94	169
ONUSAL – United Nations Observer Mission in El Salvador	1992–93	1
UNPROFOR – United Nations Protection Force (former Yugoslavia)	1992–95	4,401
UNOSOM I – United Nations Operation in Somalia I	1992–94	260 (including UNOSOM II)
UNPF – United Nations peacekeeping force (Croatia)	1995–96	162
UNPREDEP United Nations Preventive Deployment Force (Former Yugoslav Republic of Macedonia)	1995–96	808
UNTAES – United Nations Transitional Administration for Eastern Slavonia, Baranja and Western Sirmium	1996–98	16

(continued)

Mission	Duration	Total personnel
UNMOP – United Nations Mission of Observers in Prevlaka Peninsula (southern border between Croatia and the Federal Republic of Yugoslavia)	1996–2002	9
UNMIBH – United Nations Mission in Bosnia and Herzegovina	1995–2002	4
MINUGUA – United Nations Verification Mission in Guatemala	1997	3
MONUA – United Nations Observer Mission in Angola	1997–99	24
UNMIK – United Nations Mission in Kosovo	1999–	11
UNAMSIL – United Nations Mission in Sierra Leone	1999–	7
UNMEE – United Nations Mission in Ethiopia and Eritrea	2000–	15

UN-commanded operations beyond Chapter VI: de facto/de jure

Mission	Duration	Total personnel
ONUC – United Nations Operation in the Congo	1960–64	1,173
UNOSOM I and II – United Nations Operation in Somalia I and II	1992–94	260
UNTAET – United Nations Transitional Administration in East Timor	1999–2002	18
MONUC – United Nations Organization Mission in Democratic Republic of Congo	2000–	10

UN-delegated Chapter VII enforcement operations

Mission	Lead nation/ organization	Duration	Total personnel
Naval embargo against Iraq (Gulf)	USA	1991–92	350
IFOR – Implementation Force (Bosnia)	NATO	1995–96	1,777
SFOR – Stabilization Force (Bosnia)	NATO	1996	3,650
KFOR – Kosovo Force	NATO	1999	7,000
INTERFET – International Force for East Timor	Australia	1999	6
ISAF – International Security Assistance Force in Afghanistan	1. Great Britain 2. Turkey 3. Germany 4. NATO	2002–	278
Multinational Force (Iraq)	USA	2003–	300

Source: Norwegian Ministry of Defence.

Appendix 7

The Nordic countries compared

	Sweden	Finland	Denmark	Norway
Population, million (2002)	8.9	5.2	5.4	4.5
Armed forces personnel; conscripts (2002)	27,600; 12,300	27,000; 18,500	22,800; 5,700	26,600; 15,200
Total defence budget, EUR million (2002)	4,500	1,900	2,900	4,000
Costs of international activities, EUR million	115	80	145	180
Share of total costs for international activities, %	2.6	4.1	5.0	4.5
Share of total costs (excluding material, etc.) for international activities, %	4.9	4.8	5.7	6.5
Military personnel stationed abroad (2004)	1,000 (1 July)	997 (September)	1,010 (30 June)	600 (1 July)

Sources: *Finnish Security and Defence Policy 2004* (Prime Minister's Office, Government report 6, 2004), p. 96; Försvarsberedningen, *Försvar för en ny tid*. (Stockholm: Försvarsdepartementet, Ds 2004:30), pp. 306–307.

Appendix 8

Swedish military personnel in peace operations 1956–2004

UN-commanded peacekeeping and observer (Chapter VI) missions

Mission	Duration	Total Personnel
UNTSO – United Nations Truce Supervision Organization in the Middle East	June 1948–	1,057
UNEF I – First United Nations Emergency Force (Middle East)	1956–1967	12,160
UNOGIL – United Nations Observation Group in Lebanon	June–December 1958	83
UNSF – United Nations Security Force in West New Guinea (West Irian)	October 1962–April 1963	7
UNYOM – United Nations Yemen Observation Mission	July 1963–September 1964	8
UNFICYP – United Nations Peacekeeping Force in Cyprus	March 1964–1993	27,981
UNEF II – Second United Nations Emergency Force (Middle East)	October 1973–July 1979	7,642
UNIFIL – United Nations Interim Force in Lebanon	March 1978–	9,251
UNGOMAP – United Nations Good Offices Mission in Afghanistan and Pakistan	May 1988–March 1990	9
UNIIMOG – United Nations Iran–Iraq Military Observer Group	August 1988–February 1991	38
UNAVEM I – United Nations Angola Verifications Missions I	January 1989–June 1991	97
UNTAG – United Nations Transition Assistance Group in Namibia	April 1989–March 1990	75
ONUCA – United Nations Observer Group in Central America	November 1989–January 1992	30
UNAVEM II – United Nations Angola Verifications Missions II	June 1991–February 1995	55
ONUSAL – United Nations Observer Mission in El Salvador	July 1991–April 1995	19
MINURSO – United Nations Mission for the Referendum in Western Sahara	April 1991–	110

(continued)

Mission	Duration	Total Personnel
UNAMIC – United Nations Advance Mission in Cambodia	October 1991– March 1992	1,090
UNPROFOR – United Nations Protection Force (former Yugoslavia)	February 1992– March 1995	461
UNTAC – United Nations Transitional Authority in Cambodia	March 1992– September 1993	88
UNOSOM I – United Nations Operation in Somalia I	April 1992– March 1993	311
ONUMOZ – United Nations Operation in Mozambique	April 1992– December 1994	79
UNOMIG – United Nations Observer Mission in Georgia	August 1993–	62
UNPREDEP – United Nations Preventive Deployment Force (Former Yugoslav Republic of Macedonia)	March 1995– February 1999	622
UNMIBH – United Nations Mission in Bosnia and Herzegovina	December 1995– December 2002	256
UNMOP – United Nations Mission of Observers in Prevlaka Peninsula (southern border between Croatia and the Federal Republic of Yugoslavia)	January 1996– December 2002	31
MINUGUA – United Nations Verification Mission in Guatemala	January– May 1997	155
UNMIK – United Nations Mission in Kosovo	June 1999–	204
UNMEE – United Nations Mission in Ethiopia and Eritrea	July 2000–01	13

UN-commanded peace operations beyond Chapter VI: de facto/de jure

Mission	Duration	Total Personnel
ONUC – United Nations Operation in the Congo	July 1960–June 1964	6,332
UNTAES – United Nations Transitional Administration for Eastern Slavonia, Baranja and Western Sirmium	January 1996–January 1998	12
UNMIK – United Nations Mission in Kosovo	June 1996–	204
UNTAET – United Nations Transitional Administration in East Timor	October 1999–May 2002	34
UNAMSIL – United Nations Mission in Sierra Leone	October 1999–2001	9
UNMIL – United Nations Mission in Liberia	September 2003–	662

UN-delegated Chapter VII enforcement operations

Mission	Lead nation/ organization	Duration	Strength
Unified Command (Korea)	USA	July 1950– July 1953	897
Desert Storm (Kuwait)	USA	January– February 1991	525
Operation Restore Hope (Somalia)	USA	December 1992– May 1993	307
IFOR – Implementation Force (Bosnia)	NATO	December 1995– December 1996	1,749
SFOR – Stabilization Force (Bosnia)	NATO	December 1995–2001	2,531
Operation Alba (Albania)	Italy	April–August 1997	14
KFOR – Kosovo Force	NATO	June 1999–	7,200
ISAF – International Security Assistance Force in Afghanistan	1. Great Britain 2. Turkey 3. Germany 4. NATO	December 2001–	350
Operation Artemis (Democratic Republic of Congo)	France/EU	May–September 2003	200

Source: Swedish Defence Command.

Appendix 9

EU peace operations conducted under the European security and defence policy 2003–05 (March)

Operation	Mandate	Strength	Duration
EU Police Mission (EUPM) in Bosnia and Herzegovina	Chapter VI	500 police	January 2003–
EU Military Operation CONCORDIA in Macedonia	Chapter VI	400 troops	March–December 2003
EU Police Mission PROXIMA in Macedonia	Chapter VI	150 police	December 2003–
EU Military Operation ARTEMIS in Democratic Republic of Congo	UN-authorized Chapter VII	1,400 troops	July–September 2003
EU Rule of Law Mission EUJUST THEMIS in Georgia	Chapter VI	10 rule-of-law experts	July 2004–
EU Military Mission ALTHEA in Bosnia and Herzegovina	UN-authorized Chapter VII	7,000 troops	December 2004–
EU Police Mission KINSHASA in Democratic Republic of Congo	Chapter VI	30 police	January 2005
EU Integrated Rule of Law Mission EUJUST LEX in Iraq	Chapter VI	Number of trainers unspecified	July 2005 (expected)

Source: Council of the European Union.

Appendix 10

NATO peace operations 1993–2004

Mission	Duration	Mandate	Maximum strength
Sharp Guard (Bosnia)	June 1993– June 1996	UN-authorized Chapter VII	12 surface ships (June 1996)
Deny Flight (Bosnia)	April 1993– December 1995	UN-authorized Chapter VII	4,500/127 aircraft (December 1995)
Deliberate Force (Bosnia)	August– September 1995	UN-authorized Chapter VII	278 aircraft
IFOR – Implementation Force (Bosnia)	December 1995– December 1996	UN-authorized Chapter VII	60,000
SFOR – Stabilization Force (Bosnia)	1997–2004	UN-authorized Chapter VII	32,000
Allied Force (Kosovo)	March–June 1999	NATO-authorized Chapter VII	257 aircraft
AFOR – Albania Force Harbour (Albania)	April– September 1999	NATO-authorized Chapter VI	8,000
KFOR – Kosovo Force (Kosovo)	1999–	UN-authorized Chapter VII	50,000
Essential Harvest (Macedonia)	August– September 2001	NATO-authorized Chapter VI	3,500
Amber Fox (Macedonia)	September 2001– December 2002	NATO-authorized Chapter VI	700
Allied Harmony (Macedonia)	December 2002– March 2003	NATO-authorized Chapter VI	700
ISAF – International Security Assistance Force in Afghanistan	August 2003–	UN-authorized Chapter VII	8,500

Index

For Product Safety Concerns and Information please contact our EU
representative GPSR@taylorandfrancis.com
Taylor & Francis Verlag GmbH, Kaufingerstraße 24, 80331 München, Germany

www.ingramcontent.com/pod-product-compliance
Lightning Source LLC
Chambersburg PA
CBHW050410280326
41932CB00013BA/1803

9 7 8 0 4 1 5 5 4 4 9 1 7